OPERANT-PAVLOVIAN INTERACTIONS

OPERANT-PAVLOVIAN INTERACTIONS

Edited By

HANK DAVIS
HARRY M. B. HURWITZ

 LAWRENCE ERLBAUM ASSOCIATES, PUBLISHERS

1977   Hillsdale, New Jersey

DISTRIBUTED BY THE HALSTED PRESS DIVISION OF
JOHN WILEY & SONS
New York   Toronto   London   Sydney

Lawrence Erlbaum Associates, Inc., Publishers
62 Maria Drive
Hillsdale, New Jersey 07642

Distributed solely by Halsted Press Division
John Wiley & Sons, Inc., New York

Library of Congress Cataloging in Publication Data

Main entry under title:

Pavlovian-operant interactions.

    Papers and discussions presented at a conference held
at the University of Guelph, Sept. 4-6, 1975.
    Includes bibliographies.
    1. Conditioned response–Congresses.   I. Davis, Hank.
II. Hurwitz, Harry M. B.
BF319.P38   153.8'5   76-54651
ISBN 0-470-99026-0

Printed in the United States of America

Dedicated to my mother,
Sarah Davis Bushan,
and to the memory of my
father, Alfred H. Davis.

H.D.

* * * * *

In memory of C.A. Mace,
friend and mentor,
who helped me understand.

H.M.B.H.

Contents

Preface   xi
Introduction   xiii

1   ON THE ROLE OF THE REINFORCER IN ASSOCIATIVE
      LEARNING
      R. G. Weisman   1
         Introduction   1
         The Associative Process   2
         The Habituative Processes   3
         Interlocking of Innate Behavior Processes With the
            Associative Process in Classical Conditioning   6
         The Pavlovian Reinforcement Process   10
         The General Associative Process in Instrumental
            Learning   13
         Innate Behavior in Instrumental Learning   15
         The Instrumental Reinforcement Process   16
         Conclusion   19
         References   19

         Discussion   22
         References   26

2   A NOTE ON THE OPERANT CONDITIONING OF
      AUTONOMIC RESPONSES
      A. H. Black, B. Osborne, W. C. Ristow   27
         Introduction   27
         Conclusion   37
         References   39

         Discussion   40
         References   45

3 SENSITIVITY OF DIFFERENT RESPONSE SYSTEMS TO
   STIMULUS-REINFORCER AND RESPONSE-REINFORCER
   RELATIONS
   H. M. Jenkins 47
       Introduction   47
       Impurity of the Classical and Operant Paradigms   47
       Evidence on S–S* and R–S* Relations in Sign
          Tracking   48
       Interpretations and Generalizations   49
       The Comparison of Response Systems   51
       Expectations on the Origin Hypothesis   54
       Procedure and Results of the Experiment   54
       Conclusions   60
       References   61

       Discussion   62
       References   66

4 PERFORMANCE ON LEARNING TO ASSOCIATE A
   STIMULUS WITH POSITIVE REINFORCEMENT
   R. A. Boakes 67
       Introduction   67
       Behavioral Contrast and Autoshaping   69
       Discrete Trial Autoshaping with Rats   71
       Reinforcement Probability and Deprivation Level   78
       The Possibility of Superstition: A Multiple Schedule
          Procedure   81
       Comparisons Between Pigeons and Rats   84
       Autoshaping of a Loop-Pull Response by Pigeons   88
       Implication for Interactions with Instrumental
          Behavior   93
       References   96

       Discussion   98
       References   101

5 BEHAVIORAL COMPETITION IN CONDITIONING
   SITUATIONS: NOTES TOWARD A THEORY OF
   GENERALIZATION AND INHIBITION
   J. E. R. Staddon 103
       Introduction   103
       Induced Behavioral States   104
       Competition and Stimulus Control   108

Applications   113
Qualifications   120
Concluding Comments   125
References   126

Discussion   128

6   PAVLOVIAN SECOND-ORDER CONDITIONING: SOME
    IMPLICATIONS FOR INSTRUMENTAL BEHAVIOR
    Robert A. Rescorla   133
       Introduction   133
       A Demonstration of Pavlovian Second-Order
         Conditioning   135
       The Stability of Second-Order Conditioning   138
       Some Analogous Consequences for Instrumental
         Behavior   147
       Some Additional Implications: What is Learned?   158
       A Comment on the History of Second-Order
         Conditioning   160
       Conclusion   162
       References   163

7   THE SAFETY SIGNAL HYPOTHESIS
    Martin E. P. Seligman, Yitzchak M. Binik   165
       Introduction   165
       Response Suppression   168
       Problems for the Safety Signal Hypothesis   175
       References   176

       Discussion   180
       References   187

8   AVERSIVELY CONTROLLED BEHAVIOR AND THE
    ANALYSIS OF CONDITIONED SUPPRESSION
    Harry M. B. Hurwitz, A. E. Roberts   189
       Introduction   189
       Historical Antecedents   190
       Conditioned Suppression: Theory and
         Measurement   197
       The Effects of CS-US on an Avoidance Baseline:
         Conditioned Suppression or Enhancement?   202
       Conclusions   219

References   221

Discussion   224
References   231

9   RESPONSE CHARACTERISTICS AND CONTROL DURING
     LEVER–PRESS ESCAPE
     Hank Davis   233
       Introduction   233
       Background   234
       The SSDR Analysis of Escape: Its Adequacy   236
       The SSDR Analysis of Escape: Its Inadequacy   239
       Pavlovian Analysis of Escape?   241
       Research on SSDRs and Escape   244
       Response Force and Lever-Press Escape   250
       The Reinforcement of Lever Holding   257
       Relationship Between Lever-Press Escape and
         Avoidance   260
       Conclusion   263
       References   264

       Discussion   267
       References   272

10   CONDITIONING FOOD-ILLNESS AVERSIONS IN WILD
     ANIMALS: CAVEANT CANONICI*
     John Garcia, Kenneth W. Rusiniak, Linda P. Brett   273
       Introduction   273
       Historical Notes on Bait Shyness   274
       Comparative Bait Shyness   280
       The Status of Bait Shyness in Learning Theory   300
       References   306

       Discussion   311
       References   316

Author Index   317
Subject Index   325

Preface

On September 4, 5, and 6, 1975, a conference entitled "Operant–Pavlovian Interactions" was held at the University of Guelph, in Ontario, Canada. The following is an alphabetical list of conferees and their present institutional affiliations:

* Abraham H. Black, McMaster University
* Robert Boakes, University of Sussex
* Hank Davis, University of Guelph
* John Garcia, U.C.L.A.
* Harry M.B. Hurwitz, University of Guelph
* Herbert M. Jenkins, McMaster University
  Nicholas Mackintosh, University of Sussex
  Douglas Reberg, University of Western Ontario
* Robert A. Rescorla, Yale University
* Martin E.P. Seligman, University of Pennsylvania
  Sara Shettleworth, University of Toronto
  Shepard Siegel, McMaster University
* J.E.R. Staddon, Duke University
* R.G. Weisman, Queen's University

Asterisks indicate a participant who presented a paper. All persons served as discussants.

In designing the format of this book we have attempted to keep as much of the flavor of the conference as possible. The discussion material that follows each chapter has been extracted from tapes made of each 2-hour session. We trust that these discussions will provide a fuller dimension to the book, by giving the reader a further insight into both the conferees and their ideas. In editing the tapes, we tried to choose dialogue that amplified a point or enabled a speaker to criticize or present an idea not in evidence in his chapter.

We hope that readers will keep several qualifying factors in mind. The discussions are not necessarily based on the final versions of the chapters that appear in the book. In most cases, although preliminary chapter drafts were distributed to conferees, not all of these draft versions arrived in time for detailed reading prior to the conference. In fact, many of the discussions followed only from some rather brief introductory remarks, during which time the speaker might not have elaborated his position as clearly as we hope it appears in his chapter. Questions, criticisms, and occasional redundancies should be viewed in light of these conditions. Finally, Bob Rescorla was unable to attend the conference. Accordingly, his chapter appears without a subsequent discussion section.

We are thankful to Canada Council, without whose financial support our conference plans could not have materialized. We are also grateful to Wendy Spicer, who took on the joyless task of transcribing tapes, and to Susan Simmons, who helped with the indexing and last minute editorial burdens. Our thanks also to Larry Erlbaum, our publisher, for his support and confidence in this project.

A word about the subject index, which follows the text: Because of the specialized nature of this conference, certain terms and concepts are so widespread in their usage as to appear regularly in virtually every chapter. Obvious examples of such items, which have been omitted from the index, are: operant conditioning, Pavlovian conditioning, instrumental conditioning, reinforcement, law of effect, motivation, conditioned and unconditioned stimulus and response, contingency, pigeon, and rat. Reference to these items can readily be found by opening the book at random.

Introduction

The first important distinction between operant and Pavlovian conditioning was made in 1928 by Polish scientists Konorski and Miller. Unaware of their work, Skinner proposed a similar analysis in 1935 of the manner in which operant and Pavlovian conditioning might differ and interact. Konorski and Miller responded to Skinner's statement, and by 1937 the now-classic debate over "two types of conditioned reflexes" was in high gear.

In recent years, the attention of many learning theorists has returned to the fundamental question of whether there are identifiably different forms of learning. The present volume contains chapters that reassess our basic learning paradigms. They deal with the definitional problems of isolating operant and Pavlovian conditioning, as well as the attempt to analyze the inevitable interactions that follow. These issues are examined in a variety of settings: Some authors deal with operant-Pavlovian interactions directly by devising procedures to generate them; others examine operant-Pavlovian interactions by examining their possible contribution to established conditioning paradigms.

Obviously, the fundamental concerns of this book are not new. This is as it should be, for surely if the processes and definitions under consideration are *basic*, we have an enduring obligation to reexamine them in light of an expanding body of data and theory. What we hope makes this volume distinctive is its attempt to wed these traditional questions with an array of contemporary issues and research. In order to accomplish this, we called together a group of psychologists who have contributed widely to the area of learning theory. Our primary focus was to see whether these scientists had retained or could evolve a common conceptual framework despite obvious differences in their areas of interest. The reader can draw his or her own conclusions, and may find the discussion sections following each chapter particularly helpful in this regard.

* * * * *

Once together, the contributers to this book found that basic definitions of all three terms in the title seemed elusive. For example, what is meant by "operant"? A conditioning procedure? A process within the organism that results from that procedure and underlies behavioral change? A unique bit of behavior? The same holds for "Pavlovian": In what manner are we invoking the term? Once those two issues are settled, we are free to deal with the term "interaction," and it appears that we will need both hands free to uncover what it means. Generally speaking, the term "interaction" refers to the relationship between at least two events, so that knowledge of either or both events is not sufficient to understand the phenomenon under study. In fact, the interaction represents a separate principle that, itself, must be explored experimentally.

Given this array of possible definitions, what are the various levels at which we can approach an operant-Pavlovian interaction? Most simply, it might occur at an operational level. However, here even our categories form subcategories, for there are at least two ways in which this procedural interaction may happen. One is the result of an explicit attempt by the experimenter to combine two different sets of operations within a single experiment. The commonest example of this is perhaps the conditioned suppression procedure, in which the operant and Pavlovian components are explicitly programmed. It is also possible, however, that such a procedural interaction may occur implicitly by what is described in the book as "paradigm impurity." For example, a single procedure, glibly assumed to be either operant or Pavlovian, may on further analysis contain elements of both. This may result from what have been termed "autocontingencies" (see Davis, Memmott, & Hurwitz, 1975) or may occur by virtue of "implicit contingencies," arrangements that come about as a consequence of the animal's behavior. Another possibility is that we may fail to see the importance of a Pavlovian procedure, such as higher order conditioning, simply because of its vague status in the literature, and may therefore attribute some of its effects to operant manipulations.

Consider another level at which interactions may occur. A number of authors argue that operant-Pavlovian interactions occur at the "process" level. These descriptions, typically related to two-factor theory, may invoke some notion of complementary or opposing processes; for example, the Pavlovian process may take precedence over the operant process. One can (and one often does) take the additional step of assuming that these processes have direct motivational bearing. Again, if we use the example of conditioned suppression, "fear," resulting from the Pavlovian process (which results from the Pavlovian operations), takes precedence over appetitively motivated bar pressing, which reflects the operant process (which results from the operant procedure). Of course, what we actually see is an animal who stops working for food during a signal that precedes shock. It begins to be a question of how far from the world of observable events one wishes to take one's analysis.

Apropos of this point, one can approach operant-Pavlovian interactions in yet another manner by focusing on directly observable events and analyzing response incompatability. The organism obviously cannot be cowering in the rear of the cage and bar pressing in the front at the same time. For a number of reasons this approach to studying interactions is relatively rare. For one, the level of behavioral observation necessary to support such an analysis is almost totally alien to the automated behaviorist tradition. Perhaps far more fundamental a problem, however, is that no one has convincingly demonstrated an essential corollary: namely, that identifiably different response topographies result from operant vs. Pavlovian conditioning.

The problem of whether and how to distinguish between operant and Pavlovian conditioning has been aptly summarized in *Basic Principles of Learning,* a recent book by Roger Tarpy. He concludes:

> ... the general evidence for the two-process position ... is not very compelling. The converse statement seems equally true—there is little evidence which demands a one-factor interpretation. What is one to believe? There are several ways that psychologists have chosen to cope with this ambiguity. ... Perhaps the most appropriate has been to recognize the complexity of the problem and continue to search for new perspectives [1975, pp. 78–79].

We are in basic agreement with Tarpy's view and hope to have contributed to this search for "new perspectives." Within our book, the issue of operant-Pavlovian interactions has been approached by using different situations and levels of analysis. All of the examples mentioned in this introduction (e.g., conditioned suppression, implicit contingencies, higher-order conditioning, behavioral incompatability) are dealt with in the following pages (see chapters by Hurwitz and Roberts, Jenkins, Rescorla, and Staddon, respectively), as are a further variety of situations that in some arguable manner relate to, and it is hoped elucidate, the notion of operant-Pavlovian interactions.

Hank Davis
Harry M.B. Hurwitz

There is at least one philosophical problem in which all thinking men
are interested. It is the problem of cosmology: the problem of
understanding the world. . . . All science is cosmology, I believe.

> −K.R. Popper from Preface to 1959
> edition of *Logic of Scientific
> Discovery*

I aspire to the cosmos, to the throne of God, not to discovering the
laws of the two-lever Skinner box.

> −John Garcia (with characteristic humor)
> September 6, 1975, Guelph, Ontario

. . . we must select or construct an experimental space which can be
well controlled. . . . We are interested in the probability that in such a
controlled space the organism . . . will engage in the behavior
we . . . record. At first blush, such an interest may seem trivial. We shall
see, however, that the conditions which alter the probability . . . are
quite complex. Moreover, they have an immediate important bearing on
the behavior of other organisms under other circumstances, including
the organism called man in the everyday world of human affairs.

The insight into human behavior gained from research of this sort has
already proved effective in many areas. . . . It is possible that (it) will
provide us at last with the techniques we need . . . to build a better
world and, through it, better men.

> −B.F. Skinner from "The Experimental
> Analysis of Behavior," *American Scientist,*
> 1957, **45**, 343−371.

There are apparently alternate roads to the cosmos.

> −Eds.

OPERANT-PAVLOVIAN INTERACTIONS

1
On the Role of the Reinforcer in Associative Learning

R. G. Weisman

Queen's University, Canada

INTRODUCTION

Weisman's chapter addresses itself to what he terms a "paradigm shift," or a change in the form that behavior analysis has recently taken. His view of learning attempts to account for animal behavior not only in terms of reinforcement but also in terms of innate responses and cognitive processes. The following questions are dealt with in Weisman's chapter: (1) What is the evolutionary history of associative learning? (2) How are the events that generate reinforcement arranged? (3) What are the relative roles of practice effect and instinct in Pavlovian and operant conditioning? (4) What role do cognitive factors play in generating conditioned responses?

This chapter, as much a distillation of the literature as of my own beliefs, is an attempt to trace new outlines for the functions of the reinforcer in engendering behavior change in associative learning. The work has its historical impetus in the traditional distinction between learning and performance but its most important impetus is the modern view that behavior change resulting from associative learning involves, at least, a primitive but powerful knowledge acquisition system and some equally important deterministic performance rules that govern the conversion of stored knowledge into biologically relevant behaviors. In the present work the nature of the behavioral units, the roles of exercise and effect, and even the terminology of association are reassessed. Specifically, I have tried to show how innate, habituative, and associative processes interlock, one with the next, to generate the effect we attribute to reinforcers.

The Associative Process

Associative learning seems in large part a result of the ability of animals to extract correlations in time and space between events from nature. That is, animals are not merely affected by correlations between events, they learn about them. Animals can learn that the occurrences of two stimuli are positively or negatively correlated (Pavlov, 1927; Rescorla, 1968) or even that the occurrences of two stimuli are not correlated at all (Mackintosh, 1973). This ability may be usefully conceptualized as cognitive (Neisser, 1967), not simply associative, and certainly not as itself a product of its consequences for individual animals. That is, animals more or less automatically produce some central representation of events that preserves their order in time whether one event is motivationally significant or both events are rather neutral.

Sensory preconditioning.   For evidence that animals learn to associate essentially neutral stimuli one need only consult the often slighted literature of sensory preconditioning. In the sensory preconditioning experiment, the preconditioning phase correlates two motivationally trivial stimuli, say S_1 and S_2, usually in the literature a light and a tone; then the conditioning phase correlates S_2 with a reinforcer. Finally during a test phase S_1 is shown to control behavior conditioned to S_2. Of course, results obtained during the test phase should be compared against various controls to avoid mislabeling stimulus generalization, unlearned reactions, etc., as sensory preconditioning.

In a review of sensory preconditioning research Seidel (1959) concluded that the procedure generated small but reliable effects. Research conducted over the intervening 16 years (e.g., Prewitt, 1967; Rizley & Rescorla, 1972) has actively confirmed this conclusion (Mackintosh, 1974). Some further conclusions seem justified.

1. Overt behavioral mediation of association between S_1 and S_2 can be rejected as an explanation of the phenomena. Stimuli emanating from the same sound source have been associated (Kendall & Thompson, 1960) and a tone and light were associated even when rats were paralyzed by curare (Cousins, Zamble, Tait, & Suboski, 1971).

2. Motivationally powerful reinforcers are not necessary to associative learning as it occurs in the first phase of the sensory preconditioning experiment. The main consequence of preconditioning trials seems to be the construction of central representations of the stimuli.

Some sort of general associative process is integral to the present chapter and, indeed, to current thought concerned with information processing in animal learning. Nonetheless, as a verified instance of the general case sensory preconditioning remains deficient, because only evidence concerning learning about positive correlations has been reported. If sensory preconditioning is an example of the general case of which Pavlovian conditioning is an instance then animals must learn about negative and zero correlations between relatively neutral events.

It has not escaped notice that although sensory preconditioning experiments regularly produce highly reliable results, the magnitude of the difference between experimental and control groups is often quite small. Moreover, there is reason to believe that refinements in procedure, although otherwise useful, do not increase the magnitude of effect appreciably. The effectiveness of increasing the number of sensory preconditioning trials appears to reach a real limit, perhaps, imposed by the intervention of another process. Of course, one can press on, presenting many, many preconditioning trials. Indeed, Hoffeld, Kendall, Thompson, and Brogden (1960) administered up to 800 preconditioning trials to one of several groups of cats. However, across response measures four pairings of S_1 and S_2 resulted in several times as much avoidance responding to S_1 during the test phase as 800 pairings. Similar but less extreme results were reported by Prewitt (1967), who found S_1 a somewhat more effective conditioned suppressor of licking in rats after 16 preconditioning trials than after 64 trials. Thus, increasing the number of trials during preconditioning does not appear to result in ever more association between S_1 and S_2, although control of the conditioned response by S_1 remains much weaker than control by S_2.

The Habituative Processes

Implicated in the constraint of sensory preconditioning are what may be termed the habituative processes, habituation proper and latent extinction, which are at least as general as sensory preconditioning and latent learning but with opposite effects. Habituation, of course, is the waning of behavioral, and electrophysiological, responses with repeated stimulation. It occurs quite generally across behavioral categories affecting species-characteristic motor patterns to predators (Hinde, 1954) and conspecifics (Clayton & Hinde, 1968) as well as orienting reactions to tones and lights (Sokolov, 1960). There is good evidence that the neural correlates of tones and lights diminish with continued presentation, as in the preconditioning phase of the sensory preconditioning experiment (Sharpless & Jasper, 1956).

The neural correlates of repeatedly presented stimuli not only diminish but also enter into association with other stimuli less rapidly: that is, they show the effects of latent inhibition (Lubow & Moore, 1959). That nonreinforced preexposure to the conditioned stimulus retards later conditioning is well established (Lubow & Siebert, 1969; Rescorla, 1971: Siegel, 1972). It is therefore difficult to believe that repeated nonreinforced presentation of S_2 during preconditioning does not retard later learning to associate S_2 with a reinforcer. Association between S_1 and S_2 may be eventually retarded because neither is a reinforcer. Interaction between sensory preconditioning and latent inhibition has not been investigated. Perhaps, as Mackintosh (1973) suggests, animals simply learn to ignore stimuli that fail to predict reinforcers. It would appear that vague theoretical objections to sensory preconditioning research have obscured the more interesting questions this work poses. In particular, interlocking between the habituative and associative processes in sensory preconditioning experiments deserves more direct investigation than it has received so far. Covariation between latent inhibition, habituation proper, and sensory preconditioning must be studied within a single experimental setting.

Differential habituation.   Learning to associate correlated events may occur automatically and without reinforcement, but not without opposition. Opposing the general associative process are habituative processes by which animals may learn to ignore events. For example, the waning of EEG arousal and the behavioral orienting response to a tone in cats is nearly complete after a total of only 1 or 2 min of exposure (Sharpless & Jasper, 1956), whereas comparable decrements in responses to a live owl by chaffinches (Hinde, 1954) or to their litters by female mice (Noirot, 1964) may require hours or even days of exposure. There seems to be general agreement that the habituative processes operate at different rates depending on the motivational relevance of the event (Lorenz, 1965, p. 56; Hinde, 1970, p. 296; Denny & Ratner, 1970, p. 534). One need hardly point out that the reinforcers most favored in Pavlovian conditioning experiments are powerful motivational events, if not themselves releasers of species-characteristic fixed action patterns.[1] This highly adaptive feature of reinforcers has evolutionary consequences for associative learning. For it is likely that associations between neutral events and reinforcers endure with repetition, whereas associations between merely neutral events do not, in large part because of the differentially greater effect of the habituative processes on the latter events.

Some evolutionary considerations.   Even a brief survey of the diversity found in evolutionary history prompts one to speculate that natural selection "experimented" with special associative processes prior to or over the course of the phylogenetic development of the general associative process. However evidence for the notion that special associative processes, one for taste, another for vision, etc., are the "general" case is noticeably less than overwhelming. Flavor aversion may be learned in one trial but so may conditioned suppression (Wearden, 1975). Flavor aversion may follow conditioning with long CS–US intervals but so may instrumental learning in a T maze (Lett, 1975). Moreover basic phenomena common to Pavlovian conditioning with, say, food or shock as reinforcers, for example, overshadowing, blocking, latent inhibition, discrimination, and

---

[1] The question of whether habituation and satiation, as in the repeated presentation of food or water, are allied processes is not within the scope of this chapter.

extinction, are observed in flavor aversion experiments as well. Finally, quantitative differences in the speed at which animals learn to associate various CSs with various reinforcers should not be taken as strong evidence for qualitative differences in associative process. Actually, Waddington's (1953) hypothesis for the genetic assimilation of phenotypic variation seems to predict selection pressures, rather than special associative processes, to account for important between stimulus—reinforcer, and response—reinforcer, variance in learning rates. For example, in nature rats learning flavor aversions in one trial are rather more likely to survive to bear progeny than rats requiring up to 10 trials to learn the same classically conditioned aversion. Also the likelihood of actual exposure to a toxic substance may be much less from merely being in the same place as the toxic substance. Accordingly, the association of places with toxic substances proceeds somewhat slowly. This suggests that we can apply artificial selection to produce very rapid place aversion with toxic reinforcers.

It is possible to muster other quite plausible evolutionary advantages of the interlocking of habituative and associative processes. Selection may favor the genotype of animals habituating more slowly to, say, the sight of food or a mate than to the repeated presentation of some biologically trivial event. Also, the general associative process seems the simplest adaptation sufficient to permit neutral events to acquire biological significance. Of course, without selective habituative processes a quite general associative process may well be an evolutionary disaster, causing animals to fill their heads with the neural correlates of literally every correlation between events they have encountered in nature. However, the interlocking of selective habituative processes with a general associative process has adaptive features not replicated by the development of more selective associative processes. For example, as new correlations between events arise animals may automatically learn about them; if after several repetitions these events possess or acquire no biological significance then their central correlates are quite simply and automatically diminished along with the orienting reactions they originally have elicited.

A general associative process, more fully than an array of special associative processes, provides a basis for the superior functioning attributed to humans and the other higher primates. The resulting picture of animal learning not only mirrors the one the behaviorist presents for us but also provides a cognitive basis of learning that no amount of S—R obscurantism can completely conceal. However, I shall not berate the S—R behaviorists too vigorously for their suspicions concerning a general associative process, which has appeared to leave animals quite busy but not very active. Even an outright mentalist, if one should be found, must admit that natural selection can only act on what animals do and not on what they know. It seems reasonable to have doubted that natural selection has ever produced a process the primary function of which is to allow animals to learn the correlations between the neutral events in their environment.

Interlocking of Innate Behavior Processes
with the Associative Process in Classical Conditioning

The first role we have assigned to the reinforcer in associative learning is to provide resistance to the habituative processes. The preceding discussion of adaptedness leads us to consideration of a second function of the reinforcer in Pavlovian conditioning, viz., as the impetus for behavior change. Whether to consider conditioning as fundamentally a mechanism of cognitive (Tolman, 1932) or of behavioral (Skinner, 1938) change has divided students of learning for decades. The behaviorists have always insisted that behavior change is what learning is all about. Given the importance of behavior to the natural selection of the genetic determinants of an automatic associative process they can hardly have been completely mistaken. However, experimental analysts of behavior have been too interested in the effects of instrumental learning on behavior to concern themselves very much with the question of how the Pavlovian reinforcer generates behavior change. Understandably, cognitive psychologists are more interested in what their subjects know than in what they do. So after explicating the primitive knowledge acquisition function of Pavlovian conditioning they tend to fall silent. Finally, although ethologists have not shown a sustained interest in learning they have devoted considerable effort to the study of the behavior engendered by biologically important stimuli.

Units of innate behavior. Turning to the ethologists (Lorenz, 1970; Tinbergen, 1951) for a description of the Pavlovian reinforcer and the behavior it controls is hardly a rash choice. Some 15 years ago, S. C. Ratner made the same proposal during his seminars in Comparative Psychology at Michigan State University. Indeed, Pavlov (1927, pp. 9–11) himself was well aware of the possibility that his procedures might control behavior processes complex enough to be termed instincts.[2] We have more than historical precedent to guide us, however; evolutionary considerations make the ethological model attractive. Use of the ethologists' model assumes that the associative process has evolved interlocked to the innate and habituative processes that have preceded it and have already generated behavior and behavior change, respectively.

Lorenz (1965) and Tinbergen (1951) listed only two general classes of behavior: appetitive behavior, which included taxes and various basic locomotor patterns, and consummatory behavior, which included only rigidly preprogrammed motor units. Because the terms appetitive and consummatory are only roughly descriptive,[3] I have revised the list slightly to include three general,

---

[2] Distinctions between reflexes and the more centrally organized response processes could be the subject of an entire book. We shall simply assume here that complex organized behavior has both reflexive and endogenous elements.

[3] For example, it is unclear what, if anything, an aggressive display consumes or consumates.

descriptively named, mutually exclusive classes of behavior: These are orienting reactions, basic locomotor activities, and action patterns. Orienting reactions are viewed as turning reflexes that locate the animal with respect to stimuli. Locomotion, of course, is the particular behavior that brings an animal from one location to another. Action patterns, sometimes termed fixed action patterns, appear to be more or less preprogrammed complex behavioral units usually defined with reference to specific stimuli and deprivation states. Both orientation and locomotion require general status as behavioral units because they are common to the broad range of complete behavior sequences yet are quite separable from the specific action pattern seen in any particular behavior sequence. Sequences of units may be seen to occur in just the order in which they have been defined in an idealized instance of instinctive behavior, released by a biologically significant event; in practice, however, they can occur simultaneously or even alone. In general, orienting reactions steer locomotor behavior and action patterns, giving behavior a very purposive look. However, action patterns can occur unsteered and even orienting reactions can occur in the absence of appropriate external stimuli.

Some ethologists prefer to reserve the label "innate" for the fixed action pattern alone but it is easy to resist this restriction. All three units are

> ... innate in the sense that they are functions of the characteristics and the organizations of the animal's sensory, nervous, and muscular systems and are as much subject to genetical control as are structural features. It follows that in the course of evolution they have become adaptively moulded by selection in exactly the same way as has structure. [Ewer, 1968, p. 305]

I further suggest that oriented movements and action patterns are the very behavioral units the general associative process has evolved to control. There are not learned and innate behaviors; there are only learned modifications of innate behaviors.

Instincts as instrumental acts. The resemblance between highly organized complex innate behavior as described by ethologists and behavior under control of instrumental learning is really quite remarkable. Only recently have Hearst and Jenkins (1974) and Moore (1973) begun to draw the conclusion that we have often mistaken the former for the latter. Yet the taxes that direct locomotion and action patterns in birds were first described (Lorenz, 1965) over 35 years ago. Stubbornly, we have resisted the conclusions that (a) much animal behavior, even mammalian behavior, is innate,[4] and (b) animals have often not even learned the correlation between their behavior and its adaptive consequences. Ewer (1968) cites many instances of highly purposive-looking instrumental acts that on closer examination turn out to be stereotyped, built-in,

---

[4] Those who still balk at the term "innate" can substitute the words "powerful genetic determinants of the products of development."

open-loop control systems. One everyday example described by Ewer (1968, pp. 7–8) involved a common house cat burying the feces of her young. If the feces were quite near the edge of the litter box when she sniffed them, then the cat made the usual scraping movements with her forepaws outside the box. All that was needed to make her actions effective was a slight change in position, a simple enough operant, but instead she continued to scrape the floor. Someone watching a cat effectively burying feces might assume that it was an instrumental sequence reinforced, perhaps, by the removal of feces, their odor, or both. Yet as is characteristic of these otherwise adaptive innate action patterns ". . . when some slight alteration in the circumstances makes the normal pattern inappropriate and only a very minor adjustment is needed the animal obstinately persists in the old pattern" [Ewer, 1968, p. 9]. Although this may be the stuff from which the instrumental process has evolved, the fact remains that some of the adaptive behavior previously treated as the product of differential reinforcement contingencies seems instead the product of differential selection contingencies.

In the context of differential selection contingencies, it is a bit embarrassing to recall that at the center of the distinction between classical conditioning and instrumental learning has been the notion that modification of the reinforcer by an animal's behavior is a special characteristic of instrumental learning (Kimble, 1961; Rescorla & Solomon, 1967). Researchers conducting classical conditioning experiments were cautioned to exercise great care to insure that animals' conditioned and even unconditioned responses left all parameters of the occurrence of the Pavlovian reinforcer unchanged (Gormezano, 1966). In the face of such methodological purity ". . . it can be shown in most classical conditioning experiments that the conditioned response may enhance or somehow modify the reinforcing quality of the unconditioned stimulus" [Terrace, 1973, p. 101]. Salivation may increase the palatability and the digestibility of food or alternately function to dilute acid in the mouth. In a further example, "From an instrumental point of view, the dog learned to lift its leg in order to minimize either the discomfort of having its leg suddenly flexed or the pain produced by the shock although the dog cannot escape or avoid the shock completely" [Terrace, 1973, p. 78].

Consider the feeding reaction of the pigeon: The animal orients toward food, walks to it, then pecks it up. It seems difficult to escape the conclusion that this essentially innate behavior sequence was genetically selected to get the pigeon to food and to get food through the pigeon. To this end has evolved an incredibly complex and integrated pattern of sensory, muscular, central, and autonomic reactions. It is simply too late to arrange our experiments so that the components of this pattern fail to modify the Pavlovian reinforcer—probably thousands of centuries too late. The lesson is that these complex patterns, of which our experiments usually study only isolated bits, are directed (Tinbergen, 1951), preprogrammed (von Holst & von St. Paul, 1960), open-loop (McFarland, 1971), biological systems the efficiency of which in modifying the environment has been assured by countless generations of natural selection.

Exercise. The ethological view of the Pavlovian reinforcer has important implications for the roles of performance and exercise in classical conditioning. Behavior preprogrammed into animals' nervous systems should require little practice during conditioning trials. Although a complex organized species-characteristic unconditioned response may be seen as the critical antecedent of the conditioned response, the actual performance of the unconditioned response has little bearing on the outcome of the classical conditioning experiment. Dogs blocked from salivating early in conditioning by atropine salivated to the CS later after effects of the drug had dissipated (Crisler, 1930; Finch, 1938). The skeletal components of conditioned responses to the CS and unconditioned responses to the US in dogs were blocked by curare (Solomon & Turner, 1962) but the CS controlled later avoidance responding. Woodruff (1974) blocked pecking components in drinking by delivering water directly to pigeons' mandibles via an implanted cannula. Nevertheless "drink like" pecking was elicited by key light paired with an injection of water. Although sometimes cited in other contexts, these experiments have important implications for the behavior generating or performance laws of classical conditioning. Stated briefly, the basic performance rule for the Pavlovian reinforcer is that evolution, not practice, makes perfect.

Instinct Conditioning. Psychologists have pointedly ignored the adaptedness of even the isolated bits of behavior they have observed in classical conditioning experiments. Even reports (Adler & Hogan, 1963; Thompson & Sturm, 1965; Farris, 1967) of the control of fairly complete innate sequences of skeletal behavior by conditioned stimuli correlated with ethological releasers—instinct conditioning—caused hardly a ripple. Sometimes instinct conditioning was seen as only another instance of consummatory conditioning. The fact that orienting reactions, locomotor behavior, and action patterns were all included in the CR was ignored. Even after watching Howard Farris (1964) successfully conduct a sexual conditioning experiment with Japanese quail at Michigan State University, I confess to being more impressed with the wider generality of Pavlovian reinforcers the work has promised than with the associative control of innate behavior patterns. It should have been crystal clear that reflex conditioning was the special case and instinct conditioning the general case.

In any event, the implications of instinct conditioning remained largely ignored until Brown and Jenkins (1968) reported what appeared to be classical conditioning of the pigeons' key peck. This finding, more than any other, accelerated the pace of research to almost fever pitch. What was so startling about autoshaping of the pigeons' key peck? Surely, not the report that pigeons peck during a CS for food. Rats lick during a CS for water (Debold, Miller, & Jensen, 1965; Weisman, 1965), and, as any schoolboy knows, dogs salivate to a CS for food. Two aspects of the autoshaping experiment were unsettling. The first unsettling aspect of the autoshaping experiment was that the pigeons' key peck, until then viewed solely as a product of operant reinforcement, might be under the control of Pavlovian reinforcement as well. The second and more basic unsettling aspect of the autoshaping experiment was that the pigeon oriented, then walked toward the lighted key, only finally pecking at it repeatedly. We were quite unprepared for the finding that classical conditioning controlled directed actions elicited by the CS. We were unprepared because we had ignored ethological evidence that innate behavior released by such biologically significant events as reinforcers consisted of orienting reactions, locomotor activity, and action patterns. We had gone so far as to ignore relevant evidence from Pavlovian appetitive conditioning experiments (e.g., Pavlov, 1927; Zener, 1937). All in all we deserved to be unsettled and surprised.

Few of the early studies of instinct conditioning employed a localized CS but, following the reports of autoshaped key pecking, further evidence that the CR may be directed with respect to a localized CS gradually accumulated: Rackham (cited by Moore, 1973) observed courting and Wasserman (1973) saw pecking and nuzzling to a localized CS for, respectively, a mate in pigeons or a heat lamp in chicks. Evidence for the generality of the statement that classical conditioning is most often instinct conditioning is slowly accumulating. However, the need for classical conditioning research with diverse species and reinforcers can hardly be overemphasized. The work reported by Boakes and by Garcia in this volume is an encouraging step toward a broader basis for generalization.

The Pavlovian Reinforcement Process

As we have seen, the general associative process functions to organize the central representations of events, any events, but otherwise generates no behavior. The habituative processes teach animals to ignore biologically neutral events, perhaps by diminishing their central representations. The interlocking of the general associative processes with habituative processes, usually termed classical conditioning, teaches animals the correlations between neutral events and those of biological significance. We have further noted that ethological descriptions of sequences of species-characteristic behavior controlled by releasers seems to fit the most general case of behavior change engendered by the Pavlovian reinforcer.

The remaining problem, of course, is to explain how, having associated the CS with a reinforcer, animals come to respond to the CS with components of the species-specific behavior pattern released by the Pavlovian reinforcer. More specifically, why do animals respond to the CS with some components and not others of the innate pattern?

Cognitive and environmental determinants of the UR.   Let us begin by considering the question of how reinforcers themselves release behavior. An obvious but probably somewhat oversimplified answer is that the neural correlates of events more or less directly evoke preprogrammed sequences of innate behavior. The observed behavior patterns depend on the overlap between the central representation of the reinforcer an animal constructs and the form required to evoke any particular sequence of behavior. It seems quite unlikely that animals construct simply physicalistic representations of reinforcers. A rat receiving electric shock to the tail may represent the event as an attack by a conspecific in one context or by a predator in another context. Very young chicks exposed to a heat lamp may represent the event as a broody hen (Hogan, 1974). It follows that the less naturalistic the reinforcers we concoct, the more divergent our subjects' representations of them are likely to become from our own.

We must consider the results of certain studies that have elicited species-characteristic behavior by electrical stimulation of the brain. In his review of this work, Glickman (1973) emphasized the role of peripheral stimulation from environmental events for the behavior elicited by brain stimulation. Eating, drinking, or viewing and smelling a conspecific were much more likely to be observed during stimulation if objects that supported the activity were present. von Holst and von St. Paul (1960) released complex innate behavior in chickens by electrical stimulation of the brain. The more complete and detailed examples included all three innate units: orientation, locomotion, and action patterns. These sequences were released by the combination of a model and brain stimulation, not by brain stimulation alone. In general, when environmental support is absent or weak, brain stimulation may elicit only incomplete action patterns, locomotor activity or, sometimes, general motor unrest, which is a sort of vertebrate edition of kineses.

Cognitive and environmental determinants of the CR.   Now we are ready to consider the cognitive products of the associative process and classical conditioning in particular. When we say that an animal has learned the correlation between one event and another, we may in cognitive terms mean only that the central representations of one event now include information about the other event. Thus, the neural correlate of the CS becomes quite a cognitive structure, including considerable information about the reinforcer, its relationship in time to the CS, and probably at least some of its key physical, biological, and emotional characteristics. When two events are correlated positively in time the result may be the construction of a second representation utilizing information available in the first. In classical conditioning this second representation should certainly resemble an animal's representation of the reinforcer, but it is unlikely to be the same, any more than a sketch drawn from memory is likely to be identical with one drawn from life. The central representation, which evokes the UR, is constructed in the presence of the event itself, whereas the representation that evokes the CR is best viewed as a reinforcer memory, constructed only in the presence of information concerning the reinforcer encoded into the representation of the CS. The constructive transformational nature of the memorial processes may level and sharpen a reinforcer memory. The result may be more vivid but less detailed than the representation formed in the presence of the reinforcer. Reinforcer memories as described here and the US representations described by Rescorla and Heth (1975) must have common characteristics. However, it is unclear whether Rescorla and Heth have arranged for separate US representations and memories as in the present view. Eventually it is going to be necessary to account for memories evoked by conditioned stimuli negatively and randomly correlated with the reinforcer, and these may be different than the representation evoked in the presence of the reinforcer.

These cognitive considerations make exact correspondence between the CR and UR unlikely, but the mere fact that the reinforcer, or some stimulus resembling it, is not present during the CS may also result in divergence between the CR and UR. That is, neither the CS nor the environment may support all of the components of the innate behavior pattern evoked by the reinforcer memory, constructed from information stored with the CS. Pigeons exposed to an auditory or nonlocalized CS for food orient to the CS but rarely approach or peck it; but pigeons exposed to a localized visual CS orient, approach, and peck. In his demonstration of classical conditioning of sexual behavior Farris (1967) used an auditory CS. His birds directed courting responses to the partition separating them from the female, but when Rackham used a localized visual CS his pigeons directed their courting behavior to the CS. If the CS, or some other stimulus in the chamber, had the proper dimensions, animals might mount it during the CS. Given the ingenuity and diligence with which experimental psychologists proceed in these matters, I expect to read many, more formal reports of outlandish antics resembling the UR during classical conditioning experiments: dogs eating signal lamps, pigeons copulating with lighted solid objects, rats chewing tokens, and perhaps even cats attacking tone generators. However, stimulus substitution should be considered only the starting point, not the end point, for modern performance rules for classical conditioning. The reinforcer is only one determinant of the CR; the correlation between the CS and the US, the availability of other environmental events (supports) during the CS, and animals' innate response units with respect to their cognitions and memories of the CS and US are also important determinants of performance during the CS.

The survival value of the interlocking of the general associative and innate behavior generating processes has been discussed by Moore (1973). Once freed from the experimental psychologist's laboratory, animals benefit considerably from instinct conditioning. Richard Schuster has related to me what must be the most impressive case; it involves survival in the baldest sense of the word. Some herd animals show innate reactions to a conspecific's alarm call but not to any attribute of a predator. The alarm call itself is often released long after it can be of much value to the victim, but the correlation between the predator and the alarm call apparently generates powerful control of fleeing by quite specific characteristics of given predator species in other members of the herd. Classical conditioning here provides an open-ended predator recognition system that appears to play a critical role in the survival of the species. Clearly, it is time to call in question the view that classical conditioning plays no important role in the lives of animals in nature (Thorpe, 1956).

The two performance rules we have reviewed for instinct conditioning seem quite simple yet capable of generating diverse behavior changes. First, the nature of the memory of the reinforcer may vary as a result of changes in the parameters of associative learning. Second, the actual behavior released by a reinforcer memory may vary with the nature of the environmental support available for each of the three behavioral units. This second rule is especially important because it gives flexibility to the CR quite independent of the associative process. A rat may merely mouth a steel ball bearing correlated with food but chew to bits an otherwise similar nylon ball bearing correlated with food.[5] Also, of course, a change in the location of the CS will shift the direction of the CR. Classically conditioned, oriented, complex, motor behavior may therefore be modified, perhaps, even from trial to trial.

Stripped of the opportunity to display action patterns during the CS, by a low level of environmental support, animals may show general motor unrest, or sometimes merely orient occasionally toward the CS and think about, expect, the Pavlovian reinforcer. These latter possibilities imply that other ongoing behavior may be affected when a reinforcer memory evokes a preprogrammed sequence that because of environmental constraint then fails to occur.

The General Associative Process in Instrumental Learning

There is an obvious extension of the information gathering function of the general associative process to instrumental learning: Animals may learn to associate the neural correlates of their own behavior with the correlates of external events, much as they learn to associate the neural correlates of two external events (Estes, 1969, 1973). Animals appear to be able to extract information concerning the full range of correlations in time between their behavior and a reinforcer. They may learn that their behavior is correlated positively or negatively with a reinforcer. Also, they may learn that their behavior occurs independently of a reinforcer (Maier, Seligman, & Solomon, 1969). Indeed pigeons learn to differentiate between stimuli correlated with key peck-dependent and key peck-independent food (Weisman & Ramsden, 1973). Thus, animals are not merely influenced by response–reinforcer dependencies, they learn about them.

___

[5] Recently, R. A. Boakes, at Sussex University, has made laboratory observations of the misbehavior of rats with token reinforcers, for example, stimuli correlated with food and water.

Latent learning. Mackintosh (1974, p. 217) has pointed out the similarities between sensory preconditioning and latent learning paradigms. I need only remind the reader that latent learning experiments often show that arrangement of a contingency between a response and an essentially sensory event results in a change in the probability of the response when that event is later correlated with a reinforcer. The role of the reinforcer in insuring that response—reinforcer associations are not subject to latent inhibition has not been explored. One important difficulty is that few response—event correlations are biologically trivial. At the very least such correlations·teach animals to localize objects and events in the spatial environment.

Communality with classical conditioning. According to the view proposed here, the associative process is a general analyzer of events in the space—time continuum, which includes an animal's own behavior. Surely, this common associative process must be basic to many of the well-known similarities in the results of classical conditioning and instrumental learning experiments. The analyzer may apply the same rules to correlations having as their first term either responses or stimuli. However a shared associative process need not imply that differences between classical conditioning and instrumental learning are slight. The associative process is but one determinant of performance. The rules for generating behavior, the performance rules, for classical conditioning and instrumental learning may be different and may even compete for control of ongoing behavior.

Response memories. The concern for cognitive determinants of behavior control, which dominated my consideration of the role of the Pavlovian reinforcer, is most relevant to the case of instrumental learning as well. In classical conditioning reinforcer memories, but not usually response memories, play an important role in generating the CR. In authentic instances of instrumental learning the CR is selected by the response—reinforcer contingency and not merely by the releasing function of the reinforcer itself. Thus, if the instrumental CR is to reoccur, it, and not just the reinforcer, must be remembered.

Memory for the instrumental CR may be viewed as simply a special case of the central representation of motor behavior. Researchers in both ethology (Ewer, 1968, p. 325) and human performance (Keele, 1973) agree in suggesting that specific responses are the result of the enactment of stored motor programs that are more or less complexly represented in memory prior to any given instance of the response. In general the more effect controlled, detailed, and skilled the motor response, the more elaborate one supposes that its enactment code becomes (Posner, 1973, p. 25). It does not follow, however, that the entire motor program must be constructed from traces of its prior occurrence each time a response is emitted or that the entire program for a response must become an element of association.

Innate Behavior in Instrumental Learning

It is currently popular to discount evidence of instrumental control of animal behavior (e.g., Moore, 1973; Bolles, 1972). These authors, and others, now argue that simple innate sequences controlled by Pavlovian contingencies, rather than operant contingencies, may be the common result of our instrumental learning experiments. Indeed, these authors go further, suggesting that relatively little evolutionary pressure exists in favor of response–reinforcer learning. However, we must not let our newly found insight into instinct conditioning blind us to the ample evidence that animals may learn new sequences and organizations of innate behavior units by trial and error correlation with biologically important events.

Some fables. Much nonsense has been written concerning the behavioral products of instrumental learning. Two-process theorists as diverse as Skinner (1938) and Mowrer (1960) have agreed that the behavioral products of instrumental learning are freed of their antecedents, emitted, in a manner that the behavioral products of classical conditioning are not. However it seems quite reasonable to insist that environmental stimuli and animals' expectations elicit the behavioral products of both learning processes. It is sometimes suggested that because, say, rats learn to lever press both to obtain food and to escape shock the same response is associated with two different reinforcers. It is easy to resist this suggestion; perhaps animals can learn to associate the same response topography with different reinforcers, but we have scant evidence in favor of this possibility. Instead it appears (see Davis chapter in this volume) that only the microswitch closures are the same when rats lever press to obtain food and to escape shock. Lever press is not a behavior, it is only an effect of behavior. The topographically different behaviors correlated with food and shock escape are the same "lever press" only in this limited sense. Often, especially in elementary textbooks, one reads that instrumental learning leads to new behaviors. To the biologist, behavior is a substrait of the animal, part of a species' morphology, like its anatomy or pelt. In this basic sense there can be no new behavior without a new skeleton, musculature, and nervous system; these sum to a new, or at least different, species. I therefore reject the notion that instrumental learning involves new behaviors.

Evolution of voluntary control. The origin of instrumental learning seems most likely to be found in classical conditioning with the release of innate sequences of behavior by reinforcer memories. Over conditioning trials vivid Pavlovian CRs, such as sexual displays and fear reactions, may become as well associated with the reinforcer as the relatively drab Pavlovian CS. To one degree or another, any Pavlovian CR may be represented in long-term memory because of its correlation with the reinforcer during classical conditioning. In such instances, animals may be said to learn about response–reinforcer correlations without the benefit of an instrumental learning paradigm. Rescorla has presented evidence, elsewhere in this volume, that higher order Pavlovian conditioning often involves association between a second-order CS and a first-order CR. His analysis, in agreement with the present hypothesis, points to the existence of a CR memory relatively independent of reinforcer memory. The evolution of instrumental behavior modification may have been advanced considerably by the liberation of the CR from direct release by the reinforcer or even the reinforcer memory.

A review of the instrumental learning of naturally occurring species in their usual environments (Ewer, 1968) points out that the components of the instrumental response are remarkably endogenous response units. That is, the individual movements in instrumental response patterns are innate, but animals must learn to select and integrate them so as to produce the proper result. For example, squirrels' nut splitting movements and cats' oriented mouse-neck bites are innate action patterns, but individual animals become increasingly skilled in utilizing them. Even the association between the innate feeding response and having the meal must be learned by cats and squirrels (Leyhausen & Eibl-Eibesfeldt as cited by Ewer, 1968, pp. 318–320). The first time that a cat kills a mouse, therefore, the central representation of the mouse as food may be quite absent, with the response released by the correlates of form and movement only. Then, over trials, the cat becomes increasingly able to aim its attack at the correct bit of the mouse's anatomy from any direction and in an apparently deliberate manner. Similarly, squirrels learn gradually, over trials, to gnaw furrows parallel to the fiber of the nut prior to making the innate splitting movement.

The most reasonable explanation of instrumental learning seems to be that innate sequences of behavior are first released by environmental stimuli correlated with the reinforcer and then selected and arranged according to their relative validities, correlations in time, with the reinforcer. This view makes classical conditioning an evolutionary precursor of instrumental conditioning and instrumental learning the evolutionary mechanism for closed-loop feedback control of the response by its correlation with the reinforcer. Bear in mind, however, that open-loop systems based on the releasing function of the reinforcer are often sufficiently efficient and powerful that no further behavior modification results.

The Instrumental Reinforcement Process

I have recently found it instructive, if somewhat disappointing, to reread Thorndike's *Animal Intelligence* (1911). The experiments dealt with escape from a small enclosure by cats and dogs. Thorndike (1911) notes that "No one who has seen the behavior of these animals when trying to escape could doubt that

these actions were directed by instinctive impulses not by rational observations . . . a dog or cat can open a door by accidental success of its natural
impulses [p. 73] ." This view of the production of instrumental behavior varies
little from that espoused here; it appears that Bolles (1970) has only redis-
covered the importance of species-specific defense reactions.

One can applaud Thorndikes' briefly reported experiments with cats. He
describes the selection of an efficient clawing movement by its correlation with
escape and food. However, one must then react with horror to the logic by
which he, on scant evidence, has rejected response—reinforcer association, and
indeed the notion of memory itself, in favor of the well-known dogma that
reinforcers stamp in or strengthen stimulus—response connections or associations. The course of history in animal learning would have been simplified
immeasurably if Thorndike had seen the role of response selection, which the
admission of response—reinforcer associations made possible. Unfortunately, the
substitution of a response selection performance rule for a strengthening mechanism had to wait another six decades (Staddon & Simmelhag, 1971; Staddon,
1972; and Staddon, this volume). Staddon (1972) stated that "Reinforcement
acts to select properties of behavior including both stimulus and response
components. Selection is determined by relative proximity to reinforcement of
properties that vary in time or the relative frequency of reinforcement for
properties that are constant in time [p. 220] ."

The model of instrumental performance presented here utilizes both releasing
and selecting functions of the reinforcer. The releasing function of the reinforcer is, initially the proper concern of the ethologist. The selecting function of the reinforcer has been approximated, at least, in the new theories of
human motor skill (Keele, 1973; Pew, 1974; Schmidt, 1975). It is in this context
that it seems reasonable for us to view instrumental behavior as skilled motor
performance selected and arranged from the innate motor response units
released by the reinforcer.

Consider Thorndike's cats tucked away in the famous box. The situation
releases a number of innate motor reactions. One such behavior sequence opens
the door. The cat escapes and is fed. When the cat is next inside the box the
sequence correlated with escape may be remembered. However expectations of
escape and food conditioned to the situation may release behavior not present
on the first trial, these latter responses may be correlated with escape and food
as well—and so it goes. Over trials the cat may build a rough schema that
includes salient features of the box, their own behavior, and the relative validity
of these events as correlates of the reinforcer. Of course only the enactment
commands of motor programs and not "responses" are encoded. The effect is to
assemble a sequence of enactment commands which when retrieved by the
occurrence of situational and motivational cues result in a smoothly run
sequence of motor programs. This instrumental response system utilizes control
of the reinforcer in a, mainly, between trials feedback loop. That is, skilled

performance develops a unitary functional aspect, not because of feedback during the trial, but because of the selection and integration of innate motor units as a function of their inclusion in some form during prior trials.

Constraints. It seems reasonable to expect any new performance rules for conditioning and learning to account for the by now well-known "constraints on learning." Specifically, we must be able to account for failure of the correlation of a response with a reinforcer to increase the rate of that response (Bolles, 1970; Shettleworth, 1973). However one must be careful to avoid accounting for a nonphenomenon. The observation that, say, rats do not often learn to lever press to avoid shock can generate theoretical statements about constraints. When subsequent experiments show that most rats learn lever-press avoidance, although slowly, the theory is only slightly embarrassed. Then, later, when other reports show that rats may learn lever-press avoidance quite rapidly when the warning signal is not adjacent to the lever or when the safety signal has previously served as a Pavlovian inhibitor of fear, the theory may appear slightly foolish. The constraints on learning may have to be divided up between the subjects and the experimenters. Even so, it does appear likely that some responses increase in frequency more quickly than others as a function of their correlation with a biologically important event.[6] The present model of instrumental learning begins to account for constraints by recognizing the complexities of the processes involved. There are at least three junctions at which constraint may occur:

1. The response and the reinforcer may simply fail to be associated even though they are, in fact, correlated. This seems an unlikely alternative; most responses are rich in stimulus properties to be associated with the reinforcer.

2. Other responses released by reinforcer memories in concurrent classical conditioning render the instrumental response sequence unlikely. Examples given by Breland and Breland (1961), and in omission training of the pigeons' key peck (Barrera, 1974), seem to be the result of this form of interference with instrumental learning.

3. The central representation of the response memory may be insufficient to enact the behavior. This may be because only stimulus aspects of the response are encoded, because the response is only part of an action pattern and has no separate enactment code, or even because the aspect of the response for which selection is sought is not represented in memory.

Clearly we need to learn more about the enactment codes and motor programs that generate the responses we seek to control. In naturally occurring instru-

___

[6]Evolutionary pressure may be expected to result in rapid assimilation of genetical determinants of instrumental response selection of behavior sequences with especial survival value.

mental learning, the innate units selected by the response—reinforcer contingency are among the behaviors released by expectation of the reinforcer. This seems to describe the instance an instrumental response selection system evolved to control. Selection of innate response units released by other reinforcers may not be impossible but may be only a sometimes useful byproduct of instrumental learning.

Conclusion

After reading this speculative theoretical account of conditioning and learning one might well wish for a return to simpler theories, those eschewing consideration of innate behavior patterns, evolutionary mechanisms, memory, and the complexity of a response selection system as bad botany and worse mentalism. Unfortunately, however, the strengthening theories of reinforcement are falsified by evidence amply cited in this volume. The innate structures, both cognitive and motor, evolved to affect behavior change can no longer be ignored. Instead they invite, if not demand, our attention.

Acknowledgments

This chapter was prepared with support from the National Research Council of Canada while the author was a Canada Council Leave Fellow and Visiting Professor in the Laboratory of Experimental Psychology at the University of Sussex, England. I wish to thank the entire staff of the Laboratory for their kindness during my visit. I am also most grateful to Richard Schuster and Geoffrey Hall for their careful reading of an earlier draft of this chapter.

References

Adler, N., & Hogan, J. A. Classical conditioning and punishment of an instinctive response in Betta splendens, *Animal Behaviour* 1963, **11**, 351–354.

Barrera, F. J. Centrifugal selection of signal-directed pecking. *Journal of the Experimental Analysis of Behavior*, 1974, **22**, 341–355.

Bolles, R. C. Species-specific defense reactions and avoidance learning. *Psychological Review*, 1970, **71**, 32–48.

Bolles, R. C. The avoidance learning problem. In G. H. Bower (Ed.), *The psychology of learning and motivation*. Vol. 6. New York: Academic Press, 1972. Pp. 97–139.

Breland, K., & Breland, M. The misbehavior of organisms. *American Psychologist*, 1961, **16**, 681–684.

Brown, P. L., & Jenkins, H. M. Auto-shaping of the pigeon's key peck. *Journal of the Experimental Analysis of Behaviour*, 11, 1968, 1–8.

Clayton, F. L., & Hinde, R. A. The habituation and recovery of aggressive display in *Betta splendens. Behaviour*, **30**, 1968, 96–106.

Cousins, L. S., Zamble, E., Tait, R. W., & Suboski M. D. Sensory preconditioning in curarized rats. *Journal of Comparative and Physiological Psychology*, 1971, 77, 152–154.

Crisler, G. Salivation is unnecessary for the establishment of the salivary conditioned reflex induced by morphine. *American Journal of Physiology*, 1930, 94, 553–556.

Debold, R. C., Miller, N. E., & Jensen, D. D. Effect of strength of drive determined by a new technique for appetitive classical conditioning of rats. *Journal of Comparative and Physiological Psychology*, 1965, **59**, 102–108.

Denny, M. R., & Ratner, S. C. *Comparative psychology: Research in animal behavior.* Homewood, Ill.: The Dorsey Press, 1970.

Estes, W. K. New perspectives on some old issues in association theory. In N. J. Mackintosh & W. K. Honig (Eds.), *Fundamental issues in associative learning.* Halifax, N. S.: Dalhousie University Press, 1969. Pp. 162–189.

Estes, W. K. Memory and conditioning. In F. J. McGuigan & D. Barry Lumsden (Eds.), *Contemporary approaches to conditioning and learning.* Washington, D.C.: V. H. Winston & Sons, Inc., 1973. Pp. 265–286.

Ewer, R. F. *Ethology of mammals.* London: Elek Science, 1968.

Farris, H. E. Behavioral development social organization and conditioning of courting behavior in Japanese quail, *Coturnix coturnix japonica.* Unpublished doctoral dissertation, Michigan State University, 1964.

Farris, H. E. Classical conditioning of courting behaviour in the Japanese quail, *Coturnix coturnix japonica. Journal of Experimental Analysis Behaviour,* 1967, **10**, 213–217.

Finch, G. Salivary conditioning in atropinized dogs, *American Journal of Physiology*, 1938, **124**, 136–141.

Glickman, S. E. Responses and reinforcement. In R. A. Hinde & J. Stevenson-Hinde (Eds.), *Constraints on learning.* London: Academic Press, 1973. Pp. 207–241.

Gormezano, I. Classical conditioning. In J. B. Sidowski (Ed.), *Experimental methods and instrumentation in psychology.* New York: McGraw-Hill, 1966. Pp. 385–420.

Hearst, E., & Jenkins, H. M. *Sign-tracking: The stimulus reinforcer relation and directed action.* Austin, Texas: Psychonomic Society, 1974.

Hinde, R. A. Factors governing the changes in strength of a partially inborn response, as shown by the mobbing behaviour of the chaffinch: I. The nature of the response, and an examination of its course. *Proceedings of the Royal Society*, 1954, **142**, 306–331; II. The waning of the response *Proceedings of the Royal Society*, 1954, **142**, 331–358.

Hinde, R. A. *Animal behaviour. A synthesis of ethology and comparative psychology*, New York: McGraw-Hill, 1970.

Hoffeld, D. R., Kendall, S. B., Thompson, R. F., & Brogden, W. J. Effect of amount of preconditioning training upon the magnitude of sensory preconditioning. *Journal of Experimental Psychology*, 1960, **59**, 198–204.

Hogan, J. A. Responses in Pavlovian conditioning studies, *Science*, 1974, **186**, 156–157.

Keele, S. W. *Attention and human performance.* Pacific Palisades, California: Goodyear, 1973.

Kendall, S. B., & Thompson, R. F. Effect of stimulus similarity on sensory preconditioning within a single stimulus dimension, *Journal of Comparative and Physiological Psychology*, 1960, **53**, 439–442.

Kimble, G. A. *Hilgard and Marquis' conditioning and learning.* (2nd ed.) New York: Appleton-Century-Crofts, 1961.

Lett, B. T. Long delay learning in the T maze. *Learning and Motivation*, 1975, **6**, 80–90.

Lorenz, K. *Evolution and modification of behaviour.* Chicago: University of Chicago Press, 1965.

Lorenz, K. *Studies in animal and human behaviour.* Vol. 1. London: Methuen, 1970.

Lubow, R. E., & Moore, A. U. Latent inhibition: The effect of non-reinforced preexposure to the conditioned stimulus. *Journal of Comparative and Physiological Psychology*, 1959, **52**, 415–419.

Lubow, R. E., & Siebert, L. Latent inhibition within the CER paradigm. *Journal of Comparative and Physiological Psychology*, 1969, **68**, 136–138.

Mackintosh, N. J. Stimulus selection: learning to ignore stimuli that predict no change in reinforcement. In R. A. Hinde & J. Stevension-Hinde (Eds.), *Constraints on learning.* London: Academic Press, 1973. Pp. 75–96.

Mackintosh, N. J. *The psychology of animal learning.* London: Academic Press, 1974.

Maier, S. F., Seligman, M. E. P., & Solomon, R. L. Pavlovian fear conditioning and learned helplessness. In B. A. Campbell & R. M. Church (Eds.), *Punishment and aversive behavior.* New York: Appleton-Century-Crofts, 1969. Pp. 299–342.

McFarland, D. J. *Feedback mechanisms in animal behaviour.* London, New York: Academic Press, 1971.

Moore, B. R. The role of directed Pavlovian reactions in simple instrumental learning in the pigeon. In R. A. Hinde & J. Stevenson-Hinde (Eds.), *Constraints on learning.* London: Academic Press, 1973. Pp. 159–186.

Mowrer, O. H. *Learning theory and behavior.* New York: Wiley, 1960.

Neisser, U. *Cognitive psychology.* New York: Appleton-Century-Crofts, 1967.

Noirot, E. Changes in responsiveness to young in the adult mouse: I. The problematical effect of hormones. *Animal Behaviour,* 1964, **12,** 52–58.

Pavlov, I. P. *Conditioned reflexes.* New York: Oxford University Press, 1927.

Pew, R. W. Human perceptual-motor performance. In B. H. Kandowitz (Ed.), *Human information processing: tutorials in performance and cognition.* Hillsdale, N.J.: Lawrence Erlbaum Associates, 1974. Pp. 1–40.

Posner, M. J. *Cognition: An introduction.* Glenview, Ill.: Scott, Foresman, 1973.

Prewitt, E. P. Number of preconditioning trials in sensory preconditioning using CER training. *Journal of Comparative and Physiological Psychology,* 1967, **64,** 360–362.

Rescorla, R. A. Probability of shock in the presence and absence of CS in fear conditioning, *Journal of Comparative and Physiological Psychology,* 1968, **66,** 1–5.

Rescorla, R. A. Summation and retardation tests of latent inhibition. *Journal of Comparative and Physiological Psychology,* 1971, **75,** 77–81.

Rescorla, R. A., & Heth, C. D. Reinstatement of fear to an extinguished conditioned stimulus. *Journal of Experimental Psychology: Animal Behavior Processes,* 1975, **1,** 88–96.

Rescorla, R. A., & Solomon, R. L. Twoprocess learning theory: Relationship between Pavlovian conditioning and instrumental learning. *Psychological Review,* 1967, **74,** 151–182.

Rizley, R. C., & Rescorla, R. A. Associations in second-order conditioning and sensory preconditioning. *Journal of Comparative and Physiological Psychology,* 1972, **81,** 1–11.

Schmidt, R. A. A schema theory of discrete motor skill learning. *Psychological Review,* 1975, **82,** 225–260.

Seidel, R. J. A review of sensory preconditioning, *Psychological Bulletin,* 1959, **56,** 58–73.

Sharpless, S., & Jasper, H. Habituation of the arousal reaction. *Brain,* 1956, **79,** 655–680.

Shettleworth, S. J. Food reinforcement and the organization of behavior in Golden Hamsters. In R. A. Hinde & J. Stevenson-Hinde (Eds.), *Constraints on learning.* London: Academic Press, 1973. Pp. 243–265.

Siegel, S. Latent inhibition and eyelid conditioning. In A. H. Black & W. F. Prokasy (Eds.), *Classical conditioning.* Vol. II. New York: Appleton, 1972. Pp. 231–247.

Skinner, B. F. *The behavior of organisms.* New York: Appleton, 1938.

Sokolov, E. N. Neuronal models and the orienting reflex. In M. A. B. Brazier (Ed.), *The central nervous system and behaviour.* New York: Macy Foundation, 1960.

Solomon, R. L., & Turner, L. H. Discriminative classical conditioning in dogs paralyzed by curare can later control discriminative avoidance responses in the normal state. *Psychological Review,* 1962, **69,** 202–219.

Staddon, J. E. R. Temporal control and the theory of reinforcement schedules. In R. M.

Gilbert & J. R. Millenson (Eds.), *Reinforcement behavioral analyses.* New York: Academic Press, 1972. Pp. 209–261.

Staddon, J. E. R., & Simmelhag, V. L. The "superstition" experiment: A re-examination of its implications for principles of adaptive behavior. *Psychological Review,* 1971, 78, 3–43.

Terrace, H. S. Classical conditioning. In J. A. Nevin (Ed.), *The study of behavior,* Glenview, Ill.: Scott, Foresman, 1973. Pp. 71–115.

Thompson, T., & Sturm, T. Classical conditioning of aggressive display in Siamese fighting fish. *Journal of the Experimental Analysis of Behaviour,* 1965, 8, 397–403.

Thorndike, E. L. *Animal intelligence.* New York: Macmillan, 1911.

Thorpe, W. H. *Learning and instinct in animals.* (1st ed.) London: Methuen, 1956.

Tinbergen, N. *The study of instinct.* Ocford: Clarendon Press, 1951.

Tolman, E. C. *Purposive behaviour in animals and men,* New York: Century, 1932.

von Holst, E., & von St. Paul, U. vom Wirkungsgefuge der Triebe, *Naturwissenschaften,* 1960, 18, 409–422. Translated in *Animal Behavior,* 1963, 11, 1–20.

Waddington, C. H. Genetic assimilation of an acquired character. *Evolution,* 1953, 7, 118–126.

Wasserman, E. A. The effect of redundant contextual stimuli on auto-shaping the pigeon's keypeck. *Animal Learning and Behavior,* 1973, 1, 198–206.

Wearden, J. H. The effect of independent stimulus and reinforcement manipulations on the behavior produced by single trial aversive conditioning. Paper read at the annual meeting of Experimental Analysis of Behavior Group, Exeter, England, 1975.

Weisman, R. G. Experimental comparison of classical and instrumental appetitive conditioning. *American Journal of Psychology,* 1965, 78, 423–431.

Weisman, R. G., & Ramsden, M. Discrimination of a response-independent component in a multiple schedule. *Journal of the Experimental Analysis of Behavior,* 1973, 19, 55–64.

Woodruff, G. Autoshaping: a "learned release" hypothesis. Paper read at the annual meeting of the Eastern Psychological Association, Philadelphia, Pa., 1974.

Zener, K. The significance of behaviour accompanying conditioned salivary secretion for theories of the conditioned response, *American Journal of Psychology,* 1937, 50, 384–403.

DISCUSSION

Much of the discussion that followed Weisman's presentation centered on his use of sensory preconditioning as a model for the general associative process. In his words, "... the sensory preconditioning situation does not involve a reinforcer but consists of an association between events that appear in most respects to be biologically trivial or neutral."

Among the issues raised were the following:

Staddon: Ron, I'm puzzled by what you're suggesting. It sounds like a two-factor theory of sorts. On one hand, you are suggesting a general associative process which you are calling sensory preconditioning. You claim that events are associated regardless of their nature or importance. On the other hand, you postulate a habituation process. Under it, the things that we call reinforcers or important motivational stimuli may take longer to habituate than other events.

Do you propose, then, to explain all of learning with reference to these two processes? Also, that events are differentially associable only because of differences in the habituation mechanism?

Weisman: Yes to both questions.

Jenkins: I'm not convinced that there is compelling evidence to support the notion of a general associative process. Even if there is, however, I don't agree that sensory preconditioning is the best model to follow.

Seligman: I'd also like to question the notion that there is a general associative process. I can suggest four learning-related phenomena which appear to be widely different from what is held to be the typical associative process. The first is taste-aversion learning; the second is bird-song learning; the third, which we hardly ever talk about, is prism adaptation; and the fourth is the McCullough effect. I would think, for instance, that both prism adaptation and the McCullough effect require us to invoke special associative processes for the visual system.

Weisman's reply suggested the possibility that although several different response systems, each with its own unique properties (such as characteristic temporal delays) might exist, it was still reasonable to consider only a single general associative process. Therefore, the differences that prompted Seligman's question were, under Weisman's system, presumed to reflect differences in the characteristics of response systems rather than differences in underlying associative processes.

Hurwitz: You seem to be arguing that sensory preconditioning is a well-established phenomenon. Wouldn't you agree that this is an area in which a great number of negative results exist?

Weisman: Perhaps, but there has been a vast improvement in our techniques over recent years. For example, Rizley and Rescorla (1972) describe an effective technique for studying sensory preconditioning. I've also seen some impressive demonstrations of sensory preconditioning of curarized subjects in Milt Suboski's laboratory at Queen's University.

Hurwitz: When I last looked at the sensory preconditioning literature and performed an operational analysis on what people had actually done, I came to the conclusion that although there were occasional effects, they often appeared to have much to do with the nature of the two stimuli that were being associated. In successful demonstrations the two stimuli hardly ever appeared to be "biologically neutral" with respect to each other; for example, sound preceding light rather than light preceding sound. In short, why do you use these experiments to argue in favor of a general associative process? It seems to be a weak argument because the experimental evidence in this area is also weak.

Weisman: I dispute the fact that the evidence is weak. More careful work has been done on the sensory preconditioning phenomenon than on many of the so-called established facts of behavior theory.

Garcia: I see some problems with the concept of "biological neutrality." If the organism already had the information you were trying to teach it from other sources, sensory preconditioning would be redundant and unsuccessful. On the other hand, if the organism were in a sensory deprived situation, then your manipulation of the environment would be tremendously important. Many of the unsuccessful demonstrations in this literature may reflect the fact that the information contained in sensory preconditioning was useless and redundant.

Seligman: If you are proposing that what goes on in sensory preconditioning is a way of looking at the general associative process, and that sensory preconditioning is intimately related to correlation, it seems to me that we are missing some important data. For instance, we only know at best that sensory preconditioning results from pairing S_1 and S_2. We know nothing of inhibitory sensory preconditioning effects, however, and as far as I know, no one has ever run correlational studies between S_1 and S_2 and looked for the appropriate transfer effects.

Weisman: Marty, you're absolutely right. There are no such data. This is unfortunate because they would represent an ideal test of the generality of sensory preconditioning as an instance of the associative process.

In the course of discussing the general associative process proposed by Weisman, a distinction was raised between two possible effects of exposure to an association. Stating the case loosely, in the first view behavior is directly affected by the correlation between events. This may take the form of a change in the probability of response or, in the term proposed by Garcia, of a "hedonic shift." In the second view, an animal learns or gains information about the correlation that exists in the environment. Its behavior need not be affected and the predominent effect of this association may be termed cognitive. Regarding this distinction, Weisman said the following:

Weisman: I am confident that no behavior need be generated by exposure to correlation between events even though they are learned about; and I am also sure that most of the correlations that we learn have no effect on our behavior at all.

This conclusion and related points in Weisman's chapter generated the following comments:

Jenkins: If I had read only the first part of your chapter I would have thought that the animal simply learns about correlations. For example, having knowledge about a correlation between signal and food, the animal will go to where food is likely to appear in the presence of the signal. In the second part of the chapter, however, you begin to discuss the manner in which behavior is engaged by events in the environment, and it seems to me that you are shifting ground a great deal. One wonders why you have to invoke two processes: the animal (1) learning about correlations in the environment and (2) somehow deciding that the thing to do in the presence of a signal is to go after the food.

Weisman: I am not suggesting in any formal sense that a decision is involved. The animal does not decide to peck or not to peck at the key. My point is that a cognitive representation of the US is responsible for generating the behaviors we observe.

Jenkins: I take exception to your use of autoshaping as an example of this form of association. Autoshaping does not represent a cognitive process in any sense. The subject does very stupid things. However, we know that autoshaping makes sense in terms of evolution. In fact, I can't imagine how you could find any surviving trait, structure, or behavioral pattern and presume that it had no evolutionary or adaptive significance.

Davis: I would think that structures such as antlers, as well as certain behavior patterns, which evolved for perfectly good reasons, may get somewhat out of step with their present environments and appear quite "stupid," as Herb [Jenkins] has termed them. In such transitional conditions, I'm not sure we have to assume that these structures or behaviors continue to be reasonable and adaptive simply because they reflect what has once evolved.

Garcia: However, remember that the Darwinian axiom is that the contingencies in the world for any species today are by in large the same as when the species evolved. Otherwise the species would be dead. Jenkins has come close to testing this in his autoshaping experiments. He could probably starve a pigeon to death in a Skinner box because the pigeon would rather peck at a light than eat his grain.

Jenkins: We've never done it quite that dramatically but I assume it could be done.

Weisman's contention that Pavlovian conditioning was instinct conditioning generated considerable discussion. Among the comments that were made are the following:

Shettleworth: What would be an exception to the principle that Pavlovian conditioning is instinct conditioning?

Weisman: Although I believe this to be the general case, I have come across several exceptions. One is the conditioned emotional response, which I am not sure can be construed as an innate response. A second is drug conditioning, and a third is interoceptive conditioning, where no observable behaviors, as we conventionally define them, are involved.

Davis: I'm confused about the status that an instinct has after it has come through the Pavlovian conditioning process. Perhaps a more direct way of stating my question is to ask whether the implications of your position are more drastic for the learning theorist or for the ethologist. Presumably both of their sacred domains have been affected by your premise.

Weisman: I'm afraid that the implications of my position are more drastic for the learning theorist than they are for the ethologist. Unlike ethology, which has always presumed that elements of behavior could be modified without significantly affecting their innateness, psychology has bought the relatively inflexible rules associated with the reflexive model.

References

Rizley, R. C., & Rescorla, R. A. Associations in second-order conditioning and sensory preconditioning. *Journal of Comparative and Physiological Psychology,* 1972, **81,** 1–11.

2

A Note on the
Operant Conditioning
of Autonomic Responses

A. H. Black
B. Osborne
W. C. Ristow

McMaster University

INTRODUCTION

Because it was believed that autonomic responses could not be successfully conditioned by operant techniques, autonomic behavior was repeatedly used as an index of Pavlovian conditioning. In the mid-1960s, a number of researchers argued that autonomic responses could be conditioned by either operant or Pavlovian methods, therefore invalidating them as a technique for distinguishing between operant and Pavlovian conditioning. However, Miller's failure to replicate several important demonstrations of operant control of autonomic functions has forced us to face the question of whether to return to our original position, which draws parallel distinctions between operant and Pavlovian conditioning and the skeletal vs. autonomic nervous systems. In the following chapter, Black, Osborne, and Ristow argue that despite the questionable status of Miller's data, there are sufficient suggestions of operant control of some autonomic functions to keep one from distinguishing between types of conditioning in this manner.

The topic of this book is operant–Pavlovian interactions. This chapter deals with what may be described as one aspect of a subcategory of a closely related topic. The "closely related topic" is the attempt to distinguish between Pavlovian and operant conditioning. It is closely related because one must be able to tell the difference between the two if one is to study their interaction. The "subcategory" consists of the various versions of the notion that operant and Pavlovian conditioning can be distinguished by the class of responses that is affected by each. The "aspect" is concerned with whether autonomic responses should be classified with those responses that cannot be operantly conditioned. We shall make a few preliminary comments about the more general issues and then discuss the operant conditioning of autonomic responses.

One can distinguish between operant conditioning and Pavlovian conditioning on the basis of the experimental procedures employed. However, this distinction is not as interesting, perhaps, as some others:

1. Are different things learned as a consequence of the application of Pavlovian and operant conditioning procedures?
2. Is the mechanism that produces learning different in each?

If the two procedures were mutually exclusive one could hope to find answers to those questions relatively easily. Unfortunately, they are not, as we and others have pointed out *ad nauseum*. When one carries out one procedure, one usually carries out the other inadvertently (Black, 1971).[1] This difficulty, however, has not stemmed the flow of attempted answers to these questions.

The first question is the one that is relevant to the issues dealt with in this chapter. One can distinguish at least two types of answers proposing that different things are learned in Pavlovian and in operant conditioning. The members of the first class, which seems to be gaining popularity these days, suggest that associations between central representations of stimuli are formed by Pavlovian procedures and associations between central representations of the response and the reinforcer, or of discriminative stimulus, response, and reinforcer, are produced by operant conditioning. The particular response that occurs in a given Pavlovian conditioning situation is one that reflects the knowledge of the temporal relationship among the central representations of events.

Those answers in the second class suggest that associations between stimuli and specific responses are formed by both Pavlovian and operant conditioning and,

[1] Recently more use has been made of procedures that reduce the significance of this type of confounding. These procedures include omission training (e.g., Williams & Williams, 1969), which pits Pavlovian and instrumental contingencies against one another during appetitive Pavlovian conditioning, an analogous procedure developed by Gormenzano and Coleman (1973) that pits Pavlovian and operant conditioning against one another during Pavlovian aversive conditioning, and the bidirectional design that holds Pavlovian contingencies approximately constant while groups are exposed to opposite instrumental contingencies (Black, 1967; Miller & DiCara, 1967). Each of these procedures involves difficulties with respect to interpretation. Jenkins (this volume) has discussed omission training in this respect, and Black, Cott, and Pavloski (in press) have discussed problems associated with the bidirectional design.

furthermore, that different types of responses are associated with the stimulus in each. The amenability of autonomic responses to operant conditioning is of particular concern for those who support this position; if autonomic responses can be operantly conditioned the distinction between the two procedures based on the dichotomy between skeletal and autonomic responses becomes no longer valid.

The view that autonomic responses could not be operantly conditioned was held quite strongly by some—but without much empirical support. (See Black, 1971 for a review of this literature.) Then in the 1960s, a number of papers appeared which indicated that operant conditioning of autonomic responses was possible. Miller (1969) argued quite strongly that the good name of autonomic responses had been maligned in the past and that they were amenable to operant conditioning—but, as it turned out, again without much empirical support. Neither he nor his colleagues nor researchers in other laboratories have been able to replicate as yet the results on which Miller based his arguement, that is, the results on the operant conditioning of autonomic responses in curarized rats. (See chapters by Black, by Brener, by DiCara, by Hahn, by Miller and Dworkin and by Roberts et al. in Obrist, Black, Brener, & DiCara, 1974).[2]

If one holds these data on curarized rats in limbo, it turns out that there remain few well-controlled published studies on operant autonomic conditioning—particularly in infrahuman subjects. For example, conditioning of low and high heart rates has been reported only by Black (1967, 1971) in partially curarized dogs, and by Engel (1974) and Engel and Gottlieb (1970) in normal monkeys. This work suffers from certain deficiencies. For example, in none of the experiments have randomly reinforced control groups been utilized; therefore, one cannot specify precisely the effects of the reinforcement contingencies. The operant conditioning of increases in blood pressure in infrahuman subjects has been reported (again without the control group that one should like), but attempts to condition decreases in blood pressures have not been successful (Harris, Gilliam, Findley, & Brady, 1973). Furthermore, although the data on human subjects tend to be more satisfactory, (e.g., Blanchard, Scott, Young, & Haynes, 1974; Gatchel, 1974; Lang & Twentyman, 1974; Schwartz, 1975), a number of failures have been reported (e.g., Mandler, Preven, & Kuhlman, 1962; Stern, 1967), the effects of operant training have been relatively small, and the research designs have been often inadequate, as Blanchard and Young (1973, 1974) have pointed out in detail.

The current state of knowledge on operant autonomic condition can be summarized as follows. First, although the evidence suggests that operant conditioning

---

[2] A number of other people have reported successful operant conditioning of heart rate (Hothersall & Brener, 1969; Slaughter, Hahn, & Rinaldi, 1970; and Gliner, Horvath, & Wolfe, 1975), but Hothersall and Brener and Slaughter et al. have subsequently reported difficulties in replicating their findings.

does occur in some cases, more carefully controlled studies are needed—particularly studies that include control groups which provide information as to whether observed changes can be attributed to the reinforcement contingency. The bidirectional design, which seems to have become something of a security blanket for a number of researchers in this field, is useful but not sufficient by itself (see Footnote 1). Second, and this is the main point that we should like to make, even if one agrees that operant autonomic conditioning has been demonstrated in some cases, one still does not have the information that is needed in order to talk sensibly about the operant conditionability of autonomic responses. One needs to know a great deal more about the range of autonomic responses that can be conditioned; we do not think that all of them are the same in this respect (Roberts, Lacroix, & Wright, 1974). Furthermore, one needs to know more about the amount of change and the type of change that can be produced in a given autonomic response; there are not enough data to give a reasonable estimate on the limits to which particular response systems can be pushed.

Part of the reason for the absence of data on these issues can be found in the recent history of research on operant autonomic conditioning. The early published experiments employed simple procedures that led to striking effects. This success seems to have dampened the attempt to systematically develop more powerful procedures, at least until recently. As a consequence, one does not know whether the paucity of data on operant autonomic conditioning can be attributed to some refractoriness of autonomic responses to operant control or to the failure to develop and employ adequate procedures.

In research that we have been carrying out recently, we have attempted to deal with two of the issues discussed above. First, we attempted to provide data that might give us more information about the effects of the contingency between response and reinforcer by comparing rats that were reinforced for producing high heart rate or low heart rate with rats exposed to a reinforcer that was presented randomly with respect to the response. Second, we attempted to find out more about the degree to which a given response can be changed by operant conditioning procedures by comparing the efficacy of three different shaping procedures.

Rats were given 5 days of adaptation followed by either 5 or 10 days of acquisition. Training was carried out in a running wheel with brain stimulation serving as the reinforcer. A PDP-8 computer was employed to present stimuli and reinforcements and to record and analyze heart rate. An Electrocraft activity recorder and a Sony 3600 videocorder were employed to measure skeletal activity. Four groups of rats were trained as follows:

1. The shaping procedure that has been most frequently employed in research on operant autonomic conditioning can be labeled. a reinforcement density procedure. The target response is either an interbeat interval (IBI) of very short

duration (that is, fast heart rate) or an IBI of relatively long duration (that is, slow heart rate). Successive approximations (that is, IBIs of successively decreasing or increasing duration) to these target responses are reinforced. In this case, one sets some criterion level to define the first approximation to the target response and reinforcement is presented if this criterion is met or exceeded. The criterion is made more difficult when the reinforcement density becomes high or, to put it another way, when the latency of response becomes short. The criterion is made easier when reinforcement density falls below some minimum level. In this procedure, there are really two criteria, the first for determining when reinforcement is to be given, and the second for determining when the first criterion is to be changed.

We employed the following version of this procedure to train a group of four rats (two for producing high heart rates and two for producing low heart rates). Each daily session consisted of 20 100-sec trials (SD periods) preceded by one 10-min SΔ period and followed by a 10-min SΔ period. The experimenter selected a criterion heart rate level, and any four consecutive IBIs that equalled the criterion or exceeded it were reinforced. The criterion was made more difficult when an average of 10 or more reinforcements occurred on each of the previous five trials. The criterion was made easier when an average of fewer than five reinforcements occurred on each of the previous five trials. When such an automatic criterion change occurred, it was always by some fixed amount. Whenever the criterion became easier, it was always by 1 msec, and whenever it became more difficult, it was always by 2 msec.

2. A second group of eight subjects was trained (four to produce high and four to produce low heart rates) using a percentile reinforcement procedure (Platt, 1973). A procedure similar to this has been employed on curarized rats (Fields, 1970; Roberts *et al.*, 1974). In this procedure, the criterion for defining the response that is to be reinforced is determined on the basis of a continuously updated frequency distribution of response values, and this criterion is automatically adjusted so that the probability of reinforcement (computed with respect to number of responses instead of time) remains constant. We reinforced sets of four consecutive IBIs in the following way. At the beginning of the first trial on each day, IBIs were sampled until a total of 50 were collected, and these were used to construct a frequency distribution of IBI values. The four IBIs occurring next were sampled; if all four IBIs equalled or exceeded the shortest IBI in the distribution (for producing fast heart rates) or the longest IBI in the distribution (for producing slow heart rates), reinforcement occurred. Regardless of whether reinforcement occurred, the IBI that was "worst" among the four with respect to the criterion was added to the distribution of 50 and the IBI that was temporally first to be placed in the distribution of 50 was deleted. Another set of four successive IBIs was then sampled, the above procedure was repeated, and so on. This procedure guaranteed that each response of four IBIs had to equal or exceed 98% of the previous 50 responses in order to be reinforced.

3. A third group of four rats was trained using a random reinforcement procedure. Reinforcement was not contingent on any aspect of the rats' behavior but the density and pattern of reinforcement approximated that delivered to animals on the percentile reinforcement schedule.

4. A fourth group is being trained currently (four rats have been trained to produce increases and three to produce decreases in heart rate) using a procedure that combines features of the percentile reinforcement and constant criterion schedules. This schedule was identical to the percentile reinforcement schedule except for one feature: When the heart rate went above (or below) a fixed criterion level, the percentile reinforcement schedule was superseded by a constant criterion schedule in which every response exceeding the fixed criterion was reinforced. In addition, this group received longer SΔ periods during each session.

Rats trained on the reinforcement density procedure displayed neither significant increases nor significant decreases in heart rate. Three out of four rats displayed fast heart rate with respect to the pretraining baseline on Day 1 of training, and then all decreased or remained constant over days. An example of data for two rats is shown in Fig. 2.1.

We had planned to train more animals employing this procedure, but a detailed analysis of the results suggested that it was subject to a serious flaw. This flaw is revealed most clearly when one employs reinforcers, such as brain stimulation, the omission of which leads to rapid extinction. When the criterion became very difficult for rats reinforced for heart rate increases, a reduction in reinforcement density occurred. When this happened, the animals quickly became less active and the heart rate dropped; this moved the heart rate further below the criterion level and made the occurrence of reinforcement even less probable. In short, a positive-feedback loop was established that interfered with conditioning. For those rats in which slow heart rates were shaped, the opposite condition held. When the criterion reached a point at which few reinforcements were obtained, the animals would become quiet, the heart rate would drop, and reinforcement density would increase. In this case a feedback loop was established that facilitated conditioning. This asymmetry between the groups being trained to produce fast and slow heart rates interfered with learning to increase heart rate and led, we think, to a failure to find group differences with this shaping procedure. In any case, we concluded that this procedure was not particularly useful and abandoned it.

The data on the percentile reinforcement schedule were more encouraging. Data for animals run in this group and for the rats run in the random reinforcement group are shown in Fig. 2.2. At the end of training, there were significant differences between groups reinforced for increasing and decreasing heart rates, and there were not significant between-group differences in baseline heart rate. A comparison with the random control group showed a significant difference

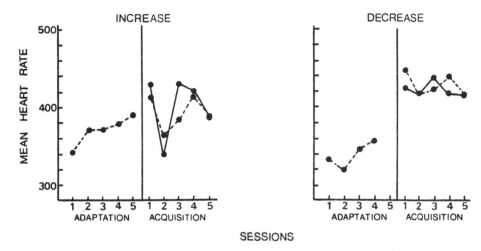

FIG. 2.1 Heart rate as a function of days of training (sessions). A reinforcement density procedure was employed during acquisition. (See text for more details on this procedure.) For rats in the "increase" group reinforcement was delivered when the heart rate was equal to or greater than a criterion level. For rats in the "decrease" group reinforcement was delivered when the heart rate fell below a criterion level. Solid lines, SD; dashed lines, SΔ.

between the increase group and the random group but not between the decrease group and the random group.

The rats' behavior immediately preceding reinforcement, obtained from video-tape for Session 5, was categorized and the profiles are presented in Fig. 2.3. As in the heart rate data, there were clear differences between increase and decrease groups and increase and random groups, but not between the decrease and random groups. As is evident from this figure, the group reinforced for increases in heart rate tended to engage in more vigorous behavior than either of the other two groups.

At first glance, these data could be taken to mean that the conditioning procedure had no effect on the behavior of the rats in the decrease group. However, further analysis of the videotapes suggested differences in the patterns of behavior exhibited by the decrease and random groups. The animals in the group in which decreases in heart rate were reinforced displayed alternation between periods of increased skeletal activity and periods of decreased activity (e.g., walking followed by slowing down), whereas the animals in the random group displayed a more irregular pattern of activity. These observations are supported by the fact that differences between the two groups in the walking category approached significance.

It seemed possible to us that animals in the decrease group engaged in the cyclical pattern of behavior because this strategy led to a higher rate of reinforcement. We thought that we could increase the likelihood of the animal's

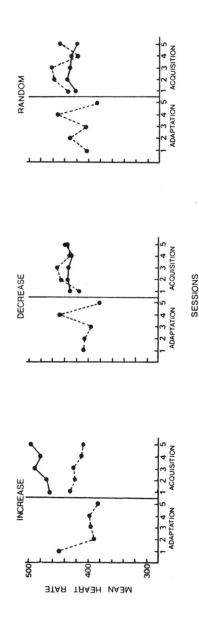

FIG. 2.2 Heart rate as a function of days of training (sessions). A percentile reinforcement training procedure was employed during acquisition. (See text for more details on this procedure.) Cardiac accelerations were reinforced in the "increased" group, and cardiac decelerations were reinforced in the "decrease" group. For the "random" group reinforcement was not contingent on behavior. Solid lines, SD; dashed lines, SΔ.

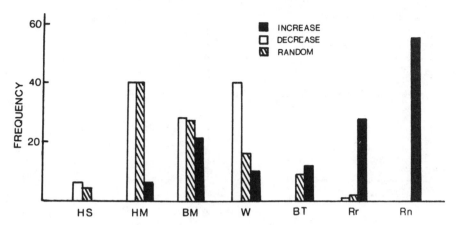

FIG. 2.3 Frequency distribution of behaviors displayed immediately preceding reinforcement by rats trained under the percentile reinforcement and random reinforcement procedures. HS, holding still; HM, head movements; BM, body movements; W, walking; BT, body turn; Rr, rearing; Rn, running.

maintaining a steady low heart rate by adding the constant criterion feature to the percentile reinforcement schedule because this feature resulted in the reinforcement of all responses below some fixed rate. At the least, it would tell us whether animals could push their heart rates lower by the alternation strategy described above than by the maintenance of steady low rates.

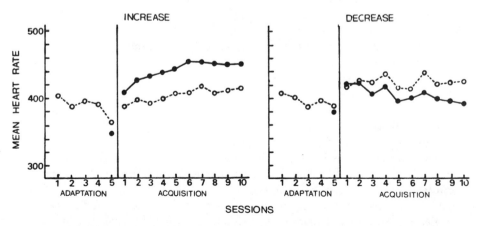

FIG. 2.4 Heart rate as a function of days of training (sessions). A program combining features of the percentile reinforcement and constant criterion procedures was employed during acquisition. (See text for more details on this procedure.) Increases in heart rate were reinforced in the "increase" group, and decreases in heart rate were reinforced in the "decrease" group.

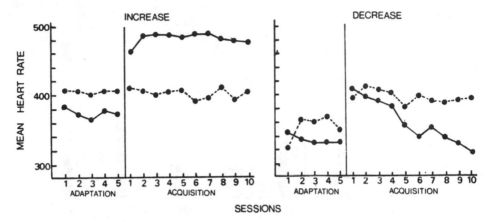

FIG. 2.5 Heart rate as a function of days of training (sessions). These data were obtained by Brener using a shock-avoidance procedure. Heart rates below a criterion level were punished in the "increase" group and heart rates above a criterion level were punished in the "decrease" group. Solid lines, SD; dashed lines, SΔ.

Animals in the percentile reinforcement plus constant criterion groups are still being trained. Therefore, we have not analyzed the results. The data on heart rate, which are shown in Fig. 2.4, do suggest two things. The increase procedure had effects which were similar to the effects of the percentile reinforcement schedule; the decrease procedure seemed somewhat more effective.

Brener (personal communication), employing a shock avoidance procedure, has obtained data on heart rate that are very similar to ours. Rats received 5 days of adaptation with each session 40 min in duration. Thereafter, they were submitted to 10 days of conditioning using a shock-avoidance procedure. SD and SΔ segments, each 10 min in duration, alternated; each session commenced with an SΔ period. Two groups of rats were trained: One was reinforced for decreasing heart rate and the other for increasing heart rate. During SD periods, a tone was presented whenever the animal failed to display criterion behavior. The animal could terminate the tone by exhibiting criterion behavior, but if it failed to do so a shock would ensue and the shock would be followed by a 10-sec time out, following which the procedure would recycle. A criterion heart rate response was defined as five successive IBIs occurring in a period that was either longer (reinforce low heart rate) or shorter (reinforce high heart rate) than an adjustable criterion interval. The tone came on following the first five-IBI sample that did not meet the criterion and the shock was presented if the animal emitted five successive samples of five IBIs that did not meet the criterion. The criterion was made more stringent whenever the animal succeeded in avoiding the shock continuously for a period of 2 min or avoiding the tone for a period of 30 sec. It was made easier whenever the animal received five successive shocks without any avoidance or postponement.

The results are shown in Fig. 2.5. They are very similar to the data we obtained using the percentile reinforcement plus constant criterion procedure.[3] In addition, Brener also found a close correlation between heart rate and skeletal activity.

Conclusion

There are four points that we should like to make in discussing these results.

1. The fact that different shaping procedures have had such different effects is, to say the least, not surprising. Nevertheless, it does reinforce the point that we have made in the introduction to this chapter: The detailed study of the effectiveness of the conditioning procedure is a worthwhile venture at this time.

2. Heart rate responses (particularly high heart rates) can be operantly conditioned in normal animals. Therefore, one cannot argue that autonomic responses are not amenable to operant control, and that autonomic responding can be employed to distinguish between Pavlovian and operant conditioning. In particular, these data make it clear that one cannot employ a change in autonomic responding that occurs during operant conditioning as an index of some nonoperant process. For example, one cannot use a change in heart rate to a discriminative stimulus for a lever pressing avoidance response as an index of "classically conditioned fear" of that discriminative stimulus.

It may, of course turn out that other autonomic responses cannot be operantly conditioned. Even if this were the case, however, one would still not be able to employ the autonomic–skeletal distinction, as it is commonly understood, to distinguish between Pavlovian and operant conditioning.

3. There is a close positive correlation between heart rate changes and skeletal activity. Such correlations have been taken as evidence for the mediation of autonomic responses by skeletal responses or by central neural processes that initiate skeletal responses; that is, for the view that skeletal activity is changed by the response–reinforcer relation and the autonomic change is merely a concomitant or consequence of the skeletal response. This interpretation may lead one to conclude that autonomic responses cannot be operantly conditioned. However, when we say that a change in some response has been operantly conditioned, we usually mean that the change in the response has been produced by the pairing of, or contingency between, response and reinforcer. If we accept this proposal, than a change in an autonomic response can be produced by operant conditioning whether mediation occurs or not as long as the response–reinforcer contingency produced the change. Because the mediating and

---

[3] It is interesting to note that Brener was successful with a reinforcement density procedure, whereas we were not. It may be that reinforcement density shaping procedures are more effective with aversive reinforcers and percentile shaping procedures are more effective with appetitive reinforcers.

mediated responses show a high correlation, it seems more correct to say that the operant conditioning procedure affected both (Black, 1974).

We disagree even more strongly with the conclusion that the mediation data permit one to employ autonomic responses as indices of nonoperant processes during operant conditioning. Suppose, for the moment, that we assume that heart rate is mediated by skeletal responses. Heart rate changes would accompany skeletal operantly conditioned responses and skeletal classically conditioned responses; therefore, one would not know which conditioning process, if either, was reflected by the heart rate change unless one knew which process had produced the skeletal response (Black & de Toledo, 1972; Roberts & Young, 1971).

4. We do not want to leave the impression that we think there is nothing to the distinction among response classes because of the demonstration of operant autonomic conditioning. For example, one can distinguish responses in terms of constraints on conditioning. Two types of constraint are especially relevant. The first type, associative constraints, which have been emphasized in the learning literature, refer to the fact that certain stimuli, responses, and reinforcers are more likely to be associated than others (Bolles, 1970; Garcia, McGowan, & Green, 1972). The second type of constraint, which we have called system constraints (Black, 1974), is a constraint on performance rather that on the formation of associations. System constraints refer to the limitations on change in a particular response that arise from the nature of the neural control system of which that response is a part. It seems to us that autonomic responses are particularly sensitive to system constraints. For example, there may be a limit on the amount of change that can be produced as a function of the homeostatic feedback systems of which most autonomic responses are a component. The fact that both we and Brener have had difficulty in obtaining decreases in heart rate below adaptation levels may be one example of this type of constraint. Also, there may be system constraints that arise from the relationship among different response systems. For example, suppose that heart rate was linked to the system controlling skeletal movement so that heart rate increases could not occur unless skeletal movement occurred. We might then limit the magnitude of conditioned heart rate increases by requiring the subject to hold still during training and so reveal a system constraint on the operant conditioning of heart rate.

The main problem is that we can see some differences among responses with respect to their amenability to operant conditioning and to the constraints to which they are subject and, at the same time, do not have enough data to develop an appropriate scheme for classifying the responses. Some classification of responses that cross-cuts the skeletal—autonomic distinction may turn out to be more relevant to the distinction between operant and Pavlovian conditioning (Mackintosh, 1974). The real problem may be, however, that the attempt to distinguish between operant and Pavlovian conditioning, beyond asking whether there are different effects of different aspects of the conditioning procedure, is itself a futile endeavor.

Acknowledgments

The research described in the paper was supported by the National Research Council of Canada Grant No. A0042 and Ontario Mental Health Foundation Grant No. 258 to A. H. Black. We would like to thank John Morley for preparing the computer programs and H. Barbaree and Mary-Ann Kasprowicz for assistance in carrying out the research.

References

Black, A. H. *Operant conditioning of heart rate under curare.* Technical Report No. 12, Department of Psychology, McMaster University, Hamilton, Ontario, October 1967.

Black, A. H. Autonomic aversive conditioning in infrahuman subjects. In F. R. Brush (Ed.), *Aversive conditioning and learning.* New York: Academic Press, 1971. Pp. 3–104.

Black, A. H. Operant autonomic conditioning: The analysis of response mechanisms. In P. A. Obrist, A. H. Black, J. Brener, & L. V. DiCara (Eds.), *Cardiovascular psychophysiology: Current issues in response mechanisms, biofeedback and methodology.* Chicago: Aldine, 1974. Pp. 229–250.

Black, A. H., Cott, A., & Pavloski, R. The operant learning theory approach to biofeedback training. In G. E. Schwartz & J. Beatty (Eds.), *Biofeedback: Theory and research.* New York: Academic Press, in press.

Black, A. H., & de Toledo, L. The relationship among classically conditioned responses: Heart rate and skeletal behavior. In A. H. Black & W. F. Prokasy (Eds.), *Classical conditioning II: Current theory and research.* New York: Appleton-Century-Crofts, 1972, 290–311.

Blanchard, E. G., Scott, R. W., Young, L. D., & Haynes, M. R. The effects of feedback signal information content on the long-term self-control of heart rate. *The Journal of General Psychology*, 1974, 91, 175–187.

Blanchard, E. G., & Young, L. D. Self-control of cardiac functioning: A promise as yet unfulfilled. *Psychological Bulletin*, 1973, 79, 145–163.

Blanchard, E. G., & Young, L. D. Clinical applications of biofeedback training: A review of evidence. *Archives of General Psychiatry*, 1974, 30, 573–589.

Bolles, R. C. Species-specific defense reactions and avoidance learning. *Psychological Review*, 1970, 17, 32–48.

Engel, B. T. Electroencephalographic and blood pressure correlates of operantly conditioned heart rate in the restrained monkey. *Pavlovian Journal of Biological Science*, 1974, 9, 222–232.

Engel, B. T., & Gottlieb, S. H. Differential operant conditioning of heart rate in the restrained monkey. *Journal of Comparative and Physiological Psychology*, 1970, 78(2), 217–225.

Fields, C. I. Instrumental conditioning of the rat cardiac control systems. *Proceedings of the National Academy of Sciences*, 1970, 65, 293–299.

Garcia, J., McGowan, B. K., & Green, K. F. Biological constraints on conditioning. In A. H. Black & W. F. Prokasy (Eds.), *Classical conditioning. Vol. II.* New York: Appleton-Century-Crofts, 1972, Pp. 3–27.

Gatchel, R. J. Frequency of feedback and learned heart rate control. *Journal of Experimental Psychology*, 1974, 103(2), 274–283.

Gliner, J. A., Horvath, S. N., & Wolfe, R. R. Operant conditioning of heart rate in curarized rats: Hemodynamic changes. *American Journal of Physiology*, 1975, **228**, 870–874.

Gormezano, I., & Coleman, S. R. The law of effect and CR contingent modification of the UCS. *Conditional Reflex*, 1973, 8(1), 41–56.

Harris, A. H., Gilliam, W. J., Findley, J. D., & Brady, J. V. Instrumental conditioning of large magnitude, daily, 12-hour blood pressure elevations in the baboon. *Science*, 1973, **182**, 175–177.

Hothersall, D., & Brener, J. Operant conditioning of changes in heart rates in curarized rats. *Journal of Comparative and Physiological Psychology*, 1969, 68, 338–342.

Lang, P. J., & Twentyman, C. T. Learning to control heart rate: Binary vs analogue feedback. *Psychophysiology*, 1974, **11**(6), 616–629.

Mackintosh, N. J. *The psychology of animal learning.* New York: Academic Press, 1974.

Mandler, G., Preven, D. W., & Kuhlman, C. K. Effects of operant reinforcement on the GSR. *Journal of the Experimental Analysis of Behavior*, 1962, **5**, 317–321.

Miller, N. E. Learning of visceral and glandular responses. *Science*, 1969, **163**, 434–445.

Miller, N. E., & DiCara, L. V. Instrumental learning of heart rate changes in curarized rats: Shaping and specificity to discriminative stimulus. *Journal of Comparative and Physiological Psychology*, 1967, **63**, 12–19.

Obrist, P. A., Black, A. H., Brener, J., & DiCara, L. V. (Eds.) *Cardiovascular psychophysiology.* Chicago: Aldine Publishing Co., 1974.

Platt, J. R. Percentile reinforcement: Paradigms for experimental analysis of response shaping. In G. H. Bower (Ed.), *The psychology of learning and motivation.* Vol. 7. New York: Academic Press, 1973.

Roberts, L. E., Lacroix, J. M., & Wright, M. Comparative studies of operant electrodermal and heart rate conditioning in curarized rats. In P. A. Obrist, A. H. Black, J. Brener, & L. V. DiCara (Eds.), *Cardiovascular psychophysiology.* Chicago: Aldine, 1974.

Roberts, L. E., & Young, R. Electrodermal responses are independent of movement during aversive conditioning in rats, but heart rate is not. *Journal of Comparative and Physiological Psychology*, 1971, 77, 495–512.

Schwartz, G. E. Biofeedback, self-regulation, and the patterning of physiological processes. *American Scientist*, 1975, **63**, 314–324.

Slaughter, J., Hahn, W., & Rinaldi, P. Instrumental conditioning of heart rate in the curarized rat with varied amounts of pretraining. *Journal of Comparative and Physiological Psychology*, 1970, 72, 356–359.

Stern, R. M. Operant conditioning of spontaneous GSRs: Negative results. *Journal of Experimental Psychology*, 1967, **75**, 128–130.

Williams, D. R., & Williams, H. Auto-maintenance in the pigeon: sustained pecking despite contingent non-reinforcement. *Journal of the Experimental Analysis of Behavior,* 1969, **12**, 511–520.

DISCUSSION

Davis: You've indicated that the autonomic–skeletal distinction may not be effective in separating between operant and Pavlovian conditioning. Assuming for the moment that we can agree that a real separation exists between operant and Pavlovian learning, do you see any other central correlates as helping to make this separation?

Black: I am not aware of such a central correlate now, and I am not sure that I would want to talk in terms of two different kinds of conditioning.

Hurwitz: Historically the point has been made, and it's come up several times at our conference, that Pavlovian conditioning refers to emotional conditioning. One might then simply say that the autonomic measures we get bear on the organism's emotional state.

Black: What you're suggesting is that I can take some electrodes and attach them to an animal's periphery, and from those recordings tell you something about the animal's emotional state. The data simply don't support this. Consider heart rate, for example. The animal might have a high heart rate simply because he's in an exercise wheel. If you don't let me look at his behavior, I might conclude simply from his heart rate that he's emotionally aroused.

Davis: Then what would have led anybody to take heart rate measures during conditioned suppression procedures, for example?

Black: I don't know. They might be interested in learning about how the cardiovascular system functions under stress.

Seligman: I think that's going too far, Abe. What you first said strikes me as reasonable: you have to know something about the context of the situation. However, once you know, for example, that the subject is in a conditioned emotional response (CER) situation, then heart rate might tell you something legitimate about emotionality.

Black: However, even data on heart rate changes during CER can best be explained by the amount of skeletal activity. I think a lot of time and effort is needlessly being spent with expensive measurement techniques. It's a lot of trouble to measure and analyze autonomic responses. You could probably get the information a good deal more easily by watching the animal.

Weisman: I agree. The ethologists say the way to find out what is an animal's emotional state is to look at the animal and see what he's doing.

Black: I think Marty's [Seligman] suggestion is that those observations would be complemented by autonomic recordings.

Weisman: What would it add? It's inconceivable to me that an animal could be cowering, for example, and not be fearful.

Seligman: There are probably three or four different ways of causing an animal to cower. You can operantly condition him to cower . . .

Weisman: We're not sure you can.

Seligman: Nevertheless, just as Abe has pointed out that heart rate can reflect a variety of causes, I think that cowering or other behavioral observations might, too. I found 49 separate indices that have been used in the literature to suggest that an organism was afraid.

Black: I agree with Marty that some measures in addition to the observation of behavior are probably useful. It's just that some measures are not going to be particularly good, and heart rate is one of them.

Davis: That isn't a general statement about the usefulness of physiological correlates?

Black: No, there are qualitative differences among them. Autonomic responses can't be employed as simple indicators of emotion any more than they can be as simple indicators of Pavlovian conditioning.

Weisman: The measurement of emotion strikes me as being not particularly interesting in any case. If you infer the emotion from the behavior, and you know the operations that generated it, I'm not sure that emotional states are necessary to explain anything.

Garcia: It's very important to investigate motivation and emotion. They represent a much more powerful technique to control incentives than controlling behavior directly. [This point is elaborated in discussion following Chapter 10, by Garcia, Rusiniak, & Brett—Eds.]

Michael Peters (a conference observer) argued that the Pavlovian approach to conditioning autonomic responses has not been as uniformly impressive as one often assumes (for example, the GSR). Similarly, within the skeletal system a considerable number of muscles do not lend themselves to operant control (for example, movement of the small toe independently from adjoining toes). Peters suggested the we would have to investigate the characteristics of target organs and response systems before neurological distinctions and generalizations could be made.

Jenkins: In a parallel sense to the autonomic–skeletal distinction, are there not some responses that can be modified by operant contingencies but not by Pavlovian contingencies? That is, instead of asking the question about physiological correlates, are there any responses which are modifiable only by one class of contingencies and insensitive to the other?

Black indicated that he thought that the approach suggested by Jenkins was a more productive direction than the pursuit of neuroanatomical distinctions. No one, however, provided a definitive answer to Jenkins' question. [The question of differential sensitivity to contingencies by different response systems is pursued further in Jenkins' chapter.—Eds.]

A. E. Roberts [coauthor of Hurwitz' chapter]: In preparing for our chapter, naturally enough I spent some time rereading the Rescorla and Solomon (1967) paper on two-factor theory. With respect to the theme of the conference, there's an explicit statement made in that paper about the manner in which operant and Pavlovian conditioning interact. The Pavlovian factor is presumed to assume control over the instrumental factor. To what extent is that conclusion characteristic of their particular view? I put this as an open question: what is the nature of the interaction which typically occurs between operant and Pavlovian conditioning?

Hurwitz [after some silence] : Is someone going to attempt an answer?

Seligman: I was going to ask a related question of Hank [Davis]. I suppose this partially expresses my answer to Roberts' question. What does the title "Operant—Pavlovian Interaction" mean? I barely understand interaction in a statistical sense.

Davis: My response to Robin's [Roberts] question is to pose yet another question which is more critical and more fundamental than his. I wonder in light of the data and analyses which have appeared in the last decade, and in light of many of the things that have been said at this conference, if it makes sense any more for any of us to get up in front of even the lowest level undergraduate class and make the statement that there are two kinds of learning: operant and Pavlovian conditioning? Can we justify that distinction anymore at a process level or even, after some of the points that Herb [Jenkins] has made, at an operational level?

Jenkins: I hope that my message wasn't that you can't distinguish between the two paradigms. They're perfectly distinguishable in terms of operations. My message was that you can't pull a relation out of one paradigm and assume that it's having the same effect as when it appears as part of another paradigm.

Davis: I got the impression that it may be impossible to isolate a pure operant or pure Pavlovian paradigm.

Weisman: We never could. Still, I think the operant—Pavlovian distinction is valid at least procedurally and it may be valid, in some sense, in the way in which behavior is controlled.

Seligman: Consider the clear distinctions we have in psychology. Rods and cones, for example. Not just the anatomical distinction, but the fact that after years of research we have the dark adaption curve and two different sets of laws. We've now spent about 40 years studying operant and Pavlovian conditioning and the research still hasn't produced two sets of laws which are nonoverlapping. The difference between two kinds of Pavlovian responses, for example, is sometimes greater than the difference between operant and Pavlovian conditioning. It seems to me that this sort of outcome does not support useful distinctions. Part of what I wanted to do when I talked about "preparedness" vs. "unpreparedness" was to establish a little more coherence than the distinction between operant and Pavlovian conditioning provides.

Jenkins: I don't agree in the sense that I don't think we're dealing with an optional question. Trying to make the distinction between whether these are separate learning processes may be an optional question, but that these two procedures have to be understood in the way that they change behavior is not optional. Broadly speaking, there are two very different things happening. On one hand, a passive organism is exposed to some stimulus arrangement in the environment and he's getting changed. On the other hand, you have an active organism flailing around his environment, and because he changes things, he gets changed. You can't just forget that those two different kinds of things are going on. So, we're going to have operant–Pavlovian conferences probably indefinitely. The terms may change but the basic issues will be the same.

Seligman: I see both shallow and deep distinctions made in a science. A procedural distinction often starts off as a nonoptional shallow distinction. It's shallow because it doesn't necessarily imply that a process difference also exists in the animal. In the present case we can't find anything that maps neatly into the distinction in terms of laws, processes, or response systems. That's the problem.

Jenkins: The present distinction may be shallow only in the sense that it doesn't have much content yet. There are these two different basic arrangements that exist in the environment. It's not a question of our having invented them and now we're stuck with them and we have to analyze them. They reflect some very Kantian categories about the world and we're going to have to learn how they work, and what systems are modified by them. It's like the topic of reproduction to the biologist. He can't decide not to study it; it's fundamental to his discipline. Psychology can probably get away without studying schedules of reinforcement. It's a man-made system and it's not necessary to get into the detailed analysis of schedule effects. However, he can't avoid studying the operant–Pavlovian distinction.

Seligman: I'm not saying not to study Pavlovian conditioning and operant conditioning. All I'm saying is there is no reason to believe there's a Pavlovian process and an operant process.

Jenkins: I agree. I don't think we have the vaguest idea what we mean by "process" in this sense.

Seligman: If we had found out that autonomic went with Pavlovian and skeletal with operant, or cognitive went with operant and noncognitive with Pavlovian, then we'd be looking at processes.

Jenkins: Even if it had broken down that simply, we still wouldn't have had any process distinctions.

Davis: What would it take, then? I think Marty has given us something of a model with his "preparedness" dimension. He's proposed we look at the degree to which cognitions are involved and the involvement of different neural substrates. In addition, we have such categories as the number of trials to reach some criterion for learning or extinction. . . . These things begin to accumulate to the point where we can begin to substantiate the notion of a process.

Black: I'd be willing to say that you might find out that two different neural systems, anatomically speaking, could be involved. However, they might ultimately work the same way. If the same mechanism was involved, I don't see how you'd be any closer to establishing differences in "process" by demonstrating different anatomical substrates.

Davis: Marty raised the question before about what the term "operant–Pavlovian interactions" meant. In what is probably a shallow sense, I think I can offer an answer. I'll borrow Herb's situation in which an animal is flailing about its environment. There are events which are produced as a consequence of the organism's behavior, and those events probably get hooked up with other events in the environment through procedures which could be described as Pavlovian. The continuous interaction of these two arrangements probably keeps the organism's behavior lawfully controlled. In a shallow sense, the analysis of that situation could be described as an operant–Pavlovian interaction. In fact, I suspect it has considerable generality to the "real world." I'd have to remain silent, though, on the deeper question of whether different processes were involved as each element of that interaction worked on the organism.

At the close of discussion, Black suggested that the controversy over whether an animal learned about correlations or was controlled directly by them, an issue that was raised repeatedly during the conference, might perhaps be one way of viewing the distinction between operant and Pavlovian conditioning.

References

Rescorla, R. A., & Solomon, R. Two process learning theory: Relationships between Pavlovian conditioning and instrumental learning. *Psychological Review,* 1967, **74,** 151–182.

3

Sensitivity of Different Response Systems to Stimulus—Reinforcer and Response—Reinforcer Relations

H. M. Jenkins

McMaster University

INTRODUCTION

Jenkins expresses some degree of pessimism about our ability to analyze the degree of control exerted by operant (response–stimulus) versus Pavlovian (stimulus–stimulus) contingencies within any single experimental arrangement, such as autoshaping. He suggests instead that a more profitable approach to understanding the role of R–S and S–S relations in the determination of behavior may involve focusing our attention on how these fundamental conditioning arrangements affect different response systems.

Impurity of the Classical and Operant Paradigms

It is widely acknowledged that the classical and operant paradigms are impure. Although in the classical experiment only an S–S* (stimulus–reinforcer) contingency is arranged, responses are followed by the reinforcer and this R–S* relation can be important. Similarly, in the operant experiment only an R–S* contingency is arranged, but certain stimuli from the site at which the response occurs are inevitably followed by the reinforcer, and the resulting S–S* relation may exert an important effect.

Autoshaping, or sign tracking, may prove especially valuable in the continuing effort to understand the joint action of S–S* and R–S* relations in learning.[1]

---

[1] "Relation" is here used as a generic term that includes arranged contingencies, secondary or implicit correlations, and temporal conjunctions.

The procedure is, or course, that of classical conditioning. In the commonest example, one arranges for a stimulus, the lighting of a disk, to predict the delivery of food to a hungry pigeon. The S–S* contingency is the only arranged contingency. The response that emerges, however, pecking at the lighted disk, is one that can also be established by an operant procedure in which only an R–S* contingency is arranged. Movements directed toward a disk that is constantly lighted and hence has no signal value are selectively reinforced until the shaping procedure produces a peck at the lighted disk. So, the same response, pecking the disk, can be established and maintained by arranging only an S–S* or only an R–S* contingency.

In the sign-tracking experiment not only are there temporal conjunctions between responses and reinforcers, but there is also a correlation between responses and reinforcers. The correlation results from the S–S* contingency and the behavior it induces. Therefore, it may be called a secondary or implicit correlation, or, to use Dave Williams' term, a "piggyback" correlation.

The relations described above are not unique to autoshaping. They occur in most classical conditioning experiments. However, the fact that the directed skeletal action of pecking a disk is apparently subject to both R–S* and S–S* influences suggests that autoshaping may be an especially good place to see the joint effects of these relations at work in the control of behavior.

Evidence on S–S* and R–S* Relations in Sign Tracking

The main findings on the role of S–S* and R–S* relations in sign tracking may be summarized, very briefly, as follows:

1. The S–S* contingency induces the peck directed at the signal. The evidence shows clearly that the appearance of the very first response is a function of the S–S* contingency (Brown & Jenkins, 1968); it is not simply a reflection of the so-called operant level for pecking a lighted disk. More than superstitious operant conditioning is involved.

2. Omission training, in which a response to a disk results in the omission of the scheduled food presentation, does not eliminate the response (e.g., Williams & Williams, 1969). However, making omission contingent on a response does reduce responding below the level obtained when the omission of the reinforcer occurs with the same frequency but independently of responding (Schwartz & Williams, 1972).

3. When the contingency between S and S* is removed by delivering food outside of the stimulus (unsignaled food) at the same rate as it is occurring inside of the stimulus, the response is quickly eliminated (Gamzu & Williams, 1973).

4. The form of the disk–contact response is controlled by, and closely resembles, the consummatory response evoked by the reinforcer. When the reinforcer is grain the contact response is a grain-seizing peck. When a water

reinforcer is used, the disk is contacted with drinking movements. The resemblance between the contact response and the reinforcer is a result of the signaling relation, or S–S* contingency, and not of a prevailing drive state because the resemblance occurs when a pigeon that is both hungry and thirsty receives one stimulus signaling food and another signaling water (Jenkins & Moore, 1973).

Interpretations and Generalizations

The evidence cited above strongly suggests that S–S* relations are dominant in the control of behavior in the sign-tracking experiment, but there has been little agreement in the literature on what further generalizations should be drawn. Here are some views, based on the kind of evidence we have briefly reviewed, as to the role of S–S* and R–S* relations in the control of learned behavior. They are ordered by increasing emphasis on the role of S–S* relations.

D. R. Williams (1974) writes:

> The Schwartz and Williams study clearly demonstrates that key-pecking is susceptible to both S–S* and R–S* conditioning relationships within the framework of a single procedure arrangement. Apparently it is not the case that the discrete-trials Pavlovian paradigm in some way operates to blot out operant relationships. Rather, it seems that key-pecking in the pigeon is sensitive to direct S–S* relationships, and maintains a sensitivity to R–S* operant linkages as well. Thus, pecking is sensitive to the conditional S–S* relationship of classical conditioning, and also to the conditional R–S* relationship of operant or instrumental conditioning.
>
> In light of these findings, it seems appropriate to refer to key-pecking as "biconditional" behavior, because its strength depends on both the conditional S–S* link of classical conditioning, and the conditional R–S* link of instrumental conditioning. A full account of its occurrence must take *both* sources of conditional control into account. [pp. 40–41 of preprint]

Mackintosh (1974) writes:

> Pavlovian reinforcement will tend to produce behaviour in anticipation of the delivery of the reinforcer that is related to the behaviour elicited by the reinforcer. Provided that the behaviour elicited by the reinforcer is the same as the behaviour specified by the experimenter as necessary for the delivery of the reinforcer, there may be little need to appeal to anything more than simple Pavlovian processes to account for the change in the animal's behaviour even if the experiment is operationally instrumental. In such a case, it is possible that no response–reinforcer associations will occur and that the animal's behaviour will not be modified because it generates reinforcing consequences. [p. 139]

Bolles (1972) writes:

> In the auto-shaping procedure generally and in the negative automaintenance [omission training] procedure particularly—the strength of the response is not controlled by its consequences. It is evidently controlled by the signalling properties of the illuminated key. [p. 185, bracketed words inserted]

And in another passage:

> Bindra's analysis [see below] appears appropriate for the learning of birds, which consists primarily of responding in old ways to new stimuli. But to account for the plasticity of mammalian behavior, it may be useful to hypothesize the possibility of both stimulus [S–S*] and response [R–S*] learning. [p. 406, bracketed words inserted]

Moore (1973), after reviewing the procedures commonly used to establish the key peck, writes:

> In summary, the pecking response can be prompted by the punch-board technique or by taping grain to the key, it can be awaited and reinforced or shaped through successive approximations; it can be re-directed from the food site; it can be auto-shaped. In every case both the acquisition and maintenance of the response follow at once from Pavlovian principles. In every case the Pavlovian process accounts for both the form and direction of the learned behaviour. The operant principle, by contrast, is in some cases patently irrelevant, and in all cases unnecessary. For these reasons, it seems parsimonious to interpret the pigeon's simple instrumental peck as a Pavlovian conditioned response. [p. 177]

Bindra (1974) writes:

> ... learning involves the development of stimulus–stimulus contingencies *only*; stimulus–response or response–stimulus contingencies are not critical in learned behavior modifications. [p. 203]

A thorough and fair discussion of the views of each of these writers would be an extensive undertaking. For the purposes of this chapter I should like to raise only two issues that are suggested by these brief quotations. The first concerns the question of what can be concluded from the results obtained under omission training about the role of S–S* and R–S* relations in the original conditioning arrangement. The question is worth close examination because experiments making use of omission training have played a critical part in strengthening the view that R–S* relations play a minor role, if any, in sign tracking.

To fix ideas, consider the question of what is established by the finding that the omission contingency does not eliminate, or even greatly suppress, the sign-tracking response. Does it follow that the R–S* relations that are normally entailed by the unmodified sign-tracking procedure do not contribute strongly to the support of the behavior? It does not follow unless one assumes that a response which is not suppressed by the removal of certain relations is not supported by the presence of those relations. There is nothing to compel that assumption. One can readily conceive that the response is normally supported either by an S–S* relation, an R–S* relation, or both together, but as soon as one relation is removed the other becomes dominant. The fact that the sign-tracking response persists despite the omission contingency only lends plausibility to the view that R–S* relations are not involved in the unmodified arrangement; it does not force that conclusion. Similar considerations apply to the question of what is established by the finding that an omission contingency does reduce the strength of a sign-tracking response. It does not follow from this fact that the R—S* relation normally entailed by the sign-tracking experiment is effective. The omission contingency does not excise discretely a previously existing relation; it introduces the new relation specified by the omission contingency. The fact that adding this explicit contingency has an effect tells us nothing for certain about the role of response—reinforcer relations in the unmodified sign-tracking experiment.

Similar arguments apply to the conclusions that may safely be drawn from the results of removing the S—S* contingency by the introduction of unsignaled food during the intertrial periods. Because this manipulation also removes the secondary response—reinforcer correlation, the elimination of the response cannot be unequivocally attributed solely to the removal of the S—S* contingency.

There is another, quite different matter that is raised by what is missing from the quotations rather than by what they contain. The authors are concerned with the effect on behavior of relations between just two terms: the stimulus and reinforcer or the response and reinforcer. Bolles is explicit in his view that nothing more is involved in animal learning than the synthesis of the expectations generated by S—S* and R—S* relations. What has happened to Skinner's most important concept, that of the three-termed relation that defines the discriminated operant? As he put it, a discriminative stimulus sets the occasion for the reinforcement of a response. The three-termed relation is, in Skinner's view, basic—it is not a byproduct of two two-termed relations. To put the matter in the language of expectancy, the animal learns to expect a certain outcome of responding (R—S*) conditional on a prior stimulus. The expectancy might be represented as S(R—S*). This conditional outcome expectancy cannot be synthesized from two separate expectancies of the form (S—S*) and (R—S*) because it has a different structure. It is interesting that most recent discussions of operant and classical conditioning have skipped over the possibility that an irreducible three-termed relation may sometimes be involved in the control of behavior. The discussion by Catania (1971) is a notable exception.

The Comparison of Response Systems

I have argued that it is very difficult to isolate the functions of various relations in a given conditioning arrangement by altering contingencies. There is a need for a different approach. Instead of asking what are the determinants of the response in a particular example of classical or operant conditioning, we may try to develop systematic data on the effects of S—S*, R—S*, and S(R—S*) relations on different response systems. Conjectures currently in circulation about what response systems are especially sensitive to what relations are based largely on comparisons across experiments. The comparisons suffer from the uncertainties introduced by a lack of comparable measures and of essential controls.

The experiment I wish to describe has been designed to provide a more direct comparison than previously has been made of the effects of certain R—S*, S—S*, and S(R—S*) contingencies on two response systems. The experiment is, of course, a very small part of what should be a large and systematic undertaking. One of the problems with getting started on such an undertaking is deciding on what "response systems" to compare. What are the right dimensions along which to describe response systems for the purpose of comparing their sensitivity to the types of relations we have been considering?

One approach is to focus on different effector systems. The continuing effort to learn whether responses mediated by the autonomic nervous system show a different pattern of sensitivity than do skeletal responses mediated by the CNS is an example of this approach. Quite a different approach is to describe response systems in terms of their origin in S–S* or R–S* contingencies. If a response originates from the arrangement of an S–S* contingency alone it is a reasonable guess that it is less sensitive to R–S* relations than a response that must be developed through an R–S* contingency. Jenkins (1973) has suggested as much, and the view expressed by Mackintosh in the previously quoted passage is that sensitivity to different relations is not a property of a response alone but of the role played by the reinforcer in setting the form of the response.

The response systems to be compared in the present experiment differed on many dimensions. Among the differences was the way in which the response originated: by virtue of an Ṡ–S* contingency or by virtue of an S(R–S*) contingency. This represents a guess about a relevant dimension of response systems for the questions at hand but it is only one of a large number of possible starting points.

One response system in the present experiment conformed to the concept of a discriminated operant. Pigeons were reinforced with food for waving their heads (head positioning) in midair, in a position well away from a peckable object, when a sound was on. The response was defined by the interruption of a pair of infrared photocell beams that intersected at right angles about 12 inches from the floor and at the center of the pigeon chamber. A sharp click produced by operating a relay mounted on one wall provided clearly audible feedback to mark the interruption of the beams. The discriminative stimulus was a white noise. After preliminary training, in which the response was shaped and the density of reinforcement was gradually decreased, the arrangement was as follows. On the average of about once a minute, the noise came on for 8 sec. In each 1-sec period there was a probability of 0.03 that if the photocell beams were interrupted, food would be delivered. Reinforcements were unavailable when the sound was off.

The behavioral sequence fits the concept of the discriminated operant because the reinforcer is jointly contingent on the discriminative stimulus and the response. The response is arbitrarily related to both the reinforcer and the discriminative stimulus in the sense that merely arranging a contingency between the discriminative stimulus and the reinforcer (S–S* contingency) would not establish the response. The response is not a naturally occurring part of the food-getting sequence and it is not directed at the initiating stimulus.

The second response system resembled the sign-tracking case except for the addition of a response–reinforcer contingency. The stimulus was the lighting of the pigeon's response key. The response was initially autoshaped by presenting the food reinforcer when the key was lighted whether or not a response occurred. As soon as the response was occurring regularly, the delivery of the food was made contingent on responding. The probability that a peck was reinforced was decreased to 0.03 in each second on a schedule that exactly paralleled the one used for the head-positioning response. Unlike the prototype of the discriminated operant, this sign-tracking response was established and could have been maintained at an appreciable level by arranging a contingency only between the lighting of the key and the delivery of food. (In fact, other pigeons were run on the identical procedure except for the absence of a response–reinforcer contingency in order to assure ourselves that the response was autoshapable with those parameters. We were assured.) Also, in contrast to the discriminated operant, the response was directed at the controlling stimulus, and because the response was pecking, it was of course closely related to a natural part of the food-getting sequence in the pigeon.

Training of the head-positioning response to noise continued for 15 50-trial sessions by which time each animal was consistently responding at a rate at least 10 times greater during the noise-on period than during the noise-off period. The key-pecking response was trained for the same number of sessions, although in this case responding was confined to the key–light on periods almost from the beginning.

At this point we have two response systems that have originated in different ways but that have in common the fact that the response is initiated by a stimulus and reinforced intermittently by response-contingent food. The experiment consists of relaxing certain aspects of the joint contingency of the reinforcer on the stimulus and the response in order to assess the role of these contingencies on each response system. The R–S* contingency can be removed by delivering the reinforcer during the stimulus independently of the response. When this is done, the S–S* correlation that arose indirectly from the joint contingency, or S(R–S*) relation, then becomes a directly arranged contingency. The S–S* contingency can be removed by presenting food during the stimulus-off periods at the same rate as during the stimulus-on periods.

The experiment permitted comparisons of performance when:

1. The reinforcer remained jointly contingent on the stimulus and response (S, R contingent) as it was in the first phase.

2. The reinforcer was contingent only on the stimulus (S contingent). The response contingency during the stimulus was removed.

3. The reinforcer was contingent only on the response (R contingent). To realize this condition, food was delivered outside of the stimulus at the same rate as it could be earned through the response contingency, which remained in

effect during the stimulus. If responding is maintained during the stimulus the food rate is approximately the same in the stimulus as out of the stimulus (as in variable-interval schedules, the reinforcer rate varies only slightly over large variations in the rate of response), and there is no positive correlation between stimulus and food. Should responding during the stimulus continue one would have to say that the stimulus is acting as an instruction: "This is the occasion on which the R–S* contingency is in effect." Or more colloquially: "Now you must earn the food you otherwise get freely." The arrangement is especially interesting because it corresponds more exactly to the one called for by the concept of a discriminative stimulus as an occasion than does the typical arrangement for discriminative operant conditioning. By virtue of the joint contingency in the typical arrangement the discriminative stimulus is positively correlated with the reinforcer and part or all of its function may depend on that correlation.

4. The reinforcer was contingent on neither the stimulus nor the response (noncontingent). In this case food was delivered at the same rate in and out of the stimulus without regard to responses.

Expectations on the Origin Hypothesis

It may be of interest to consider what effects these manipulations can be expected to have on the basis of what I call the origin hypothesis. The origin hypothesis says that if the response can be established and maintained by a stimulus–reinforcer contingency alone, and if the response resembles the one elicited by the reinforcer, then control of the response is dominated by the S–S* relation and is only weakly if at all affected by R–S* relations. Conversely, the control of a response that requires for its establishment an R–S* contingency, and the form of which is arbitrarily related to the response elicited by the reinforcer, is largely controlled by R–S* relations and little, if at all, affected by S–S* relations. The origin hypothesis is essentially the view expressed in the previously quoted passage from Mackintosh.

The origin hypothesis leads us to expect that when the R–S* contingency in S is removed while the S–S* contingency remains, the sign-tracking response will be reduced less than the discriminated operant, if at all. In contrast, removal of the S–S* contingency only, leaving the R–S* contingency intact during S, should virtually eliminate the sign-tracking response but have little if any effect on the discriminated operant. In the completely noncontingent case only temporal conjunctions between S and S* and between R and S* remain in both cases. The origin hypothesis says nothing about the possibility of a differential effect of this condition on the response systems.

Procedure and Results of the Experiment

Throughout the experiment each session consisted of 50 8-sec trials. A punched tape was used to set a probability of .03 in each 1 sec of the stimulus that a reinforcer would be available. When the reinforcer was response contingent in the stimulus, an available reinforcer was held until the response occurred. When the reinforcer was not contingent on responses, all available reinforcers were delivered as soon as the code for an available reinforcer was read. Each reinforcer consisted of four 45-mg Noyes pellets, Formula C, delivered in 1 sec into a cup mounted near the floor on the center of the key panel. Intertrial intervals were variable with a mean of 30 sec.

The mean baseline rate for the head-positioning response was 2.4 responses per 8-sec trial. The mean rate of intertrial responses was 0.2 responses in 8 sec. In the case of key pecking, the mean baseline rate was 10.3 responses per 8-sec trial and the mean rate of intertrial responses was .08 in 8 sec. The head-positioning response occurred at a lower rate than did the key peck and the discrimination between trial and intertrial was less complete. None of the manipulations in subsequent phases resulted in a significant increase in the rate of intertrial responding.

During the last eight sessions of the baseline phase, the mean total number of reinforcements actually obtained in the 50 8-sec trials of a session was 9.9 in the head-positioning groups and 13.0 in the key-pecking groups. Although the expected number of reinforcements made available with $p = .03$ in each second for 50 8-sec trials is 12, the tapes actually made available an average of 14.8 reinforcements during the trials. When reinforcers were delivered noncontingently the actual rates were therefore somewhat higher than the obtained rates and the discrepancy was greater for the head-positioning response than for key pecking. This is not a desirable feature of the procedure but examination of the data for individuals reveals no detectable effects from these relatively small variations in the rates of reinforcement.

The design of the experiment is summarized in Table 3.1. The first phase, in which the reinforcer was jointly contingent on the stimulus and response, established baseline levels of performance. The effect of altering the contingencies on the rate of response relative to the baseline levels was assessed in subsequent phases by means of both within- and between-group comparisons.

Consider first the effects of (1) removing the response part of the joint contingency, thereby putting into effect a directly arranged S–S* contingency, and of (2) removing all contingencies. The relevant data are provided by between-group comparisons in Phase 2, and are shown in Fig. 3.1. When the joint contingency remained, the baseline rate was, as expected, maintained with little change from the end of the previous phase for both types of responses. In the case of the head-positioning response (DO groups), removal of the response–reinforcer contingency within the stimulus, leaving (in a sense creating) a direct S–S* contingency, caused a drop in rate. The rate did not, however, fall as rapidly as when all contingencies were removed. A qualitatively similar picture resulted from the same manipulations on key pecking (ST groups). Removal of the response contingency caused a reduction in rate but not as great a reduction as was caused by removal of all contingencies.

TABLE 3.1

Contingencies in Each Phase of Training for the Peck Response (ST Groups) and the Head-Positioning Response (DO Groups) (N = 4 for each group)

	Key peck (sign tracking)[a]			Head positioning (discriminated operant)[a]		
Phase	Group ST-1	Group ST-2	Group ST-3	Group DO-1	Group DO-2	Group DO-3
1	S, R	S, R	S, R	S, R	S, R	S, R
2	S, R	S	N	S, R	S	N
3	R	S	S	R	S	S
4	S, R	N	N	S, R	—	—

[a]S,R, stimulus and response contingent; R, response contingent in S only; S, stimulus contingent only; N, noncontingent.

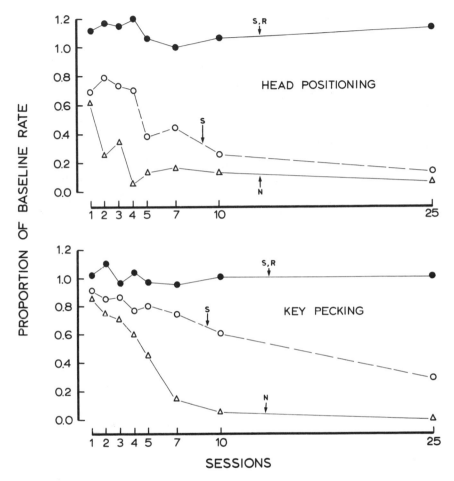

FIG. 3.1 Median rate of response relative to rate at the end of Phase 1 when the joint contingency of reinforcer on stimulus and response (S,R) was maintained; when the response–reinforcer contingency was dropped, leaving only a stimulus contingency (S); or when both response and reinforcer contingencies were dropped (N).

The principal difference between the results of head positioning and key pecking lies in the level at which the response was maintained by the S–S* contingency. Key pecking was maintained at a higher proportion of its baseline level than was head positioning. Both responses eventually ceased to occur when all contingencies were removed, but the key peck showed greater persistence than did head positioning.

Further data on the effect of the stimulus contingency alone come from certain within-group comparisons on the effect of restoring only the stimulus contingency following exposure to 25 sessions of noncontingent reinforcement (Group ST-3 and Group DO-3 from the end of Phase 2 to Phase 3). The data are shown in Fig. 3.2. The head-positioning response showed some recovery (three or four animals showed a clear but partial recovery). The key peck showed a greater recovery. These results are consistent with the previous between-group comparison in showing that both the discriminated operant and the sign-tracking response are sensitive to the S–S* contingency. Not surprisingly, the sign-tracking response was supported by the S contingency alone at a level closer to the level maintained by the joint S,R contingency.

We consider next the effect of removing the stimulus contingency while the response contingency remains within the stimulus presentation. It will be recalled that this is accomplished by delivering food outside of the stimulus at the same rate as food can be produced via the S–R* contingency within the stimulus. The relevant data come from Group ST-1 and DO-1 in Phases 2, 3, and 4. The data are shown in Fig. 3.3. Even though the R–S* contingency remained

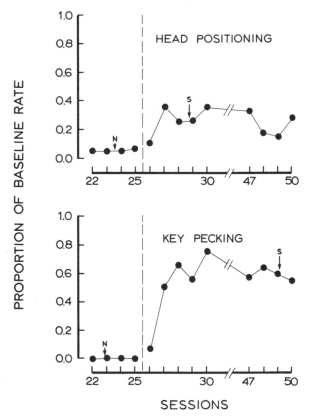

ΓIG. 3.2 Effect of restoring only the stimulus contingency on the median rate of response relative to baseline rate (N = noncontingent, S = stimulus contingent only).

in the stimulus, the head-positioning response was quickly eliminated by the removal of the stimulus part of the joint S–R contingency. Because the response dropped out, food was not delivered during the stimulus and the result was a negative correlation between the stimulus and the reinforcer (the reinforcer was then being delivered only during stimulus-off periods). When the joint contingency was restored (reinforcers removed from the stimulus-off periods) there was a rapid recovery of the response. The stimulus part of the joint stimulus–

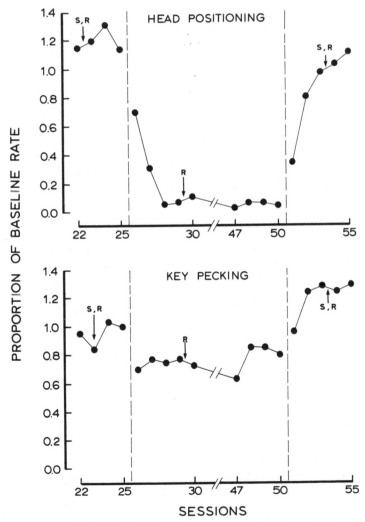

FIG. 3.3 Effect of removing the stimulus part of the joint (S,R) contingency, leaving a response contingency during the stimulus only (R), on the median rate of response relative to baseline rate.

response contingency was necessary to the continued performance of the head-positioning response.

The results for key pecking were quite different. Although removal of the stimulus part of the joint contingency caused an immediate drop in the median rate, a very substantial rate was nevertheless maintained by the R–S* contingency alone throughout the extended exposure to that condition. Because virtually all of the potentially available reinforcers were earned, reinforcers were being delivered at the same rate in and out of the stimulus. When the joint contingency was restored, the median rate increased to a level somewhat higher than its previous level under the joint contingency.

Conclusions

The head-positioning response under the discriminative control of sound, which we took to be a prototype of the discriminated operant, and the key peck directed to and controlled by the lighted key, which we took to be the prototype of a sign-tracking response, showed qualitatively similar changes when the joint contingency of the reinforcer on both stimulus and response was altered in various ways. Each response was sensitive to an S–S* contingency, to an R–S* contingency, and to a three-termed S(R–S*) contingency.

These response systems differed not in the kinds of relations to which they were sensitive, but in the levels at which they were supported by reduced contingencies, relative to the levels maintained by a fully contingent arrangement. Key pecking, the prototype of the sign-tracking response, was supported at a higher proportion of its baseline level than was head positioning, the prototype of the discriminated operant, by either an S–S* contingency alone or by an R–S* contingency alone.

I take these results to mean that the origin hypothesis of the relative sensitivity of different response systems to S–S* and R–S* relations is at best inadequate and is more likely just plain wrong. The response we took to be a prototype of sign tracking was supposed to be relatively indifferent to R–S* contingencies. It turns out, however, that the response has exactly the property called for by the concept of the discriminated operant. When the discriminative stimulus does not predict, and is not correlated with, the delivery of the reinforcer, it can nevertheless function as an occasion on which responses are made by virtue of the R–S* contingency. I take this to mean that the three-termed relation identified by Skinner is alive and well and is not reducible to a pair of correlations. It is ironic that the relation should be so nicely displayed by the key-peck response in view of the recent tendency to remove it from the rapidly shrinking company of what are taken to be operantly reinforceable responses.

The present results do not allow us to identify the role of S–S*, R–S*, or S(R–S*) relations within any single procedure, such as the standard autoshaping or sign-tracking paradigm. One can assess the effect of introducing new contingencies or removing certain contingencies (and thereby altering others) on a response system, but that unfortunately does not establish what role the various relations were exerting in the original arrangement. That is simply because changing the contingencies provides an opportunity for new learning.

At the risk of laboring the point, I should like to return to the question of what can be concluded about the control of a response system from the effects of an omission contingency. The present experiment did not, of course, involve an omission contingency but it is virtualy certain that head positioning would be quickly eliminated by that contingency since, as we have seen, it was eliminated when the R–S* contingency was simply removed. Although the presumed outcome would certainly demonstrate that the system was sensitive to a response–reinforcer relation, it would not, of course, mean that the response was being supported solely by, or even predominately by, positive R–S* relations that existed prior to the introduction of the omission contingency. The head-positioning response was, in fact, not supportable by an R–S* contingency in the stimulus unless the reinforcer was jointly contingent on the stimulus as well as on the response. The behavior of the key-pecking response shows the other side of the coin. The response was supportable by R–S* relations alone even though it is known to be a response that is difficult to suppress by the omission contingency. A response readily suppressed by an omission contingency may nevertheless not be supported by an R–S* contingency alone, whereas a response that continues to occur despite an omission contingency may nevertheless be supported by an R–S* contingency alone. There is not a direct relation between the suppressibility of a response by the omission contingency and its supportability by a positive R–S* contingency.

The present experiment does not take us very far toward the identification of the properties of response systems that may account for differences in the way they are affected by contingencies. The response systems in the present experiment differ along many dimensions. For reasons that cannot be developed here I favor the hypothesis that responses which are directed at a localizable, controlling stimulus are more readily supported by S–S* and R–S* relations than are those which, although conditional on a controlling stimulus, are not directed toward it. In any case, I conclude with a sure thing: very little is known as yet about the properties of response systems that make them more or less suppressed by, or supportable by, reduced contingencies among stimuli, responses, and reinforcers.

References

Bindra, D. A motivational view of learning, performance, and behavior modification. *Psychological Review*, 1974, 81, 199–213.

Bolles, R. C. Reinforcement, expectancy, and learning. *Psychological Review*, 1972, **79**, 394–409.

Brown, P. L., & Jenkins, H. M. Auto-shaping of the pigeon's key peck. *Journal of the Experimental Analysis of Behavior,* 1968, **11,** 1–8.
Catania, A. C. Elicitation, reinforcement, and stimulus control. In R. Glaser (Ed.), *The nature of reinforcement.* New York: Academic Press, 1971. Pp. 196–220.
Gamzu, E., & Williams, D. R. Associative factors underlying the pigeon's keypecking in auto-shaping procedures. *Journal of the Experimental Analysis of Behavior,* 1973, **19,** 225–232.
Jenkins, H. M. Effects of the stimulus reinforcer relation on selected and unselected responses. In R. A. Hinde & J. S. Hinde (Eds.), *Constraints on learning.* New York: Academic Press, 1973. Pp. 189–203.
Jenkins, H. M., & Moore, B. R. The form of the auto-shaped response with food or water reinforcers. *Journal of the Experimental Analysis of Behavior,* 1973, **20,** 163–181.
Mackintosh, N. J. *The psychology of animal learning.* New York: Academic Press, 1974.
Moore, B. R. The role of directed Pavlovian reactions in simple instrumental learning in the pigeon. In R. A. Hinde & J. Stevenson-Hinde (Eds.), *Constraints on learning.* London: Academic Press, 1973. Pp. 159–186.
Schwartz, B., & Williams, D. R. The role of the response-reinforcer contingency in negative automaintenance. *Journal of the Experimental Analysis of Behavior,* 1972, **17,** 351–357.
Williams, D. R. Biconditional behavior: Conditioning without constraint. Unpublished manuscript, 1974.
Williams, D. R., & Williams, H. Auto-maintenance in the pigeon: Sustained pecking despite contingent nonreinforcement. *Journal of the Experimental Analysis of Behavior,* 1969, **12,** 511–520.

DISCUSSION

Jenkins argued that one cannot identify the role played by S–S and R–S relations within a procedure, such as autoshaping, by the introduction of new or altered contingencies, such as omission training. The changes resulting from these new relations allow for the possibility of new learning and hence the results cannot be used to reconstruct the contribution made by S–S and R–S relations in their original context. He made the following suggestion:

Jenkins: An alternative is to compare different response systems, such as key pecking and head positioning in the pigeon, and to subject these to parallel manipulations in order to explore the contribution made by the R–S and S–S relations to the performance of the subject. It is a strategy that has not been systematically applied.

As part of the advocacy to look toward new paradigms, Jenkins suggested that we should eschew traditional labels for codifying behavioral variables and procedures, a viewpoint that was challenged on several occasions. In answer to Davis' question whether it was reasonable to continue using the word "reinforcer" to indicate both response-contingent events and Pavlovian unconditioned stimuli, Jenkins replied that one's descriptive vocabulary should not tie one to a particular interpretation of the events.

Davis: However, shouldn't our labels indicate not only whether, for example, something is edible, but also the procedure under which the edible object became available?

Seligman: Along with Hank's point, I'm curious about whether there is some reason for talking about S–S and R–S relations rather than using the more traditional terminology of Pavlovian and operant conditioning.

Jenkins: I am not uncomfortable with the fact that the term "reinforcer" is arguably vague as to which conditioning procedure is involved. I have come to the point of using the term "reinforcer" without implying either R–S or S–S relations. In fact, I use such labels as R–S and S–S relations because the term "relations" is generic to cover the whole area of arranged contingencies, implicit correlations, temporal conjunctions, and so forth. We need a vocabulary to describe these relations without getting involved in traditional preconceived interpretations brought about by such labels as "conditioned stimulus."

A number of participants proposed alternative explanations for some of the results that are reported in Jenkins chapter.

Weisman: Herb's results show only some of the ways that experiments comparing S–S and R–S correlations can turn out. For example, the duration of instrumental training and the amount of food deprivation during such training dramatically affects discrimination between response dependent variable interval and response independent variable time components of a multiple schedule (Weisman & Ramsden, 1973). So, very well-trained or very hungry birds will continue to peck on response-independent food schedules. Your results may therefore be determined not only by the interactions between response systems and stimulus–reinforcer relations.

Jenkins: Your point is well taken and I see that there may be a useful parallel which I didn't see before between the work on multiple schedules involving response-dependent and response-independent components and the work I've been doing.

Staddon: Yours is a most intriguing and subtle result. However, I think it becomes less puzzling if one recognizes that a response–reinforcer contingency exerts its effects in part through indirect effects on stimulus–reinforcer contingencies. This line of thought has led me (Staddon, 1976) to the notion of response elasticity: An elastic response is one, such as head positioning, that is strongly affected by what I consider to be stimulus contingencies; for example, relative and absolute frequency of reinforcement. An inelastic response is one, such as pecking, that is not much affected by changes in either relative or absolute rate of reinforcement.

This notion can be made more precise by considering the four positive functions shown in Fig. 3.4. The two solid, negatively accelerated functions represent the properties of pecking, an inelastic response. The top curve, P(EXT), shows how rate of pecking varies with rate of food delivery in one VI component of a multiple schedule when there is no food delivered in the other component. The lower solid curve, P(VT), shows how pecking varies when there is a fixed rate of "free" food in the other component. Because pecking is, by the hypothesis, inelastic, the shift from EXT to VT has little effect and the two curves are close together. The rising function labeled "VI schedule function" shows the effect of the instrumental response on the rate of food delivery, i.e., the properties of the VI schedule. It shows that over the typical range of peck rates a change in the rate of pecking has little effect on the rate of food delivery. Therefore, the decrease in peck rate caused by the shift from EXT to VT in the other component shifts the equilibrium point only slightly, from A to B, a small decrease in response rate.

The situation for an elastic response, such as head positioning, is very different. Here, the shift from EXT to VT greatly decreases response rate. The new response rate, in turn, cannot sustain the previous food delivery rate, so that a new equilibrium is established at a much lower point, D, well below the previous equilibrium at C.

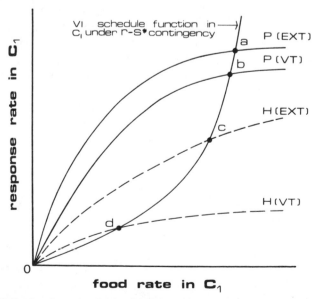

FIG. 3.4 Distinction between elastic and inelastic responses proposed by Staddon. See text above for elaboration.

I agree that Herb's elegant experiment demolishes what he terms the "origin hypothesis." I suggest instead that something such as the "elasticity" dimension may be a more useful way of characterizing different response systems.

Seligman: If one conceived of some of the food reinforcement schedules as avoidance of time out, could it be that the kind of response you require contributes to the effects you have described? There may well be "good" operants for the avoidance of time out, just as we have evidence that there are "good" operants for getting food.

Jenkins: I understand the words but not the operations which would bear on the issue raised by Marty. I assume you are asking whether key pecking is a more "prepared" response than head positioning for the avoidance of time out from food. The results certainly tell us that key pecking is more readily supportable, but whether that means it's more "prepared" or not I don't know. We need a way of identifying degrees of preparedness that's independent of the results we're trying to explain with the concept of preparedness.

In later discussion Jenkins suggested the relevance of Garcia's notion of a hedonic shift, which results from a Pavlovian conditioning procedure. For example, behavior previously appropriate to the reinforcer may under certain conditions become targeted to the signal, and such behavior may be maintained because of the continuing hedonic significance of the signal. One consequence may be to make any behavior supported in this way relatively insensitive to response—reinforcer contingencies, as in the case of key pecking. The notion that the signal may take on attributes of a "desired object" has therefore to be seriously considered.

Hurwitz: In the case of the pigeon one can see how an illuminated disk could develop attributes associated with food. However, I find it very difficult to understand how a sound could function in the same sense as a target stimulus for food-appropriate behaviors. There may be some animals where the reverse would hold: where visual stimuli are unlikely to be targets or desirable objects, but where sound stimuli might develop such functions.

Jenkins: That may well be. However, in the case of pecking in the pigeon I doubt that sound, whether localized or not, could serve as the target for the pecking response. A sound stimulus might serve to initiate a pecking response directed at some targetlike feature of the environment. Perhaps a response directed at a lighted key, under control of a sound stimulus, would act much like the autoshaped key-peck response where the lighted key serves as both the initiating stimulus and the target response. That's a possibility that would be interesting to explore. [See related remarks by Hurwitz following Boakes, Chapter 4.—Eds.]

Despite the fact that Jenkins' results indicated the importance of the R—S relation in supporting the key-peck response, Staddon suggested that S—S relations may ultimately have considerable importance in behavioral control.

Staddon: There are many experiments which seem to say that temporal changes in the frequency of food over time are the essential factor influencing an animal's performance. All the other variables become of secondary importance. A subject's behavior may drift once food frequency changes but ultimately his responding always comes under the food frequency variable.

Jenkins: You put too much emphasis on the importance of S–S* contingencies. Why can't we accept that an animal can learn not only these but can also respond to reinforcement contingencies, joint contingencies, and so forth? Why restrict the system to one alternative?

Staddon: I am only talking about a dominant mechanism.

Jenkins: I am convinced that on the basis of the experiment I have outlined, responses which to all the world look like conditioned Pavlovian responses are indeed sensitive to response–reinforcement relations. The animal is flexible enough to pick up any of these relations, so it would be a mistake to go for a model that insisted on a single dominant mechanism.

References

Staddon, J. E. R. Learning as adaptation. In W. K. Estes (Ed.): *Handbook of learning and cognitive processes,* Vol. 2. Hillsdale, N.J.: Lawrence Erlbaum Assoc., 1976.

Weisman, G. & Ramsden, M. Discrimination of a response-independent component in a multiple schedule. *Journal of the Experimental Analysis of Behavior,* 1973, **19**, 55–64.

4
Performance on Learning to Associate a Stimulus with Positive Reinforcement

R. A. Boakes

University of Sussex

INTRODUCTION

As Boakes notes in the introduction to his chapter, we do not presently have an adequate performance model for Pavlovian conditioning, which leaves us in a less than ideal position to understand the nature of operant–Pavlovian interactions. Boakes suggests that the attention directed to the autoshaping of pigeons has been something of a mixed blessing. On the one hand, it has caused us to reconsider a range of experimental situations and puzzling phenomena. On the other hand, however, the dependence of interpretations of autoshaping on pigeon key-pecking data has perhaps lead to an unwarranted emphasis on the stimulus substitution theory, which Boakes feels is an inadequate performance model for Pavlovian conditioning in general.

Any comprehensive theory of classical conditioning needs to contain two parts: a model of associative learning and a performance model. Recent years have seen a considerable increase of interest in classical conditioning and developments of sophisticated models of associative learning. However this progress has not been accompanied by a parallel development of our understanding of the way in which the learning of an association affects behavior.

Because associations are not directly observable, some set of performance rules is obviously required in order to obtain any sort of empirical evidence on associative learning. As long as an associative model is developed within the context of some highly standardized experimental preparation a limited set of simple performance rules may be adequate. For example, the considerable body of research that has stemmed from Kamin's discovery of the blocking phenomenon has been mainly limited to the situation in which the phenomenon was first obtained, namely conditioned suppression in rats (Rescorla & Wagner, 1972; Wagner & Rescorla, 1972; Mackintosh, 1975). In testing their model in the context of conditioned suppression Rescorla and Wagner need to assume only that the V value, the parameter corresponding to associative strength, is correlated with the degree of suppression that a stimulus exerts on behavior maintained by a standard schedule of appetitive reinforcement. Now this is perfectly satisfactory and indeed probably the only way to proceed if one's primary interest is in the rules governing the formation of associations. If Rescorla and Wagner had simultaneously attempted to analyze the way in which response suppression was determined not only by the V value of a stimulus, but also by the parameters of the schedule maintaining the baseline behavior, the deprivation state of their subjects, and so on, then little progress would likely have been made in the study of associative processes. By holding such factors constant, then, with the assumption that they do not interact in an important way with variables determining associative strength, a simple set of performance rules may be sufficient.

However, in seeking an answer to the general question of how a temporal relationship between a stimulus and a reinforcer affects the behavior of an animal, we need not only to understand how the animal learns to associate the two events but also what the behavioral consequences of such learning are.

The main point of this chapter is to suggest that we are in a poor position to obtain a general understanding of how the effects of classical conditioning interact with instrumental conditioning because we lack an adequate performance model for the behavioral effects of classical conditioning procedures. The need for such models has perhaps not seemed pressing for two rather different reasons. Until quite recently interest in interactions between classical and instrumental conditioning has been largely confined to psychologists working in the tradition of two-factor theory with its emphasis on the analysis of avoidance learning (e.g., Rescorla & Solomon, 1967). Within this tradition the main interest has been in interactions at an associative level (see chapters by Rescorla and by Seligman in this volume) so that transfer effects that may have been mediated by the association of specific responses to stimuli in the situation have received little attention.

Much recent research on the interactions between classical and instrumental conditioning has been stimulated by the discovery of autoshaping (Brown & Jenkins, 1968). This too has led to the neglect of performance rules but for a rather different reason. Research on autoshaping has largely used a particular situation, in which it turns out that a rather simple performance model appears to be adequate. The model is that of "stimulus-substitution theory," which states that when an animal learns to associate a CS with a UCS, the CS comes to evoke at least part of the response pattern previously evoked only by the UCS. As applied to a standard autoshaping situation there is some ambiguity in the model with respect to the direction of the conditioned behavior, as discussed by Hearst and Jenkins (1974), but it works well, for example, in accounting for the way the conditioned response changes as the kind of reinforcement employed is varied (e.g., Jenkins & Moore, 1973).

Various kinds of evidence, including the two sets of experiments described later in this chapter, have persuaded us that the standard situation used in the study of autoshaping is a special case and that the apparent adequacy of stimulus-substitution theory as a general performance model for classical conditioning disappears when other situations are examined. Before we discuss this claim in more detail it may be helpful to explain how we have become interested in the problem.

Behavioral Contrast and Autoshaping

We had been carrying out a number of studies of behavioral contrast at Sussex, some of which involved the presentation of free reinforcement (Halliday & Boakes, 1972; Boakes, 1973), when we were struck by the similarities between the procedures we were using and those used by Gamzu and Williams (1971) to study autoshaping. This similarity, together with Westbrook's (1973) finding in the same laboratory that behavioral contrast did not occur with pigeons when a lever-press response was used, suggested that the two phenomena might be closely related. We soon learned that this idea had already occurred to many others (e.g. Gamzu & Schwartz, 1973; Keller, 1974; Hearst & Jenkins, 1974).

The explanation of behavioral contrast that this idea has suggested is based on a rather simple theory of behavioral interactions between classical and instrumental conditioning. Because both the theory, termed "response additivity" by Schwartz and Gamzu (in press) and by Boakes, Halliday, and Poli (1975a), and the evidence for it have been widely discussed in the above references, only a brief description is given here. The theory proposes that in the conventional situation used for studying discrimination performance in the pigeon, pecking directed at the positive stimulus under differential conditions of reinforcement is maintained by two contingencies: that between the stimulus and reinforcement and that between the response and reinforcement. That is, the pigeon pecks both because the stimulus is predictive and because pecking produces reinforcement. However under comparable nondifferential conditions, where reinforcement is available at the same frequency whatever stimulus is present, only one of these contingencies, the response—reinforcer contingency, is present. Consequently pecking toward the positive stimulus occurs at a lower rate under nondifferential than under differential conditions; which is the effect known as behavioral contrast. From this point of view, therefore, behavioral contrast is an example of an additive interaction between the effects on behavior of classical and instrumental conditioning.

It should be noted that most discussions of this explanation have in effect assumed that a stimulus substitution model explains how the stimulus–reinforcer contingency affects behavior. The standard pigeon situation is regarded as containing two features crucial for the appearance of contrast: the use of an operant response, pecking, which resembles the consummatory response to the reinforcer, grain, thus insuring that the behavior produced by the stimulus–reinforcer contingency is also pecking; and the positioning of discriminative stimuli on the key, which insures that this pecking is directed at the key. In fact, there are no data indicating that both conditions are necessary for obtaining a behavioral contrast effect with pigeons; it is possible, for example, that the location of the stimuli is the only important factor.

The most important lesson from the study of autoshaping has been that caution is needed before general conclusions are drawn about operant conditioning from the results of studies in which hungry pigeons have been reinforced with grain and pecking has been the instrumental response. It is clear that in this particular experimental situation stimulus–reinforcer contingencies may play at least as large a part in determining behavior as the instrumental contingencies programmed by the experimenter. Now, most of the research on autoshaping supporting the stimulus–substitution model has used this kind of situation. It is noteworthy that one of the most problematical set of results for such a view has been obtained by Wasserman (1973), using chicks as subjects and heat as the reinforcer: He found that the chicks would peck at a key light that regularly preceded the onset of a heatlamp, even though no such behavior was elicited by the heatlamp itself. It seemed to us that caution was similarly needed before general conclusions were derived about the behavioral effects of stimulus–reinforcer contingencies from one particular situation and, therefore, that the response additivity view of behavioral contrast should be tested in conditions that differed from the standard pigeon situation.

One obvious body of data presenting difficulties for a simple application of the theory was that from studies of discrimination learning in rats. Whereas in many studies using lever pressing by rats behavioral contrast has not been clearly obtained (e.g., Pear & Wilkie, 1971), as is consistent with the theory, there is a sufficient number of clear positive cases (e.g., Henke, Allen, & Davison, 1972; Mackintosh, Little, & Lord, 1972; Gutman, Sutterer, & Brush, 1975) to make one wonder about its generality. There is a clear need to determine the conditions under which contrast does or does not occur when rats are used as subjects.

The second problem that interested us was the effect of using responses other than pecking with pigeons. Given that performance on multiple schedules by the pigeon has been studied for only two responses, key pecking and lever pressing (Westbrook, 1973; Hemmes, 1973), there are limited empirical grounds for assuming, as does the response additivity theory, that pecking is the special case and lever pressing the norm. It seemed well worthwhile to investigate some further response and the one we decided on was a vertical pull on a loop suspended from the ceiling of the conditioning chamber.

In neither situation did it seem completely obvious what behavior would arise as a result of stimulus—reinforcer contingencies alone. Consequently a necessary preliminary step was to attempt to answer this question before we investigated the behavioral interactions between stimulus— and response—reinforcer contingencies presumed to be present in a discrimination situation.

Although our work on this subject has started from an interest in behavioral contrast, the need to understand the way in which stimuli correlated with appetitive reinforcers affect behavior is not confined to this specialized problem, nor is it to the study of the effects of explicitly superimposing Pavlovian conditioned stimuli on instrumentally maintained behavior. The implication of research on autoshaping, as pointed out by Hearst and Jenkins (1974), is that in any conditioning situation, even one in which the contingencies explicitly programmed by the experimenter involve responses, the behavior of the animal may be affected by the particular type of stimuli, by the type of response used as an operant, and also by the type of reinforcer employed. The results that follow suggest that behavior arising from any explicit or implicit stimulus—reinforcer contingency may interact with the behavior demanded by a response contingency in various complex ways.

Discrete Trial Autoshaping with Rats

A note on terminology is appropriate here. "Autoshaping" has been used, like many other terms in animal psychology, to describe both a procedure and a phenomenon. Hearst and Jenkins (1974) have pointed out a number of unsatisfactory features of this label and have advocated that "sign tracking" be used as a replacement. However this introduces a new problem because unlike, for example, the procedure of extinction, witholding reinforcement, which almost inevitably results in the phenomenon of extinction or a reduction in responding, the use of a "sign-tracking" procedure far from guarantees behavior that can appropriately also be labeled "sign tracking," as is to be illustrated. Because the term "autoshaping" has been so widely adopted, we continue to use it here, but as the description of a procedure only. Its definition is identical to that of a classical conditioning procedure, namely, one in which the primary explicit contingency is between stimuli and reinforcement. The only possible merit of continuing to use the term "autoshaping" is that it does at least emphasize the interest in effects on responses that may very easily serve as operants with an instrumental conditioning procedure; for example, such responses as approach toward or contact with some form of manipulandum, as opposed to such responses as salivation or eye blinking, which do not normally affect the external environment of an animal. In the present context of behavioral interactions this emphasis is an important one. It should be noted that this usage includes the procedures employed in some studies that are not normally considered to be examples of autoshaping. What are usually termed studies of classically conditioned licking would be one such case (e.g., Patten & Rudy, 1967), and furthermore one that can be profitably compared with studies that are more conventionally labeled "autoshaping."

In contrast, the term "sign tracking" is used here to describe a certain phenomenon, namely the occurrence of conditioned behavior directed toward a localized stimulus employed in an autoshaping procedure. The reasons for this usage of the two terms is that, as found in the present study, the same procedure can produce two different forms of conditioned behavior. One is directed toward the stimulus, whereas the other is directed toward the place at which the reinforcer is about to arrive. For the sake of symmetry, and of retaining the Tolmanian flavor of "sign tracking," the equivalent generic term for this second form of behavior should perhaps be "goal tracking." Although this has not hitherto attracted as much attention as the sign-tracking phenomenon, it has seemed to us to be equally worthy of study.

A number of attempts have been made to develop a situation for rats where an autoshaping procedure would produce results similar to those obtained from pigeons. Most successful attempts have included, as at least part of the CS, the insertion of a retractable lever (e.g., Peterson, Ackil, Frommer, & Hearst, 1972; Savage, 1975). Such a stimulus is not very suitable for the study of performance in a multiple schedule, either one incorporating response-dependent schedules of reinforcement or the multiple version of autoshaping used first by Gamzu and Williams (1971). Consequently, in collaboration with Jose Linaza we tried to develop a stationary object that when illuminated as a signal for food, would consistently elicit some kind of manipulative response. A variety of attempts had been disappointing, when we learned of very similar, but successful, work at Oxford by Leslie and Ridgers (Leslie, 1974; Leslie & Ridgers, in preparation). Having produced a version of their lever, shown as Type A in Fig. 4.1, and mounted it in the kind of chamber they were using, a standard rat chamber manufactured by Camden Instruments Ltd., we began to record consistent behavior from our rats. This particular commercial chamber has an important feature, a vertical flap covering the food tray aperture, the movement of which operates a microswitch. Such switch operations, which are here termed "tray-entry" responses, have been systematically recorded as have depressions of the lever.

The standard procedure for three of the experiments using this apparatus was one in which 40 trials occurred in each daily session at variable intervals averaging 1 min. On each trial the lever was illuminated for 7 sec (CS period) and under autoshaping conditions the offset of this light was followed immediately by the delivery of a food pellet. These events were entirely independent of the

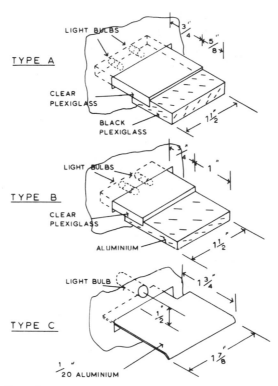

FIG. 4.1 Lever dimensions and arrangements of lever lights. Type A was used in Experiments 1 and 2 and Types B and C were used in Experiments 3 and 4.

rats' behavior, except under later omission conditions described below. In addition, subjects were also given a random condition, identical to the above except that lever illumination and pellet delivery were independent events.

The principal aim of Experiment 1 was to compare behavior under these two conditions. Twelve rats served as subjects. Six were first given 12 autoshaping sessions, followed by 12 random sessions; for the other six the order of conditions was reversed.

The results were in one sense very consistent, in another very noisy. They were consistent in that all 12 subjects responded to the CS at a higher frequency in the autoshaping than in the random condition. They were noisy in that the kind of conditioned behavior obtained varied from subject to subject. As is seen from the individual data from six subjects presented in Fig. 4.2, some rats pressed the lever during the CS period, some only operated the tray flap, whereas many made both responses.

The measure of behavior used in this figure is the percentage of trials in which at least one response, either lever press or tray entry, has occurred. Rates of

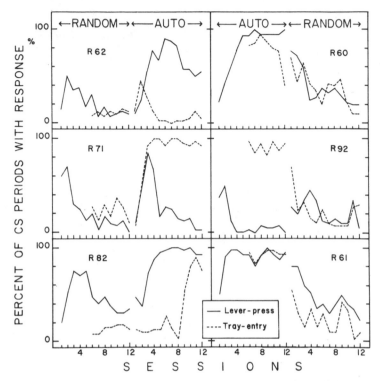

FIG. 4.2 Experiment 1: Results for six subjects from the first phase of the experiment illustrating various individual patterns of behavior. The top pair are subjects for which lever pressing was the more frequent response in the final autoshaping sessions; for the middle pair the tray-entry response was more frequent, and the bottom pair frequently made both responses during the CS. Rats receiving the random condition first are shown on the left and those receiving the autoshaping condition first are on the right.

responding during CS periods were also analyzed in this and subsequent experiments and the pattern of results was essentially the same. Thus, in Experiment 1 over all subjects the mean rate of lever pressing during CS periods, eight responses a minute for the final three sessions of the autoshaping condition was higher than the mean, three responses a minute for the last three sessions of the random condition ($p < 0.05$); and similarly the mean tray-entry rate of 12 responses a minute for the autoshaping condition was higher than the mean of three responses a minute for the Random condition ($p < 0.01$).

A similarly varied pattern of results was obtained from 12 further rats that served as subjects in Experiment 2. In this study all subjects were first given eight sessions of the random condition, followed by 12 sessions of autoshaping. Only the averaged results are presented in Fig. 4.3, where it is seen that both

FIG. 4.3 Experiment 2: Mean percentages of CS periods with a lever-press or tray-entry response for the first phase of the experiment.

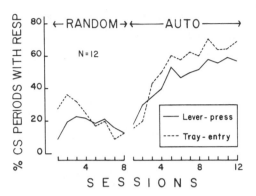

lever pressing and tray entry again occurred at a significantly higher frequency in the autoshaping than in the prior random condition.

The pattern of results obtained in these two experiments differs from that observed in typical autoshaping studies with pigeons as subjects or in studies with rats in which insertion of a lever serves as the CS (e.g., Peterson *et al.*, 1972). However frequent tray entries were also reported by Leslie and Ridgers (in preparation) and approach during the CS to the site of reinforcement was observed by Hearst in an unpublished experiment cited in Hearst and Jenkins (1974, p. 38). A varying mixture of what we are now labeling sign-tracking and goal-tracking behavior was also observed by Zener (1937) in what can be considered to be the first study of this kind. The occurrence of variable behavior under highly controlled conditions often turns out to be the result of conflicting processes or of undetected variables. It seemed appropriate to see whether this was true in the present case.

One possible way of pursuing the idea that the two response tendencies might be in competition was to attempt to suppress one response by means of an omission contingency. The 12 subjects from Experiment 1 were given 12 sessions of each of three omission conditions. The basic procedure continued as in the first part of the experiment, but in addition a further contingency was introduced: in the lever omission condition (LO) no pellet was delivered at the end of a CS period if one or more lever presses were made during that CS period; in the tray omission condition (TO) no pellet was delivered if a tray entry was made; and in the double omission condition (DO) the occurrence of either response prevented pellet delivery. The six rats showing the greatest tendency to press the lever were given lever omission first and the remainder started with tray omission. The omission contingencies were effective in reducing the frequency of the target response, or responses, although rarely eliminated them. With the lever omission condition the average frequency of trials with a lever response was reduced to 16% in the final three sessions, and with tray omission the comparable figure for tray entries was 9%. With double omission both responses were reduced to a slightly lower level, with again the lever press showing slightly more resistance to the omission contingency.

The aspect of most interest in the present context was that in some cases suppression of the target response was accompanied by an increase in the alternative response to a level higher than at any time before: thus, as shown in Fig. 4.4, for R62 a high level of tray responding was obtained under LO conditions and for R71 and R92 a high level of lever pressing was obtained under TO conditions (cf. Fig. 4.2). Reversals in the relative strengths of the two responses with the change from LO to TO, or vice versa, also occurred in five other subjects.

An observed reciprocal relationship between two responses as a result of some experimental manipulation such as the present one does not necessarily imply that normally the two responses are in conflict. Some form of behavior is always likely to appear to fill the void left by reducing one previously frequent response. However these result at least provide some support for the idea of conflict between two response tendencies. From the initial parts of the two

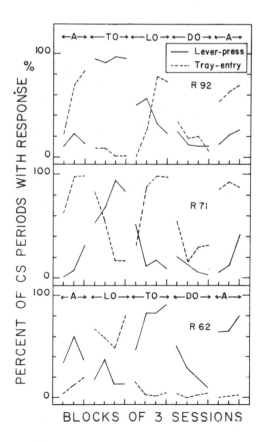

FIG. 4.4 Experiment 1: Effects of various omission contingencies on the performance of three subjects in the second phase of the experiment. For R92 and R71 initial autoshaping sessions (A) were followed first by the tray omission (TO) condition and then by the lever omission (LO) condition. For R62, LO preceded TO. For all subjects and double omission (DO) condition was the final omission contingency.

experiments it seems that a common resolution of this conflict is for an animal to make both responses during the CS period (see Fig. 4.2).

The effect of omission conditions was studied further with the 12 subjects of Experiment 2. Because the introduction of an omission contingency leads to a change in reinforcement frequency, as well as the presence of a negative response contingency, we wished to determine the relative importance of the two factors by employing a yoked design. Subjects were assigned to pairs, which were matched as far as possible in terms of their performance under autoshaping conditions. One member of a pair, the master subject, was given the double omission condition; the other member served as a yoked subject, receiving reinforcement at the same frequency and time as the master subject but in the absence of any response contingency.

Each pair was given 18 sessions of the above conditions and, as is shown for the master subjects in Fig. 4.5, the double omission procedure again had a marked suppressive effect, on both responses. Again, however, only in one case, R1, were both responses effectively eliminated. In the yoked subjects the frequency of lever pressing was little affected by the changes in reinforcement probability induced by the performance of their master subjects. For all six pairs the reduction in lever-press frequency was markedly greater in the master subject

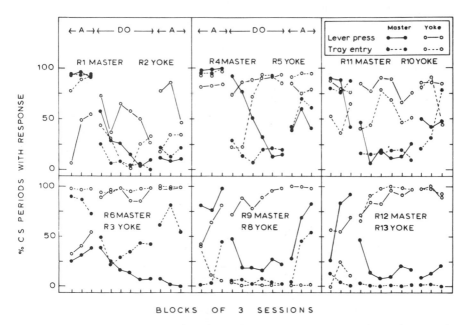

BLOCKS OF 3 SESSIONS

FIG. 4.5 Experiment 2: Comparison between the performance of master subjects given double omission conditions and that of their yoked partners given identical reinforcement conditions but no response–reinforcer contingency.

and it therefore appears that this reduction was mainly determined by the negative response contingency and not by changes in reinforcement probability. This conclusion cannot be drawn so confidently for the tray-entry response, because for two yoked subjects, R2 and R5, there was a large reduction in tray-entry frequency following the large change in reinforcement probability when the omission condition was first introduced for their master subjects.

Reinforcement Probability and Deprivation Level

In the last section some evidence was presented for considering the lever-press, or sign-tracking, response and the tray-entry, or goal-tracking, response as competing forms of behavior. Such a viewpoint would be more compelling if factors other than selective omission conditions could be shown to have differential effects on the two responses. In addition there remains the puzzling question of why only sign tracking is seen in most pigeon studies. Were there any crucial variables, apart from the difference in species and in apparatus, that distinguished the conditions described so far from those normally used with pigeons?

One possible candidate was motivational level. Whereas in experiments of this kind it is normal practice to deprive pigeons to the fairly severe level of 75–80% of their free feeding weights the rats in the present Experiments 1 and 2 were only moderately, and possibly also variably, deprived: they were housed together in batches of two or three and maintained on a 22-hour feeding schedule. If therefore seemed possible that with increased deprivation the lever-press response might dominate.

A second possible factor was suggested by the results of the yoked subjects from the final part of Experiment 2, where in some subjects the tray-entry response was weakened by a drop in reinforcement probability. In addition, we had found that tray-entry responding was almost absent in a multiple schedule version of autoshaping, as described in the next section, and this also suggested that the predictability of reinforcement might affect tray entry much more than lever pressing.

These two factors were investigated in Experiment 3. The subjects were 16 rats that were individually caged. Eight were highly deprived to 75% of their free feeding weights and eight lightly deprived to the 90% level. The procedure was exactly the same as that for the autoshaping condition in Experiments 1 and 2, except that for a group of four high-deprivation subjects and a group of four low-deprivation subjects reinforcement occurred after only half the CS periods on a semirandom basis. Reinforcement occurred after every CS period for the remaining two groups. In addition to the two chambers previously used, which were now fitted with a modified version of the original lever, Type B in Fig. 4.1, two additional Camden chambers were used, in which the lever lights were mounted just above instead of within the levers, as shown as Type C in Fig. 4.1. Within each group half the subjects had a Type B and half a Type C lever.

The most important variable turned out to be the probability of reinforcement. As is seen in the right-hand half of Fig. 4.6, tray-entry responding during CS periods by the eight subjects given 50% reinforcement steadily decreased and disappeared almost completely in the highly deprived subjects, whereas the opposite occurred with the eight subjects given 100% reinforcement. With the latter subject CS tray entries steadily increased, and with highly deprived subjects, eventually at least one tray entry occurred on almost every trial. This large effect of reinforcement probability on the tray-entry response appears to be responsible for the rather paradoxical effect on the lever-pressing response, shown on the left-hand side of Fig. 4.6. In this case with the 100% groups the response, although more rapidly acquired in the early sessions, subsequently drops in frequency to a level well below that of the 50% group. Thus, reinforcing only half the trials turns out to be more effective for producing sign tracking in this situation than reinforcing every trial.

A measure we used for the relative strengths of lever pressing and tray entry in individual subjects was the difference between the percentage of trials with a lever press and the percentage of trials with a tray entry. On this measure an animal that pressed the lever on all 40 trials in a session and never made a tray entry would score +100 and one that on all trials made only tray entries would score −100. This measure, the "lever−tray difference," is used in Fig. 4.7. Here

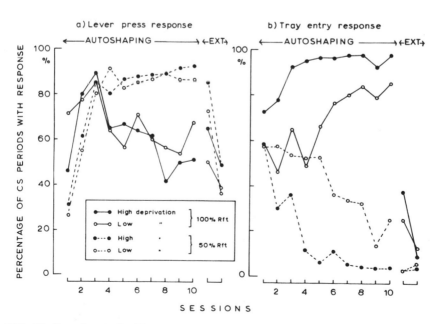

FIG. 4.6 Experiment 3: Frequency of lever-pressing response (a) and of tray-entry (b) response in all four groups in the first two phases of the experiment.

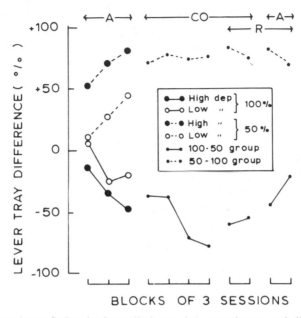

FIG. 4.7 Experiment 3: Results from all phases of the experiment, excluding two sessions of extinction, expressed in terms of mean "lever–tray difference" scores. The score for each subject was obtained by subtracting the percentage of trials on which a tray-entry response was made from the percentage of trials with a lever press. Following the first two phases the two 100% groups (high and low deprivation) were combined to form a single "100–50" group ($N = 8$). Similarly the two 50% groups were combined to form a single "50–100" group ($N = 8$).

the data shown in Fig. 4.6 are represented in this manner for the initial condition, A, for simple autoshaping and are averaged over blocks of three sessions for the final nine sessions. The clear dominance of lever pressing in the 50% groups and of tray entry in the 100% groups can again be seen.

Because many of the subjects in the 100% groups frequently made both responses in a single CS period, their scores did not differ greatly from zero and it was not clear which response was dominant in such cases. Consequently we introduced a contingency designed to eliminate one of the responses in these subjects. This compound omission (CO) procedure was an added contingency whereby no reinforcement occurred at the end of a CS period in which both responses had been made. All subjects were now maintained at 80% of their free-feeding weights in this and the following phases of the experiment, so that with the introduction of the compound omission contingency there were just two groups; one continuing with 50% reinforcement and one with 100% reinforcement.

Because few 50% subjects made both responses within a single CS period this added contingency was not expected to affect their performance very much and, as is seen in Fig. 4.7, the lever–tray score for this group (50–100) remained constant during the second phase of Experiment 3. In the group receiving 100% reinforcement (100–50), where many subjects made both responses, the CO contingency tended to reduce lever pressing and thus, as Fig. 4.7 shows, to decrease further the lever–tray score. Only median scores are given in this figure: Of the eight subjects in the 100–50 group six showed a marked decrease in lever pressing, with tray entries continuing at the same frequency; one subject showed a reduction in both responses; and with one final subject of the CO contingency led to the elimination of tray entries, leaving lever pressing intact.

These results provide further evidence for considering the two responses to be in competition: Lever pressing dominates with 50% reinforcement and, although also occurring with 100% reinforcement, is the weaker of the two responses under these conditions. A final attempt to gain further evidence on the effects of reinforcement probability was made by reversing the probabilities of reinforcement for the two groups, but, as is seen for the final two phases shown in Fig. 4.7, this was not very successful.

The implications of these results are discussed later. The following section is concerned with a rather different problem.

The Possibility of Superstition: A Multiple Schedule Procedure

We have not yet raised the question of whether the frequent and continuously maintained behavior that has been obtained in the experiments so far described is in fact controlled by the stimulus–reinforcer contingencies explicitly programmed in each experiment. It appears that orienting toward the CS can often become a stable response in the type of salivary conditioning experiment commonly performed in East European laboratories, but for Konorski at least such behavior was seen as a "parasitic"–or in western terminology, "superstitious"–instrumental response (Konorski, 1967, p. 268). Similarly a reader committed to the idea that such responses as pressing a lever or operating a flap are primarily governed by response–reinforcer contingencies may well suspect the present data to reflect the influence of possible implicit response–reinforcer contingencies (see Jenkins, this volume). That is, the subjects of these three experiments may have been superstitious rats instead of Pavlovian rats.

When an autoshaping procedure is successfully used with pigeons an analysis of their behavior in terms of superstitious conditioning may seem to provide a plausible answer, at least superficially, to the question of why they continue to peck, but this analysis is less convincing as an account of why they start to peck in the first place. Pigeons rarely peck an illuminated disk unless it is explicitly paired with grain. However, in the case of rats this particular difficulty for the superstitious analysis does not arise, for as seen in Experiments 1 and 2 (see Fig. 4.2 and 4.3), rats both press a lever and operate the tray flap at a moderate frequency in the absence of any contingency. Because initially these responses occur at a higher rate when the lever is illuminated and because any response during the CS period is shortly followed by reinforcement, it seems that the law of effect may be sufficient to account for maintained lever pressing and tray entry.

This possibility is further strengthened by other observations. Watching the animals it was hard to see in what way their behavior differed from that of animals that had been trained by conventional instrumental procedures. Early in training they sniffed at and attempted to contact the light; depression of the lever was apparently an accidental byproduct of such attempts. Later on the usual pattern was pressing the lever with a single forepaw while alternately orienting toward the light and the food tray. No gnawing of the lever was ever directly observed and, although one of the levers in the first experiment was eventually half eaten away, in general damage to the levers was surprisingly slight. In another situation (Boakes, Poli, & Lockwood, 1975b) we have found that rats can demolish a much tougher material very rapidly. Similarly, Leslie and Ridgers (in preparation), in their related work on autoshaping, have noted that absence of gnawing of the lever, despite the fact that the brightest part of their lever is the projecting face.

One type of evidence that in other situations has been employed to test for the presence of superstitious conditioning has been the introduction of an omission contingency (e.g., Sheffield, 1965). If a response is acquired despite an omission contingency, or shows little decrement when such a condition is introduced, as is often the case with pigeons (e.g., Williams & Williams, 1969), then it can be concluded that the behavior is primarily determined by the stimulus–reinforcer contingency. However, the elimination of some response by an omission contingency provides ambiguous evidence: It may indicate that the response was formerly maintained only by superstitious conditioning, or that any effect of the formerly important stimulus–reinforcer contingency was weak compared to the opposing effect of the new negative response–reinforcer contingency. As we have seen earlier, the introduction of various omission conditions in Experiments 1 and 2 led to a marked, although gradual, decrease in lever pressing and tray entry, but in most cases the responses were not completely eliminated. This suggests that the behavior was at least partly maintained by stimulus–reinforcer contingencies, but the evidence is not decisive.

A third finding has indicated that superstitious conditioning is of little importance in determining the behavior of pigeons in an autoshaping situation. Gamzu and Williams (1971) employed a multiple schedule form of autoshaping, where free reinforcement occurred at irregular intervals in the presence of an illuminated response key, but not when the key was dark. They found that pigeons pecked at the lit key with this differential condition and that the rate of pecking was subsequently greatly reduced with the subsequent introduction of a nondifferential condition, where free reinforcement occurred at the same rate in the absence of the signal. Here one has a transition from a situation in which both stimulus–reinforcer and implicit response–reinforcer contingencies may be effective to one in which the stimulus–reinforcer contingency has been removed, whereas the response–reinforcer contingency may remain intact. Consequently, if there is little change in responding during such a transition, for example, this indicates that the behavior is primarily maintained by superstitious conditioning.

It seemed of interest to discover whether the behavior previously obtained with the discrete trial procedure of the first three experiments would also develop with this form of autoshaping, and if it did, to find out to what extent it would be affected by such a transition from differential to nondifferential conditions.

In Experiment 4 the same chambers were used as in the previous experiment, with Type B levers in two of the chambers and Type C levers in the other two. Throughout the experiment periods of 30-sec duration in which the lever light was present (S1 periods) alternated with periods of 2-min duration in which the lever-light was absent (S2 periods). Each session started with an S2 period and consisted of a total of 15 of each period. In the differential condition pellets were delivered at variable intervals with a mean of 30 sec only in S1 periods (*mult* Free VI 30-sec EXT), whereas in the nondifferential condition pellets were delivered at the same frequency in both S1 and S2 periods (*mult* Free VI 30-sec Free VI 30-sec).

A total of 16 naive rats was maintained on a 22-hour feeding schedule. Eight were arbitrarily assigned to the Type B chambers ("light within lever" condition) and eight to the Type C chambers ("light above lever" condition). Within each group the sequence of differential and nondifferential phases was varied as shown in Fig. 4.8. Rates of lever pressing are given in this figure, but tray-entry responding is not shown because this remained at a low level throughout.

There are three aspects of these results which show that superstition plays at most a minor role in this situation. First, lever pressing occurred at moderate rates only in the differential condition and in all subjects S1 rates were higher than those in S2 periods. There was a tendency for more responding to occur with the Type B arrangement (light within lever), but overall the results suggested that the Type C arrangement (light above lever) was almost as effective.

Second, response rates in nondifferential session were not only low when this was the initial condition, but also when this followed a block of differential sessions. For the two groups shown in the right-hand panels of Fig. 4.8, therefore, S1 rates in the final phase that followed the block of differential sessions were little higher than in the first nondifferential phase. Because any implicit response–reinforcer contingency remains constant with a change from differential to nondifferential conditions, this aspect of the results also indicates that lever pressing was primarily maintained by the stimulus–reinforcer contingency.

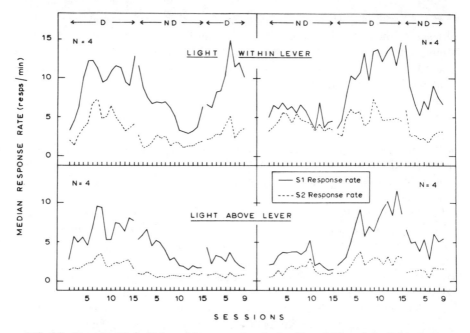

FIG. 4.8 Experiment 3: Rates of lever pressing during S1 and S2 periods. Subjects given the Type B lever are shown in the upper panels and those given Type C levers in the lower panels. The left-hand panels show the performance of the two groups for which the differential (D) condition was the first condition, and the right-hand panels show the two groups experiencing the nondifferential condition (ND) first.

Third, S2 rates were also higher in the differential than in the nondifferential condition, even though somewhat paradoxically reinforcement occurred during S2 periods only in the nondifferential condition.

It seems reasonable to generalize from these results and also assume that with the discrete trial procedure of Experiments 1, 2, and 3 responding was primarily controlled by the explicit stimulus–reinforcer contingencies.

Comparisons between Pigeons and Rats

In many respects the behavior of the rats in these four experiments resembled that of pigeons in comparable studies. A form of sign-tracking response, that is, behavior directed toward a localized stimulus, developed and continued indefinitely as long as that stimulus consistently preceded the delivery of a reinforcer. As with pigeons, this behavior was reduced, but not eliminated, by the introduction of a negative contingency between the response and reinforcement. The same behavior also developed when reinforcement occurred at irregular intervals only in the presence of the stimulus. Finally, following acquisition in such a differential condition, the subsequent introduction of reinforcement in the absence of the stimulus, as in a nondifferential condition, produced a marked reduction of this behavior; the data shown in Fig. 4.8 closely resemble those obtained by Gamzu and Schwarz (1973, Fig. 2, but see below) using a similar procedure, but with pigeons as subjects and key pecking as the response.

Other aspects of the results differ from those normally obtained from auto-shaping studies with pigeons. Although, as we have seen, a conditioned response consisting of approach to the site of reinforcement has been recorded in other rat studies, this form of behavior has not usually been reported with pigeons. Admittedly, few pigeon chambers are fitted with flaps over the food aperture of with any other device for recording approach toward the grain hopper. Neverthe-less, in watching pigeons in a number of standard autoshaping studies we have never seen any tray-directed behavior during the CS. Reports from other labora-tories confirm this observation. Where pecking drifts away from the key light it appears as likely to be directed to one side of the key as down toward the tray aperture.

Earlier the question was raised as to whether some procedural difference was responsible for the appearance of tray approach responses in the present situa-tion. The results of Experiment 3 indicated that deprivation level was not a critical variable in this respect. In the first part of this experiment increasing the deprivation level decreased the variability of behavior and tray-entries were most pronounced in the condition most comparable to that of pigeon studies, namely with high deprivation and 100% reinforcement.

Are there any other procedural factors that might account for the difference, or, to put the question in another way, in what kinds of autoshaping situation may pigeons behave like the rats of the first three experiments?

One situation in which we have observed pigeons to approach the tray area when a response key is illuminated as a signal for food has been in a large chamber where the signal is a distance of 75 cm from the food aperture. The situation was based on Jenkins' "long box" experiment, reported in Hearst and Jenkins (1974), in which it was found that subjects would peck at the signal despite the delay of reinforcement imposed by the distance they subsequently had to travel in order to obtain grain.

Some of our subjects behaved in this manner. Others would wait, apparently paralyzed by indecision, halfway between the signal and the food aperture. However many, especially after considerable training, approached the food aperture when the key light was switched on. A photocell system had been installed to monitor occasions on which the pigeon inserted his head into the aperture. However, unlike rats, pigeons rarely made this response, even though standing close by.

One possible reason for the frequent occurrence of approach to the tray in this study, but not in earlier work, arose from discussion with Jenkins about detailed procedural differences. In the present study an intense house light was used, to facilitate TV monitoring, and this had the probably critical effect of making the tray light far less salient than is usual. Peron (personal communication) has suggested that the presence of a highly discriminable stimulus correlated with the presence of grain in the conventional pigeon situation may be an important difference between this and other autoshaping studies.

A second situation, in which pigeons have been reported to approach or insert their heads into the food aperture in an autoshaping situation, has been described by Wasserman (1973) and by Mackintosh (1974, p. 107).[1] As many researchers unexpectedly found, when Brown and Jenkins' (1968) discovery of autoshaping first became known, little key pecking occurs if there is no house light in the chamber. Although Wasserman and Mackintosh have suggested explanations of this finding that are not related to the present issue, we felt that competition from tray approach tendencies may play some part in preventing key pecking in this situation. In collaboration with E. M. Peron, a preliminary investigation of autoshaping of pigeons in a dark chamber was carried out in which the effect of reinforcement probability was studied; however, no clear effect of this variable was obtained. Unfortunately, although insertions of the head into the food aperture could be recorded by an infrared photocell, these did not occur frequently in many subjects, and the use of a standard spatial arrangement of response key and aperture made it impossible to separately record approach to the aperture.

These two studies suggest two distinct sources for the difference in tray-entry responding between pigeons and rats. First, the conventional arrangement for pigeons in which the signal is usually vertically above the tray aperture prevents any dissociation between approach toward the signal and approach toward the tray. Possibly in a situation in which the signal was displaced horizontally from the tray, deprivation and reinforcement probability would have the same effects on the relative strengths of sign tracking and tray approach in pigeons as were found with rats in Experiment 3. Second, it appears that even when pigeons do make a distinct tray approach, unlike rats they rarely insert their heads into the aperture. This is probably because the presence of food is associated with a stimulus that, because it is visual, is far more salient for the pigeon than for the rat. Varying the illumination of the food tray was found to have little effect on the rats that served as subject in Experiments 1 and 2. It seems likely that substantial effects of such a manipulation can be found with pigeons as subjects.

To summarize this discussion, it seems premature to conclude that the absence of tray approach behavior in standard pigeon autoshaping studies indicates a fundamental difference between the performance of rats and pigeons when they learn to associate a stimulus and a reinforcer. It seems possible that the appropriate values of at least two variables—distance from signal to food, and house light intensity—may produce a situation in which a pigeon's behavior

---

[1] This was kindly pointed out to me by both E. M. Peron and R. G. Weisman.

resembles that of a rat. Stimulus duration and tray illumination may also be important factors.

In this section the main concern so far has been with tray-entry responding. There are three further differences between the results of the present experiments and those obtained with pigeons. The first two will be introduced only briefly.

Although no mention of it has been made in the text, the reader may have noticed from Fig. 4.6 that two extinction sessions were introduced immediately after the first phase of Experiment 3. Because two groups had received 100% reinforcement and two 50% reinforcement, it was possible to examine the effect of reinforcement probability on the course of extinction. Whereas previously we have found in autoshaping work with pigeons that key pecking is far more persistent in extinction after 50% reinforcement, as is found in the vast majority of instrumental conditioning studies, there is no indication of the standard partial reinforcement effect in Experiment 3.

This may be related to the presence or absence of competition from the tray-entry response, which extinguishes very rapidly compared to the lever-press response. However this question requires further research and in general extinction following autoshaping deserves more attention than it has hitherto received, especially in the light of the variable effects of partial reinforcement on classical conditioning (see Mackintosh, 1974; pp. 72–75).

In Experiment 4, where the multiple procedure was used, acquisition of lever pressing under differential conditions was as rapid for the eight rats that had previously received 15 sessions of nondifferential training as for the eight that were given differential training in the first phase of the experiment. In this respect the results, as shown in Fig. 4.9 below, differ from those obtained by Gamzu and Schwartz (1973) using a similar procedure with pigeons. They found that extended exposure to nondifferential reinforcement severely interfered with the subsequent development of sign tracking. This does not appear to be the case with rats, as is also indicated by the present failure in the discrete-trial situation of Experiments 1 and 2 to detect any effects attributable to prior exposure to the random condition.

The final comparison between pigeons and rats concerns the similarity between conditioned and unconditioned response obtained in most autoshaping studies with pigeons and the apparent lack of any such relationship in the present experiments. As discussed earlier, the fact that with pigeons the topography of the key peck closely resembles that of the consummatory response has led to the wide acceptance of a stimulus substitution model for the performance of animals in an autoshaping situation. Gnawing of the lever by rats has been observed when lever insertion has served as the CS and this did not occur under comparable conditions when brain stimulation instead of food was used as reinforcement (Peterson *et al.*, 1972). Nevertheless, neither in the present experiments nor in those by Leslie and Ridgers (in preparation), which appear to be the only two studies employing lever illumination (as opposed to lever insertion) as the CS, was the conditioned response clearly related to the kind of reinforcement used. In one experiment, Leslie and Ridgers (personal communication) used sucrose solution as reinforcement instead of food pellets. They did not observe the differences in behavior that would be expected from stimulus substitution theory or, for example, from Jenkins and Moore's (1973) results from pigeons.

The obvious question to ask is why the behavior of rats is not so clearly determined by the nature of the reinforcer as is the behavior of pigeons. Perhaps a more fruitful question is to ask, as we did earlier in this section, whether the apparently consistency of pigeon behavior in this respect results from the repeated use of a particular, highly standardized situation. The section that follows is concerned with this question.

Autoshaping of a Loop-Pull Response by Pigeons

As with the experiments using rats described earlier, the work with pigeons that is described in this section has started from our interest in behavioral contrast. In some earlier preliminary work with Keith Denby, which examined a variety of potential manipulanda, we had found that a vertical pull on a steel ring suspended from the ceiling appeared to be a promising alternative to key pecking or lever pressing to use in discrimination studies. The response was relatively easy to shape, especially compared to a response that consisted of some movement of the foot, and no problem arose in maintaining it on interval schedules of reinforcement.

Finding a suitable response was not enough. We also wished to have a manipulandum that could contain the discriminative stimuli. Because previous experiments that have examined the role of response factors in behavioral contrast, such as Westbrook (1973), have used nonlocalized stimuli, the significance of failing to obtain contrast with a lever-press response is weakened by the fact that the effect is small, or nonexistent, even with a key-pecking response (e.g., Redford & Perkins, 1974). Consequently a device was needed that could serve as a source of visual stimuli and that could be manipulated in at least two different ways; it would allow the recording of pecking directed at it and also of some response that bore no relation to the behavior elicited by the reinforcer. In terms of the classification we proposed in Boakes *et al.* (1975a), we wished to be able to compare discrimination performance in a Type A situation, where the stimulus is located on the manipulandum and the effective response resembles the consummatory response, with that in a Type D situation, where the stimulus is also located on the manipulandum but the response is unrelated to the reinforcer.

The device eventually used consisted of a U-shaped loop of clear plexiglass tubing projecting from the bottom of a hollow cylinder suspended from above the ceiling. This cylinder was painted matte black outside and silvered inside. It contained a 1-W bulb that illuminated only the loop. The cylinder was mounted in such a way that horizontal displacements of the loop toward the food tray—the "peck" response—and vertical displacements downward—the "pull" response—could be recorded separately.

Being at the time convinced of the applicability of stimulus substitution theory to autoshaping, we fully expected that, when the looplight served as a signal for food, a pigeon would peck but not pull at the loop. Furthermore, if behavioral contrast and autoshaping were intimately related, the use of a peck as the operant in a discrimination situation might give rise to contrast, whereas in an otherwise identical situation the use of the pull as the operant would not.

In a pilot experiment with Mark Lockwood that employed a discrete-trial autoshaping procedure, six of the eight naive pigeons employed as subjects soon began to peck at the loop when it was illuminated as a signal for food. What came as a surprise was that many subjects also made the pull response; with two subjects pulling was more frequent than pecking. In an attempt to eliminate pull responses, the occurrence of which we then regarded as unfortunate and probably artifactual, various adjustments to the loop mounting and associated circuitry were made, ending with the following arrangement in each chamber. A horizontal force of 15–20 g was required to trigger a peck response, and a vertical force of 37–40 g was required to trigger a pull response. The responses were made mutually inhibitory, in the sense that once a peck response had been initiated no pull response could occur until the loop had returned to its resting position, and vice versa. These technical details are included to indicate the attempt made to minimize the possibility that what was being recorded as a pull response was not some late component of a peck movement. Observation of the birds strongly suggested that the pull was a distinct response. In making a pull response most birds seized the bottom of the loop with their beaks and made a vigorous tug downward.

Despite these changes the pull response still occurred frequently in three subjects by the end of 11 autoshaping sessions. In these subjects, moreover, the response was fairly resistant to the double omission contingency introduced during a further seven sessions. With this contingency, as in Experiments 1 and 2, the occurrence of either response during a CS period canceled reinforcement at the end of that period.

A further eight naive pigeons served as subjects in a further study, Experiment 5, where the response requirements were kept constant at the values given above. As before, each session contained 40 trials, occurring at average intervals of 1 min. On each trial the loop light was illuminated for 6 sec and this was immediately followed by reinforcement, a 4-sec presentation of the grain hopper. Eight autoshaping sessions were followed by 12 double omission sessions.

Almost no responding at all was recorded from two subjects. The individual performances of the remaining six naive subjects are shown in Fig. 4.9. Two subjects, P403 and P411, displayed the pattern we had originally anticipated,

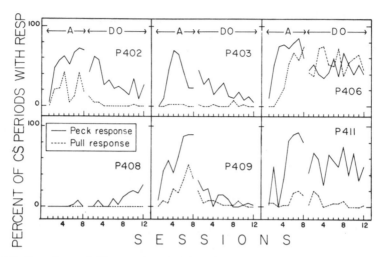

FIG. 4.9   Experiment 4: Frequencies of trials with peck and with pull responses for six of the eight naive pigeons in the experiment.

namely in the autoshaping condition a high incidence of pecking, which was somewhat suppressed by the subsequent omission contingency, with little pull responding at any stage. However, as observed in the pilot experiment, with three subjects the pull response occurred frequently in the autoshaping condition even though the stringent definition of this response was in effect here from the outset. In one pigeon, P406, this response was as resistant to the omission contingency as the peck response.

Because we suspected that prior experience might be important in determining behavior in this situation, a further six pigeons also served as subjects in Experiment 5. These had been previously been shaped to pull the loop and had received about 10 further sessions of training in which loop pulling had been reinforced on a variable-interval schedule. Given this prior training it was hardly surprising that pull responses were much more frequent in this group than in the naive group, as can be seen in Fig. 4.10. In the double omission condition the results for these subjects were similar to those for the naive subjects. With one exception, P146, pulling was more greatly suppressed than pecking.

Data from an earlier experiment using a conventional pigeon arrangement with a key light as the signal and a simple omission condition, but otherwise very similar stimulus and reinforcement schedules, made it possible to compare the final levels of pecking in the two situations. Although the mean percentage of trials was initially far lower in the present experiment, results from the final three omission sessions were very comparable to those from the situation in which pecks at a response key were recorded: for both groups of six pigeons in

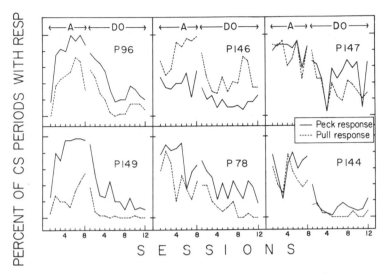

FIG. 4.10 Experiment 4: Frequencies of trials with peck and with pull responses for the six pigeons with previous instrumental training on the pull response.

the present study and for the 16 pigeons in the conventional one, the mean percentage of trials with a peck was approximately 25%.

In summary, the data for all groups of subjects given this discrete trial procedure were consistent in indicating that, both in terms of the relative frequencies of the two responses during simple autoshaping and in terms of their resistance to omission, pecking was the more dominant response. Nonetheless, in many ways the pull response, although weaker, appeared to show similar properties to the peck response.

In the earlier discussion on the possible role of superstitious conditioning in the rat experiments it was suggested that a multiple autoshaping procedure can be of particular interest. The importance of a stimulus–reinforcer contingency in maintaining a response can be assessed by examining the effects of a transition from a differential condition, where reinforcement occurs only in the presence of a stimulus, to a nondifferential condition, where reinforcement occurs equally frequently in the absence of the stimulus. Consequently an experiment of this kind was carried out to determine what kind of contingency maintained the pull response in the pigeon situation.

Experiment 6 was carried out in collaboration with Felix dal Martello and used a procedure very similar to that of Experiment 4. The loop light was on during the 12 S1 periods of each session. These were of 20-sec duration and alternated with S2 periods of 2-min duration, in which the loop light was off. The differential condition of the first 15 sessions was one in which reinforcement occurred at mean intervals of 30 sec only in S1 periods (*mult* Free VI 30-sec EXT). The nondifferential condition of the final nine sessions was one in which reinforcement occurred at the same rate throughout the session (*mult* Free VI 30-sec Free VI 30-sec). The eight subjects were again naive pigeons maintained throughout at 80% of their free-feeding weights.

Two subjects rarely responded at all. The response rates for each of the remaining six subjects are shown in Fig. 4.11. As with the discrete trial procedure of Experiments 5, pecking was the more common response and occurred in all six birds. As can be seen, four subjects also pulled the loop at moderate rates in the differential condition. The introduction of the nondifferential condition effectively eliminated both responses in five subjects, but had little effect on D8. One presumes that for this subject superstitious conditioning played a major part in maintaining the behavior.

The individual variability obtained here makes it impossible to draw very firm conclusions from these data. However, in combination with the results of the two previous experiments, it seems fair to conclude that the pull response, even though less frequent than pecking, was no less controlled by the stimulus–reinforcer contingency than was the peck response.

Thus, if the stimulus arrangement differs from the conventional one, the use of an autoshaping procedure may produce a conditioned response that bears little relation to the consummatory response, even when the subjects are hungry pigeons and the reinforcement is grain. Consequently the lack of any obvious correspondence between conditioned and unconditioned response in the earlier studies using rats is not an exceptional case.

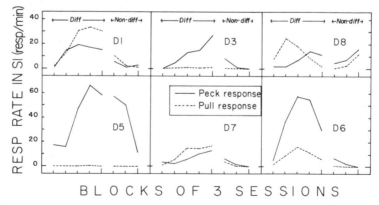

FIG. 4.11 Experiment 5: Rates of pecking and of pulling in the S1 component (loop light on) for six pigeons in the experiment. Response rates in the S2 component (loop light off) rarely exceeded one response a minute. A negligible amount of responding in either component occurred in the two remaining pigeons.

Implication for Interactions with Instrumental Behavior

A variety of experimental results obtained at Sussex in the last couple of years has been cited, some in detail and others in outline. The emphasis has been on those studies directly concerned with questions about the kind of behavior that develops when a classical procedure is applied in situations of the kind normally employed in the study of instrumental conditioning. Rather than to provide here a summary of the data, it seems more useful to describe the general picture of autoshaping that the jigsaw pieces of evidence from this and other laboratories suggest at present.

The schema is as follows. In any situation where an animal learns to associate some localized stimulus—a light or the presence of some object—with a positive reinforcer, two types of response are likely to develop: sign-tracking behavior and goal-tracking behavior. Each can be considered to contain two components, on approach component and a terminal component, as illustrated in Fig. 4.12. The relative strengths of these two responses and the nature of the terminal components are probably affected by a wide variety of factors, some rather general and others highly specific to the situation.

Among those suggested by the research reported here, it seems likely that the effects of reinforcement probability and of the incentive value of the reinforcer on the relative strengths of sign tracking and goal tracking are very general ones. Similarly, it is probably a general rule that an omission contingency confined to one response tends to increase the probability of the other's occurring. Such a contingency may be explicitly programmed or may be implicit in the situation, as when a classical procedure is superimposed on some instrumentally maintained behavior so that, for example, a high frequency of approaches to the signal results in a reduced frequency of reinforcement. In the same way the spatial relationship between signal and reinforcer may be a further general factor that introduces an implicit omission contingency: A considerable distance

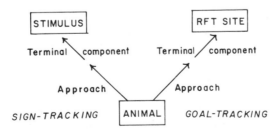

FIG. 4.12 Schematic illustration of the two types of behavior, sign tracking and goal tracking, that can be generated by a classical conditioning procedure and their suggested segmentation into approach and terminal components.

between stimulus and reinforcer may make a high frequency of sign tracking lead to a reduction in the immediacy or the amount of reinforcement obtained and thus produce a decrease in the relative strength of the sign-tracking response.

There are probably further general factors that have similar effects. The duration and salience of the signal are both likely to affect the balance between sign tracking and goal tracking. For example, in contrast to the present studies with rats, the fact that tray approach has not been reported in autoshaping studies employing the insertion of a lever as a signal may be accounted for by assuming that such an event is more salient to the rat than the illumination of a lever.

The nature of the terminal components of each response appears to depend much more on specific aspects of a given situation. What an animal does when it has approached close to the site of imminent reinforcement while the CS is still present probably depends on the physical arrangements for delivering the reinforcer and on whether there is a highly discriminable stimulus correlated with its presence.

Similarly, what an animal does when it has approached close to the signal depends on the local physical properties of the signal and its surround: in the case of pigeons whether a light appears behind a small vertically mounted disk at head height, in a loop above the head, or on the floor (Gilbertson, 1974) and whether, instead of a light, a localized noise is used as the signal (Hearst & Jenkins, 1974). As an example of this, we might mention that in the pilot work that preceded the rat autoshaping studies reported here, we found that to obtain lever pressing it was essential to prevent light from being visible from below the lever, because otherwise rats would tend to go under the lever and lever raising was not a response the equipment could record.

The terminal component may also depend on whether there is an omission contingency in effect and possibly on the animal's past history: if the animal has formerly learned some form of instrumental behavior in this or a highly similar situation, it seems likely that this behavior may be incorporated into the terminal part of the sign-tracking response and now be maintained by stimulus–reinforcer contingencies. Finally the terminal component is affected by the factor that has hitherto attracted the most attention, namely, the type of reinforcer used.

The schema outlined here will no doubt seem to many to permit a distressing degree of latitude to predictions about the outcomes of particular experiments. In this respect it compares unfavorably with the crisp certainties of stimulus-substitution theory. Unfortunately, the data we have reviewed seem to require just this degree of latitude. Stimulus substitution, indeed, can be seen to constitute a special case of our more general account: Under a special set of circumstances, the conditioned response conforms to that expected from the principle of stimulus substitution.

If the situation is one in which the sign-tracking response is preponderant and the physical arrangement is one that is compatible with a considerable fraction of the consummatory response, then the conditioned response is likely to resemble the unconditioned response and is affected by changes in the type of reinforcer employed. Without these special conditions the relationship between conditioned and unconditioned response is not likely to be a close one. Two examples illustrate this point. In studying behavior in a situation modeled on some of the reports by Breland and Breland (1961) of misbehavior we noted that thirsty rats that had to exchange a ball for water would chew the ball, rather than lick it, although chewing less than hungry rats rewarded with food (Boakes et al., 1975b). Timberlake and Grant (1975) have provided a more dramatic illustration of what is presumably the same point; when the presence of one rat serves as the CS signaling food for a second rat, the latter does not gnaw the CS rat, it exhibits social behavior.

There remain two questions: what form can a performance model of classical conditioning take, and what are the implications for interactions between classical and instrumental conditioning.

The use of "model" is possibly unfortunate in evoking the idea of a rather formalized theory. Although explanations of how associations are acquired may be best expressed in symbolic form, this seems unlikely to ever be an appropriate representation for their behavioral effects. The most one can perhaps aim for is a set of empirical generalizations, of which a few may be quantifiable, to describe the effects of a number of factors on, say, the relative strengths of signal and tray responses. As for the precise nature of the terminal components it seems that only a few, rather vague generalizations are possible; such as, if the arrangement of the signal is appropriate, the sign-tracking response is likely to resemble the consummatory response.

The consequences of this view of autoshaping for our understanding of the way that stimulus–reinforcer contingencies affect instrumentally maintained behavior are rather alarming. Insofar as such interactions operate at the response level, it suggests that whether the instrumental behavior is enhanced or suppressed by a stimulus–reinforcer contingency is affected by a large number of factors. Furthermore, a change in either direction may occur for different reasons. For example, in one situation suppression may occur because of competition from a strong tray-approach response, whereas in another where, say, reinforcement probability or deprivation level is different, suppression may occur because of a strong sign-tracking response directed toward a signal that is displaced from the manipulandum.

To end on a more positive note, the research reviewed here has taught us at least one very definite lesson: we should resist the temptation of taking from the shelf equipment that can immediately be plugged in; instead we should devote time to exploring new situations, for this can stimulate one to think about familiar situations in new ways.

Acknowledgments

Much of the research reported here was supported by a grant from the United Kingdom Medical Research Council to Dr. M. S. Halliday and myself. As well as being a collaborator throughout most of the experiments, Sebastian Halliday's comments made a major contribution to the preparation of this chapter. I wish also to thank especially Nick Mackintosh and Andrew Ridgers in this respect.

A number of people contributed at various times to the experimental work. These included Denis Kemp, whose technical skills were invaluable, and research assistants Keith Denby and Mark Lockwood, whose ability to remain cheerful and utterly reliable, despite a grueling daily routine, was remarkable as well as essential.

Finally I would like to thank the three people whose participation in this work was made possibly by awards from the European Training Programme in Brain and Behaviour Research: Jose Linaza, Erminielda Mainardi Peron, and Felix dal Martello.

References

Boakes, R. A. Response decrements produced by extinction and by response-independent reinforcement. *Journal of the Experimental Analysis of Behavior*, 1973, **19**, 293–302.

Boakes, R. A., Halliday, M. S., & Poli, M. Response additivity: effects of superimposed free reinforcement on a variable-interval baseline. *Journal of the Experimental Analysis of Behavior*, 1975, **23**, 177–191. (a)

Boakes, R. A., Poli, M., & Lockwood, M. J. A study of misbehavior: token reinforcement with rats. Paper delivered at the Psychonomic Society, Colorado, 1975. (b)

Breland, K., & Breland, M. The misbehavior of organisms. *American Psychologist*, 1961, **16**, 661–664.

Brown, P. L., & Jenkins, H. M. Auto-shaping of the pigeon's key-peck. *Journal of the Experimental Analysis of Behavior*, 1968, **11**, 1–8.

Gamzu, E., & Schwartz, B. The maintenance of key-pecking by stimulus contingent and response-independent food presentation. *Journal of the Experimental Analysis of Behavior*, 1973, **19**, 65–72.

Gamzu, E., & Williams, D. R. Classical conditioning of a complex skeletal response. *Science*, 1971, **171**, 923–925.

Gilbertson, D. Courtship as a reinforcer in the pigeon. Unpublished M.Sc. thesis, Oxford University, 1974.

Gutman, A., Sutterer, J. R., & Brush, F. R. Positive and negative behavioral contrast in the rat. *Journal of the Experimental Analysis of Behavior*, 1975, **23**, 377–383.

Halliday, M. S., & Boakes, R. A. Discrimination involving response-independent reinforcement: implications for behavioral contrast. In R. A. Boakes & M. S. Halliday (Eds.), *Inhibition and learning*. London: Academic Press, 1972. Pp. 73–97.

Hearst, E., & Jenkins, H. M. *Sign-tracking: the stimulus–reinforcer relation and directed action*. Austin, Texas: Psychonomic Society, 1974.

Hemmes, N. S. Behavioral contrast in pigeons depends on the operant. *Journal of Comparative and Physiological Psychology*, 1973, **85**, 171–178.

Henke, P. G., Allen, J. D., & Davison, C. Effects of lesions in the amygdala on behavioral contrast. *Physiology and Behavior*, 1972, **8**, 173–176.

Jenkins, H. M., & Moore, B. R. The form of the autoshaped response with food and water reinforcers. *Journal of the Experimental Analysis of Behavior*, 1973, **20**, 163–182.

Keller, K. The role of elicited responding in behavioral contrast. *Journal of the Experimental Analysis of Behavior*, 1974, **21**, 249–257.

Konorski, J. *Integrative activity of the brain.* Chicago: University of Chicago Press, 1967.

Leslie, J. C. The mechanism of conditioned suppression. Unpublished doctoral thesis, Oxford University, 1974.

Leslie, J. C., & Ridgers, A. Autoshaping, omission training and differentiation training in rats. In preparation.

Mackintosh, N. J. *The psychology of animal learning.* London: Academic Press, 1974.

Mackintosh, N. J. A theory of attention: Variations in the associability of stimuli with reinforcement. *Psychological Review*, 1975, **82**, 276–298.

Mackintosh, N. J., Little, L., & Lord, J. Some determinants of behavioral contrast in pigeons and rats. *Learning and Motivation*, 1972, **3**, 148–162.

Patten, R. L., & Rudy, J. W. Orienting during classical conditioning: acquired versus unconditioned responding. *Psychonomic Science*, 1967, **7**, 27–28.

Pear, J. J., & Wilkie, D. M. Contrast and induction in rats on multiple schedules. *Journal of the Experimental Analysis of Behavior*, 1971, **15**, 289–296.

Peterson, G. B., Ackil, J. E., Frommer, G. P., & Hearst, E. Conditioned approach and contact behavior for food or brain stimulation. *Science*, 1972, **177**, 1009–1011.

Redford, M. E., & Perkins, C. C. The role of autopecking in behavioral contrast. *Journal of the Experimental Analysis of Behavior*, 1974, **21**, 145–150.

Rescorla, R. A., & Solomon, R. L. Two-process learning theory: relationships between Pavlovian conditioning and instrumental learning. *Psychological Review*, 1967, **74**, 151–182.

Rescorla, R. A., & Wagner, A. R. A theory of Pavlovian conditioning: variations in the effectiveness of reinforcement and nonreinforcement. In A. H. Black & W. F. Prokasy (Eds.), *Classical conditioning II: Current research and theory.* New York: Appleton-Century-Crofts, 1972.

Savage, A. Autoshaping and omission training in rats as a function of type of reinforcer. Unpublished doctoral dissertation, University of Sussex, 1975.

Schwartz, B., & Gamzu, E. Pavlovian control of operant behavior: An analysis of autoshaping and its implications for operant conditioning. In W. K. Honig & J. E. R. Staddon (Eds.), *Handbook of operant behavior.* Englewood Cliffs, N.J.: Prentice Hall, in press.

Sheffield, F. D. Relation between classical conditioning and instrumental learning. In W. F. Prokasy (Ed.), *Classical conditioning.* New York: Appleton-Century-Crofts, 1965. Pp. 302–322.

Timberlake, W., & Grant, D. L. Autoshaping in rats to the presentation of another rat predicting food. *Science*, 1975, **190**, 690–692.

Wagner, A. R., & Rescorla, R. A. Inhibition in Pavlovian conditioning: Application of a theory. In R. A. Boakes & M. S. Halliday (Eds.), *Inhibition and learning.* London: Academic Press, 1972. Pp. 301–336.

Wasserman, E. A. The effect of redundant contextual stimuli on autoshaping the pigeon's key-peck. *Animal Learning and Behavior*, 1973, **1**, 198–206.

Westbrook, R. F. Failure to obtain positive contrast when pigeons press a bar. *Journal of the Experimental Analysis of Behavior*, 1973, **20**, 499–510.

Williams, D. R., & Williams, H. Auto-maintenance in the pigeon: Sustained pecking despite contingent non-reinforcement. *Journal of the Experimental Analysis of Behavior*, 1969, **12**, 511–520.

Zener, K. The significance of behavior accompanying conditioned salivary secretion for theories of the conditioned response. *American Journal of Psychology*, 1937, **50**, 384–403.

DISCUSSION

In discussing his experiments, Boakes claimed several reasons for thinking that the results might have little to do with Pavlovian conditioning. For example, rats operate the lever whether it is illuminated or not; the illumination merely enhances such behavior and, in the words of one of the participants, "allows the law of effect to grind away." Nevertheless, the results of the fourth experiment clearly showed that lever pressing was maintained by the stimulus–reinforcer contingency. Boakes argued that an analysis in terms of "stimulus substitution" was generally inapplicable to the present situation. He further suggested that in general stimulus substitution theory cannot account for autoshaped behavior. Boakes cited an experiment by Timberlake and Grant in which a rat sits waiting for food in a standard autoshaping situation. The conditioned stimulus in this case is the arrival of a second rat, which comes down a slide a few seconds before the food pellet arrives. Although stimulus substitution theory predicts cannibalism, Timberlake and Grant report the emergence of social behavior. Furthermore, if a block of wood is used as the CS such social behavior does not occur. As Garcia suggested during discussion, a Pavlovian conditioning procedure could transfer positive hedonic value to some object, but what kind of behavior would be observed would also depend on the nature of the object.

Weisman: Can you tell us why your model is not simply a stimulus substitution approach? You've added the notion of environmental support which, as you know, I'm quite partial to. Yet my question remains.

Boakes: Stimulus substitution is an inadequate model because it does not tell you anything about the direction the behavior is going. Except in special instances, it does not even tell you what form the behavior will take.

Weisman: Yes, it does. The rat will do as much of the unconditioned behavior to the CS as you will let him. Don't forget, the rat's consumatory behavior is considerably more complicated than a pigeon's. For instance he uses his paws. If you want to know what gets substituted you should watch rats eat and then you'll know what to expect.

Jenkins: Does stimulus substitution theory predict that the light substitutes for the food, or does the animal act in the presence of the light as if some food were in the food tray?

Weisman: The question of whether the animal is directed to the lever, light, or food tray is separate from the question of what he does when he gets to the location of his choice. The point is, surely whether behavior appropriate to the unconditioned stimulus (food) will also be seen.

Jenkins: Are you saying then, that the concept of stimulus substitution does not tell us to expect that the animal will move toward the signal or to the tray, but that no matter where he moves, when he finally gets there he will do something as much like the unconditioned response as the object will allow?

Weisman: Yes. There are three parts to what the animal does: he orients toward things, he moves toward objects, and he does things when he gets there. There is nothing in stimulus substitution theory that predicts that the rat in Boakes' experiment will orient to either tray or lever. However, when he gets to either place, he does things that are rather specific. To tell whether stimulus substitution is a good rule is to have lexicon of what rats do when they eat various kinds of foods and to match up this lexicon to what is seen in the presence of the object which serves as the conditioned stimulus. [Note the difference between the preceding view of stimulus substitution expressed by Weisman and the position that John Garcia expresses in the discussion following his chapter. Whereas Weisman's emphasis was on unconditioned responses made to the US, the "lexicon of what rats do" that Garcia would no doubt have us make would involve behaviors that naturally occurred to the CS, rather than to the US.—Eds.]

Much of the discussion that followed concerned the nature of contingencies and correlations that occur within autoshaping in general and in Boakes' procedure in particular. Jenkins repeatedly stressed the importance of the first response made by the organism on the assumption that if it could be shown that the so-called conditioned stimulus could be held responsible for leading to the lever response, then maintenance of this response could be explained in terms of an implicit correlation with reinforcement. Because such a mechanism had also been used to account for "superstitious behavior," however, the question was raised as to whether a response that had been autoshaped should be viewed as an instance of superstition.

Jenkins: There are data having to do with the acquisition of the first response and the extent to which it is sensitive to the stimulus contingency. This, to my mind, makes it very clear that the implicit "piggy back" correlations are not an account for the acquisition of autoshaped responses.
Boakes: You would need something else to account for the first occurrence of the response that forms part of your implicit correlation.

Seligman: What exactly is an implicit correlation?
Jenkins: It is really a redundant correlation; a correlation which is only maintained because of some behavioral facts. It is one that you can always get rid of if you conditionalize your contingency table on some other variable. If you look at your contingency table you will find that you have arranged a contingency between a stimulus and a reinforcer, but the stimulus does something to the animal and this establishes a behavior—reinforcement contingency.
Staddon: So what the animal is doing as a consequence of his behavior is adding a correlation?
Jenkins: Right! The subject is in fact not keeping track of the correlations accurately. He does not have a record which says if I respond or not respond

during a stimulus, the reinforcer occurs nevertheless at the same rate. Once he gets going, unless he is like an experimenter and tries responding or not responding to see whether the rate of reinforcement is the same, he is going to be hooked.

Staddon: Well, in the autoshaping situation we can look and see how many of the CS occurrences are actually accompanied by a response. For example, what if you can show that during acquisition he does not respond every time the CS occurs, and yet he always gets food. Then there would really be no basis for saying there is a correlation between the response and food during the early trials.

Jenkins: True, the correlation may not be perfect, but he never gets food outside the stimulus, whereas sometimes he gets food when he is responding in the stimulus. This is the basis for claiming that there is a correlation between these events.

Staddon: However, he also responds outside the stimulus and he does not get food.

Jenkins: We don't know whether what the animal does in one stimulus condition is quite different from what he does in another, and whatever he does in the stimulus condition we call CS will generate the correlation between his behavior and reinforcement. This I believe to be of critical importance. If he is responding in both stimuli, in the CS and in the non-CS periods, however, then he will not be working under an implicit correlation.

Hurwitz: It seems to me that in order to understand what is going on in Boakes' experiment with rats, we must invest effort in a more fine grained analysis. I would therefore make the following suggestion; that we describe not only the events themselves, but their order of occurrence. If you present a stimulus in advance of every pellet of food, then the stimulus may begin to control a variety of activities that center around the location where the food is dispensed. If this stimulus is proximal, then part of the subject's behavior will be directed toward this location. The behavior may even begin to antedate the presentation of the stimulus, and this may be critical in generating a "piggy back" or implicit correlation.

The case we have been discussing is one in which the stimulus attracts the subject and becomes an "object" or a "manipulandum." When this happens, behavior directed to the object may then be maintained by food being made available. Two additional questions remain, however. First, what happens in those instances where the stimulus which predicts the availability of food is not traditionally suitable as a manipulandum; e.g., a diffused light. Can approach behavior be autoshaped? Second, what happens in the case where there are other objects in the environment that are available as manipulanda and that have some relationship to the signaling stimulus (e.g., a lever below the light)? Is behavior readily transferred to these stimuli and autoshaped?

Seligman: Tell me what people like Mackintosh and I should do since we believe that animals can learn a negative correlation; that is, that there are stimulus conditions under which behavioral events have no influence.

Jenkins replied by saying that such cases did, of course, occur, but the critical conditions under which this kind of "helplessness" learning took place as compared to cases where superstitious behavior occurred were not really known. He reaffirmed our need to investigate the boundary conditions under which implicit correlations would develop and throw the animal into "superstitious behavior," as opposed to situations in which the animal learned that its behavior was not instrumental in changing the environment.

Reference

Timberlake, W., & Grant, D. L. Autoshaping in rats to the presentation of another rat predicting food. *Science,* 1975, **190,** 690–692.

5
Behavioral Competition in Conditioning Situations: Notes Toward a Theory of Generalization and Inhibition

J. E. R. Staddon

Duke University

INTRODUCTION

John Staddon's chapter is an attempt to quantify the processes that occur during stimulus generalization and during inhibition. Staddon points out that most of the research on stimulus control that has proceeded from Guttman and Kalish's 1956 demonstration using a free-operant technique has done so in the absence of u unifying model or theory. Whether or not Staddon's model is to be successful in filling this void is a matter for speculation at present. His model is not a final product but involves some preliminary notions that he hopes will stimulate research. In this way the utility of the model can be more fully evaluated.

The approach to inhibition that Staddon has proposed trades heavily on his 1971 Psychological Review *paper with Simmelhag, in which the distinction between "interim" and "terminal" behaviors is formally proposed. The manner in which these antagonistic classes of behavior interact and compete becomes the basis for Staddon's quantified approach to stimulus control and inhibition.*

The 10-year period following Guttman's demonstration (Guttman & Kalish, 1956) of an operant method for directly measuring stimulus generalization gradients saw a massive production of experimental papers exploring the limits of the technique. This spate of experiment was not matched by a corresponding edifice of integrative theory. Now, 20 years later, the central theoretical concept in the area is still Spence's (1937) idea of interacting gradients of inhibition and excitation (cf. Hearst, Besley, & Farthing, 1970; Rilling, 1977). Promising approaches in terms of multidimensional perceptual space (e.g., Cross, 1965; Shepard, 1964) do not appear to have been as useful in ordering the animal literature as was at one time hoped. As in any field that persists for long without a general theory, new experiments seem now to confuse and complicate almost as much as they clarify. Perhaps for this reason, in recent years the topic of stimulus generalization has moved away from center stage.

Although many uncertainties remain, experiments using the Guttman and Kalish technique have nevertheless revealed a number of well-established properties of generalization gradients. The purpose of this chapter is to examine the peak shift, behavioral contrast, and the relative slopes of excitatory and inhibitory gradients, from the point of view of two simple assumptions. The first is that different activities may be under the control of different stimuli, which may or may not overlap in their effects. The second assumption is that activities tend to compete with each other for the available time. Neither of these assumptions is novel, and both have been mentioned from time to time in discussions of stimulus control and generalization. However, recent experiments on the inducing effects of periodic food suggest something about the origin of these competing behaviors, their sources of stimulus control, and the nature of the competition among them. Moreover, the implications of the assumptions of separate stimulus control and competition do not seem to have been systematically explored. I hope to show that the discrimination phenomena just mentioned can be derived from these two assumptions.

The present contribution is not in any sense a finished account. Much more empirical work is needed to test the implications of the two basic assumptions, and a number of subsidiary quantitative assumptions have had to be made to derive predictions. It is unlikely that the quantitative choices I have made will all turn out to be optimal, even if the general approach has merit. I hope that this first attempt to understand the implications of competition among independently controlled behaviors for our understanding of generalization and discrimination will at least direct attention to the problem, and encourage others to seek better ways of grappling with it.

Induced Behavioral States

Periodic presentation of food to a hungry animal (a fixed-time schedule or temporal conditioning) is the simplest kind of classical conditioning procedure. Observation of animals exposed to this procedure has shown that they reliably develop stereotyped patterns of behavior within each interfood interval (Davis & Hubbard, 1972; Skinner, 1948; Staddon & Ayres, 1975; Staddon & Simmelhag, 1971). This schedule-induced behavior is typically synchronized with the periodic food deliveries in such a way that it can be divided into two classes: terminal responses, which occur in anticipation of food toward the end of the interfood interval; and interim activities, which occur earlier in the interval. Staddon and Simmelhag (1971) suggested that these two classes of activity can be identified with antagonistic states, a food-related state associated with the terminal response, and a state associated with motives other than hunger, such as thirst and aggression, which is associated with interim activities.

In temporal conditioning there is no external stimulus: food (the US) and its absence are signaled by different values of postfood time. However, the concept of antagonistic states can be extended to more typical conditioning situations in which external stimuli signal food (CS+) or its absence (CS−). Pavlov (1927) believed that conditioned inhibition was due to a direct effect of stimuli on inhibitory brain processes. However, almost immediately after his work became widely known in the West, the concept of inhibition as being due to the excitation of an antagonistic motor system was proposed (e.g., McDougall, 1929; Wendt, 1936). More recently, Konorski (1967), Anokhin (1974), and others trained in the Pavlovian tradition have turned to the competition view. Although couched in quasi-physiological terminology of "drive centers" and "CR [conditioned response] arcs," the similarity of Konorski's (1967) position to the one being advanced here is obvious:

> ... an important conclusion may be reached: that both the [Pavlovian] terms "internal inhibition" and "inhibitory CR" are not adequate and should be abandoned. The CR established by food non-reinforcement of a given stimulus is based on two *excitatory* CR arcs. One arc runs from the CS units to the no-food taste units which are reciprocally related to the food taste units. The other arc runs from the CS units to the units of hunger antidrive center situated in the higher level of the emotive brain and reciprocally related to the higher level hunger center [p. 327].

On the next page, Konorski (1967) points out that the concept of inhibition should refer not to sensory connections but to built-in reciprocal relations between incompatible modes of behavior:

> ... what we do now is merely to stress that we do not have evidence of *inhibitory connections being formed* in the course of negative training, as was accepted in our previous work. . . . inhibitory interconnections established in ontogeny between antagonistic centers of the brain are *utilized* in any conditioning procedure, as they are in the unconditioned activity of the organism [p. 328]

In the context of operant discrimination learning, Terrace (1972) has proposed that behavior antagonistic to that occurring in S+ develops in S−, provided that the discrimination is learned with "errors." Terrace suggests that the antagonistic behavior controlled by S− represents a conditioned "emotional" response evoked by nonreinforcement. Jenkins (1965) earlier made a similar suggestion without taking any position on the origin of the incompatible response.

The present view is that the antagonistic behavior in S− reflects the development of a motivational state antagonistic to that associated with S+ and is perhaps an evolutionary adaptation that allows animals to avoid places associated with food at times when food is unavailable. This idea, and the evidence in its support from experiments with periodic food, has been reviewed elsewhere (Staddon, 1977; Staddon & Simmelhag, 1971) and need only be summarized here. On food schedules during interim (S−) periods rats drink or chew nonfood objects and pigeons may attack a target conspecific; presentation of food during this time may not result in eating. Dogs presented with food during an alimentary CS− delay eating or refuse to eat, and this procedure sometimes leads to "experimental neurosis" (Konorski, 1967). Animals will learn an instrumental response to obtain an aggression target or water during interim periods. During terminal (S+) periods, only food-related behaviors occur and only food acts as a reinforcer.

Factors Affecting the Strength of Terminal and Interim Behaviors

In a constant environment, the "strength" of a behavioral state can be identified with the frequency of behaviors associated with that state. If schedule-induced drinking is taken as a measure of the strength of the interim state, and the frequency of a terminal response such as lever pressing or key pecking (either schedule-induced or instrumental[1]) measures the strength of the terminal state, then it appears that the relation between terminal and interim states is reciprocal. Such factors as rate of food delivery and food deprivation affect the level of interim and terminal activities similarly (see Staddon, 1977, for a review). For example, Fig. 5.1 shows rate of induced drinking as a function of rate of food delivery (i.e., frequency of eating episodes, in future referred to as food rate) on various fixed-time schedules of food delivery. The rate of drinking increases with food rate. As Catania and Reynolds (1968) and others have shown, the function relating rate of an instrumental response to food rate is also a monotonically increasing one.

There is considerable evidence that as the rate of food delivery increases, the fraction of time taken up by induced activities increases (Staddon, 1977). One piece of evidence is illustrated in Fig. 5.1, which shows that the rate of wheel running (and the fraction of time taken up by this activity) decreases as food rate increases. Running is not a schedule-induced activity, and rate of running decreases on a schedule of periodic food by comparison with a preschedule or extinction baseline. This suppression suggests that running is increasingly displaced by the induced terminal and interim "states," which therefore must come increasingly into competition with each other as food rate increases.

---

[1] Generalization gradients are typically obtained following training with an instrumental response. However, I have recently reviewed the evidence suggesting that a response contingency has little effect on maintained behavior, whose strength is almost entirely determined by motivational variables, such as deprivation and relative rate of reinforcement (Staddon, 1975, 1977). Hence it is reasonable to assume that induced states develop on any procedure in which reinforcement availability is associated with differential signals, either temporal or exteroceptive.

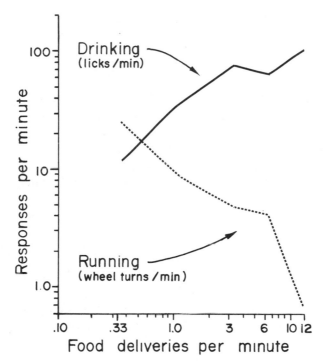

FIG. 5.1 Average rate of running and drinking for a group of rats exposed to several fixed-time schedules of food delivery. Both axes are logarithmic (redrawn from Staddon, 1977).

There are two other kinds of evidence for competition between activities on food schedules: (a) If, on a periodic food schedule an interim activity such as drinking is temporarily prevented, the terminal response (e.g., bar pressing) tends to occur earlier in the interval. (b) Induced activities occur in a regular temporal sequence on periodic schedules. However, there is some variation in the starting and ending times of activities. Correlations between the ending time of an activity and the time to the next activity are generally negative for both rats and pigeons. The later a given activity ends, therefore, the sooner the next one begins. Similarly, the later an activity begins, the shorter its duration. Both these negative correlations suggest reciprocal inhibition (competition) between successive activities.

Thus, the stereotyped activities observable on maintained schedules of reinforcement appear to be jointly determined by two sets of factors: (a) controlling stimuli proper to each class of activity (e.g., the water bottle, for drinking; the response key, for pecking; and time, for all activities), and (b) competition from other activities.

Competition and Stimulus Control

With this background, it is possible to develop a tentative hypothesis about the behavioral mechanisms underlying generalization and inhibition. The elements to be taken into account are as follows.

1. Stimulus control of each activity. For any pair of activities such stimulus control can be either disjoint or conjoint. Disjoint control means that variation in the property or properties of one stimulus affects the level of one of the activities but has no direct effect on the level of the other.[2] Conjoint control is the opposite: Variation in a stimulus property has some direct effect on both activities. Because the present approach assumes only excitatory control by external stimuli (inhibitory gradients can be explained as indirect effects), direct control of an activity by a stimulus dimension is indicated by the production of a decremental generalization gradient as the stimulus is varied.

2. Competition. As the previous discussion indicates, activities induced by periodic food compete with one another, so that as the causal factors (controlling stimuli) for one activity are weakened its place is taken up, more or less completely, by other activities. This approach assumes that such competition is quite general in procedures involving food reward. Various activities occur, one of which may be the instrumental response (the terminal response); others may be induced "interim" or "adjunctive" behaviors and still others may be activities, such as grooming or running, that are not directly related to the schedule of food delivery at all (facultative activities: Staddon, 1977). These activity classes will, I suggest, usually be found to vary reciprocally in strength: As the causal (stimulus) factors for one activity are reduced, the level of activities in antagonistic classes should increase. The function describing the reciprocal relation between two antagonistic activity classes is here termed a "competition function."

3. Effect of discrimination versus nondiscrimination procedures. The present approach, unlike Blough's (1975) process model for steady-state generalization, does not deal directly with learning. Nevertheless, if it is to explain such phenomena as contrast it must incorporate assumptions about the effects of discrimination procedures on stimulus control. For example, any activity occurring in a discrimination situation is likely to have at least two separable sets of controlling stimuli: (a) stimulus aspects selected for variation by the experimenter (these will usually be dimensions of the discriminative stimuli, such as wavelength, intensity, or orientation) and (b) all other features of the situation that exert any control over the response under consideration. In addition to

---

[2] Such nonoverlapping stimuli (e.g., stimuli with few common dimensions, such as a tone and a color) are often referred to as "orthogonal." However, the term has implications relating to Cartesian space that may not be warranted, and the term disjoint seems less exceptionable.

"apparatus cues," these include aspects of the discriminative stimuli not explicitly varied in a generalization test. The effect of varying a discriminative stimulus aspect, both on responses that it controls directly, and on other activities, depends on the relative contribution of contextual cues. One effect of a discrimination procedure may be on the distribution of control between discriminative stimuli (and among discriminative stimuli) and contextual cues. I will show that given reciprocal interactions among activities, a relatively modest reallocation of stimulus control is sufficient to yield contrast effects.

There are three principal areas of uncertainty in applying this approach to real experimental situations:

1. The definition of an activity class. No hard and fast rule can be given. Behaviors that covary, under the manipulations of interest, are usually considered here as members of the same activity class. If a given behavior covaries with others under some conditions but not under other conditions, the explanation (in terms of my approach) may lie either in wrong identification of behavior classes or in interactions among a larger set of activity classes and their controlling stimuli. Obviously, if the model is to be useful, activity classes should correspond to easily identifiable behaviors, such as pecking, lever pressing, drinking, and running.

2. Two other related issues are the nature of the competition function and the time scale to be considered. In considering moment by moment transitions from one activity to another the usual "strength" model assumes a strictly discrete transition: When the strength (level of causal factors) for activity A exceeds that of ongoing activity B, A immediately supplants B (e.g., Atkinson & Birch, 1970; McFarland, 1974; Staddon, 1977). In this case there is no competition function in the present sense. An activity is either occurring or not, and no graded relation between two activities is possible. Whether or not this simple model corresponds exactly to the real mechanisms underlying moment by moment behavior change, there are good adaptive reasons to suppose that abrupt transitions are desirable. In most situations, decisive action is better than a half-hearted response or none, and a real Buridan's ass would not long survive.

Studies of generalization and discrimination do not usually deal with behavior at this molecular level. Instead, concern is with the average level (instances per minute, percent of time taken up) of activities as stimulus factors are varied. Under these conditions a graded relation between the level of one activity and the level of others becomes possible. I hypothesize molar competition functions of this sort. However, this does not preclude the possibility that molar functions are an outcome of more molecular processes involving changes in particular response tendencies with time or trials (cf. Atkinson & Birch, 1970; Blough, 1975). Until a really unified theory is established, it seems prudent to pursue both approaches.

3. The idea that a given behavior class has two or more independent sources of stimulus control (such as discriminative stimuli and contextual cues) is central to the present model. This assumption at once raises the question of the composition rule that best describes the combined action of two stimuli. The simplest rule is algebraic, i.e., that a given source of stimulus control produces a constant increment in the level of responding, independently of other stimulus sources (the "law of heterogeneous summation": Seitz, 1940). In the quantitative sections of the chapter this principle is assumed, but like all other quantitative assumptions it is subject to revision in light of experimental results.

Competition Hypothesis

With these preliminaries, it is possible to summarize the relations among factors affecting behavior on discrimination procedures in the form of a competition hypothesis, as follows:

1. The presentation of food or any other hedonic stimulus in a given situation induces in animals two antagonistic "states": The terminal state is associated with stimuli or times predictive of food (S+ or CS+). The interim state is associated with stimuli or times predictive of no food (S− or CS−).
2. The "strengths" of these states (i.e., the frequencies of behaviors associated with them) are directly related to reinforcement variables, such as the relative and absolute frequency of food, the size of food portions, and the hunger of the animal.

From these two assumptions it is possible to infer that terminal, interim, and other states, and the activities associated with them, compete; and that this competition becomes more severe as food rate increases.

This model is illustrated in Fig. 5.2 for a standard successive discrimination situation in which S+ is a stimulus associated with variable-interval food reinforcement and S− is a successively presented stimulus associated with extinction. The terminal state (T) is assumed to be jointly controlled by S+ and contextual factors, and the antagonistic interim state (I) to be controlled by contextual factors and S− (arrowed lines). Thus S+ and S− are disjoint, although I and T have contextual stimulus factors in common. The figure also shows reciprocal inhibitory relations (competition) between the two states, indicated by the lines with filled circles on the ends.

Linear Inhibition

In order to follow out the implications of an interactive model of this sort, it is helpful to make quantitative assumptions about the form of the competition function (the reciprocal inhibitory effects of T on I and vice versa) and about the rule describing how the effects of discriminative stimuli (S+ and S−) and contextual factors summate. As a first step, linear inhibition is assumed for the

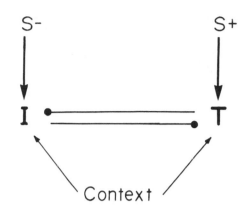

FIG. 5.2 Postulated interactions between tendencies to engage in incompatible terminal (T) and interim (I) activities in a discrimination situation with disjoint S+ and S–. Arrows show positive effects; lines with filled circles show inhibitory effects.

competition function: As the strength of state (activity) T increases, the strength of activity I decreases in linear fashion. This is the simplest kind of competitive interaction and has been employed extensively in analyses of lateral inhibition in the *Limulus* eye (e.g., Ratliff, 1974; Wolbarsht & Yeandle, 1967).

There is some experimental evidence in favor of a simple algebraic composition rule for combining stimulus control from several sources (e.g., Heiligenberg, 1965; Leong, 1969), and this is also assumed.

All quantitative, and some qualitative, predictions are undoubtedly going to be affected if either of these simple assumptions turns out to be false. However, the power of the approach to integrate a range of results from several different experimental situations does not appear to depend on the particular form of these two functions, providing it is monotonic.

Disjoint control. The basic simultaneous equations for the disjoint case can be derived directly from Fig. 5.2. Let T equal the rate of the class of activities controlled by S+ (the terminal or instrumental response) and I equal the rate of the class of activities controlled by S– (interim activity); then,

$$T = L_T - k_1 I + C_T \qquad (5.1a)$$

$$I = L_I - k_2 T + C_I \qquad (5.1b)$$

where L_T and L_I are the contribution to T and I of discriminative stimulus factors, C_T and C_I are the contribution of contextual factors, and k_1 and k_2 are "coupling constants" representing the inhibitory effect of I on T and vice versa. Because we are ultimately interested in predicting the effects of stimulus manipulations, the constants L_T and L_I should be replaced by functions representing the dependence of T and I on the relevant disjoint dimensions of S+ and S–. Therefore $f_T(S_T)$ and $f_I(S_I)$ are defined as similarity functions, describing the dependence of T and I on stimulus dimensions S_T and S_I. These functions are assumed to vary between 0 and 1, where $f_T(S+) = f_I(S-) = 1$. Because control in this case is disjoint, $f_T(S-) = f_I(S+) = 0$; that is, for the dimensions S_I and S_T, S+ makes no contribution to I and S− makes none to T. With these assumptions incorporated, the inhibition equations become:

$$T = af_T(S_T) - k_1I + C_T \qquad (5.2a)$$

$$I = \beta f_I(S_I) - k_2T + C_I$$
$$(5.2b)$$

where α and β are scaling constants that take account of the relative contribution of the stimulus aspect being varied to the total strength of behaviors T and I.

Consider now the rate of T and I in the presence of the S+ dimension (S_T, i.e., in the absence of S_I). Because S_T and S_I are disjoint, $f_I(S_T) = 0$ for all S_T. Therefore, combining Eqs. (5-2a) and (5-2b) and eliminating I yields T as a function of S_T.

$$F_T(S_T) = \frac{\alpha f_T(S_T) + C_T - k_1 C_I}{1 - k_1 k_2} \qquad (5.3)$$

which is a positive linear function of $f_T(S_T)$. The relation between I and S_T can be derived in the same way:

$$F_I(S_T) = \frac{C_I - k_2[\alpha f_T(S_T) + C_T]}{1 - k_1 k_2} \qquad (5.4)$$

which is a negative linear function of $f_T(S_T)$.

Finally, the relation between I and T as the controlling stimulus for $T(S_T)$ is varied can be derived directly from Eq. (5.2b) given that $f_I(S_I) = 0$ in the absence of S_I:

$$I = C_I - k_2 T \qquad (5.5)$$

Equations (5.3), (5.4), and (5.5) define the expected empirical relations between T, I, and stimulus values along the S_T continuum. The similarity function $f_T(S_T)$ is usually assumed to be decremental in form; that is, $f_T(S_T)$ decreases as the difference between S_T and S+ increases. Hence, Eq. (5.3) describes an excitatory (decremental) generalization gradient in terms of T, and Eq. (5.4) describes an inhibitory (incremental) gradient in terms of I. Equation (5.5) restates the linear inhibition assumption: as T is varied, I varies in a complementary fashion.

Conjoint control. In this case, both T and I are controlled by the same stimulus dimension. However, in general the point of maximum control will be different for the two behavior classes. For example, in the typical wavelength discrimination situation, S+ might be 550 nm and S− 600 nm. In the simplest case the form of the two similarity functions, $f_T(S)$ and $f_I(S)$, does not depend on the location of their peak values on the stimulus dimension.[3] In this case the functions for T and I, respectively, can be represented as $f(S)$ and $f(S + D)$, where D is the stimulus difference between S+ and S− (50 nm in the example).

Therefore, the basic equations for the conjoint case (which describe the relations between the rates of T and I and values on the stimulus dimension, S) are

$$F_T(S) = \alpha f(S) - k_1 F_I(S) + C_T \tag{5.6a}$$

$$F_I(S) = \beta f(S + D) - k_2 F_T(S) + C_I \tag{5.6b}$$

Combining and rearranging yields the function relating T to S:

$$F_T(S) = \frac{\alpha f(S) + C_T - k_1 [\beta f(S + D) + C_I]}{1 - k_1 k_2} \tag{5.7}$$

Equation (5.7) represents the effects on the gradient of a discrimination procedure in which S+ and S− have a common dimension. Equation (5.3) is the comparable function when a dimension of S+ not shared by S− is varied.

The next section applies the relations just derived to various discrimination and generalization situations. With the aid of testable assumptions about the effects of experimental operations on the parameters of the model and on controlling stimuli, a number of effects can be brought together.

Applications

Contrast and Discrimination

Consider a pigeon trained to peck a key for food on a simple VI 1-min schedule in the presence of light of a certain wavelength. The rate of pecking will be substantial but less than the maximum possible. The present view implies that peck rate is less than maximal because of competition from at least two classes of other activities: activities in which the animal always has some tendency to engage ("facultative" activities, e.g., preening), and specific induced activities, interim activities, antagonistic to the food-motivated response (cf. Rachlin, 1973). Like pecking, these other activities are under the control of contextual cues and the discriminative stimulus on the response key. There are no other stimuli, so granted that we are here considering steady-state, habitual behavior

---

[3] There is still some uncertainty about the proper form for the similarity function, and this assumption may be false for some dimensions. For example, both the JND function and the color space have been suggested as possible similarity functions for wavelength. Here the form of the similarity function is not independent of the location of S+ on the stimulus dimension (wavelength). However, in most cases it can be made so by appropriate transformations of the stimulus scale (e.g., Shepard, 1965), permitting the present simplified approach.

(i.e., behavior completely under the control of external stimuli) there are no other alternatives. Discriminative control of pecking and the other competing activities (lumped together for convenience into a single "I" category) is conjoint here, because there is only one stimulus, and both similarity functions, $f_T(S)$ and $f_I(S)$, must peak at the same value. Thus the rate of pecking as a function of the stimulus value is described by Eq. (5.7) with $D = 0$:

$$F_T(S) = \frac{f(S)(\alpha - k_1\beta) + C_T - k_1 C_I}{1 - k_1 k_2} \tag{5.8}$$

In the presence of the training stimulus, $f(S+) = 1$; hence

$$F_T(S+) = \frac{\alpha + C_T - k_1(\beta + C_I)}{1 - k_1 k_2} \tag{5.9}$$

Consider now what is likely to happen if the pigeon is shifted to a standard multiple-schedule successive discrimination, in which it continues to receive food for pecking in the presence of the original S+, but this stimulus is alternated with another, disjoint stimulus (S−) in the presence of which no food is received. One effect of this procedure is that the bird soon ceases to peck S−. Moreover, many, if not all, the activities in the "I" category tend to occur preferentially in S−. It is reasonable to assume, therefore, that the relevant similarity function for I centers on S−, and S+ now makes no contribution to the strength of I. Therefore, the rate of pecking in the presence of S+ is now described not by Eq. (5.7) but by Eq. (5.3), the disjoint case. Setting $f_T(S+) = 1$ yields

$$F_T(S+) = \frac{\alpha + C_T - k_1 C_I}{1 - k_1 k_2} \tag{5.10}$$

Comparing Eq. (5.10) with Eq. (5.9), and assuming that the four parameters α, β, k_1, and $,k_2$ and the contributions of contextual cues do not change, shows that the rate of pecking in the presence of S+ is increased by the discrimination procedure by an amount equal to $k_1\beta/(1 - k_1 k_2)$, i.e., positive behavioral contrast.

The keys to this result, which does not depend on these quantitative details, are the assumptions (a) that the T and I behaviors exert a more or less constant reciprocal influence on each other; and (b) that following discrimination, control of the I behaviors shifts from the old S+ to S− so that the factors contributing to the strength of I in the presence of S+ are reduced. If the strength of I in the presence of S+ is reduced, so is its inhibitory influence on T. Hence, even if nothing else changes, T increases via disinhibition.

If these two assumptions are true, therefore, one might expect contrast to be a fairly general phenomenon, quite apart from species-specific "autoshaping" effects (Boakes, this volume; Rachlin, 1973; Schwartz & Gamzu, 1977), although these may also play a role.[4] Contrast would not be expected, by the present view, if the behavior that comes to occur in S− following the shift to a discrimination procedure does not include any of the I-class behavior competing with T in the prediscrimination phase. This issue can only be settled by careful observation, but there are some data consistent with the present position. Terrace (e.g., 1972) has reported that the occurrence of positive contrast depends on the type of behavior that comes to occur in S−. If the behavior is of a relatively novel type, as seems to be the case in learning without "errors," contrast is weak or nonexistent. In a later experiment, using human subjects and a joystick response, Terrace (1974) reports that positive contrast is directly related to the level of antagonistic (i.e., physically opposite to the instrumental response) responses in S− in the discrimination phase. On the assumption that such responses occurred in the prediscrimination phase this finding is also consistent with the present view. Of course, even if the antagonistic behavior is one that occurred in S+, the present model allows for the possibility of contrast failing to occur if S+ makes only a very small contribution to the strength of I in the prediscrimination phase (small β), or if I has only a weak inhibitory effect on T (small k_1).

Slope of Inhibitory Generalization Gradients

Spence's model of tranposition has been applied to the phenomenon of the peak shift by Hearst (1969) and others (cf. Rilling, 1977, for a review). The model explains transposition (a shift in preference, or the point of maximum responding, away from S+ in a direction opposite to S−, when both are on the same stimulus dimension) by postulating opposing excitatory and inhibitory gradients whose resultant is the observed performance. It can be expressed in the terms I have been using as

$$F_T(S) = f_T(S) - f_I(S) \qquad (5.11)$$

where $f_T(S)$ and $f_I(S)$ are now the underlying "response strength" gradients. It is easy to show that if these gradients are assumed to be continuous and unimodal,

---

[4] Autoshaping and the additivity theory of contrast can be incorporated within the present approach by means of the assumption that the I and T states are associated with different types of behavior, depending on the strength of the states. For example, pigeons show autoshaped pecking only if they are very hungry, if food delivery is frequent, or if the stimulus signaling food is brief relative to the intertrial interval (Schwartz & Gamzu, 1977; Staddon, 1977). By the argument of the preceding paragraph, the strength of T in the presence of S+ is increased because of disinhibition following the shift to a discrimination procedure. If a high strength of T (i.e., the behavioral state related to food) is associated, in pigeons, with pecking, the appearance of autoshaped pecking following the shift from periodic food to periodic food alternated with extinction (as in an experiment by Gamzu & Williams, 1971) is explained.

a peak shift is only obtained if the slope of the inhibitory gradient between S+ and S+' (the peak of the shifted gradient) is greater than the slope of the excitatory gradient over that range.

This model has two well-known defects: (a) it predicts a generally lower, rather than higher, overall rate of responding following discrimination training; this is the problem of behavioral contrast, dealt with in the preceding section, and (b) empirically obtained inhibitory gradients are generally shallower, instead of steeper, than excitatory ones.

Spence's model deals with simultaneous inhibitory and excitatory tendencies activated by a given stimulus dimension. This comparison of simultaneous tendencies is easily made in terms of the present model, since Eq. (5.5) gives the rate of the competing (I) response as the controlling stimulus for the instrumental response (T) is varied: $I = C_I - k_2 T$. The slope of the excitatory gradient measured in terms of I is therefore $1/-k_2$. k_2 is, I assume, generally less than one, because the inhibition of one response by another is likely to be less than total. Although the present simplified argument considers only two classes of behavior at a time, more than two are likely to occur in a given situation. Hence, reduction in the level of one activity is likely to yield increases in several others. Therefore, the increase in any one is likely to be less than the decrease in the first, assuming that the units are comparable (cf. Jenkins, 1965). This point is discussed more fully later. This model, therefore, can accommodate easily to findings that inhibitory gradients have a shallower slope than excitatory ones.

However, excitatory and inhibitory gradients are not in fact usually measured in the simultaneous way implied by Spence and by the analysis just described. Instead, separate groups of animals are tested with complementary procedures (e.g., Honig, Boneau, Burstein, & Pennypacker, 1963; Jenkins & Harrison, 1962). Both groups receive successive discrimination (multiple schedule) training and the instrumental response (T) is the only one recorded. For one group, a disjoint dimension of S+ is varied in a generalization test, and for the other a disjoint dimension of S− (usually the same dimension, such as line tilt) is varied. The inhibitory gradients obtained from the S− group are then compared with the excitatory ones obtained from the S+ group. Typically the inhibitory gradients are shallower than the excitatory ones. In this case, the gradient of responding as S+ is varied is given by Eq. (5.3):

$$F_T(S_T) = \frac{\alpha f_T(S_T) + C_T - k_1 C_I}{1 - k_1 k_2} \qquad (5.3)$$

The comparable gradient of responding as the disjoint S− dimension is varied can be derived from Eqs. (5-2a) and (5-2b), given that $f_T(S_T) = 0$ in the absence of the S_T dimension:

$$F_T(S_I) = \frac{C_T - k_1 [\beta f_I(S_I) + C_I]}{1 - k_1 k_2} \qquad (5.12)$$

These equations are linear in $f_T(S_T)$ and $f_I(S_I)$. If it is assumed that the similarity functions have the same form (as they should, because the same dimension is varied in both cases), then the slope of the excitatory gradient (Eq. 5.3) relative to the inhibitory gradient (Eq. 5.12) is $\alpha/-k_1\beta$. If $f_T(S_T)$ is set equal to $f_I(S_I)$ and these two functions are eliminated from Eqs. (5.3) and (5.12), the relation between response rate in S_T as this dimension is varied (T_T) and response rate in S_I as it is varied (T_I) can be derived. The result is the linear function

$$T_I = \left(\frac{C_T - k_1 C_I}{1 - k_1 k_2}\right)\left(1 + \frac{k_1\beta}{\alpha}\right) - \frac{k_1\beta T_T}{\alpha} \qquad (5.13)$$

whose slope is $k_1\beta/\alpha$, the relative slope of the two generalization gradients just discussed. If the situations for the S+ and S− groups are truly symmetrical, then α and β can be assumed to be equal and the slope of the function relating T_I to T_T is therefore k_1, that is, less than one. The inhibitory gradient will be shallower than the excitatory one.

It is not possible to estimate α and β from available empirical results. However, there are data which allow a partial test of the prediction of linearity embodied in Eqs. (5.5) and (5.13). The X's in Fig. 5.3 show data from an experiment by Catania, Silverman, and Stubbs (1974) in which pigeons were trained to peck two keys for food, delivered according to a concurrent VI schedule. Responding

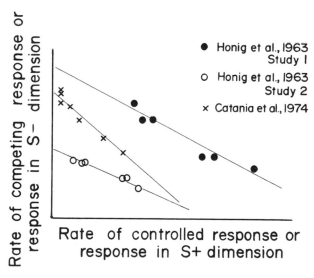

FIG. 5.3 Terminal response rate plotted as a function of interim (competing) response rate as the stimulus controlling the terminal response is varied. Redrawn from data due to Honig *et al.* (1963) and Catania *et al.* (1974). Axes in arbitrary rate units. See text for details.

on the right key was controlled by line orientation, on the left key by a color. In a generalization test, the orientation of the line on the right key was varied, and response rate as a function of orientation was measured on both keys. Figure 5.3 shows response rate on the right (the response controlled by line orientation) plotted as a function of response rate on the left (the competing response), for the group average data. The relation is approximately linear, as Eq. (5.5) predicts. The slope of the function is close to -1, suggesting strong competition between the two responses ($k_2 = 1$). This is consistent with the fact that the responses were topographically similar, were reinforced equally, and the total rate of reinforcement in the situation was relatively high. Thus, a decrement in one response was taken up almost completely by an increase in the other.

Figure 5.3 also shows data from the experiment by Honig et al. (1963). Response rate as the line-tilt dimension was varied for the group trained with vertical as S$-$ (T_I) is plotted vs. rate in the same tilt for the group trained with vertical as S+ (T_T). Again the relation is approximately linear in both studies, as predicted by Eq. (5.13). The only difference between Study 1 (filled circles) and Study 2 (open circles) is that the birds in Study 1 had previous experimental experience, whereas those in Study 2 had none. The similar slopes of the two lines in Fig. 5.3 indicate that parameters k_1, α, and β were not significantly different between the two groups. The most likely difference is in the contributions of contextual factors: Either a decrease in C_I with experience or an increase in C_T could produce the higher intercept for the experienced group show in Fig. 5.3.

The linear inhibition model therefore appears to be consistent with empirical inhibitory generalization gradient data and, unlike Spence's model, is not constrained to predict steeper inhibitory than excitatory gradients.

Peak Shift

The predicted form of the postdiscrimination gradient is easily derived from Eq. (5.7), which describes conjoint control, once the form of the similarity function, $f(S)$, is known. For simplicity, a Gaussian function is assumed in the following analysis:

$$f_T(S) = \exp -[(S - M)/\mathcal{S}]^2 \qquad (5.14)$$

for the terminal response, where M corresponds to S+. The function for the interim response is therefore

$$f_I(S) = \exp -[(S - M - D)/\mathcal{S}]^2 \qquad (5.15)$$

The key assumptions of the present approach are competition, embodied in the values of the coupling coefficients (k_1, k_2), and overlapping stimulus control, embodied in the form of the similarity function and the separation (D) between S+ and S$-$. In this preliminary treatment, therefore, I describe the dependence of contrast (rate in S+) and the peak shift (mode of the postdiscrimination gradient) on the value of the coupling coefficients and the separation between S+ and S−, holding all other parameters constant. For simplicity, α and β are assumed equal to 1, context effects are neglected ($C_I = C_T = 0$), and k_1 is assumed equal to k_2. These assumptions yield the following expression for the postdiscrimination gradient:

$$F_T(S) = \frac{f(S) - kf(S + D)}{1 - k^2}$$

(5.16)

Substituting Eqs. (5.14) and (5.15) into Eq. (5.16) and setting $\mathcal{S} = 1$, $M = 5$, and $D = .5$ (S− = 5.5), yields the postdiscrimination gradient shown in Fig. 5.4. The two underlying similarity functions are also shown.

Several properties of these gradients are of interest:

a. The reciprocal inhibition between the instrumental response and its antagonist allows the animal to discriminate perfectly between S+ and S− even though the two similarity gradients overlap substantially.

b. The postdiscrimination gradient is considerably sharper than the underlying similarity gradients, quite apart from differences in peak response rate.

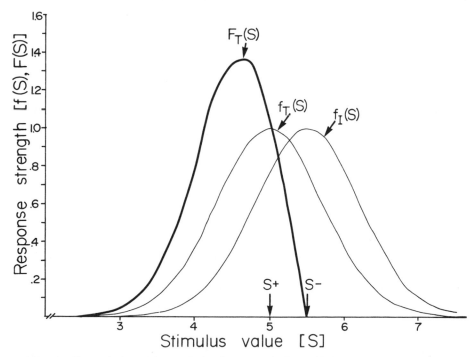

FIG. 5.4   Theoretical Gaussian similarity functions $f_T(S)$ and $f_I(S)$ and the postdiscrimination gradient $F_T(S)$ predicted by the linear inhibition model. The axes are in arbitrary units. $f_T(S) = \exp\left[-(S-5)^2\right]$, $f_I(S) = \exp\left[-(S-5.5)^2\right]$.

c. The peak of the postdiscrimination gradient is shifted away from S+ in a direction opposite to S– (peak shift).

d. With the value of k chosen so as to produce zero responding to S–, the linear model predicts positive contrast, i.e., a higher response rate in S+ after discrimination training than before. This prediction can be derived as follows: Before discrimination training, $D = 0$ (i.e., both I and T activities are under the control of the same value on the S+ dimension). Substituting in Eq. (5.16) and simplifying yields

$$F_T(S+) = f(S+)/(1 + k) = 1/(1 + k) \qquad (5.17)$$

Because $F_T(S+) = 1$ in the postdiscrimination phase, the result is positive contrast if k in the prediscrimination phase is greater than 0. All four of these characteristics are typical of gradients obtained following free-operant successive discrimination training, with S+ and S– lying on the same stimulus dimension (e.g., Hanson, 1959). An analogous set of calculations allows the negative peak shift (Guttman, 1965) to be deduced from the model.

Figure 5.5 shows the relations among k, response rate in S+, and the peak of the postdiscrimination gradient. Considering first the relation between k and rate in S+ (contrast), these curves show the function for three values of D (the separation between S+ and S–) for the similarity functions shown in Fig. 5.4. When D is small (e.g., .5), rate in S+ is nonmonotonically related to k, with rate in $S+$ varying little as k varies from .1 to .7. Thereafter, rate in S+ increases rapidly as k increases. For large values of D, rate in S+ increases sharply with k over most of the range.

The functions for peak shift are quite different, especially for small values of D (where a peak shift is, in fact, most likely). When $D = .5$, peak shift increases approximately linearly with k over a range when rate in S+ is changing little. Moreover, there is a substantial peak shift when $k = .5$, when rate in S+ is a minimum. If k is chosen so that response rate in S– is zero, then k becomes smaller for larger values of D; hence the peak shift decreases as D increases, as is usually found. A similar decrease is predicted even if k remains constant as D increases.

Therefore, the peak shift and contrast effects do not necessarily covary according to the model, as they do not in fact. Contrast can occur without a peak shift (as when D is large in relation to the spread of the similarity functions), and vice versa (as when D is small, and k is intermediate), and both these dissociations have been reported (cf. Mackintosh, 1974, for a review).

Qualifications

My objective has been to present a prima facie argument for the utility of the concept of competition among activities as an essential component of any

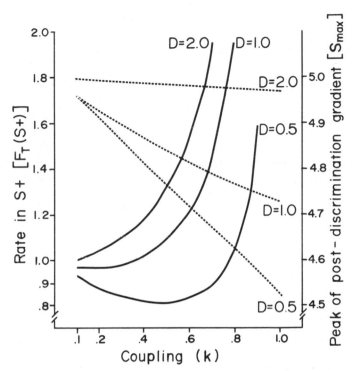

FIG. 5.5 Theoretical curves derived from Eqs. (5-14), (5-15), and (5-16) in the text showing rate in S+ (solid lines) and the location of the peak of the postdiscrimination gradient (dashed lines) as a function of the coupling constant, k, for three values of D (separation between S+ and S−). The other parameter values are the same as in Fig. 5.4.

theory of generalization and inhibition. However, in order to draw out the implications of this idea, several simplifying assumptions have had to be made.

The assumption that there are only two classes of antagonistic activities.   This is certainly false. For example, rats on periodic food schedules anticipate food, drink, run, and engage in "comfort" activities such as grooming. Only drinking and food anticipation are directly related to rate of food presentation, although the increasing percentage of time taken up by these two activities may be the primary cause of competitive interaction among all activities. The algebra for the multiresponse case is cumbersome, but it does not seem likely that any of the conclusions drawn on the basis of an analysis of two responses are going to be invalidated by consideration of more complex cases, although the model may then become less convenient. It does seem likely that extension to the N-response case can allow this approach to deal with a wider range of data.

The assumption of an invariant competition function. The quantitative sections of this chapter assume linear inhibition between activities. This assumption can be challenged on at least two grounds: first, that inhibition between activities may not be linear[5]; and second, that the form of the inhibition between any pair of activities may not be independent of the level of other activities, i.e., there may be no invariant competition function. If many activities are competing for expression, competition measured between any pair may be more severe (e.g., the coupling coefficients may be higher) than when the number of competing activities is less. This question can be studied empirically by establishing independent control of two activities A and B by disjoint stimulus dimensions A* and B*. The level of A and B can then be measured as A* and B* are varied with and without the opportunity to engage in a third activity, C, not directly affected by A* and B*. If the interaction between A and B is invariant, then the same function should result with and without C (although the range covered will be different in the two cases). The same experiment also allows direct measurement of the competition function.

The present model is related to the notion of behavioral conservation discussed recently by Allison (1974) and implicit in Herrnstein's account of the matching law for concurrent operant schedules (see de Villiers, 1977, for a review). The argument behind this view is as follows. Any activity takes a certain amount of time. Hence it is obvious that the rate of a recurrent activity cannot increase without limit. When more than one activity can occur in a situation, a relation of the following form may hold:

$$g_1(A_1) + g_2(A_2) + \ldots + g_N(A_N) = 1 \qquad (5.18)$$

where the A_i are rates of each of N activities that can occur. This kind of relation can be termed a conservation relation, because it affirms that there is some limit on the total amount of activity.

A linear conservation relation is the simplest. Suppose, for two mutually exclusive and exhaustive activities, that each occurrence of each activity takes a fixed amount of time. If the first activity occurs N_1 times in a session of length L, and the second activity occurs N_2 times, then the following relation must hold:

$$\frac{N_1 k_1}{L} + \frac{N_2 k_2}{L} = 1 \qquad (5.19)$$

---

[5] The concept of a competition function is closely related to the economic concept of an indifference curve, because both describe how a decrease in the amount of one entity (amount of a good, rate of an activity) is replaced by an increase in another. The linear functions assumed here correspond to perfect substitutability, in an economist's terms. Substitutability is usually imperfect, however, and real indifference curves are usually convex to the origin. Such curves are often well fit by a hyperbola and therefore can be rendered linear by a logarithmic transformation of the axes. Hence this discrepancy may not be critical for the present approach. See Rapport (1971) for an application of the economic approach to animal behavior.

where k_1 and k_2 here are the times taken up by each instance of the two activities. If the rates of the activities are denoted by T and I, then Eq. (5.19) reduces to

$$k_1 T + k_2 I = 1 \qquad (5.20)$$

or, rearranging,

$$I = \frac{1}{k_2} - \frac{k_1}{k_2} T \qquad (5.21)$$

which is of the same form as Eq. (5.5).

There are several features of linear conservation that make it hard to use in practice. First, it requires knowledge of the entire repertoire of the animal in a given situation, and estimation of weighting factors for each activity, before it can be applied. Second, additional assumptions are needed to incorporate the effects of stimuli (these are an integral part of the present approach). Third, conservation says nothing about which activities will increase to fill up the gap left by a decrease in the level of one activity. The simplest possibility, often discussed (e.g., Dunham, 1971), is that the other activities change so as to maintain fixed proportions among themselves. However, this rule is not in good agreement with experimental results (e.g., Staddon & Ayres, 1975) and cannot allow for either the appearance of new activities or the disappearance of old ones.

Despite these caveats, it is clear that the inhibitory relations between activities postulated by the linear inhibition model are not unrelated to time-sharing restrictions. The times typically taken up by each activity in a conditioning situation impose constraints on the parameters of the model that can perhaps best be worked out empirically.

Restriction to two discriminative stimuli. The present analysis has dealt with only two discriminative stimuli. However, it is possible that even if only two stimuli are actually presented by the experimenter, the number of effective stimulus aspects may be greater. For example, Davis (1971) and Lyons (1969) have reported data showing that if pigeons are trained with a hue S+ and a vertical line as S− and then tested with the S− dimension superimposed on S+, excitatory gradients, with a peak at S− but at a lower rate than that shown to S+ alone, can be obtained. One way this may come about is illustrated in Fig. 5.6, which shows the stimulus factors controlling I (a behavior that competes with pecking) and T (pecking) controlled by three kinds of stimulus: S+ is the hue which facilitates pecking alone; S− is the vertical orientation which, because the pigeons in these experiments continued to peck (at a low rate) on S−, may also have controlled pecking; and S−* is a hypothetical second component of S− (perhaps simply the presence of something on the response key), which may have controlled the behavior competing with pecking in S− and be responsible for the lower peak rate in that stimulus. When the S− dimension is superimposed

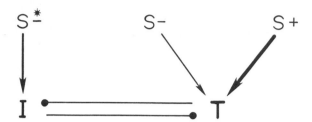

FIG. 5.6 Postulated interactions to explain anomalous compound gradients obtained by Davis (1971) and Lyons (1969). See text for details.

on S+, S+ has a constant positive effect, and the facilitatory effect of the S– dimension on pecking decreases as S varies away from S–. Hence, as line tilt (the S– dimension) is varied, the balance shifts in favor of the constant contribution by S–* (which does not vary with orientation), and an excitatory gradient on the S– dimension is therefore obtained.

This example emphasizes the necessity of observing animals in generalization experiments so as to estimate how many, and what, stimuli are operating and what aspects of behavior they have come to control.

Restriction to a performance model. The present approach is a model of "what is learned," in the tradition of Spence's original interacting gradients idea. It lacks "learning assumptions," such as those embodied in Blough's recent analysis of steady-state generalization gradients, which describe the process by which the animal reacts to changes in reinforcement contingencies. It also lacks rigorous assumptions relating behavior to reinforcement variables in the steady state, such as those offered by Herrnstein and others in their analyses of operant choice behavior (cf. de Villiers, 1977, for a review). However, there are ways in which reinforcement variables can be applied to this model and two of these have been briefly discussed: the probable effect of frequency of food reinforcement on the strength of competitive interaction among behaviors; and the possible role of shifts in stimulus control in positive behavioral contrast. Better assumptions about the way in which relative reinforcement rate affects stimulus control and the values of coupling coefficients can allow the model to deal with negative contrast as well. However, it seems pointless to hypothesize along these lines until more experimental analyses of competitive interactions have been carried out. My present intent is simply to pull together several well-authenticated findings from the Guttman–Kalish transfer paradigm and relate them to simple assumptions about the "structure" of learned behavior. Questions of parameter estimation and quantitative prediction belong to a later stage. First it is necessary to see to what extent the behavior of the model resembles the behavior of pigeons and rats in a qualitative way across a range of situations.

Restriction to a stimulus–response analysis. This approach makes no attempt to deal with "true" relational responding of the sort that Spence tried to rule out in his original account. Some apparently paradoxical results can be incorporated, however. For example, Honig (1962) found a peak shift using a successive (multiple schedule) procedure but not using a comparable simultaneous (concurrent) procedure. It is obviously easier to compare two stimuli that are both present simultaneously than to compare a single stimulus with the memory of one not present. This difference may be reflected in the form of the similarity functions in the two situations. A sharper function for the simultaneous case (equivalent to a large value for D in Fig. 5.5) could obviously account for Honig's failure to find a peak shift in that case. However, other properties of simultaneous discriminations, such as some animals' ability to solve the "intermediate-size problem," cannot be handled within the present framework without additional assumptions. This kind of simplification is necessary as a first approach. If the general idea is fruitful, ways to extend it are likely to become clear later.

Concluding Comments

Activities occur in time, and it is clear that animals engage in more, and more vigorous, activities in some situations than others. If hungry pigeons are given frequent, periodic access to small quantities of food, for example, vigorous stereotyped activities soon develop between food deliveries, and there is much evidence that these activities compete with each other for the available time. The phenomena of generalization and discrimination are typically studied in intermittent food situations of this sort.

The activities that occur in conditioning situations do not occur equally at all times and in the presence of all stimuli. On the contrary, some activities characteristically occur at times when food delivery is improbable (interim activities) and others when it is probable (terminal responses). If these times are signaled by distinctive stimuli, these stimuli come differentially to control competing activity classes. This chapter has explored the implications of competition among independently controlled behaviors for the phenomena of discrimination, inhibition, and generalization. With the aid of a simple quantitative model, the properties of inhibitory generalization gradients, behavioral contrast, and the peak shift have been derived from these two basic premises. The model incorporates untested assumptions about the form of behavioral competition and the effects of stimulus combinations. Nevertheless, its general agreement with the qualitative properties of generalization and discrimination phenomena suggests that the approach is potentially useful.

Acknowledgments

This research was supported by a grant from the National Science Foundation to Duke University.

References

Allison, J. A. conservation model for the facilitation and suppression of responding by controlled-time contingencies. Paper presented at the Psychonomic Society Meeting, Boston, 1974.

Anokhin, P. K. *Biology and neurophysiology of the conditioned reflex and its role in adaptive behavior.* (Translated by S. A. Corson.) New York: Pergamon, 1974.

Atkinson, J. W., & Birch, D. *The dynamics of action.* New York: Wiley, 1970.

Blough, D. S. Steady state data and a quantitative model of operant generalization and discrimination. *Journal of Experimental Psychology: Animal Behavior Processes,* 1975, **104**(1), 3–21.

Catania, A. C., & Reynolds, G. S. A quantitative analysis of the responding maintained by interval schedules of reinforcement. *Journal of the Experimental Analysis of Behavior,* 1968, **11**, 327–383.

Catania, A. C., Silverman, P. J., & Stubbs, D. A. Concurrent performances: Stimulus-control gradients during schedules of signalled and unsignalled concurrent reinforcement. *Journal of the Experimental Analysis of Behavior,* 1974, **21**, 99–107.

Cross, D. V. Metric properties of multidimensional stimulus generalization. In D. I. Mostofsky (Ed.), *Stimulus generalization.* Stanford: Stanford University Press, 1965. Pp. 72–93.

Davis, H., & Hubbard, J. An analysis of superstitious behaviour in the rat. *Behaviour,* 1972, **43**, 1–12.

Davis, J. M. Testing for inhibitory stimulus control with S– superimposed on S+. *Journal of the Experimental Analysis of Behavior,* 1971, **15**, 365–369.

de Villiers, P. A. Choice in concurrent schedules and a quantitative formulation of the law of effect. In W. K. Honig & J. E. R. Staddon (Eds.), *Handbook of operant behavior.* Englewood Cliffs, N.J.: Prentice-Hall, 1977.

Dunham, P. J. Punishment: method and theory. *Psychological Review,* 1971, **78**, 58–70.

Gamzu, E., & Williams, D. R. Classical conditioning of a complex skeletal response. *Science,* 1971, **171**, 923–925.

Guttman, N. Effects of discrimination formation on generalization measured from a positive-rate baseline. In D. I. Mostofsky (Ed.), *Stimulus generalization.* Stanford: Stanford University Press, 1965.

Guttman, N., & Kalish, H. I. Discriminability and stimulus generalization. *Journal of Experimental Psychology,* 1956, **51**, 79–88.

Hanson, H. M. Effects of discrimination training on stimulus generalization. *Journal of Experimental Psychology,* 1959, **58**, 321–334.

Hearst, E. Excitation, inhibition and discrimination learning. In N. J. Mackintosh & W. K. Honig (Eds.), *Fundamental issues in associative learning.* Halifax: Dalhousie University Press, 1969.

Hearst, E., Besley, S., & Farthing, G. W. Inhibition and the stimulus control of operant behavior. *Journal of the Experimental Analysis of Behavior,* 1970, **14**, 373–409.

Heiligenberg, W. The effect of external stimuli on the attack readiness of a chichlid fish. *Zeitschrift für Vergleichende Physiologie,* 1965, **49**, 459–464.

Honig, W. K. Prediction of preference, transposition and transposition-reversal from the generalization gradient. *Journal of Experimental Psychology,* 1962, **64**, 239–248.

Honig, W. K., Boneau, C. A., Burstein, K. R., & Pennypacker, H. S. Positive and negative generalization gradients obtained after equivalent training conditions. *Journal of Comparative and Physiological Psychology,* 1963, **56**, 111–116.

Jenkins, H. M. Generalization gradients and the concept of inhibition. In D. J. Mostofsky (Ed.), *Stimulus generalization.* Stanford: Stanford University Press, 1965.

Jenkins, H. M., & Harrison, R. H. Generalization gradients of inhibition following auditory discrimination learning. *Journal of the Experimental Analysis of Behavior*, 1962, **5**, 435–441.

Konorski, J. *Integrative activity of the brain.* Chicago: University of Chicago Press, 1967.

Leong, C. Y. The quantitative effect of releasers on the attack readiness of the fish *Haplochromis burtoni* (Chichlidae, Pisces). *Zeitschrift für Vergleichende Physiologie,* 1969, **65**, 29–50.

Lyons, J. Stimulus generalization as a function of discrimination learning with and without errors. *Science*, 1969, **163**, 490–491.

Mackintosh, N. J. *The psychology of animal learning.* London: Academic Press, 1974.

McDougall, W. The bearing of Professor Pavlov's work on the problem of inhibition. *Journal of General Psychology*, 1929, **2**, 231–262.

McFarland, D. J. Time-sharing as a behavioural phenomenon. In D. Lehrman, R. Hinde, & E. Shaw (Eds.), *Advances in the study of behavior.* New York: Academic Press, 1974.

Pavlov, I. P. *Conditioned reflexes.* (Translated by G. V. Anrep.) London: Oxford University Press, 1927.

Rachlin, H. Contrast and matching. *Psychological Review*, 1973, **80**, 217–244.

Rapport, D. J. An optimization model of food selection. *American Naturalist*, 1971, **105**, 575–588.

Ratliff, F. (Ed.) *Studies on excitation and inhibition in the retina.* New York: Rockefeller University Press, 1974.

Rilling, M. Stimulus control and inhibitory processes. In W. K. Honig & J. E. R. Staddon (Eds.), *Handbook of operant behavior.* Englewood Cliffs, N.J.: Prentice-Hall, 1977.

Schwartz, B., & Gamzu, E. Pavlovian control of operant behavior: An analysis of auto-shaping and of interactions between multiple schedules of reinforcement. In W. K. Honig & J. E. R. Staddon (Eds.), *Handbook of operant behavior.* Englewood Cliffs, N.J.: Prentice-Hall, 1977.

Seitz, A. Die paarbildung bei einingen Cichliden. *Zeitschrift für Tierpsychologie*, 1940, **4**, 40–84.

Shepard, R. N. Attention and the metric structure of the stimulus space. *Journal of Mathematical Psychology*, 1964, **1**, 54–87.

Shepard, R. N. Approximation to uniform gradients of generalization by monotone trans-formations of scale. In D. I. Mostofsky (Ed.), *Stimulus generalization.* Stanford: Stanford University Press, 1965.

Skinner, B. F. "Superstition" in the pigeon. *Journal of Experimental Psychology*, 1948, **38**, 168–172.

Spence, K. The differential response in animals to stimuli varying in a single dimension. *Psychological Review*, 1937, **44**, 435–444.

Staddon, J. E. R. Schedule-induced behavior. In W. K. Honig & J. E. R. Staddon (Eds.), *Handbook of operant behavior.* Englewood Cliffs, N.J.: Prentice-Hall, 1977.

Staddon, J. E. R. Learning as adaptation. In W. K. Estes (Ed.), *Handbook of learning and cognitive processes.* Vol. 2. Hillsdale, N.J.: Lawrence Erlbaum Associates, 1975.

Staddon, J. E. R., & Ayres, S. L. Sequential and temporal properties of behavior induced by a schedule of periodic food delivery. *Behaviour*, 1975, **54**, 26–49.

Staddon, J. E. R., & Simmelhag, V. L. The "superstition" experiment: A re-examination of its implications for the principles of adaptive behavior. *Psychological Review*, 1971, **78**, 3–43.

Terrace, H. S. By-products of discrimination learning. In G. Bower & J. Spence (Eds.), *The psychology of learning and motivation.* New York: Academic Press, 1972. Pp. 195–265.

Terrace, H. S. On the nature of non-responding in discrimination learning with and without errors. *Journal of Experimental Analysis of Behavior*, 1974, **22**, 151–159.

Wendt, G. R. An interpretation of inhibition of conditioned reflexes as competition between reaction systems. *Psychological Review,* 1936, **43**, 258–281.

Wolbarsht, M. L., & Yeandle, S. S. Visual processes in the *Limulus* eye. *Annual Review of Physiology,* 1967, **29**, 513–542.

DISCUSSION

A number of issues were raised concerning the varied definitions of inhibition and their relevance to Staddon's model:

Davis: One definition of inhibition that might pose some difficulty for your model involves a situation in which the subject is exposed to a negative contingency. Assume that the subject learns about a relationship in the environment rather than learning particular behaviors; for example, that stimulus X predicts the absence of event Y. Although this might be construed as inhibitory learning in the sense described by Rescorla (1967), I can't see how your model would handle such a situation.

Weisman: Let me put Hank's [Davis] question another way. Is it possible to get inhibitory control without affecting behavior? Or is it possible to teach an animal about a relationship in one situation that will have a direct bearing on his behavior in a later situation?

Staddon: What you're really asking is: "Suppose one can't observe any behaviors. Should one assume, for example, that the subject is really thinking about drinking and that's why he's not eating?" Obviously this is very unsatisfactory. I'd say that this is an open question. If the model were firmly established and one found a unique situation that was so impoverished that no behaviors could be observed, then we might extrapolate and say presumably something is functioning as an interim behavior and inhibiting everything else.

Jenkins: It seems to me that the historical concept of inhibition which comes out of the physiological literature involves the simultaneous presence of excitatory and inhibitory stimuli. For example the cell body will fire if given excitatory input but will not fire when inhibitory input is applied at the same time. To be consistent with this historical use of the term "inhibition," from which psychology drew its model, your position should have at its core some requirement involving the concurrent presentation of S+ and S−. This does not seem to be the way in which your model operates, however.

Seligman: Are you saying that anytime you have not programmed an explicit CS+ at the same time as CS−, you can't bring the concept of inhibition into the analysis?

Jenkins: In the purest historical sense, that's true.

Staddon: I think I've dealt with that in an implicit way. What I've done in a sense is to take that into account by assuming that contextual cues retained by the organism provide the continuous presence of an S+ against which all other events, such as the appearance of S−, are recorded.

Moreover, the model readily allows prediction of the effects of combining S+ and S−. If $f_T(S+) = 1$, and $f_I(S-) = 1$, then from Eqs. (5-2a) and 5-2b), the rate of response T in the presence of both S+ and S− is given by:

$$T = \frac{\alpha - k_1(\beta + C_I) + C_T}{1 - k_1 k_2} \qquad (1)$$

which is clearly less than the expression for response rate in S+ alone, derivable from Eq. (5-3) in the text:

$$T = \frac{\alpha + C_T - k_1 C_I}{1 - k_1 k_2} . \qquad (2)$$

The model therefore satisfies the operational definition of inhibition, because the addition of S− reduces the rate of the measured response to S+.

Seligman: You appear on one hand to use your model to investigate Pavlovian inhibition, but on the other hand you set up a situation that involves physical competition or antagonism. Such processes may have no relevance to inhibition in the Pavlovian sense.

Staddon: On the contrary, as I point out in the paper, Konorski and others in the Pavlovian tradition argue that physical (and motivational) antagonism is precisely the mechanism of inhibition in Pavlovian situations. And, of course, these antagonistic behaviors simply develop in conditioning situations. We make no attempt to "set them up" in any way.

Staddon spent considerable time, in both his chapter and his conference presentation, discussing the role of antagonism and physical competition between events. The precise level at which this process occurred was the subject of some discussion.

Jenkins: It appears that your discussion of antagonism is centered on the behavioral level but your earlier comments regarding Konorski suggest that competition may also occur at a motivational level within this system. I see no reason, however, why I should assume that there is any difference in the motivation of an animal which is engaging in so-called "interim activities" and one which is emitting the "terminal" response. In short, I don't see why motivation has to change throughout this interval in a way which corresponds to observed behavioral change.

Staddon: Let me cite two observations relevant to this point. One is the informal observation that if animals are working on a schedule for periodic presentations of food and you give them a surprise food presentation at a time when food is not normally available they won't eat it. The second observation is Konorski's, who reports that it's extremely difficult to get animals to eat during CS− with which food had never been paired. I'm not sure, however, how central the motivational aspect is to anything I'm going to say about this model, although these data would seem to support it to some extent.

This led Jenkins to question the form taken by the equations proposed in Staddon's system.

Jenkins: When there are some interim activities occurring, presumably there are stimuli that accompany or occasion these behaviors. Why not simply write all of these equations in stimulus terms? You appear at present to have a mixture; some of the terms refer to behavior, whereas others refer to the stimulus conditions which surround behavior.

Staddon: I considered that possibility while I was developing this system but finally dismissed it. I felt that in the long run it wasn't quite as sensitive to all the events which I wanted to portray. It may still be possible. I was less comfortable, though, claiming that stimuli themselves were interacting. It appeared more reasonable that the interaction of stimuli occurred through the behaviors they occasioned.

A number of points were raised concerning the generality and utility of Staddon's model.

Davis: I thought at first that your equations took into account all the behaviors that might possibly interact or compete within the experimental situation. When I realized that a third class of behavior existed (i.e., neither "interim nor "terminal" responses), which you claim may be only indirectly affected, I wondered about the generality of the model. Can you envision a situation in which only two sets of responses are possible contenders for the behavioral "final common pathway"?

Staddon: Yes I can. I think this happens in situations where the interreinforcement interval is quite brief. In such a situation drinking and eating might be the only responses worth considering within the framework of this system. There are probably even more extreme situations in which only a single response might be available to the organism. The escape data which you've presented at this conference probably typify such a case. Of course, the approach can easily be extended to more than two response classes.

Davis: Part of the thrust of your model is an attempt to provide information about inhibition. Would you go so far as to say that if your model were perfected we would actually be learning more about the processes that underlie inhibition? Or is this simply another way of juggling numbers and making predictions about response rates?

Staddon: No. I think that the assumption about competition does say something about mechanisms. The model is a way of describing what the animal has learned in the discrimination procedure. Obviously peak shift data suggest that the animal has learned something beyond going to a stimulus and pecking during S+. The animal does more than sit passively and wait for periods during which he will be reinforced. There are other behaviors that occur during the presence of particular stimuli and that compete actively with the responses you happen to be measuring. The model is a first attempt to grapple with the interacting roles of all of these behaviors.

Black: I know you would put it more strongly, but in a sense what you are doing is using what you've termed "interim behaviors" or behaviors other than the reinforced response to provide a measure of the inhibitory strength of S−.

Staddon: I am putting it more strongly. What I'm saying is that the inhibitory strength of S− acts through its effect of inducing incompatible (i.e., interim) behaviors.

Black: But couldn't one essentially use the same formulas without making your assumptions about the role of incompatible behaviors?

Staddon: Obviously the formulas can be used without justification. However, the model then becomes a sort of curve fitting. It seems to me much more useful to try and identify the real mechanisms by which stimuli, and the "states" they induce, interact. The formulas here are just a way of putting these ideas together so as to derive predictions. If there is value in this approach, it lies more in the basic notions of competition and differential stimulus control than in the particular simplified mathematical apparatus I have employed. The trouble with most mathematical models is that the formulas work (more or less), but the interpretations of parameters do not. Consequently, the domain of data to which a given model is supposed to apply is often not clear. Disconfirmation of a prediction can leave the experimenter unsure about whether the model is wrong or he has simply applied it improperly. One antidote to this is to make sure that the approach has some comprehensiveness and can integrate a range of data, before worrying about details of function forms and parameter estimation.

6
Pavolovian Second-Order Conditioning: Some Implications for Instrumental Behavior

Robert A. Rescorla

Yale University

INTRODUCTION

In the following chapter, Rescorla approaches the topic of operant–Pavlovian interactions by examining the role of second-order conditioned reflexes. Rescorla suggests that second-order conditioning has received unjustified "bad press" and cannot simply be dismissed as the weaker version of first-order conditioning. He offers compelling evidence for its stability and resistance to a change by a variety of key independent variables. Finally, Rescorla suggests a number of ways in which experimental operations performed within the context of instrumental conditioning may yield effects that are actually mediated through the establishment of second-order conditioning.

Historically, the focus of North American studies of learning has been instrumental behavior. Our principal empirical and theoretical efforts have intended to account for goal-directed behaviors in which the consequence of those behaviors is demonstrably important for their occurrence. Until very recently this orientation has drawn attention from what many view as the more elementary associative learning that occurs in Pavlovian conditioning. At the same time, however, accounts of instrumental behavior have repeatedly appealed to our knowledge of Pavlovian conditioning to explain that behavior.

The basis for that appeal is both operational and theoretical. Operationally, despite our best efforts to independently specify the conditions for instrumental and Pavlovian learning, it remains apparent that virtually all instrumental learning situations have embedded within them the requisites for Pavlovian conditioning. Theoretically, accounts of instrumental behavior given purely in terms of the relations between that behavior and its primary consequences have seemed inadequate. Those accounts have appeared to need bolstering in two ways. First, many of the behaviors seem to occur either in the total absence of primary rewards or with rewards so delayed as to be only implausible determinants of the behaviors. Second, in many instances there is evidence for motivational determinants of the instrumental behavior other than those induced by changes in elementary deprivation states. To many theorists the embedded Pavlovian relations have offered an account of both these additional rewards and motivations.

This state of affairs is clearly illustrated in accounts of instrumental avoidance behavior. Many theories have noted that the warning signals and aversive outcome typically used in avoidance situations bear Pavlovian relations to each other (Miller, 1948; Mowrer, 1960; Rescorla & Solomon, 1967; Schoenfeld, 1950). As a consequence, it has been popular to suppose that warning signals become Pavlovian fear elicitors which provide motivation (by their occurrence) and reward (by their removal) for the avoidance response. For many theories, therefore, Pavlovian fear conditioning bears the primary responsibility for the occurrence of instrumental avoidance behavior.

A similar description can be given for instrumental behaviors that terminate in appetitive rewards. The execution of a typical instrumental behavior involves the occurrence of a sequence of responses, each of which occurs in the presence of some stimulus and additionally changes the stimulus environment by its occurrence. Many theories have acknowledged that the rewards in which those sequences terminate are likely to be Pavlovian USs which can condition the preceding stimuli (e.g., Bindra, 1974; Hull, 1952; Konorski, 1967; Spence, 1956). As a consequence, the stimuli occurring in the course of an instrumental behavior have been presumed to take on both motivational and rewarding properties.

When we reviewed some of the theories and data in this literature several years ago, Solomon and I argued that these applications often fail to do justice to the underlying Pavlovian conditioning (Rescorla & Solomon, 1967). Not only do they take our knowledge of conditioning as already established, thus discouraging its own empirical investigation, but more seriously, these theories have often adopted a primitive and highly dated description of the laws of conditioning. We argued that current empirical research in Pavlovian conditioning displayed it to be a very rich phenomenon, but that theories of instrumental behavior rarely exploited that richness. In particular, we pointed to the occurrence of Pavlovian conditioned inhibition as greatly expanding the applicability of conditioning in ways that instrumental learning theories are yet to fully appreciate.

The intent of this chapter is to direct attention to another aspect of Pavlovian conditioning that may have important implications for the account of instrumental behavior: second-order conditioning. Although it has often been acknowledged that many applications of Pavlovian principles to instrumental behaviors must involve higher-order conditioning, little has been made of that observation. The involvement of conditioning beyond the first order has not appeared to demand special attention because we have normally assumed that the rules of higher-order conditioning are essentially parallel to those of first-order conditioning. As I have argued elsewhere (Rescorla, 1973a), however, and as is illustrated below, there is reason to doubt that assumption. Furthermore, the doubts raised may have interesting implications for the application of Pavlovian conditioning to instrumental behavior.

To anticipate the argument, I suggest that whereas completed first-order Pavlovian conditioning is highly sensitive to various experimental assaults involving changes in motivation and current value of its reinforcer, second-order conditioning is relatively impervious to such assaults. I shall display evidence that shows second-order conditioning to be remarkably stable in the face of drastic changes in the original US, the motivational state, and the value of its own first-order reinforcer. I then point to a number of implications of this stability for the motivating and rewarding role that second-order conditioning may play in instrumental performance. Those implications are compared with a number of initial investigations within instrumental settings. I hope to show that the facts of second-order conditioning can make understandable a number of counterintuitive findings from the instrumental literature. Furthermore, it may provide the underpinnings for instrumental performance more successfully than can first-order Pavlovian conditioning.

A Demonstration of Pavlovian Second-Order Conditioning

The phenomenon of second-order conditioning is observed when a stimulus serves as a Pavlovian reinforcer only by virtue of its own prior relation to the unconditioned stimulus. Although Pavlov (1927) devoted some energy to its description, the notion has historically labored under the weight of a bad press. Several years ago when we began our investigation of second-order conditioning, we could find very few sound demonstrations that it occurred with sufficient magnitude to be worthy of attention. Consequently, we carried out several experiments to illustrate that even in the context of adequate control procedures, substantial second-order conditioning of fear could be produced (Rizley & Rescorla, 1972). However, the history of skepticism about its existence and magnitude has been long enough that it still seems necessary to begin any discussion of second-order conditioning with an illustration of its occurrence. To indicate that second-order conditioning is not confined to our previously emphasized fear conditioning experiments, I pick this illustration from an appetitive conditioning situation. Indeed, throughout this chapter I emphasize the appetitive case because it provides some particularly interesting examples of the importance of second-order conditioning for instrumental behavior.

The appetitive situation that we have been using involves measurement of the rat's general activity in anticipation of the receipt of food. It is based on the commonly made laboratory observation that hungry animals often remain quiescent until the caretaker enters the room to feed them. At that time, they become highly agitated; as it turns out this agitated behavior is partially in response to the caretaker as a CS that has been repeatedly followed by a food US. Following the work of Sheffield and Campbell (1954) and of Zamble (1967), we have adapted that observation for systematic study of Pavlovian conditioning.

The particular apparatus we use is a standard Skinner box with the lever withdrawn and housed in a sound- and light-resistant shell, within which tones and lights may be presented. That Skinner box is set on the activity measuring device, which consists of two horizontal plexiglass sheets separated by ball bearings, such that the top sheet is displaced horizontally as the animal moves about. To detect that movement, a metal plum bob is suspended from the top sheet in such a way that it normally rests within a metal ring. Movement causes the bob to swing, hitting the sides of the ring; we simply count the number of contacts as a measure of activity. This is a crude but highly effective device.

Using this technique, Holland and Rescorla (1975a) carried out a three-group experiment designed to demonstrate second-order appetitive conditioning. Twelve experimental animals received initial presentations of a 10-sec flashing of the house light, each of which terminated in the delivery of two 45-mg food pellets. This was a purely Pavlovian procedure, intended to establish first-order conditioning to the light. They then received repeated presentations of a 10-sec clicker, each of which was followed by a nonreinforced presentation of the light. The intention was to observe the response to the clicker for evidence of second-order conditioning. Because pairing was used in both stages, this group was designated PP.

However, as we have argued elsewhere (Rescorla, 1973a), the simple observation of behavior to the clicker is not by itself sufficient for the conclusion that second-order conditioning has occurred. One needs to be assured that the behavior depends both on the clicker being paired with the light and on the light having previously been paired with the food. If the clicker–light relation were unimportant, one could challenge that this was an example of conditioning; if the light–food relation were unimportant, one could challenge this as an example of second-order conditioning. Consequently, Holland and Rescorla ran two comparison groups, for one of which light was initially paired with food but then the clicker and light were presented in unpaired fashion (Group PU); for the other, the clicker and light were paired but the light had previously been presented in an unpaired relation for the food (Group UP). Comparisons of the response to the clickers in these groups with that in the experimental animals should provide the kind of evidence needed to demonstrate second-order appetitive conditioning.

The outcomes of this experiment are shown in Fig. 6.1. We have plotted activity counts per minute for the final day of first-order conditioning and the 16 trials of second-order conditioning. The data at the left present the pre-CS (open symbol) and during-CS (closed symbol) results for responding to the light at the end of first-order conditioning. The important points to notice are that the pre-CS rates are low and that the two groups which received light–food pairings (Groups PU and PP) both showed increased activity during the light.

The results of more interest, for second-order conditioning, are shown to the right of Fig. 6.1. Although the pre-CS rates remained low, there was initially substantial responding to the second-order CS in all groups. However, as second-order conditioning proceeded, the response in comparison groups dropped to the level of the pre-CS activity. In contrast, the animals in Group PP showed increases in activity to a level substantially higher than that of the comparison groups.

There are a number of other interesting features of this experiment, but this is sufficient description for our present purposes. The experiment illustrates that in comparison with reasonably stringent control procedures, substantial second-order conditioning can be obtained with a food US. Let me emphasize that this is one of a large number of experiments from our laboratory that display potent second-order conditioning. We regularly observe such conditioning with a variety of appetitive and aversive USs.

Moreover, systematic investigation reveals that in many respects second-order conditioning obeys laws parallel to those typically observed with modern first-order preparations. For instance, it displays the same sort of sensitivity to temporal variables as does first-order conditioning. Conditioning is best with forward, rather than backward, procedures; but as in first-order conditioning, backward second-order conditioning can be produced. Similarly, although both delayed and trace paradigms generate substantial second-order conditioning, the former yields superior effects. Second-order conditioning is also sensitive to such attentional effects as those measured in a latent inhibition procedure. Finally, second-order conditioning is governed by many of the same informational principles as is first-order emotional conditioning. We have recently observed both overshadowing and blocking in the second-order preparation (Zimmer-Hart, 1974). In fact, we have found the Rescorla–Wagner model, which describes many of these effects for first-order conditioning, to be entirely suitable as a description for the outcomes of second-order conditioning experiments.

Consequently, we need no longer fear that second-order conditioning is not a real or powerful phenomenon. In most regards it is similar to first-order conditioning, yielding levels of responding comparable to those produced by first-

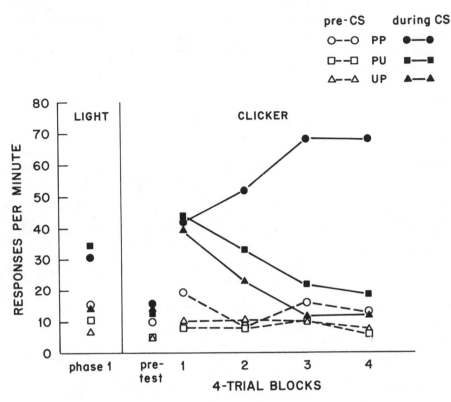

FIG. 6.1 Mean response rates during first- and second-order conditioning. The left panel shows responding during the light CS and pre-CS periods on the final day of first-order conditioning. The right panel shows responding during the clicker CS and pre-CS periods during second-order conditioning. (From Holland & Rescorla, 1975a. Copyright 1975 by the American Psychological Association. Reprinted by permission.)

order conditioning with moderate USs. In what follows, however, I argue that second-order conditioning is not simply a weaker form of first-order conditioning. It introduces features of its own that make it in some ways superior as a controller of behavior.

The Stability of Second-Order Conditioning

Together with the belief that second-order conditioning is weak and difficult to demonstrate has gone the impression that it is so transient and unstable as to be of only minor interest. The preceding section displayed evidence against the former set of beliefs. This section suggests that the latter is also incorrect, that instead second-order conditioning is highly stable and remarkably resistant to a variety of experimental attempts to reduce its power. Indeed, some of the examples I use below show second-order conditioning to be more stable than is first-order conditioning. I discuss in detail two kinds of experimental assault on second-order conditioning: changes in the value of the original unlearned reinforcer and changes in the value of the first-order stimulus responsible for second-order responding.

Changes in the Original Reinforcer's Value

Our laboratory has recently been engaging in a number of experiments aimed at uncovering the elements that are associated as a result of Pavlovian conditioning. We have begun by adopting a popular casual view of that process, according to which internal representations of the CS and US are formed and joined by an associative connection. According to this view, postconditioning manipulation of the US representation may be expected to result in changes in the ability of the CS to evoke a response. If the signal is associated with an event, changes in the value of the event should be reflected in response to that signal.

I have reported a number of experiments investigating this possibility in a conditioned suppression situation (Rescorla, 1973a, b, 1974). For instance, I have attempted to devalue the US by its repeated presentation, intending to habituate the animal to it. I have also attempted to inflate the value of a shock US after conditioning by simply exposing the animal to shocks of a much stronger value. Both of these manipulations, if carried out prior to first-order conditioning, sharply affect the ability of the US to establish conditioned suppression. Moreover, these manipulations have retroactive effects on first-order fear conditioning: US habituation depresses and US inflation augments the response that a previously conditioned first-order CS produces. These findings obviously have interesting implications for the nature of first-order fear conditioning. They support the proposition that the representation of the US is sufficiently central to the learned association that its modification affects responding.

What is more relevant in the present context, however, is our failure to find parallel changes in the response-producing power of previously conditioned second-order CSs. Despite postconditioning manipulation of the aversive US value, second-order CSs were unchanged in their suppressive power. They appeared to have taken on a kind of value of their own, an independence of the value of the original US.

Because of the importance of these findings both for interpretations of Pavlovian conditioning and for the application of those interpretations to instrumental behavior, Holland and I have recently completed parallel experiments with the appetitive activity conditioning situation described above. This situation is especially interesting in the present context because it permits both experiential and motivational modifications of the US evaluation.

By way of illustration, I describe here two experiments that follow essentially identical designs (Holland & Rescorla, 1975b). In both experiments first- and second-order Pavlovian appetitive conditioning were carried out, then the US evaluation was changed, and finally the CSs were assessed for their ability to produce a conditioned response. The experiments differed only in the technique used to change the US evaluation. In one experiment this was accomplished by pairing food with another US that induced internal malaise. In the other, food was made less valuable by satiation.

The design of the satiation experiment is described in detail in Table 6.1. Four groups of eight rats each initially received first-order conditioning with a 10-sec light CS and a two-pellet US. Then two of those groups (2-D and 2-S) received second-order conditioning in which a tone was repeatedly followed by that light. Two other groups (1-D and 1-S) received first-order conditioning to that same tone. All this training was accomplished with the animals reduced to 80% of their normal body weight. Then one group from each of the above pairs (2-S and 1-S) was satiated, whereas the other group from each pair (2-D and 1-D) remained deprived. Satiation took 6 days and was accomplished by free access to the normal Purina diet, supplemented by unlimited access to a dish of the Pavlovian reinforcing pellets just prior to the normal running time. While under these motivational states, all groups were tested for the response to the tone presented alone. It is, of course, the performance at this time that is of major interest.

Figure 6.2 shows the results of these manipulations. The points to the left of that figure show the terminal levels of conditioning prior to satiation. High, and relatively comparable, levels of conditioning were attained in the first- and second-order groups. The middle portion of the figure shows the results of the extinction test under either satiation or deprivation. Looking first at the first-order CSs (filled symbols), it is clear that satiation markedly attenuated the response to the first-order conditioned tone. There was a substantial initial effect of satiation that became larger and then disappeared during the course of testing.

The results of the second-order conditioned tone, shown in open symbols, were quite different. There was no evidence that second-order conditioning was adversely affected by satiation. Indeed, if one compares the response to the tone in the two satiated groups (triangles), it is clear that under satiation, the

TABLE 6.1
Design of a Pavlovian Satiation Experiment

Group	Phase					
	1	2	3	4	5	6
1-D	L → food	T → food	Deprivation	T	Deprivation	T
1-S	L → food	T → food	Satiation	T	Deprivation	T
2-D	L → food	T → L	Deprivation	T	Deprivation	T
2-S	L → food	T → L	Satiation	T	Deprivation	T

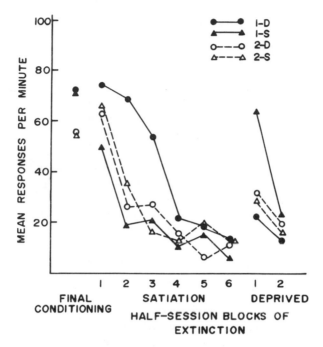

FIG. 6.2 Mean response rates during the tone CS at the end of conditioning, during extinction testing under satiation, and during extinction testing after redeprivation. Group labels indicate whether the tone was first order (1) or second order (2) and whether animals were satiated (S) or deprived (D) during initial extinction. (After Holland & Rescorla, 1975b. Copyright 1975 by the American Psychological Association. Reprinted by permission.)

second-order tone produced more responding than did the first-order CS. Despite the fact that prior to satiation the first-order response was larger, second-order conditioning sustained the impact of satiation much better than did first-order conditioning.

The far right-hand portion of Fig. 6.2 shows the results of a final set of test sessions under redeprivation. All groups showed evidence of spontaneous recovery, presumably as a result of the intervening period needed for redeprivation. However, the magnitude of that recovery was differential only in the first-order groups. Those first-order animals extinguished under satiation and then tested under redeprivation showed a very substantial response; the other groups were much more modest in their recovery. This is a point to which I return later.

The finding of principal interest from this experiment is that second-order conditioning was not affected by satiation of the original drive. A reduction in level of motivation substantial enough to greatly attenuate the first-order conditioned response left the second-order one fully intact. Consequently, satiation may be a decremental operation to which second-order conditioning is substantially more resistant than is first-order conditioning.

The results of a second technique for reducing the organism's evaluation of the food US support these conclusions. In this second experiment satiation was replaced by the pairing of the food with an illness-inducing event. By this means we hoped to change the US value through associative experiential processes. For this purpose we selected as our new US high-speed rotation, a treatment that reduces the intake of foods with which it is paired but which does not leave long-term debilitating effects.

First- and second-order conditioning were carried out in four groups treated identically to those of the previous experiment. Then one first-order (1-E) and one second-order (2-E) group each received presentations of 50 food pellets, each of which was followed by 5 min of rotation at 120 rpm. After 15 such pairings spread over 5 days, consumption of the offered pellets was reduced to about 50%. Control animals with first-order (1-C) and second-order (2-C) conditioning of the tone received only rotation without the prior offering of pellets. Then all animals were tested by nonreinforced presentation of the tone CS in the activity situation.

Figure 6.3 shows the outcomes of these manipulations. As in the preceding experiment, conditioning was substantial and comparable for the first- and second-order groups. Furthermore, like satiation, food-rotation pairings markedly interfered with the response to the first-order CS. From the outset of extinction testing Group 1-E was suppressed relative to Group 1-C. However, also like satiation, this treatment did not adversely affect the response to the second-order CS; Groups 2-C and 2-E are comparable throughout testing. Moreover, in animals that had received food—rotation pairings, the second-order CS generated more activity than did the first-order CS. Again in this case, second-order conditioning sustained an insult on the US better than did first-order conditioning.

The right-hand portion of Fig. 6.3 shows the results of additional extinction testing of the tone after intervening attempts to restore the value of the food US in the experimental groups. This was accomplished simply by giving repeated offerings of the pellets without subsequent rotation; the intention was to provide a manipulation parallel to redeprivation for restoring the food's value. The results are again parallel to those for satiation. This increase in the value of food did not benefit second-order conditioning but did improve the response to the first-order CS.

These results are therefore entirely confirmatory of those obtained previously with aversive USs. Once conditioning is completed, changes in the value of the US by a variety of means seem to have profound effects on first-order conditioning but to leave virtually untouched second-order conditioning. In this sense, second-order conditioning is not only stable, it is more stable than is first-order.

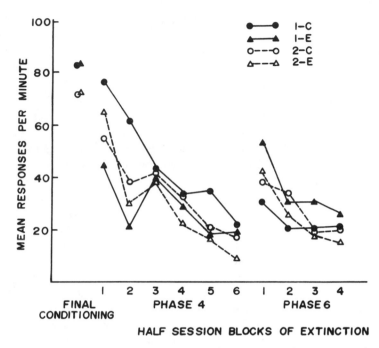

FIG. 6.3 Mean response rates during the tone CS during Phase 4 extinction testing after rotation and during Phase 6 after food-alone presentation. Labels indicate the order of conditioning to the tone and whether the rotation was paired (E) or unpaired (C) with rotation prior to Phase 4. (From Holland & Rescorla, 1975b. Copyright 1975 by the American Psychological Association. Reprinted by permission.)

It is worth pausing briefly to note several additional implications of this pair of experiments. First, these results provide interesting information on the role of motivation in Pavlovian conditioning. The parallel between the outcomes of satiation and pairing the original US with an oppositely valued reinforcer suggests that in the present situation changes in drive can be mimicked by associative manipulation of the value of the US representation. This encourages the thought that in some Pavlovian situations drives may have their primary impact by simply changing the evaluation of the representation of goal objects.

Indeed the pattern of results seems incompatible with a variety of popular alternative accounts of the manner in which drives function. For instance, drives have been suggested as general energizers (Hull, 1943), activating those associations attached to the presented CS. However, the failure of changes in food deprivation to affect the level of second-order responding suggests that any such activation must be substantially less than general in its effects. Responses and associations as closely related as the first- and second-order consequences of the same US were differentially affected. Another common account of the role of drives appeals to their stimulus properties, arguing that they participate in the stimulus complex to which conditioning has taken place. When deprivation states are changed, so are those stimuli, and consequently performance changes. However, it is difficult to see why the stimuli arising from a drive state should participate more heavily in the CS evoking first-order responding than they do when the same CS evokes second-order responding.

It may be commented in passing that modern evidence about the kinds of stimuli which control Pavlovian conditioning does not support this stimulus view of the operation of drive in any case. The logical relation that a drive stimulus has in a Pavlovian paradigm is one of a background stimulus in the presence of which some signal is differentially reinforced. That is, it bears the formal relation of A in an A−/AX+ conditioning paradigm. From what we know of such paradigms, A gains little associative strength and so can control little responding. Consequently, the hypothesis that drive stimuli are just like any other stimuli, acquiring and losing associative strength, does not in any case enable one to describe the consequences of drive manipulations for many instances of Pavlovian conditioning.

The alternative favored by these data is that drives have their major effect by modifying the evaluation of goal event representations. It is, of course, common to suppose that drives modify the evaluation of current events, increasing or decreasing the current impact of a US. However, the implication of these experiments is stronger—that it modifies the evaluation of internal representations of past events. At least for first-order conditioning, this seems consistent with the view advocated by Tolman (1932).

A second implication of these studies for Pavlovian conditioning concerns extinction. Notice that in both experiments the amount of extinction accomplished by the first set of test sessions depended entirely on the level of responding evoked by the CS during those sessions. As measured by the amount of responding during the second set of test sessions, when all animals had equivalent US evaluations again, both techniques of temporarily changing the US value also resulted in the protection of the CS from extinction. Nonreinforced CS presentations under conditions where the original US was reduced in value did not generate much extinction. This observation fits with a broad range of results indicating that a nonreinforcement decrements associative strength only when it occurs in the context of being unanticipated.

These extinction results also have consequences for the historically fascinating notion of a generalized reinforcer. Many have suggested that a particularly powerful derived reinforcer could be obtained by pairing a stimulus, in Pavlovian fashion, not with one but with many different positive USs (e.g., Skinner, 1953). However, there is a logical puzzle surrounding this proposal. How are we to pair a CS with several different USs on different occasions without each pairing with one US also constituting a nonpairing extinction trial with the others? The present results may provide an answer: Change the deprivation state so that it is appropriate to the US being used. Then those CS presentations constitute only weak extinction trials for USs on which the organism is satiated. Indeed, designs in which the organism is throughout deprived of several USs can be expected to yield only weak generalized reinforcers. This may partially account for the failure to provide strong evidence for this notion.

Finally, it is worth noting that the independence that second-order conditioning shows of satiation-induced changes in the US value may be especially relevant for the theoretical use to which conditioning has been put in explaining instrumental behavior. One of the original intentions of theorizing about learned motivations was to account for sustained performance in the face of dramatic changes in primary drives. Notice, however, that such theorizing gains us little if the learned drives themselves vary when the original motivations change. Yet any learned motivations that are dependent on first-order Pavlovian conditioning would appear to have this property. Therefore, it is exactly the fact that second-order conditioning seems to be independent of the original motivational conditions that makes it a powerful theoretical tool for applications to instrumental behavior.

Changes in the Value of the First-Order Stimulus

There is a second kind of decremental operation to which second-order conditioned responses are surprisingly insensitive. One may think that although modifications in drive state and the value of the US are ineffective, nevertheless changes in first-order stimuli may have an effect. By analogy to first-order conditioning, in which changes in the reinforcer apparently affect the response, in second-order conditioning similar changes in its reinforcer, i.e., the first-order CS, may affect the response. This turns out, however, not to be the case. Rescorla (1973a) has previously reported for aversively based second-order conditioning that neither increasing or decreasing the aversion controlled by the first-order stimulus changes the response to the second-order stimulus. In the present context, it may be helpful to illustrate this point by reference to another experiment using an appetitive US.

In one of their activity conditioning experiments, Holland and Rescorla (1975a) established a second-order response to a clicker CS in two groups of rats. This was accomplished by repeatedly pairing the clicker with a light that had previously been paired with food. After the completion of second-order conditioning, they presented the light repeatedly without food, with the intention of extinguishing its first-order CR. They then tested the animal's activity response to the second-order clicker. Figure 6.4 shows the results of these treatments, together with those of a control group treated identically but without intervening extinction of the light CS. Both groups showed rapid acquisition of second-order conditioning. More importantly, both showed maintenance of that response, despite the intervening extinction treatment of the light in Group E. Furthermore, both showed similar extinction curves for the

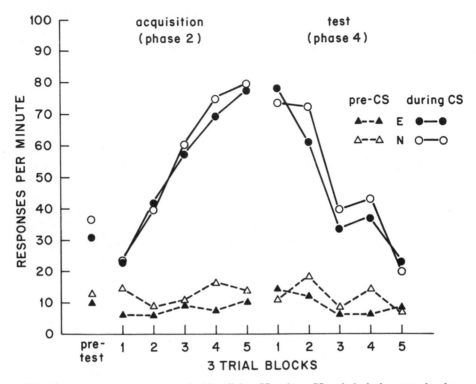

FIG. 6.4 Mean response rates during the clicker CS and pre-CS periods during second-order conditioning and extinction. In Group E, extinction intervened between acquisition and testing of the second-order stimulus. (From Holland & Rescorla, 1975a. Copyright 1975 by the American Psychological Association. Reprinted by permission.)

second-order clicker, indicating the impotence of changes in the response to the light for modifying the response to the second-order CS.

Of course, these results may well have been anticipated on the basis of those reported in the previous section. There we described several manipulations that had decremental effects on first-order stimuli but not on second-order stimuli. Had the maintenance of the first-order reinforcer been important for the production of a second-order response, then those results could not have been obtained. Both kinds of CS would have been reduced in effectiveness.

This experiment, together with results previously reported (e.g., Rescorla, 1973a; Lindberg, 1949), point to a second sense in which a second-order CS seems to take on a kind of independence of its origins. Unlike first-order conditioning, the second-order CS is relatively unaffected by changes in the value of its reinforcer. I discuss below a view of conditioning that may make these differences comprehensible. First, however, I turn to some experimental implications of these results for the application to instrumental behaviors.

Some Analogous Consequences for Instrumental Behavior

Suppose that we grant the common assumption that Pavlovian conditioning participates in instrumental performance in two ways: by establishing incentive motivation, which instigates behavior, and by constructing derived reinforcers, which strengthen it. Furthermore, suppose we agree to the proposition that instrumental behaviors usually involve sequences of responses, only the final member of which is actually coincident with the primary goal event. Then it seems plausible to conclude that much of the responsibility for establishing incentive motivation and learned reinforcement rests with higher-order Pavlovian conditioning. To be sure, stimuli early in a sequence are often similar to those present at the final goal and consequently we can expect some of these properties to accrue to such stimuli by simple generalization. Additionally, however, they should gain their potencies by higher-order conditioning.

If one accepts these arguments, then there are a number of relatively straightforward implications of the previously described Pavlovian findings for instrumental behavior. The next several sections point to some of these implications and give some illustrative evidence. Our intention here is by no means to offer a complete account of instrumental behavior or even of the involvement of Pavlovian conditioning in that behavior. Instead, our concern is to point to some novel implications introduced by attention to the detailed features of higher-order conditioning.

Changes in the Goal Event

A simple analogy to the Pavlovian studies would lead us to expect a number of consequences from changing the value of the goal event in an instrumental learning situation. First, we might expect that to the degree that second-order Pavlovian incentive motivation is responsible for motivating the instrumental performance, that performance should be relatively insensitive to changes in the organism's evaluation of the goal event. So we should not be startled by instances in which performance continues relatively unaffected even though the evaluation of the goal has been drastically altered. Second, the behaviors involved in most instrumental sequences should be supported by a mixture of first- and second-order Pavlovian conditioning. However, those behaviors more distant from the goal should involve a larger proportion of higher order conditioning; consequently, they should be especially insensitive to changes in the value of the goal event.

Satiation. As noted above, one particularly interesting way of changing the goal event is through changes in deprivation state. Because historically Pavlovian incentive motivation has played a particularly prominent role in accounting for behaviors in the absence of primary drives, Gordon Shulman and I decided to examine these implications when the goal event was modified by satiation.

For this purpose, we thought it desirable to use an instrumental learning task sufficiently extended in time to permit measurement of its component parts. Consequently we returned to the historically well-studied maze. Hungry rats were trained to obtain a 4 45-mg Noyes pellet reward by completing a maze composed of four successive T units. The correct choices involved a LRRL sequence in which the correct arms were designated by distinctive wall and floor coverings. The floors were composed of sandpaper, hardware cloth, or grid bars in one of two orientations; the walls were decorated by vertical or horizontal stripes, or by white and black paint. Except for the area of the correct arm within 18 cm of the choice points, the maze was white. The point of such distinctive stimuli was to enhance the role played by higher-order conditioning relative to that by stimulus generalization. Each T unit had a 48-cm stem and arms of the same length. Photocells placed 7.5 cm after each choice point and just outside the start box permitted measurement of the time to complete each successive choice.

Initial training consisted of one trial per day for 26 days, with the eight animals at 80% of their *ad libidum* weight. Then all animals received *ad libidum* Purina chow in their home cage for 7 days. In addition, twice each day they received a dish of approximately 150 Noyes pellets to ensure satiation on the reward used in the maze. On the next 5 days satiation was continued and the animals were tested in the maze with each daily trial terminating in the four-pellet reward. Our rather simple question is to what degree various aspects of the performance would be maintained in the face of satiation.

The left-hand side of Fig. 6.5 shows the performance during the final day of acquisition. This figure plots, on a log scale, the median running time for each of the four choice points (segments) of the maze. It is clear that terminal acquisition performance was skillful; the time to complete the first choice was slightly above 2 sec, whereas each of the other choices was made in about 1 sec. This is apparently near asymptotic performance because it was essentially unchanged over the final 5 days of acquisition. By this index, the initial behavior was terminally somewhat weaker than subsequent members of the response chain. In this regard, it is relevant to note that these animals displayed the kind of backward elimination of errors and reduction of times historically described for maze performance. The final choice was by far the most rapidly learned.

The performance during the 5 days of satiation testing is shown in the middle five curves. Several aspects of this performance are worthy of note. First, there was initially very little consequence of satiation. Despite the fact that on the first satiation test day the animals' weight was over 100% of that prior to beginning the experiment, they showed only a slight disruption. Second, over the course of testing under satiation the performance deteriorated, so that by Day 5 half the animals failed to complete at least one choice with an arbitrarily imposed maximum of 2 min. Third, the disruption produced by satiation was systematically distributed through the segments of the maze. Although it was

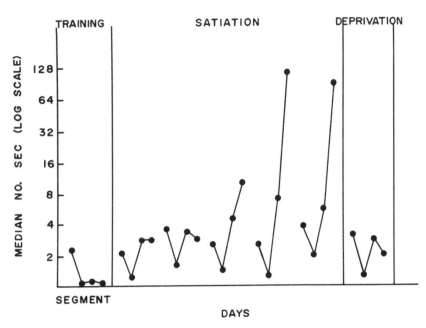

FIG. 6.5 Median number of seconds to complete each successive segment in the multiple maze, at the end of training, during 5 days of satiation, and during redeprivation.

the weakest component at the end of acquisition, the performance at the initial choice point was the least affected by satiation. Indeed, it was only on the final test day that a reliable increase in the time of the initial choice could be detected. In contrast, disruption at the final choice point was reliable, although small, on the first test day; furthermore, it was very substantial by the end of testing. Clearly, satiation acted to selectively increase the choice times for those behaviors nearest the goal.

Following the fifth satiation test day, the animals were redeprived over the course of 6 days and again tested. The performance under redeprivation is displayed in the final curve of Fig. 6.5. It is clear that redeprivation led to substantial improvement in choice times, but it is equally clear that the improvement was primarily in the later choice point performance. Although every animal was faster in the final choice time during redeprivation than on the preceding satiation day, half of the animals were faster and half slower in making their initial choice. Just as satiation selectively depressed later performance, redeprivation selectively restored that performance.

These findings are largely in agreement with those expected on the basis of an analysis employing Pavlovian higher-order conditioning. The instrumental performance continued despite considerable reduction in the original deprivation state; and this continuation was especially good for behaviors early in the sequence.

Furthermore, with redeprivation the behaviors that should more heavily involve first-order conditioning were most restored.

It is of interest to ask why, in terms of the present analysis, the effect of satiation through the sequence should develop over the course of testing. Two points are relevant. First, as those who have used satiation know, it is very difficult to guarantee complete satiation. Despite free access to the Noyes pellet rewards prior to each run, one may wonder about the adequacy of our satiation procedure. Fortunately, by continuing the reward during satiation testing, we have evidence relevant to this issue. It turns out that in terms of the reward consumed on Test Day 1 we were only moderately successful; the animals ate an average of two out of the four pellets on that day. However, by the third day and thereafter the average dropped to less than one-half pellet per animal. Consequently, although we were ultimately reasonably successful in producing rejection of the reward, it may be that some of the development of long latencies over testing came as a result of the development of satiation. In this regard it is worth noting that one may view the pellet consumption itself as one of the latest members of the instrumental sequence. Although it is difficult to compare depression in consumption with increase in choice times, the present evidence is not inconsistent with the notion that consumption was one of the most affected members of the sequence.

Second, detailed consideration of the present analysis reveals that it anticipates the development of the effects of satiation during testing. Notice that although the simple occurrence of a response to a second-order conditioned stimulus does not depend on the continued value of either the original US or the first-order CS, nevertheless maintenance of that response to a repeatedly presented second-order CS is dependent on its being regularly followed by an effective first-order CS. If the second-order CS is presented alone, without the first-order CS, or is followed by a neutral stimulus, then it loses its value. Furthermore, it seems likely, especially in the light of historical estimates of the time intervals over which instrumental reinforcers are directly effective, that all of the choice points in the maze involve a mixture of both first- and second-order conditioning; only the proportion may vary. In that case, the continued second-order incentive and reward may initially maintain substantial behavior even in the later choice points. However, as those stimuli are followed by a first-order stimulus made ineffective by satiation, then they would extinguish and so lose their effectiveness. Thus with satiation the first-order CSs would lose their strength and so be unable to sustain antecedent higher-order conditioning. The consequence is a backward deterioration in performance under satiation. Although we did not carry testing far enough to make this determination with certainty, the present results seem consistent with this expectation.

The most striking aspect of this experiment is the mismatch between the animal's initial performance and his later choices and consumption. It is quite startling to see an animal speed out of the start box and make the first two choices in about 2 sec each, only to begin losing interest and often fail to complete the trial or consume the offered reward. This kind of observation does not fit well with a causal description of instrumental behavior that attributes the performance to goal directedness.

The results of this particular satiation experiment are not alone in giving rise to such observations. Morgan (1974) has reviewed a widely scattered literature under the heading of "resistance to satiation." In that review, Morgan musters evidence that even complete satiation, leading to rejection of the original goal object, does not necessarily produce immediate deterioration of the anticipatory instrumental behavior. Furthermore, although the evidence on this point is less firm, Fantino (1965) has found that behaviors earlier in a free-operant chain are less depressed than are later behaviors when the animal is satiated on the goal object.

Such results as these suggest a context in which the classical notion of functional autonomy (Allport, 1937) can be viewed. Behaviors that become independent of their original goals may often do so because higher-order Pavlovian incentive motivation replaces the original motivation. As noted above, the power of higher-order conditioning for establishing motivation rests precisely on its apparent independence of the original motivations.

This same independence belies, of course, the casual description of instrumental behavior as goal directed. It seems inconsistent with a class of explanations in terms of the organism performing a response because it expects a particular goal. At the same time it shows a way in which the attempt to explicate the notion of expectation in terms of Pavlovian conditioning mechanisms benefits from a more sophisticated understanding of those mechanisms. Anticipation, in terms of antedating Pavlovian behaviors, may indeed play an important role in governing instrumental performance. However, our casual language may not describe accurately the rules for the acquisition and loss of such anticipatory mechanisms.

Other changes in the goal event. There are, of course, a number of other procedures that have been employed to change the organism's evaluation of primary goal events. I shall mention here three other procedures and briefly refer to some scattered data.

Perhaps the most natural technique parallels the rotational experiment described above for the pure Pavlovian case. One could easily use associative techniques, pairing the original goal event with a new US, subsequent to initial instrumental training. Experiments of this sort have been reported by Garcia, Kovner, and Green (1970) and by Holman (1975). Both of these investigations paired a food reward with an illness-inducing drug after first teaching an instrumental response for that food as the reward. Both found no decremental consequences for the instrumental behavior of that pairing, despite a profound reduction in consumption of the goal object. Unfortunately from the present

point of view, neither report indicates whether terminal behaviors in the instrumental sequence may have been reduced but not systematically measured by the
experimenter, although both report failure of consumption in the instrumental
situation.

A second technique for modifying the evaluation of a goal event has been
thoroughly explored under the rubric of successive contrast. In experiments of
this sort, initial instrumental training with one reward is followed by additional
training with a shifted reward value. The data of interest are the rapidity of
change in the performance and the level which that performance attains. Most
experiments of this sort, beginning with those reported by Crespi (1942), have
found rapid changes in performance, especially when the goal is reduced in
value. However, this result is somewhat difficult to interpret in the present
context because, unlike the other procedures discussed here, the instrumental
response occurs repeatedly in the presence of the new reward value. Therefore,
the changes induced may well involve more than simple Pavlovian adjustments.
Furthermore, it is interesting to note that although changes in performance after
a single trial with the new reward are often observed, they are usually quite
small. This may, of course, be due in good part to the gradual acquisition of the
new US value, but it may also reflect the role of second-order incentive, which is
insensitive to such changes. In this context, it is worth noting that many
investigators report that responses late in the sequence are the first to change
when reward is shifted (e.g., Ison, Glass, & Doly, 1969; Spear & Spitzner, 1966).
While this is intuitively not surprising, it is also in agreement with a description
that attributes the motivation for·the early members of the sequence to goal-
independent higher-order conditioning.

Finally, consider one particular case of reward shift—extinction. We have
argued elsewhere that when a Pavlovian CS is repeatedly presented without
reinforcement, not only does its associative structure change but also the
representation of the US undergoes a degradation in value (Rescorla & Heth,
1975). If a similar change takes place during the extinction of instrumental
activity, then we would anticipate that the incentive motivation late in the
response chain would be depressed especially rapidly. Consequently, extinction,
like acquisition, should occur first near the goal and only later move toward the
start box. Although data bearing directly on this possibility are surprisingly
difficult to find in the literature, some reports are consistent with this expectation (e.g., Wagner, 1961). Data collected in our laboratory with the multiple
choice maze described above have generally supported this proposition. Performance near the goal deteriorates rapidly, so that a few extinction trials generate
slow final choice times despite unchanged early choice times. Of course, this
outcome can be expected on a number of theoretical grounds, but it is also
comforting to the present position.

All of the data mentioned here are only suggestive, of course. Considerably
more data have to be gathered before one can comfortably conclude that early

behaviors in an instrumental sequence are relatively immune to modifications in the goal representation, much less that such immunity is attributable to second-order conditioning. However, that suggestiveness is exactly one value of this analysis.

Changes in the Value of Subgoals

Our analysis of instrumental behavior involves first-order Pavlovian conditioned stimuli as both establishers of higher-order incentive and reinforcers of antecedent instrumental responses. This latter function is particularly captured by the historical reference to such stimuli as "subgoals." In this context it is of particular interest to ask whether the continued value of those first-order stimuli is important to the production of previously trained instrumental responses. That is, we can ask about the importance of learned subgoals in the same way we asked about that of the original goal object. The results of the purely Pavlovian experiments described earlier suggest that the answer is also likely to be similar; the present value of those stimuli should be of little importance.

Extinction of the secondary reinforcer. The reasoning can perhaps be most clearly displayed in discussing behaviors that are entirely supported by subgoals, without confounding reinforcement attributable to the ultimate goal. Suppose that one first pairs a tone with food, setting up first-order Pavlovian conditioning. If he then made that tone contingent upon the prior production of an instrumental response, it should enhance that response. However, notice that procedurally the instrumental response is treated similarly to a second-order Pavlovian CS; both are regularly followed by the first-order CS in such a way that changes can be attributed to that stimulus alone. The Pavlovian result is that the learned value of the second-order CS does not depend on the current status of the first-order one. We might then think that the changed likelihood of the response would similarly persist despite changes in that stimulus.

To provide information on this possibility, we recently carried out an instrumental training experiment in which only stimuli previously paired with food served as differential reinforcers for a response. The experiment, which is entirely analogous in principle to the one reported by Rizley and Rescorla (1972) for Pavlovian conditioning, had two intentions. The first was to demonstrate the presence of such secondary reinforcement in sufficient magnitude to permit its study. Second, we wished to examine the effect on such established behavior of extinguishing the value of the secondary reinforcer.

The experiment employed a procedure like that reported by Zimmerman, Hanford, and Brown (1967). The 16 rat subjects in the experimental group were permitted to press a lever in a Skinner box to earn a 2-sec 1,800-Hz tone; intermingled with that performance, the experimenter randomly presented other 2-sec tones, which were each followed by a one-pellet food reward. Thus, although responses earned only tones, the same stimulus was concurrently paired with food to endow it with positive reinforcing power. However, the animal's response was irrelevant to the occurrence of the primary food reward. In order to maximize the resultant behavior without a large number of tone presentations, variable interval (VI) schedules were used. The rats could earn tones on a VI 1-min schedule by bar pressing; tone—food pairings were freely delivered on an independent VI 2-min schedule.

To determine the degree to which the responding observed under these arrangements could be attributed to instrumental reinforcement, we employed two types of control groups, analogous to those described for the Pavlovian experiments in our laboratory. The first group was intended to assess the role of the bar press—tone contingency. Like the experimental animals, these rats received tone—food pairings on a VI-2 schedule, but unlike the experimental animals their bar presses did not earn tones. Instead, they received additional freely delivered tones programmed on a response-independent VI 1-min schedule. Consequently, they served as a kind of yoked control, receiving the same independent events but without the relation to bar pressing. The second control group was intended to assess the degree to which the tone acquired its reinforcing power because of its concurrent relation to food. That group, like the experimental group, earned tones on a VI-1-min schedule; but unlike the experimental group it otherwise received tones and food presented freely on unrelated response-independent VI 2-min schedules. The first comparison group permits us to decide whether the experimental animal's tone is a reinforcer, whereas the second allows decision on whether that reinforcement has been learned.

These regimes were imposed for three daily 1-hr sessions. Prior to the first session, all animals had received simple bar-press training for food reinforcement until they had earned 50 pellets on a continuous reinforcement schedule. This device was intended simply to generate a reasonably high level of initial pressing to guarantee adequate contact between our treatments and the animal's behavior.

After the third acquisition session with secondary reinforcement, the experimental animals were divided into two groups. One group received extensive extinction experience with the tone. On each of 4 days they were placed in chambers identical to the Skinner boxes, but without levers, and received 60 nonreinforced presentations of the 2-sec tone. The other group of experimental animals received the same treatment but with the tone presentations omitted. Both control groups received nonreinforced tone presentations like those of the first experimental group.

Finally, on the next day, all animals were returned to the Skinner boxes and given a brief opportunity to bar press. During this test session, no tones or food pellets were presented. This means of testing permitted us to assess the strength of the behavior as previously trained, without the confounding presence of the currently differently valued tones. It does, however, subject the behavior to extinction, requiring a rapid assessment of the performance.

The left-hand side of Fig. 6.6 shows the mean responses per minute generated by these treatments over the three acquisition days. It is clear that pretraining with food resulted in relatively high initial bar-pressing rates in all groups. However, over the three acquisition days, the response rate fell markedly in the control groups, whereas it was maintained at a relatively higher level in the experimental animals (dotted lines). This quite substantial difference between the behavior of the experimental and control animals constitutes reasonably strong evidence for the role of the tone subgoal in generating the former group's behavior.

Some observers may object to this conclusion on the grounds that no increase in response rate was produced by this supposed secondary reinforcer; but the demand that a reinforcer show an absolute increase in probability or rate of some behavior has never seemed particularly convincing. Without information about how that behavior may have changed in the absence of reinforcement, it is difficult to know whether or not to expect a reinforcer to produce an increase in absolute rate. A more tenable demand is that a reinforcer should generate more

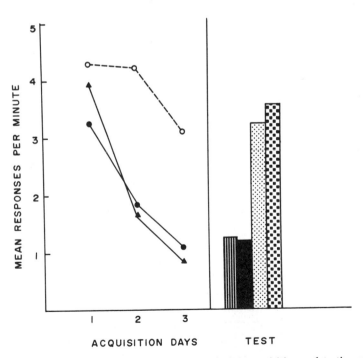

FIG. 6.6 Mean number of bar presses per minute during acquisition and testing of secondary reinforcement. During acquisition the experimental animals (o———o) received paired tones and food and food contingent on bar pressing. The other groups omitted one of these contingencies. Prior to testing both control groups (vertical lines and solid bar) and half the experimental animals (large dots) received extinction experience with the tone; the remaining experimental animals (small dots) did not.

behavior when it is made contingent on a response than when similar conditions failing to arrange that contingency are in effect. The present demonstration clearly meets that criterion.

Consequently, it is of interest to ask about the impact of extinction with the tone on the behavior of these groups. The response rates during the first 4 min of the postextinction test are shown in the right-hand portion of Fig. 6.6. After that initial period, responding had been reduced by extinction to too low a level to warrant display. We have separately displayed the performance for the two experimental groups, one with intervening extinction on the tone (large dots) and one without that experience (small dots). It is clear that such extinction produced very little effect. Both experimental groups continued to show substantially more behavior than did either of the controls, and the two experimental groups were essentially the same. Therefore, intervening extinction of the secondary reinforcer did not seem to undermine the performance of responses previously trained by that reinforcer. In this regard the instrumental response reinforced by a first-order Pavlovian CS seems parallel to the Pavlovian CS reinforced by that same stimulus.

As in the case of the Pavlovian paradigm, these results might well have been expected from the preceding satiation experiment. In that maze study, disruption of behavior late in the maze was not accompanied by disruption earlier in the sequence. To the degree that the former indicates loss of the value for stimuli late in the maze, the maintenance of earlier behavior suggests that those stimuli are not essential.

One particular value of the present experiment it that it separates out the reinforcing consequences of those stimuli for special attention. In this context, it is of interest to recall an early experiment by Schlosberg and Pratt (1956). They used the sight of food as a (learned) reward for hungry rats. After initial training, the animals were satiated and then subjected to additional trials. Although there was eventual depression of this secondarily reinforced behavior under satiation, there was no initial effect. So there is some direct evidence that changing the value of the subgoal through satiation may leave behavior previously reinforced by that subgoal unchanged.

Some related paradigms. Until now the discussion in this section has dealt with behaviors that are rewarded entirely by derived reinforcers. There are, of course, a number of related paradigms in which subgoals that occur during a chain of behavior terminating in primary reinforcement are also manipulated. It is worth pausing briefly to comment on two particular kinds of such experiments.

The first is latent extinction, in which a sequence of instrumental behavior initially ends in food reward, delivered in a particular location. The animal is then simply exposed to that location without food, in an attempt to reduce its value as a subgoal. Finally, the animal's performance of the instrumental sequence is again tested, typically by subjecting it to standard extinction procedures. In apparent conflict with the present results, a common finding is that such intervening extinction of the subgoal facilitates subsequent extinction of the behavior chain.

However, clear interpretation of such studies within the present context is complicated by the practice of continuing the subgoal's presentation during the course of extinction testing. That continuation means that only the initial test trial is relatively uncontaminated by the presence of differential reinforcement during testing. There is, of course, little question that secondary reinforcers of different strength act to differentially retard the extinction of behavior upon which they are contingent. However, the current issue is whether previously rewarded behaviors are retroactively affected by changes in the subgoal when they are tested under comparable conditions. A number of authors who have found no effects of a latent extinction treatment on the initial test performance (e.g., Coate, 1956) have made this point, although it has apparently escaped the attention of some commentators (e.g., Mackintosh, 1974).

The continuation of the subgoal during testing can affect even interpretation of the first trial, however. As latent extinction experiments are commonly carried out, the subject has visual exposure to the subgoal during the response sequence; consequently, its incentive value could affect response execution even on the first trial. The measure of most interest is performance early in the chain, therefore, when such effects should be minimized. Beginning with Seward and Levy (1949), who carried out one of the first latent extinction experiments, a number of authors have reported that subgoal extinction produced no initial effect on behaviors early in the sequence, despite profoundly disrupting goal entry. However, a particularly well-run experiment by Gonzales and Shepp (1965) did find first-trial disruption for starting times in a runway experiment.

It should be noted of course that it is not here argued that subgoals are entirely responsible for either the behaviors or the incentives which compose instrumental response sequences. Surely, many of the behaviors in a sequence fall within the effective range of the primary reinforcer and much of the incentive appears early in the chain by virtue of stimulus generalization (cf. Spence, 1956). Consequently, we would not expect chains that terminate in the delivery of a primary reinforcer to be entirely immune to changes in the value of subgoals. Historically, the emphasis of latent extinction experiments has been on the observation that such manipulations produce some effect. In the present context, however, it is equally relevant to note that the effect may not be large, immediate, or uniform throughout the instrumental performance.

A related experimental paradigm should also be mentioned. Early in the history of latent learning experiments, a number of authors attempted to change the value of goal-related stimuli by pairing them with oppositely valued reinforcers. Both Miller (1935) and Tolman and Gleitman (1949) initially trained rats to run in a maze to food reward. They then paired the previously rewarded goal box with shock and tested their animals on a single trial. Both found that such treatment disrupted performance earlier in the sequence in such a way as to indicate that the animal anticipated a particular goal box at the time of making an earlier choice. Consequently, under some circumstances a change in the value of later members of a sequence can retroactively modify earlier performance. These experiments differ, of course, in many respects from the ones described here. Perhaps one particular difference is of interest, however: Those experiments took special pains to ensure that the goal-box stimuli in question were highly salient in their own right. As is suggested below, under those circumstances stimuli late in the chain may participate in the Pavlovian learning in a way not dissimilar from that of primary reinforcers.

Despite some unclarities and only a scattering of evidence, the present results suggest that sometimes instrumental behaviors may become independent of their subgoals as well as of their final goals. The fact that this expectation was generated by the application of a Pavlovian analysis emphasizing second-order conditioning lends plausibility to the present analysis.

Some Additional Implications: What Is Learned?

The preceding discussions have emphasized the outcomes of posttraining manipulations of instrumental goal events that closely parallel those previously explored for Pavlovian conditioning. However, we have said little in the way of explaining the pattern of Pavlovian outcomes or about the general implications of such an explanation for instrumental training.

An important theoretical issue concerns why second-order Pavlovian conditioning should be so much more resistant to the kinds of intrusions described above than is first-order conditioning. We have elsewhere (Rescorla, 1973a) suggested one possibility, that first- and second-order conditioning involve the association of different contents. First-order conditioning apparently involves associations between the CS and some representations of the US, because postconditioning changes in that US change the response to the first-order CS. However, many examples of second-order conditioning probably do not importantly involve associations with either of the obvious possible stimuli, the US or the first-order CS, because the current status of neither matters for the production of the second-order response. Instead, we have previously argued that second-order conditioning may involve an association between the stimulus and the organism's reaction to the first-order CS. The animal is presented with a second-order CS, which is followed by a massive emotional reaction; perhaps he learns the association between the two.

One way to think of this possibility is to conceptualize reinforcing events as having multiple properties, any of which can potentially be associated with the CS. However, it seems likely that the most salient properties of that reinforcer would predominate. In simple first-order conditioning, the reinforcer has potent stimulus properties, as well as producing a strong emotional reaction. In that case, either or both of these properties may become associated with the CS. By contrast, in the usual second-order conditioning experiment, we have selected the first-order CS precisely because it is not a potent event in its own right; but we have then endowed it with the ability to produce a strong reaction. So after each second-order CS the organism experiences a weak stimulus together with a potent response. Furthermore, the original US is typically not even presented on such second-order trials. With these contingencies in effect, it would not be particularly surprising if the organism learned to associate the second-order CS with his own response. However, associations involving that response might well be insensitive to the kinds of stimulus-oriented decremental intrusions investigated here.

This description suggests that in some cases first- and second-order conditioning may involve very different learned contents. Second-order conditioning may not simply be less learning of the same thing as is first-order conditioning. Although similar in principle, the two procedures may encourage the organism to learn quite different things. This possibility suggests that the multiplicity of potential reinforcers and motivators governing instrumental performance is real, in the sense of involving different kinds of learning.

Such a possibility may importantly affect the way we think about the role of Pavlovian conditioning in establishing derived rewards. We have assumed that most instrumental behaviors can be viewed as rewarded by a mixture of learned and unlearned reinforcers. Notice, however, that many independent variables which are commonly manipulated in instrumental learning situations seem likely to affect the relative proportion of reinforcement attributable to these two kinds of sources. For instance, systematic variation in delay of reinforcement seems likely to affect the contribution of secondary reinforcement. Likewise, if the interval between a response and the ultimate reinforcer is inconsistent, learned reinforcers probably bear an increased responsibility. Similarly, the administration of primary reinforcement on only some trials may enhance the contribution of derived reinforcement on the other trials (see Denny, 1946). Even as we vary the number of reinforcements in the normal course of acquisition we may alter the relative contribution of primary and secondary reinforcers. As noted earlier, comments of this sort have not previously been considered troubling as long as derived and unlearned reinforcers differ only in strength. However, the present analysis suggests that they may also differ in content, so that mixtures of the two may be more analogous to administering multiple primary reinforcers. As in that case, we may need to take seriously the problem of describing how these different reinforcers combine to increase performance.

Similar comments can be made about the supposed anticipatory motivational role of Pavlovian conditioning. If the motivation is a mixture of first- and second-order conditioning processes that involve different learned contents, then our view of expectation must be reasonably complex. It no longer seems plausible to view goal expectances as anticipating unitary events; instead, the organism may learn to expect multiple and even qualitatively separable outcomes. Moreover, those different aspects of his Pavlovian anticipation may be differentially encouraged by experimental contingencies and differentially susceptible to experimental intrusions.

In general, of course, the difference between first- and second-order conditioning may be only the most obvious case in which different aspects of reinforcers are encoded. Consequently, one important long-term role that investigations of second-order conditioning may serve is to encourage analysis of the multiplicity of aspects of reinforcers which may be represented in learning, both Pavlovian and instrumental.

A Comment on the History of Second-Order Conditioning

Finally, some comment should be made about why, when the research from our laboratory demonstrates such a strong and stable second-order conditioning, psychologists have historically been so skeptical about its very existence. As many have noted, the key to the establishment of second-order conditioning is the maintenance of a strong response to the first-order CS. Indeed, as the previous section suggests, and as a variety of experiments from our laboratory indicate, the repeated pairing of the second-order CS with a strong response is *the* important condition for second-order conditioning.

However, the procedures under which we have demanded that second-order conditioning be demonstrated have typically made this guideline difficult to satisfy. Quite reasonably, we have insisted that demonstrations of second-order conditioning not admit of reinterpretation in terms of the direct action of the US on the supposed second-order stimulus. Consequently, the standard second-order paradigm involves first pairing S1 with a US and then pairing S2 with S1 in the absence of additional US presentations. As has often been noted, this procedure is guaranteed to extinguish the response to S1 at the very time it is being used to condition S2. Most historical attempts to produce second-order conditioning have apparently stumbled over just this problem. Those difficulties have been especially magnified by the fact that many Pavlovian preparations show remarkably rapid extinction of first-order conditioning. Moreover, in many cases that rapid extinction has been further accelerated by the use of highly sophisticated subjects. For instance, Pavlov's studies of higher-order conditioning used dogs who were long-time veterans of salivary experiments. Such animals showed such rapid readjustment to changed reinforcement contingencies that one- or two-trial extinction was not at all unusual.

By contrast, the preparations that we have used for the study of second-order conditioning show relatively slow extinction. With our earlier conditioned suppression experiments, this is probably attributable in part to the use of potent

USs. In that preparation it is easy to show a dependence of the magnitude of initial second-order conditioning on the strength of the original US. With the activity preparation used in many of the experiments reported here, it may be that the measure of conditioning is considerably more sensitive to any learning than is the salivary measure. In any case, the relatively slow loss produced by nonreinforcement, combined with the rapid acquisition produced by reinforcement enables these preparations to establish substantial second-order conditioning prior to the loss in response to the first-order CS.

One can use, of course, a number of techniques to "artificially" maintain the value of S1 in the course of a second-order experiment. Indeed, in our opinion the standard second-order experiment unnecessarily encourages extinction of the response to S1. The intention of removing the US from the experiment at the time of S2–S1 pairings is to prevent the charge of subtle first-order conditioning of S2. However, that intention is equally well served if one retains the US but in such a way that it could not reinforce S2 but could help S1 retain its value. One means of accomplishing this is to intermix with S2–S1 pairings separate "refresher" trials on which S1 is separately paired with the US. With only the most rudimentary knowledge of conditioning, we should be able to make those trials sufficiently distant from S2 as to make implausible any action of the US on it. Such a procedure can, in the preparations discussed here, maintain S1 at a sufficiently high value to deliver effective reinforcement to an antecedent S2 for many trials (Holland & Rescorla, 1975a; Rescorla, 1973a). As those studies show, the danger is not that the US in some subtle way reinforces S2, but just the opposite; the organism eventually discriminates between S1 presentations that are preceded by S2 (and therefore not reinforced) and those that are not (and are therefore reinforced). Consequently, S2 eventually becomes a conditioned inhibitor.

Another means of maintaining the value of S1 is to embed second-order conditioning in a sequence of the form: S2–S1–US. If this is done, one could presumably pick an S2–US interval of sufficient length that, in the absence of the intervening S1, no conditioning would be obtained. However, if S1 fills the S2–US interval, it might then be sufficiently close to the US to receive first-order conditioning and also to S2 to dispense second-order conditioning to it. Although this procedure has not been widely used in the study of second-order conditioning, it presumably describes reasonably well the Pavlovian paradigm involved in most instrumental learning situations. Consequently, the problem of loss of S1 value seems less severe in those situations to which the present application of Pavlovian second-order conditioning is made.

Aside from the real problem of maintenance of the value of S1, our belief in the demonstration of second-order conditioning has suffered from two pieces of bad propoganda. The first was initiated by Pavlov himself. He often described second-order conditioning as temporary and unstable. Given the virtual absence of demonstrations of second-order conditioning since his work, Pavlov's statements have had a powerful negative effect on the reputation of the phenomenon. We have already commented on aspects of Pavlov's experiments that might have led him to underestimate the potency of second-order conditioning. However, it is also worth noting that Pavlov's conception of temporary was somewhat different from that we might employ today. In Pavlov's laboratory experiments were of very long duration, often several years. Over such time periods first-order conditioning was capable of being sustained; by comparison, the fact that second-order conditioning disappeared, often only after many trials, led Pavlov to view it with perhaps undue disdain.

The second piece of misleading propoganda may be described as guilt by association. The phenomenon of secondary instrumental reinforcement has been notorious both in its technical difficulties and its elusiveness of demonstration. One set of reasons for this can be found in the points discussed above; the problem of S1 extinction is especially difficult in instrumental training because the organism typically has considerable control over the frequency of S1's presentation. Moreover, it has only been in recent years that procedures have been developed for the maintenance of S1's value during its use to reinforce antecedent response. However, the failure of many authors to distinguish between second-order Pavlovian conditioning and secondary instrumental reinforcement has cast the shadow of some of those difficulties on the Pavlovian case. This shadow has been particularly important since few Pavlovian studies have been carried out.

Conclusion

The intention of this chapter has been to point to a number of novel implications of second-order Pavlovian conditioning for the performance of instrumental behavior. We have reviewed several studies that illustrate the power and magnitude of second-order Pavlovian conditioning. We have further indicated that such conditioning is surprisingly resistant to changes that might be induced by motivational changes, associative changes in the US value, and changes in the value of the first-order stimulus. Armed with that information, we suggested that the incentive motivational and rewarding role of second-order stimuli may make aspects of instrumental performance equally insensitive to such intrusions. Preliminary results were reported, indicating that indeed responses early in instrumental sequences may be relatively insensitive to motivational changes and that behaviors reinforced by conditioned reinforcers may be insensitive to the current status of those reinforcers. Finally, we suggested that in some instances the manipulation of independent variables in the context of instrumental learning experiments may result in differential establishment of first- and second-order Pavlovian conditioning. Those in turn may emphasize different learned contexts and consequently different bases for that instrumental performance.

Acknowledgments

The research reported here was supported by National Science Foundation Grant GB-28703X. Conversations with Peter C. Holland and C. Donald Heth have helped shape many of the ideas discussed here.

References

Allport, G. W. *Personality: A psychological interpretation.* New York: Henry Holt & Co., 1937.

Bindra, D. A motivational view of learning, performance, and behavior modification. *Psychological Review*, 1974, 81, 199–213.

Coate, W. B. Weakening of conditioned bar-pressing by prior extinction of its subsequent discriminated operant. *Journal of Comparative and Physiological Psychology,* 1956, 49, 135–138.

Crespi, L. P. Quantitative variation of incentives in performance in the white rat. *American Journal of Psychology*, 1942, 55, 467–517.

Denny, M. R. The role of secondary reinforcement in a partial reinforcement learning situation. *Journal of Experimental Psychology*, 1946, 36, 373–389.

Fantino, E. Some data on the discriminative stimulus hypothesis of secondary reinforcement. *Psychological Record*, 1965, 15, 409–415.

Garcia, J., Kovner, R., & Green, K. S. Cue properties versus palatability of flavors in avoidance learning. *Psychonomic Science*, 1970, 20, 313–314.

Gonzales, R. C., & Shepp, B. E. The effect of end box-placement on subsequent performance in the runway with competing responses controlled. *American Journal of Psychology*, 1965, 78, 441–447.

Holland, P. C., & Rescorla, R. A. Second-order conditioning with food unconditioned stimulus. *Journal of Comparative and Physiological Psychology*, 1975, 88, 459–467. (a)

Holland, P. C., & Rescorla, R. A. The effect of two ways of devaluing the unconditioned stimulus after first- and second-order appetitive conditioning. *Journal of Experimental Psychology: Animal Behavior Processes*, 1975, 1, 355–363. (b)

Holman, E. W. Some conditions for the dissociation of consumatory and instrumental behavior in rats. *Learning and Motivation*, 1975, 16, 358–366.

Hull, C. L. *Principles of behavior.* New York: Appleton-Century-Crofts, 1943.

Hull, C. L. *A behavior system.* New Haven: Yale University Press, 1952.

Ison, J. R., Glass, D. H., & Daly, H. D. Reward magnitude changes following differential conditioning and partial reinforcement. *Journal of Experimental Psychology*, 1969, 81, 81–88.

Konorski, J. *Integrative activity of the brain.* Chicago: University of Chicago Press, 1967.

Lindberg, A. A. The report of the Wednesday meeting of November 2, 1932. *Pavlovskie Sredy: Protokoly i stenogrammy fiziologicheskikh besed.* Vol. 1. Moscow: Academy of Sciences of the USSR, 1949. P. 240.

Mackintosh, N. J. *The psychology of animal learning.* New York: Academic Press, 1974.

Miller, N. E. A reply to "sign-Gestalt or conditioned reflex." *Psychological Review*, 1935, 42, 280–292.

Miller, N. E. Studies in fear as an acquirable drive: I. Fear as motivation and fear-reduction as reinforcement in the learning of new responses. *Journal of Experimental Psychology*, 1948, 38, 89–101.

Morgan, M. J. Resistance to satiation. *Animal Behavior*, 1974, 22, 449–466.

Mowrer, O. H. *Learning theory and behavior.* New York: Wiley, 1960.

Pavlov, I. P. *Conditioned reflexes.* (Translated by G. V. Anrep.) London: Oxford University Press, 1927.

Rescorla, R. A. Second-order conditioning: Implications for theories of learning. In F. J. McGuigan & E. B. Lumsden (Eds.), *Contemporary approaches to conditioning and learning.* Washington, D.C.: V. H. Winston, 1973. (a)

Rescorla, R. A. Effect of US habituation following conditioning. *Journal of Comparative and Physiological Psychology*, 1973, **82**, 137–143. (b)

Rescorla, R. A. Effect of inflation of the unconditioned stimulus value following conditioning. *Journal of Comparative and Physiological Psychology*, 1974, **86**, 101–106.

Rescorla, R. A., & Heth, C. D. Reinstatement of fear to an extinguished conditioned stimulus. *Journal of Experimental Psychology: Animal Behavior Processes*, 1975, **104**, 88–96.

Rescorla, R. A., & Solomon, R. L. Two-process learning theory: Relationships between Pavlovian conditioning and instrumental learning. *Psychological Review*, 1967, **74**, 151–182.

Rizley, R. C., & Rescorla, R. A. Associations in second-order conditioning and sensory preconditioning. *Journal of Comparative and Physiological Psychology*, 1972, **81**, 1–11.

Schoenfeld, W. N. An experimental approach to anxiety, escape and avoidance behavior. In P. H. Hoch & J. Zubin (Eds.), *Anxiety.* New York: Grune and Stratton, 1950.

Schlosberg, H., & Pratt, C. H. The secondary reward value of inaccessible food for hungry and satiated rats. *Journal of Comparative and Physiological Psychology*, 1956, **49**, 149–152.

Seward, J. P., & Levy, N. Latent extinction: Sign learning as a factor in extinction. *Journal of Experimental Psychology*, 1949, **39**, 660–668.

Sheffield, F. B., & Campbell, B. A. The role of experience in the "spontaneous" activity of hungry rats. *Journal of Comparative and Physiological Psychology*, 1954, **47**, 97–100.

Skinner, B. F. *Science and human behavior.* New York: Macmillan, 1953.

Spear, N. E., & Spitzner, J. H. Simultaneous and successive contrast effects of reward magnitude in selective learning. *Psychological Monographs*, 1966, **80**(Whole No. 618).

Spence, K. W. *Behavior theory and conditioning.* New Haven, Connecticut: Yale University Press, 1956.

Tolman, E. C. *Purposive behavior in animals and men.* New York: Century, 1932.

Tolman, E. C., & Gleitman, H. Studies in learning and motivation: I. Equal reinforcements in both end-boxes, followed by shock in one end-box. *Journal of Experimental Psychology*, 1949, **39**, 810–819.

Wagner, A. R. Effects of amount of percentage of reinforcement in number of acquisition trials on conditioning and extinction. *Journal of Experimental Psychology*, 1961, **62**, 234–242.

Zamble, E. Classical conditioning of excitement anticipatory to food reward. *Journal of Comparative and Physiological Psychology*, 1967, **63**, 526–529.

Zimmer-Hart, C. L. An investigation of first-order principles in second-order conditioning. Unpublished doctoral dissertation, Yale University, 1974.

Zimmerman, J., Hanford, P. Z., & Brown, W. Effects of conditioned reinforcement frequency in an intermittent free-feeding situation. *Journal of the Experimental Analysis of Behavior*, 1967, **10**, 313–340.

7
The Safety Signal Hypothesis

Martin E. P. Seligman
Yitzchak M. Binik

University of Pennsylvania

INTRODUCTION

This chapter stems from Seligman's continuing interest in the psychological consequences of different shock delivery procedures. It is now widely accepted that the procedural conditions surrounding delivery of an aversive event are at least as important in determining its effect on behavior as the physical properties of the aversive event itself. Seligman has focused on two dimensions along which shock delivery procedures may vary: predictability of shock and the degree to which the subject can control the onset or offset of shock.

The following chapter describes and compares three hypotheses that deal with the disruptive effects of unpredictable and uncontrollable shock on an organism's behavior. After considering the role of preparatory responses and uncertainty reduction, Seligman and Binik opt for an explanation that streses the role of safety signals in modulating the effects of aversive events.

What is the psychological difference between predictable and unpredictable aversive events? Three hypotheses have been offered: Preparatory response, safety signal, and uncertainty reduction. We shall opt for the safety signal hypothesis and in doing so shall present the direct and indirect evidence for it. Along the way, we shall compare the safety signal hypothesis to the other theories. We begin by explicitly spelling out the safety signal hypothesis.

When aversive events are presented to animals, fear and pain occur. The safety signal hypothesis specifies why fear is limited in space and time. Consider a typical Pavlovian conditioning situation, where a CS+ reliably predicts a US. The probability of the US given the CS+ is 1.0, and the probability of the US given the absence of the CS+ is zero. If the US is an aversive event, such as electric shock, the CS+ perfectly predicts danger and the absence of the CS+ perfectly predicts safety. Safety is defined as US free periods. So after asymptotic exposure to this situation, the safety signal hypothesis predicts fear during the CS+ and no fear in its absence.

We shall usually talk about situations with one explicit CS, such as a tone; but the logic of the argument applies *in toto* to situations in which more than one explicit CS occurs and to situations in which a temporal pattern or feedback from a response is the CS.

In contrast, consider a situation in which the US is unpredictable. Here by definition the probability of the US given any event is equal to the probability of the US in the absence of that event. In this situation, no stimulus reliably predicts safety. The safety signal hypothesis predicts, in the absence of a reliable predictor of safety, the subject to remain chronically in fear. So the fundamental psychological event that limits fear is the perception of being in the presence of stimuli that reliably predict the absence of aversive events.

It has become clear in the past decade that animals in Pavlovian conditioning situations learn not only that a stimulus predicts a US (excitation) but also that a stimulus paired with the absence of the US predicts no US (inhibition). (See, for example, Boakes & Halliday, 1972; Bolles, 1970; Denny, 1971; Maier, Seligman, & Solomon, 1969; Rescorla, 1967.) Stimuli paired with the absence of shock, safety signals, can inhibit shock avoidance behavior (e.g., Rescorla & Lolordo, 1965) and can serve as positive reinforcers (e.g., Weissman & Litner, 1971). Figure 7.1 illustrates the relationship of predictable and unpredictable USs.

The uncertainty reduction hypothesis (Berlyne, 1960) claims that organisms are motivated to reduce uncertainty. This hypothesis makes very similar predictions to the safety signal hypothesis, with two exceptions:

1. Uncertainty reduction directly predicts that organisms will choose predictable over unpredictable shock. Similarly, the safety signal hypothesis makes the same prediction with the trivial assumption that less fear is preferred to more fear. The uncertainty reduction hypothesis, however, does not directly predict more fear to occur in unpredictable shock situations; it needs the nontrivial additional assumption that uncertainty results in fear.

2. The uncertainty reduction hypothesis is more general than the safety signal hypothesis. It predicts preference for predictability over unpredictability regardless of the hedonic sign of the US—aversive, appetitive, or even "neutral."

We believe that uncertainty reduction, unlike the safety signal hypothesis, predicts preference for a situation in which the $p(US/CS) = 1.0$ and $p(US/\overline{CS}) = 0$ over a situation in which $p(US/CS) = .5$ and $p(US/\overline{CS}) = 0$, where equal numbers of USs occur in both situations. We know of no experiment that has tested this. Otherwise, because of the overlap in predictions of the two hypotheses, we shall have little more to say about uncertainty reduction.

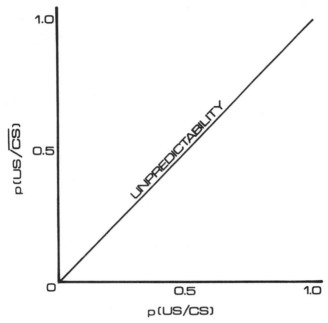

FIG. 7.1 The US is unpredictable when the probability of the US given the CS(p[US/CS])
is equal to the probability of the US given the absence of that CS(p[US/$\overline{\text{CS}}$]). Whenever the
situation does not fall along the 45° line, either the CS or its absence makes the US
relatively predictable.

The preparatory response hypothesis (Perkins, 1955) claims that when events
are predictable the subject can make an instrumental response during the CS+,
which modifies the intensity of the US. In the case of aversive USs, the
preparatory response renders them less painful, whereas it renders appetitive USs
more pleasurable. This hypothesis, like the other two, directly predicts preference for predictable aversive events. However, it needs a major additional
assumption to account for more fear occurring in unpredictable situations:
overall, somewhat more fear may occur when USs are unpredictable because the
US is more intense. As to the temporal distribution of the additional fear,
however, the hypothesis is silent.

It should be noted that all studies comparing predictable and unpredictable
shock cannot be evaluated by all theories. Neither the safety signal nor the
uncertainty reduction hypothesis makes direct predictions about the unconditioned response to a signaled versus unsignaled US, whereas the preparatory
response hypothesis does. Furthermore, the safety signal hypothesis is only
relevant to studies where there is a clear demarcation for the subject between
signaled and unsignaled shock. This excludes many studies that randomly pre-

periods of signaled and unsignaled shock. This excludes studies that randomly present signaled and unsignaled shocks to the same subject (e.g., Furedy, 1970; Furedy & Doob, 1971, 1972; Lykken, 1962). In such studies, the absence of the CS is not a safety signal, because unsignaled shocks can occur during this period. In addition, none of the three hypotheses is relevant to studies where signaled vs. unsignaled differences do not reflect associative factors (e.g., Badia & Culbertson, 1971; Badia, Culbertson, Defran, & Lewis, 1971; Badia, Lewis, & Suter, 1967; Badia, Suter, & Lewis, 1967).

Response Suppression

The most direct confirmation of the safety signal hypothesis comes from observations of the amount and temporal distribution of fear during predictable and unpredictable shock. Several dependent variables have been used as indices of "fear" in these studies: suppression of bar pressing for food (CER), suppression of licking or "basal emotional level" (BEL), and galvanic skin response (GSR). This is not the place to dispute the relationship of these measures to the hypothetical construct of "fear." Suffice it to say that we find "fear" as viable a construct as such notions as "hunger" or "learning."

Azrin (1956), Brimer and Kamin (1963), Davis and McIntire (1969), Holmes, Jackson, and Byrum (1971); Seligman (1968), Seligman and Meyer (1970); Shimoff, Shoenfeld, and Snapper (1969), and Weiss and Strongman (1969)[1] all compared suppression of instrumental responding for food during predictable or unpredictable shock. The results of all studies have been uniform, so here we only detail the Seligman (1968) study. Two groups of hungry rats first learned to bar press for food on a VI schedule. The predictable (PR) group then received 15 50-min sessions during which three 1-min CSs ended in .88 mA shock. The unpredictable group (UN) received the same CS and shocks but randomly interspersed. Food was available on the VI schedule throughout. At first, the PR group suppressed in both the presence and the absence of the CS. As they learned to discriminate between CS+shock and no CS+no shock periods, they suppressed only during the CS and pressed for food during the safety signal. In contrast, the UN group stopped pressing completely both during CS and during its absence and did not recover. Figure 7.2 presents these results.

Davis and McIntire (1969) found some recovery of bar pressing in their unpredictable group. Seligman and Meyer (1970), however, speculated that recovery might have been caused by the fact that a constant number of shocks (three) occurred in each session. The rats might have learned that after the third shock, no further shock—safety—would occur. Therefore, recovery would occur only after the third shock and would actually confirm the safety signal hypo-

---

[1] See also MacDonald and Baron (1973) and Hoffman and Fleshler (1965) for evidence that unpredictable shocks produce more generalized suppression than predictable shocks.

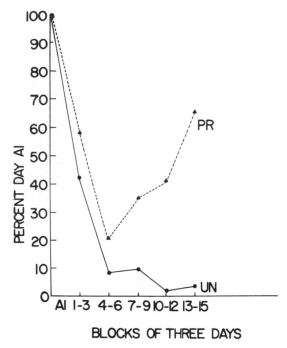

FIG. 7.2   Mean percentage of Day A1 (baseline) bar pressing for blocks of 3 days.

thesis. A paper by Davis, Memmott, and Hurwitz (1975) extends this analysis and offers additional support for the safety signal hypothesis.

Seligman and Meyer (1970) therefore gave two groups 70 sessions of unpredictable shock. One group received exactly three unpredictable shocks per day, whereas the other received a mean of three shocks with a range of one to five unpredictable shocks. During the last 30 days, the three-shock group showed some recovery: they did 61.6% of all their bar pressing during the 25% of the session that occurred after the third shock. The one- to five-shock groups did not recover: they did 25.1% of what little bar pressing they did during the 25% of the session that remained after the third shock. So rats apparently can "count" to three and use the occurrence of the third shock as a safety signal.

Imada and Soga (1971) confirmed these results with Japanese rats using suppression of licking (BEL). As with bar pressing, thirsty rats receiving unpredictable shock showed greatly reduced licking over 36 days and showed no signs of recovery.

Several studies have looked at GSR in humans during predictable and unpredictable shock sessions (Averill & Rosenn, 1972; Geer, 1968; Glass & Singer, 1972; Price and Geer, 1972). Unpredictable shock groups showed more arousal as measured by GSR during intershock intervals than the predictable groups during their non-CS intervals. This directly indicates more fear in the absence of a safety signal than its presence.

In a behavioral study, Badia and Culbertson (1970) delivered predictable and unpredictable shock to rats in both between and within group designs. Between shocks, rats in the predictable group were in the presence of a safety signal, the absence of the signal for shock. During this period they explored the chamber. In contrast, rats receiving unpredictable shock had no safety signal between shocks, and they explored the chamber less (see also Bolles & Moot, 1970). In this study bar pressing escaped shock for both groups. The unpredictable group tended to hold on to the bar for much more of each session than the predictable group. If we assume that fear of shock has motivated bar holding, it follows that the group in chronic fear, the unpredictable group, should hold the bar more than the group that has had a safety signal.

Paré and Livingston (1973) monitored stomach acidity during predictable and unpredictable shock and found that unpredictable shock inhibited gastric secretion of acid more than predictable. In addition, restraint inhibited acid more than no restraint, and shock inhibited acid more than no shock. This suggests that acid inhibition may reflect increased fear. If we make this tentative assumption, these results follow directly from the safety signal hypothesis. However, the validity of this measure is yet to be confirmed.

The fact that more fear occurs with unpredictable shock and that the temporal locus of this fear is the intershock interval, during which no safety signal is present, directly support the safety signal hypothesis. Uncertainty reduction might be consistent with the greater amount of fear if it added the premise that uncertainty caused fear. Because the locus of uncertainty is the intershock interval, more fear would then occur during this period. This version of the uncertainty reduction hypothesis is virtually identical with the safety signal hypothesis. As mentioned above, the preparatory response hypothesis could be made consistent with greater overall fear in the unpredictable group. However, we do not see how it can encompass the fact that fear is uniformly high in the intershock interval.

Studies of stomach ulceration also provide strong evidence for the safety signal hypothesis (Caul, Buchanan, & Hays, 1972; Mezinskis, Gliner, & Shemberg, 1971; Price, 1972; Seligman, 1968; Seligman & Meyer, 1970; Weiss, 1970, 1971a, b, c). These studies generally show more ulcers with unpredictable shock, and we shall assume that more ulcers reflect more fear. Because ulceration studies only yield one final measure of stress, they do not provide as direct evidence as the studies reviewed above, which monitor fear continuously.

Weiss' work is most extensive, so we shall detail it here. In a series of experiments, Weiss (1970) studied a variety of stress responses to predictable and unpredictable shock. Triads of rats were restrained and exposed to predictable, unpredictable, or no shock delivered through attached tail electrodes in one extended session. Rats receiving unpredictable shock formed many more ulcers than rats receiving predictable or no shock. Increased body temperature and elevated plasma corticosterone were also associated with unpredictable shock, but not as strikingly. Mezinskis *et al.* (1971) confirmed these ulceration findings with both fixed and variable shock durations. Price (1972) confirmed these results using a 6 hr on, 6 hr off stress schedule. When rats were unrestrained, however, ulceration differences did not occur and gastric pathology was generally mild.

Seligman (1968) and Seligman and Meyer (1970) measured ulceration along with CER in their studies of unrestrained rats. After many repeated 50-min sessions, rats receiving unpredictable shock had more ulcers than rats receiving predictable shock. A note of caution is in order, however. Because the rats receiving unpredictable shock suppressed bar pressing more, they had less food in their stomachs during the shock sessions. This may have artifactually amplified ulceration differences.

Weiss (1971a, b, c) has reported a set of intriguing data on the effects of the availability of a coping response on ulceration. We find Weiss' theory needlessly elaborate and argue that it reduces to the safety signal hypothesis. Weiss (1971a) exposed triads of rats to escapable/avoidable, inescapable, or no shock. A wheel was present in the small chamber for all groups but served as the instrumental response for only the escape/avoidance group. Shocks are either signaled, "progressively signaled," or unsignaled. We shall omit consideration of the "progressively signaled" group, because its results do not differ from the signaled group. Therefore, we basically have the 3 X 2 factorial design seen in Table 7.1.

a. *Predictability difference.* There were more ulcers with unsignaled than with signaled shock for both yoked and escape/avoidance groups.

b. *Controllability difference.* There were more ulcers with yoked inescapable shock than with escape/avoidance in both signaled and unsignaled conditions. Strangely, and without comment, Weiss (1971c) failed to replicate this in the unsignaled condition.

TABLE 7.1
Mean Number of Wheel Turns and Stomach Ulcers[a, b]

	No shock	Escape/avoidance	Yoked
Signaled shock	1.0 60	2.0 3,717	3.5 1,404
Unsignaled shock	1.0 51	3.5 13,992	6.0 4,357

[a]From Weiss (1971a).
[b]Top left numbers indicate median ulcers; bottom right numbers indicate median wheel turns.

c. *Wheel turning frequency.* More wheel turns were made in the unsignaled than in the signaled groups in both yoked and escape/avoidance conditions. More wheel turns were made in escape/avoidance than in yoked conditions, in both signaled and unsignaled groups.

d. *Correlation of wheel turning with ulcers.* The increased ulceration with unpredictability corresponded to more wheel turns with unpredictability. Weiss claimed, but failed to document adequately, that the more responses an individual subject made in any group, the more ulcers he showed.

Weiss (1971a) proposed two multiplicative factors to account for these results: (a) the less "relevant feedback," the more ulcers; (b) the more "coping" responses a subject makes, the more ulcers.

We believe that these two factors boil down to the safety signal hypothesis. Consider first the concept of "relevant feedback" that is proposed to account for the controllability differences. "Relevant feedback" is defined as a stimulus, which follows the response, that is not associated with the stressor. In fact, the stimuli to which Weiss (1971a, c) refers are associated with the absence of the stressor. They are safety signals. Therefore, an animal that escapes shock presents himself with a safety signal, the absence of shock, and this reduces ulceration.

The second factor, "the more 'coping' responses the more ulcers," is proposed to account for the predictability difference and the purported correlation of ulcers and number of wheel turns. Now there are two very different ways this factor can be construed, causally or correlationally. Causally, it would mean that actually making more responses produces more ulcers, with the message that if you force yourself to sit passively through shock you are not likely to ulcerate. This is the interesting sense that Weiss seems to opt for. The other is more descriptive and shallow but more tenable: that some third factor causes both high response rate and ulceration. There is a prime candidate for such a third factor, which Weiss himself proposes to criticize Brady's (1958) executive monkey study: Animals that are more emotional, more afraid, or more pained by the shock both are more reactive (turn the wheel more) and ulcerate more (Sines, Cleeland, & Adkins, 1963).

Recall that rats receiving unpredictable shock ulcerated more and responded more than rats receiving predictable shock in the corresponding controllability conditions. Weiss would have us believe that they ulcerated more because they responded more. In contrast, the safety signal hypothesis explains both why they ulcerated more and why they responded more (a question that Weiss never addresses). If turning the wheel is an index of fear, as bar holding seems to be in the Badia and Culbertson (1970) study, then unsignaled groups should wheel turn more because they have no safety signal. Signaled groups should wheel turn only during their danger signal. So the greater amount of fear caused by the absence of a safety signal produces both more wheel turning and more ulceration.

As for the correlation between individual wheel turning and ulceration, it if exists, it is reasonable to believe that more emotional subjects are likely to wheel turn more. (This is part of the substance of Weiss' 1971c, criticism of Brady, (1958.) This greater emotionality will produce both more ulceration and, as a byproduct, more wheel turning. Therefore, it will not do you any good to refrain from responding to prevent ulcers.

In summary, Weiss' theory reduces to the safety signal hypothesis. Relevant feedback is synonymous with safety signals, and the amount of responding reflects the lack of safety signals.

Preference for Predictable Shock

All three hypotheses under consideration predict preference for predictable over unpredictable shock. The safety signal hypothesis predicts this because unsignaled shock engenders chronic fear, whereas signaled shock engenders fear only during the signal for shock and no fear in the absence of the signal. So, with conventional parameters, in which duration of ITI is much greater than duration of the danger signal, less total fear occurs with signaled shock. The uncertainty reduction hypothesis also predicts this preference, because there is less uncertainty about what is to happen during signaled shock. Different amounts of fear do not mediate the preference, and it is not clear to us what mechanism is supposed to do so. The preparatory response hypothesis predicts preference for signaled shock because the subject can make a well-timed preparatory response during the signal, which lessens painfulness of the shock. The presence of safety is a matter of indifference. We know of no well-defined hypothesis that does not predict a preference for signaled shock.

A number of studies have examined this preference in rats (Badia, Coker, & Harsh, 1973; Badia & Culbertson, 1972; Badia, Culbertson, & Harsh, 1973; Furedy & Walters, 1970; Lockard, 1963, 1965; Perkins, Seymann, Levis, & Spencer, 1966). All of these studies point in the direction of preference for signaled shock. Badia and his collaborators have performed the most extensive and methodologically exemplary studies (see also Arabian and Desiderato, 1975). They also gathered evidence that teases apart the safety signal and preparatory response hypotheses. We detail one typical study here (Badia & Culbertson, 1972, Experiment Two.) Seven rats are exposed to a choice between signaled versus unsignaled 0.5-sec inescapable shocks. During unsignaled shock, a correlated stimulus (e.g., a white light) was present and shocks occurred at random intervals averaging 2 min. No warning stimulus predicted exactly when the shock would occur, so no safety was present during the correlated stimulus. Pressing a bar brought the rat into the presence of the complementary stimulus (e.g., the absence of the white light). This stimulus was correlated with signaled shock: The same density of shocks as above occurred, but now each shock was immediately preceded by a tone. Therefore, the absence of light without the tone is a safety signal, and the absence of light with the tone is a danger signal. All rats developed a marked preference for the signaled shock.

Three extinction (Ext) procedures were then run. In the first, pressing the bar no longer changed the schedule, so that the rat remained in the unsignaled condition no matter what he did. All rats stopped pressing. In the second and most intriguing extinction condition, bar pressing produced the stimulus correlated with signaled shock (absence of light), but unsignaled shock now occurred. Here the rats are in the presence of the safety signal but cannot prepare themselves for shock because the tone does not occur. This procedure plays the power of the safety signal off against the power of the preparatory response. All rats showed a strong preference for the safety signal, even without the tone. This preference could not have been caused by a preparatory response, because it was precluded by the absence of the tone. In the third extinction procedure, a bar press produced shock preceded by the tone but did not produce absence of light. Here, the safety signal (absence of light) did not come on, but shocks were preceded by the danger stimulus. Again preparatory responses are played off against safety signals, because the rats can now prepare themselves during the tone if they press the bar, but they get no safety signal. The rats did not press the bar. So producing a safety signal is necessary (Ext 3) and sufficient (Ext 2) for preference, and having the opportunity to make a preparatory response is neither necessary (Ext 2) nor sufficient (Ext 3). Similar experiments by Badia and his colalborators have also shown that four to nine times as long a signaled shock is preferred to an unsignaled shock, as well as two to three times as intense a shock (Badia, Coker, & Harsh, 1973; Badia, Culbertson, & Harsh, 1973). It would take a mighty effective, unobserved, preparatory response to explain this quantitative difference, whereas the safety signal hypothesis easily explains it.

Studies with humans conflict on the preference for predictable shock. Pervin (1963), Jones, Bentler, and Petry (1966), and Lanzetta and Driscoll (1966) find preference for predictable over unpredictable shock periods. Badia et al. (1967), however, found at best a weak preference for signaled shock, and Averill and Rosenn (1972) found that half their subjects consistently preferred predictable and half unpredictable shock. When preference for predictable shock is found, two subjective reports are prominent: Subjects say (a) that they can better prepare for the shock when it is signaled and (b) when the safety signal is present they can relax (Pervin, 1963; Badia et al., 1967). We should mention that the safety signal hypothesis and the preparatory response hypothesis are not mutually exclusive. It is possible that an individual can both lessen shock by some preparatory response and relax during safety.

There exists a literature on preference for immediately delivered shock over fixed or variably delayed shock. All three hypotheses predict a preference for immediate shock because the onset of shock is more predictable with immediate than with delayed shock. Using humans, Badia, McBane, Suter, and Lewis (1966), Cook and Barnes (1964), D'Amato and Gumenik (1960), Hare (1966), and Maltzman and Wolff (1970) all find a preference for immediate over delayed shock. The animal literature, however, conflicts: Knapp, Kause, and Perkins (1959) have found that rats prefer immediate to delayed inescapable shock. Renner and Specht (1967) and Renner and Houlihan (1969), however, found preference for delayed shock when the rats were forced to remain in the shock chamber following immediate shock. Only when the rats were allowed to leave the chamber following immediate shock did a preference for immediate shock occur. Interestingly, with extended trials (approximately 500), the preferences disappeared. Frankly, we do not know what the resolution of the apparent contradiction between Renner et al. and Perkins et al. is, but it is indifferent to the comparison of the three hypotheses, which all predict preference for immediate shock.

In general, therefore, preference is found for predictable over unpredictable shock. This evidence does not differentiate among the three hypotheses, with the exception of Badia's evidence (and Arabian and Desiderato's), which points toward the safety signal hypothesis.

Problems for the Safety Signal Hypothesis

It would be nice to stop here and conclude that direct measurement of fear and preference data generally favors the safety signal hypothesis. Instead we must point out two kinds of problems this hypothesis has: (a) empirical and (b) logical.

Weight loss has often been taken as a measure of stress, and we may expect greater weight loss with unpredictable than with predictable shock. Only Weiss (1970, Experiment Three; 1971a) and Price (1972) have reported such a finding. In contrast, Brady and Esty (1963); Brady, Thornton, and DeFisher (1962); Friedman and Ader (1965); and Weiss (1970, Experiment Four; 1971b, c) either find no significant difference or the opposite effect. Similarly, Spigel and Ramsay (1970) reported a greater excretory alkalai metal response (EAMR) in the turtle with temporally patterned as opposed to unpatterned shocks. EAMR has occasionally been thought to indicate stress in rats. Finally, Bowers (1971) reported a lower heart rate when humans expected a temporally uncertain shock than when they expected a certain one. We conclude that the relationship of weight loss, EAMR, and increased heart rate to "stress" remains unclear.

The safety signal hypothesis also has a couple of logical problems. The first has to do with vagueness in specifying intensity of fear during unpredictable shock. Recall that the preference for signaled shock depended on there being less total fear during signaled shock. In a typical signaled shock procedure, the total duration of danger signals is far less than the total duration of ITI safety signals (e.g., three 1-min CS+s versus 47 min of ITI in a 50-min session). In contrast, the duration of fear would be 50 min in an unsignaled procedure. However, is the intensity of fear during any moment of the CS+ the same as the intensity during any moment of the more extended fear in the unsignaled procedure? We do not yet know. When it is 3-min versus 50-min intensity, differences should not matter much. With longer durations of signaled shock, however, differential intensities might be seen. If we increased the number of shocks and the duration of CSs in a signaled procedure of fixed session length, we would not be surprised to find a point at which indifference or preference for unsignaled shock occurred. Such results would show that acute fear could be more intense than chronic fear and might yield a method for scaling their respective intensities. Seligman and Meyer (1970) found that when shock was mild, amount of suppression to the CS predicting shock was greater than chronic suppression in the unpredictable condition. When shock was intense, chronic and acute suppression were both complete, indicating a ceiling effect. These data indicate that at least with mild shock, acute fear is more intense than chronic fear.

Finally we would pose the strange but deep question of why a stimulus paired with unpredictable shock should produce chronic fear as opposed to chronic relief? After all both shock and its absence occur during the stimulus. To highlight this question, consider the appetitive parallel: food is presented unpredictably to a hungry animal. [Predictable food, incidentally, seems to be preferred to unpredictable food (e.g., Prokasy, 1956).] The stimulus occurs both with hunger and its offset. One could predict unpredictable food to result either in chronic hunger or in chronic relief of hunger depending on whether one emphasized the unpredictability of the food onset or the unpredictability of the duration of the hunger. No straightforward "safety signal" prediction is demanded in the appetitive case (see Seligman, Maier, & Solomon, 1971, pp. 385–386, versus Hershiser & Trapold, 1971 for opposite deductions). Therefore, if the background stimuli in an unpredictable shock situation co-occur with shock onset, offset, and absence, why do the fear-evoking properties of shock onset become conditioned instead of the relief properties of offset and absence? Our answer is not wholly satisfactory: Animals happen to be built that way. It makes evolutionary sense that in a situation in which noxious events occur unpredictably, animals remain in fear until they find a reliable predictor of safety instead of remaining complacent until they find a more reliable predictor of danger.

Acknowledgments

This contribution was supported by National Institute of Mental Health Grants MH19604 and MH0829, a Guggenheim Foundation Fellowship and National Science Foundation Grant SOC 74-12063.

References

Arabian, J., & Desiderato, O. Preference for signaled shock. A test of two hypotheses. *Animal Learning and Behavior,* 1975, **3**, 191–195.

Averill, J. R., & Rosenn, M. Vigilant and nonvigilant coping strategies and psychophysiological stress reactions during the anticipation of electric shock. *Journal of Personality and Social Psychology*, 1972, **23**, 128–141.

Azrin, N. H. Some effects of two intermittent schedules of immediate and non-immediate punishment. *Journal of Psychology*, 1956, **42**, 3–21.

Badia, P., Coker, C., & Harsh, J. Choice of higher density signalled shock over lower density unsignalled shock. *Journal of the Experimental Analysis of Behavior*, 1973, **19**, 25–31.

Badia, P., & Culbertson, S. Behavioral effects of signalled vs. unsignalled shock during escape training in the rat. *Journal of Comparative and Physiological Psychology*, 1970, **72**(2), 216–222.

Badia, P., & Culbertson, S. Stimulus induced attenuation of rat vocalization to shock. *Psychonomic Science*, 1971, **22**, 267–268.

Badia, P., & Culbertson, S. The relative aversiveness of signalled vs. unsignalled escapable and inescapable shock. *Journal of the Experimental Analysis of Behavior*, 1972, **17**, 463–471.

Badia, P., Culbertson, S., Defran, R., & Lewis, P. Attenuation of rat vocalizations to shock by a stimulus: Sensory interaction effects. *Journal of Comparative and Physiological Psychology*, 1971, **76**, 131–136.

Badia, P., Culbertson, S., & Harsh, J. Choice of longer or stronger signalled shock over shorter or weaker unsignalled shock. *Journal of the Experimental Analysis of Behavior*, 1973, **19**, 25–33.

Badia, P., Lewis, P., & Suter, S. Suppression of rat vocalizations to shock by an auditory CS. *Psychological Reports*, 1967, **20**, 1063–1067.

Badia, P., McBane, B., Suter, S., & Lewis, P. Preference behavior in an immediate vs. variably delayed shock situations with and without a warning signal. *Journal of Experimental Psychology*, 1966, **72**, 847–852.

Badia, P., Suter, S., & Lewis, P. Preference for warned shock: Information and/or preparation. *Psychological Reports*, 1967, **20**, 271–274.

Berlyne, D. E. *Conflict, arousal and curiosity*. New York: McGraw-Hill, 1960.

Boakes, R. A., & Halliday, M. S. (Eds.) *Inhibition and learning.* New York: Academic Press, 1972.

Bolles, R. C. Species specific defense reactions and avoidance learning. *Psychological Review*, 1970, **77**, 32–48.

Bolles, R. C., & Moot, S. A. Response repertoire changes to signalled and unsignalled shock. Paper presented at the Psychonomic Society Meeting, San Antonio, Texas, November 1970.

Bowers, K. S. The effects of UCS temporal uncertainty on heart rate and pain. *Psychophysiology*, 1971 **8**(1), 382–389.

Brady, J. P., & Esty, J. F. Social parameters of anxiety in the rat. *Recent Advances in Biological Psychiatry*, 1963, **5**, 175–183.

Brady, J. P., Thornton, D. R., & DeFisher, D. Deleterious effects of anxiety elicited by conditioned pre-aversive stimuli in the rat. *Psychomatic Medicine*, 1962, **24**, 590–595.

Brady, J. V. Ulcers in "executive" monkeys. *Scientific American,* 1958, **199**, 95–100.

Brimer, C. J., & Kamin, L. J. Disinhibition, habituation, sensitization, and the conditioned emotional response. *Journal of Comparative and Physiological Psychology*, 1963, **56**, 508–510.

Caul, W. F., Buchanan, D. C., & Hays, R. C. Effects of unpredictability of shock on incidence of gastric lesions and heart rate in immobilized rats. *Physiology and Behavior*, 1972, **8**, 669–672.

Cook, J., & Barnes, L. W. Choice of delay of inevitable shock. *Journal of Abnormal and Social Psychology*, 1964, **68**, 669–672.

D'Amato, M. R., & Gumenik, W. E. Some effects of immediate versus randomly delayed shock on an instrumental response and cognitive processes. *Journal of Abnormal and Social Psychology*, 1960, **60**, 64–67.

Davis, H., & McIntire, R. W. Conditioned suppression under positive, negative, and no contingency between conditioned and unconditioned stimuli. *Journal of the Experimental Analysis of Behavior*, 1969, **12**, 633–640.

Davis, H., Memmott, J., & Hurwitz, H. M. B. Autocontingencies: A model for subtle behavioral control. *Journal of Experimental Psychology: General*, 1975, **104**, 169–188.

Denny, M. R. Relaxation theory and experiments. In F. R. Brush (Ed.), *Aversive conditioning and learning.* New York: Academic Press, 1971. Pp. 235–295.

Friedman, S. F., & Ader, R. A. Parameters relevant to the experimental production of stress in the mouse. *Psychosomatic Medicine*, 1965, **27**, 27–30.

Furedy, J. J. A test of the preparatory-adaptive-response interpretation of aversive classical autonomic conditioning. *Journal of Experimental Psychology*, 1970, **84**, 301–307.

Furedy, J. J., & Doob, A. N. Autonomic responses and verbal reports in further tests of the preparatory-adaptive-response interpretation of reinforcement. *Journal of Experimental Psychology*, 1971, **89**, 403–404.

Furedy, J. J., & Doob, A. N. Signalling unmodifiable shock limits on human informational cognitive control. *Journal of Personality and Social Psychology*, 1972, **21**, 111–115.

Furedy, J. J., & Walters, B. C. Preference for signalled, supposedly-unmodifiable shock as a function of scrambling the grid. Paper presented at the Psychonomic Society Meeting, San Antonio, Texas, November, 1970.

Geer, J. H. A test of the classical conditioning model of emotion: the use of non-painful aversive stimuli as UCSs in a conditioning procedure. *Journal of Personality and Social Psychology*, 1968, **10**, 148–156.

Glass, D. C., & Singer, J. E. *Urban condition: Experiments on noise and social stressor.* New York: Academic Press, 1972.

Hare, R. D. Preference for delay of shock as a function of its intensity and probability. *Psychonomic Science*, 1966, **5**, 393–394.

Hershiser, D., & Trapold, M. A. Preference for unsignalled over signalled direct reinforcement in the rat. *Journal of Comparative and Physiological Psychology*, 1971, **77**(2), 323–332.

Hoffman, H. S., & Fleshler, M. Stimulus aspects of aversive controls: The effects of response contingent shock. *Journal of the Experimental Analysis of Behavior*, 1965, 8, 89–96.

Holmes, P. A., Jackson, D. E., & Byrum, R. P. Acquisition and extinction of conditioned suppression under two training procedures. *Learning and Motivation*, 1971, **2**, 334–340.

Imada, H., & Soga, M. The CER and BEL as a function of the predictability and escapability of an electric shock. *Japanese Psychological Research*, 1971, **13**(3), 116–123.

Jones, A., Bentler, P. M., & Petry, G. The reduction of uncertainty concerning future pain. *Journal of Abnormal Psychology*, 1966, **71**(2), 87–94.

Knapp, R. K., Kause, R. H., & Perkins, C. C. Immediate vs. delayed shock in T-maze performance. *Journal of Experimental Psychology*, 1959, **58**, 357–362.

Lanzetta, J. T., & Driscoll, J. M. Preference for information about an uncertain but unavoidable outcome. *Journal of Personality and Social Psychology*, 1966, **3**, 96–102.

Lockard, J. S. Choice of warning signal or no warning signal in an unavoidable shock situation. *Journal of Comparative and Physiological Psychology*, 1963, **56**, 526–530.

Lockard, J. S. Choice of a warning signal or none in several unavoidable shock situations. *Psychonomic Science*, 1965, **3**, 5–6.

Lykken, D. T. Preception in the rat: Autonomic response to shock as function of length of warning interval. *Science*, 1962, **137**, 136–137.

MacDonald, L., & Baron, A. À rate measure of the relative aversiveness of signalled vs. unsignalled shock. *Journal of the Experimental Analysis of Behavior*, 1973, **19**, 33–38.

Maier, S. F., Seligman, M. E. P., & Solomon, R. L. Pavlovian fear conditioning and learned helplessness. In B. A. Campbell & R. M. Church (Eds.), *Punishment and aversive behavior.* New York: Appleton, 1969. Pp. 299–343.

Maltzman, I., & Wolff, C. Preference for immediate versus delayed noxious stimulation and the concommitant GSR. *Journal of Experimental Psychology*, 1970, 83, 76–79.

Mezinskis, J., Gliner, J., & Shemberg, K. Somatic response as a function of no signal, random signal, or signalled shock with variable or constant durations of shock. *Psychonomic Science*, 1971, 25(5), 271–272.

Paré, W. P., & Livingston, A. Shock predictability and gastric secretion in the chronic gastric fistula rat. *Physiology and Behavior*, 1973, 11, 52–56.

Perkins, C. C. The stimulus conditions which follow learned responses. *Psychological Review*, 1955, 62, 341–348.

Perkins, C. C., Seymann, R., Levis, D. J., & Spencer, R. Factors affecting preference for signal shock over shock signal. *Journal of Experimental Psychology*, 1966, 72, 190–196.

Pervin, L. A. The need to predict and control under conditions of threat. *Journal of Personality*, 1963, 31, 570–585.

Price, K. P. Predictable and unpredictable aversive events: Evidence for the safety signal hypothesis. *Psychonomic Science*, 1972, 26, 215–216.

Price, K. P., & Geer, J. H. Predictable and unpredictable aversive events: Evidence for the safety signal hypothesis. *Psychonomic Science*, 1972, 26, 215–216.

Prokasy, W. F. The acquisition of observing responses in the absence of differential external reinforcement. *Journal of Comparative and Physiological Psychology*, 1956, 49, 131–134.

Renner, K. E., & Houlihan, J. Conditions affecting the relative aversiveness of immediate and delayed punishment. *Journal of Experimental Psychology*, 1969, 81, 411–420.

Renner, K. E., & Specht, L. The relative utility or aversiveness of immediate and delayed shock and food. *Journal of Experimental Psychology*, 1967, 75, 568–579.

Rescorla, R. A. Pavlovian conditioning and its proper control procedures. *Psychological Review*, 1967, 74, 71–79.

Rescorla, R. A., & LoLordo, V. M. Inhibition of avoidance behavior. *Journal of Comparative and Physiological Psychology*, 1965, 59, 406–410.

Seligman, M. E. P. Chronic fear produced by unpredictable electric shock. *Journal of Comparative and Physiological Psychology*, 1968, 66(2), 402–411.

Seligman, M. E. P., Maier, S. F., & Solomon, R. L. Unpredictable and uncontrollable aversive events. In F. R. Brush (Ed.), *Aversive conditioning and learning*. New York: Academic Press, 1971. Pp. 347–400.

Seligman, M. E. P., & Meyer, B. Chronic fear produced by unpredictable shock. *Journal of Comparative and Physiological Psychology*, 1970, 73, 202–207.

Shimoff, E. H., Schoenfeld, W. N., & Snapper, A. A. G. Effects of CS presence and duration on suppression of positively reinforced responding in the rat. *Psychological Reports*, 1969, 25, 111–114.

Sines, J. O., Cleeland, C., & Adkins, J. The behavior of normal and stomach lesion susceptible rats in several learning situations. *Journal of Genetic Psychology*, 1963, 102, 91–94.

Spigel, I. M., & Ramsay, A. Extinction of the excretory alkali metal response (EAMR) to stress in a reptile. *Psychonomic Science*, 1970, 19(5), 261–263.

Weiss, J. M. Somatic effects of predictable and unpredictable shock. *Psychosomatic Medicine*, 1970, 32(4), 397–409.

Weiss, J. M. Effects of coping behavior in different warning signal conditions on stress pathology in rats. *Journal of Comparative and Physiological Psychology*, 1971, 77, 1–13. (a)

Weiss, J. M. Effects of punishing the coping response (conflict) on stress pathology in rats. *Journal of Comparative and Physiological Psychology*, 1971, 77, 14–21. (b)

Weiss, J. M. Effects of coping behavior with and without a feedback signal on stress pathology in rats. *Journal of Comparative and Physiological Psychology*, 1971, 77, 22–30. (c)

Weiss, K. M., & Strongman, K. T. Shock-induced response bursts and suppression. *Psychonomic Science*, 1969, 15(5), 238–240.

Weisman, R. G., & Litner, J. S. Role of the intertrial interval in Pavlovian differential conditioning of fear in rats. *Journal of Comparative and Physiological Psychology*, 1971, 74, 211–218.

DISCUSSION

Jenkins: Suppose that the CSs were very short. Would that make a difference to the animal in terms of safety? Is the animal concerned about the fact that the safety signal is not the stimulus in the presence of which he gets shocked, or that the safety signal predicts a certain amount of time free from shock?

Seligman: I can give you an empirical answer. I think it does matter how short the CS is. We have some unpublished data which were collected in a conditioned suppression situation. I think we used 0.5 sec CS prior to shock. What we found was that half the animals gave us what looked like normal conditioned suppression, while the other half behaved as if no CS had been presented. They simply remained suppressed throughout the session.

Jenkins: So in the limiting case, assuming there is a temporal factor, the CS is so short that the animal behaves as if there were no safety at all and shock were completely random. It seems important if we are to have a safety signal hypothesis to be able to make the following distinction. Is it time per se that makes the animal feel safe, i.e., "I never get shocked for at least t seconds when I hear the safety signal," or is it the signal itself that makes him feel safe; for instance, "I never get shocked when the safety signal is present"? This seems to be an important issue for the safety signal hypothesis.

Some discussion evolved concerning the manner in which a number of parameters interacted in order to produce what Seligman termed "safety" or "fear." For example, in addition to CS duration, the duration of the intertrial interval as well as the length of the session were both suggested as variables that might qualify any simple statement about safety signals and their effects on baseline behavior.

Staddon: This seems similar to the problems which operant conditioners have had in their attempts to measure stimulus contingencies in multiple schedules. This is precisely the type of thing which Gibbon, Berryman, and Thompson (1974) have written about in trying to quantify the effects of contingency. It's not really solved at all. All we have are qualitative statements about the ways in which length of components mix in with relative rates and probabilities of reinforcement in predicting what the animal is going to do. One might as well recognize this limitation at the outset.

Seligman: In fairness I should qualify my hypothesis by saying that we are talking about a fairly limited set of parameters that people conventionally use in conditioned suppression experiments.

Davis: Regarding your findings about the effects of brief duration signals we also have unpublished data which suggest that the 2-sec value may be something of a breaking point. Our animals also showed approximately a 50–50 split in terms of whether or not conventional conditioned suppression occurred or whether the subject remained suppressed throughout the session. There are some very real problems, however, regarding the measurement of conditioned suppression when extremely brief duration warning signals are used. In fact, a conventional suppression ratio is virtually useless.

Seligman: I agree, but if you use long intertrial intervals you can report the degree of suppression between signals, which is the measure of interest to the safety signal hypothesis.

Davis: That's my main point. An often overlooked portion of the session which is extremely sensitive to the degree of aversion is the baseline itself and its degree of suppression from preshock values. For some reason this has not been exploited as a meaningful measure in the conditioned suppression literature.

Boakes: I'm not sure I understand the connection between the ulceration data you cite and the safety signal hypothesis. You seem to be comparing two groups which differ not necessarily in the amount of fear they experience, but in the temporal distribution of that fear. Specifically, one group might experience relatively intense fear for the brief time that the CS is on, whereas the other group might experience considerably less fear averaged over the entire session. Since we don't really understand the relationship between fear and ulceration, there is no definitive way to apply the outcome of such a comparison to notions of predictability in general, and the safety signal hypothesis in particular.

Seligman: I must agree that what you are proposing may represent a major problem for the safety signal hypothesis. It's obvious, for example, that if the degree of fear during the CS were enormous and only mild fear were experienced when spread out through the session then you might somehow get the opposite result. There is that degree of freedom in the theory. The data that I think are relevant, however, are Weiss's, and I think it is important that these data came out in the direction that is consistent with the safety signal hypothesis.

Boakes: However, my point is that you might have made an equally plausible case for your hypothesis had the data come out in the other direction. This is not to impugn your hypothesis, but your use of ulceration data to support it.

Staddon: Aren't you assuming that fear increases in a negatively accelerated manner with shock probability and quickly reaches some asymptotic value? So the difference between 50% shock and 100% shock is actually very small in terms of the amount of fear generated.

Seligman: I think there is some monotonic relationship between the probability of shock and the amount of fear.

Staddon: I think you have to assume it's not linear. If it were, then twice the shock for half the time would produce an identical amount of fear. You would be forced into a number of untenable positions.

Weisman: That isn't necessarily so. I think we have to consider the possibility that different URs are generated in response to increasing amounts of shock. In other words there may be a qualitative as well as a quantitative difference here. The UR which is elicited by a brief signal prior to shock may be quite different from the UR which occurs in the presence of random or unsignaled shock. When you speak of fear and measuring it, you have to consider the possibility that there is more than one "it." I've always thought of unpredictable shock as generating "terror" rather than fear. Terror may be quite removed from fear.

Staddon: How much terror equals how much fear?

Weisman: I'm not sure that they can be measured in comparable terms. They may differ in some important ways.

Seligman: I think there may be something to that suggestion. All we can say at this point is that both terror and fear, whatever they are, map in the same direction on to all the measures we use.

Weisman: Do you think that there is only one continuum and that terror and fear are the same UR?

Seligman: I don't know.

Davis: Isn't this a central problem in using such a term as fear, which is essentially a metaphor? It has considerable intuitive appeal, but we begin to treat it as if it had established quantitative properties as well. It's a metaphoric motivational state which even at its lowest levels seems to produce adequate avoidance performance and some degree of ulceration. How do we deal with it in a manner which even approaches being systematic? As shock increases, do we assume there is fear, then more and more fear, until we reach the undeniable point at which we realize we need another metaphor? Then somebody suggests that beyond "fear" there is "terror" and the whole metaphoric progression begins again. I think we're establishing an intuitive dimension which has no place in our analysis of behavior.

Seligman: I'm going to argue very strongly against that notion toward the end of the session if I get time. [Unfortunately he did not—Eds.] For the time being let me say that I agree with you that fear is an ill-defined term. It's an open-ended term, but intentionally so. I think it is scientifically useful and necessary at this stage of our analysis.

Discussion touched on recent data reported by Badia and his colleagues in which preference for signaled shock was reported even in situations that involved the animal's electing to take far more intensive shock in order to produce a warning signal.

Weisman: These data leave the safety signal and uncertainty reduction hypotheses unscathed but seem to argue strongly against the preparatory response hypothesis.

Seligman: You'd have to invoke an extremely strong preparatory response in order to handle the preference for these very intense shocks. I think it's highly unlikely and am unwilling to support such an argument. I would like to conclude that the preparatory response hypothesis is almost dead because of data such as these, but there are rational men who continue to argue in its support.

Davis: The preparatory response hypothesis is certainly alive in the sense that we're describing a situation in which an unrestrained subject is presented with a CS prior to each US. It's hard to believe that some sort of operants or CRs aren't going to occur under these conditions. The question is what function will these responses have? Can they be regarded as preparatory?

Seligman: Right, but the data question is "Do those responses, if they exist, control the preference data?" I think that the answer is no. I would not argue that a safety signal view is mutually exclusive from a preparatory response view. Preparatory responses might still occur, but the point is that they have minor relevance with respect to the issues we're addressing.

Reberg: I wonder if you have any thoughts about whether safety signals which are based on more intense shocks become stronger safety signals in some testable way than safety signals based on relatively mild shock?

Seligman: We'd have to generate a situation in the absence of any shock in order to test an animal's preference between two safety signals which had previously been paired with relatively mild and strong shock intensities. I don't know of any such data. It somehow seems counterintuitive that he would prefer a signal which had in any way been associated with the more intense shock.

Davis: It's not counterintuitive in the sense that more intense shock may also lead to more intense "relief" or "safety" in the presence of the signal.

Staddon: I think the subject would want as little to do with the situation surrounding intense shock as possible.

Davis: I agree, but what could have less to do with shock than the CS which signaled its absence?

Weisman: I think it's quite possible that safety signals only have meaning within a context which involves some degree of aversion. If you attempt to test, as we've been suggesting, in a situation in which shock is withheld, I wouldn't be surprised if the subject wanted very little to do with either safety signal. You might simply see no preference at all.

Davis: The safety signal hypothesis seems to take into account only the CS as a predictor of shock. There appears to be no mention of what predicts onset of the CS itself, which presumably has become a conditioned aversive stimulus. Even in a situation where the CS has a perfectly respectable duration, say 30 sec, I submit that there is still some degree of residual fear. You have concluded differently in your paper when you speak of "no fear in the absence of CS+." I disagree strongly with this and would argue that there is still fear during the session, even when safety signals are available. If nothing else, there is still fear of onset of the CS+, which is a predictor of shock. This CS occurs unpredictably, which, within you system, is ample reason for fear. The shock may be predictable, but the CS which signals it is not.

Seligman: Then why do baselines during conditioned suppression return to 100%?

Davis: I don't believe they do. We've been running studies using the conditioned suppression procedure for nearly 10 years now and have hardly ever had an animal recover its preshock baseline. Lately we've been focusing directly on baseline recovery and have found that animals rarely recover beyond 60 or 70% after 30 sessions. We've even run animals for up to 180 sessions and have failed to get 100% recovery of baseline. I therefore question your finding that subject reliably return to preshock baselines, and I take our results to suggest that some degree of fear, probably related to the CS, remains even when you have a reliable predictor of shock.

Seligman: This is quite an important point, of course, and I'm not sure what to say. I haven't seen your baseline data before and as far as I can tell they are in considerable conflict with the measures we've taken in this respect. As far as I recall, Meyer and I (1970) did observe a return to preshock baseline following 70 experimental sessions.

Mackintosh: Even if that's true, it's hard to tell what those preshock baselines might have become had they been allowed to develop for 70 sessions in the absence of shock.

Seligman: I agree, those control data are missing. In any case, Hank and I may well have a data conflict here.[1]

Davis: I'm not sure that my argument depends on a data base at this point. It seems more important that a logical hole exists in the safety signal hypothesis.

Seligman: Right, that there may be residual fear because the animal is afraid of the CS. You may be right.

A considerable debate emerged over whether the safety signal hypothesis, which involved only an S+, during which fear was excited, and an S−, during which fear was presumably inhibited (i.e., safety), was an adequate formulation,

---

[1] Lachlan MacFadden has suggested a possible explanation. Because the density of reinforcement delivered by Davis and his colleagues has typically been higher than that programmed by Seligman (VI 30 sec *vs.* VI 1 min), it may have been easier to recover the lower initial response rates which occurred under Seligman's procedure.

either logically (in terms of what is known of inhibition) or empirically. The following statements illustrate some of the major arguments that were raised.

Hurwitz: I don't think the safety signal hypothesis is a hypothesis in any formal sense. Instead, it seems to be an attempt to propose, or perhaps sustain, a view of behavior which I hold to be untenable. You appear to be couching the whole thing in motivational terms rather than behavioral terms. This is doubly confusing since not only can I not be sure of what behavior results direct from "fear," but also I'm not sure about what S− produces either at a motivational or a behavioral level. It simply isn't enough to say that S− produces the absence of what is produced by S+. To say that S− inhibits fear is not to specify any class of behavior, nor is it to specify any class of motivation. Inhibition of fear is not a motivational state, it tells me that motivation is no longer there. How can I translate this into behavioral terms? Although I am less happy hearing about motivational states than I am about behaviors, I would still profit from hearing what kind of motivational state is elicited by S− within the safety signal hypothesis. Until I hear this, I cannot see that the safety signal hypothesis is anything more than a warmed-over restatement of drive reduction theory.

Seligman: In terms of a strict Pavlovian analysis we define the classes of behavior that CS−, an inhibitory stimulus, elicits as being the opposite or the absence of the classes of behavior that are elicited by CS+. In terms of my hypothesis the kinds of data which are controlled by the CS− are quite easy to itemize. Since CS+ controls the suppression of barpressing, CS− controls the absence of suppression of barpressing. If CS+ controlled the suppression of drinking, then CS− would control absence of the suppression of drinking. When CS+ controls the suppression of gastric secretion, CS− releases or controls the lack of suppression of gastric secretion. I could go on listing these classes of behavior, which seems to be the point of your question. However, I want to go further than that. It seems to me that something coherent comes from all of these measures. It's useful, I think, to call the set of indicies that the CS+ controls "fear." Similarly, we can call the indicies that are controlled by CS− the "lack of fear." Others have called it "relaxation," although I'm not sure whether or not that's true.

Hurwitz: However, "relaxation" implies a different class of response. All along, your other answers involved only a single class of response: its presence or absence.

Seligman: I'm perfectly happy with stating the system in terms of the presence or absence of fear. I'm using it as more than just a notational shorthand. Instead, I think it's a generative shorthand. It tells you the things to look for. It also maps into ordinary language questions such as "Why is Johnny afraid of school?" "Why is it when we're afraid we don't eat?" I therefore think there's value in retaining the concept of fear and its absence as the basis for the safety signal hypothesis. Although fear is an open-ended concept, in terms of this hypothesis I think the behavioral classes to which it is relevant are pretty well spelled out.

Hurwitz: I'm still troubled by the concept of suppression of inhibition of a response. I'm not as interested in the fact that a particular response has waned as I am in knowing what other response or class of responses has been pulled out of the organism to displace the behavior that has been inhibited or suppressed.

MacKintosh: How do you know any responses have been displaced?

Hurwitz: It's a theory. I'm assuming an alternative model. I'm questioning the utility of a model which refers to one class of behavior or motivation only.

Seligman: I don't see why it's important to the safety signal hypothesis to specify what other class of behaviors might have taken the place of a behavior which was inhibited or suppressed.

Staddon: I agree with Marty [Seligman]. The model Hurwitz is proposing does not allow for motivational or behavioral voids. I tend to share this view in the model which I have presented at this conference. However, this argument appears to have no relevance to the system that Marty has suggested and may not compromise his logic at all.

Seligman: Perhaps the issue which you're raising is dealt with implicitly in my hypothesis. For instance when the animal is released from fear he may be free to do other things. What those other things are may be interesting in some sense, but is not directly relevant to the logic of the safety signal hypothesis.

Jenkins: One thing which I find troubling about the safety signal hypothesis is that it's unclear whether S− has significance beyond counteracting the effects of S+. Could it control a separate class of behavior or motivation or is it only relevant in context with S+?

Weisman: It seems pointless to debate the question of whether or not animals can learn that stimuli are negatively correlated. The amount of evidence in support of such a finding is embarassingly overwhelming.

Jenkins: The logic of Seligman's system requires at least three states: CS+, CS−, and the absence of either. Absence of a CS+ is not adequate to serve as an inhibitory stimulus insofar as the concept of inhibition involves opposition.

Boakes: However, surely what Marty is saying involves the implicit assumption that the absence of CS+ is itself an active inhibitory stimulus which may oppose CS+ and produce inhibition.

Weisman: It seems to me that there might be real difference between inhibition derived from an explicit stimulus that can be made part of a compounding procedure of the sort Herb is describing, and inhibition that results from removal of an excitor. This seems like a point which should be dealt with in elaborating the safety signal hypothesis.

Jenkins: Within the two-state system you are describing, why not talk about the CS+ as disinhibiting fear? That's the kind of confusion you're likely to engender in the absence of a system which has three states. There is little reason to believe that the kinds of behavioral change one would find in a two-state system would be comparable to what one would find in a system involving a prevailing baseline state against which behavior change could be induced by presenting either CS+s or CS−.

Seligman: Would the following situation meet the criterion for the three-state system you are describing? We first establish a stable behavioral baseline within a conditioned suppression procedure. We then introduced upon that baseline both a CS+ and a CS−, one of which was reliably paired with shock and the other with absence of shock. Assuming we could show reliable changes in response rate, suppression to CS+, and acceleration to CS−, would this constitute the sort of situation you are describing?

Jenkins: It would.

[Ed. note: a survey of the literature, as well as a recent conditioned suppression experiment (Davis, Memmott, and Hurwitz, 1976) suggests quite strongly that simultaneous suppression and acceleration cannot be demonstrated reliably within a conditioned suppression context.

References

Davis, H., Memmott, J., & Hurwitz, H. M. B. Effects of signals preceding and following shock on baseline responding during a conditioned suppression procedure. *Journal of the Experimental Analysis of Behavior*, 1976, 25, 263–277.

Gibbon, J., Berryman, R., & Thompson, R. L. Contingency spaces and measures in classical and instrumental conditioning. *Journal of the Experimental Analysis of Behavior*, 1974, 21, 585–605.

Seligman, M. E. P., & Meyer, B. Chronic fear and ulceration in rats as a function of unpredictability of safety. *Journal of Comparative and Physiological Psychology*, 1970, 73, 202–207.

8

Aversively Controlled Behavior
and the Analysis
of Conditioned Suppression

Harry M. B. Hurwitz

University of Guelph

A. E. Roberts

Catawba College

INTRODUCTION

The chapter by Hurwitz and Roberts deals primarily with the effects of super-imposing an aversive Pavlovian procedure on an operant avoidance baseline. This modified conditioned suppression procedure has generated a rather inconsistent body of results, which is a point of central concern for Hurwitz and Roberts. In addition to surveying and reanalyzing much of the data in this area the authors attempt to extract and criticize some of the theoretical underpinnings of these experiments. Hurwitz and Roberts direct much of the thrust of their argument against two-factor theory, which has most recently been articulated and defended by Rescorla and Solomon (1967). The authors conclude by proposing an alternative conceptual framework to handle the conditioned suppression of avoidance and related behavioral data.

This chapter approaches the theme of the text by examining behaviors observed when a Pavlovian and an avoidance procedure are brought together. Much of our work has concerned the nature of behavior change found when a conditioned aversive stimulus is superimposed on a baseline of avoidance. We have used frequency of shock rather than the rate of response as the measure of such behavioral change. There is a mystique about rate of response when applied to avoidance phenomena that needs discussion, and we shall try and demystify this. Regardless of whether the rate of response remains unaffected, whether it increases or declines during a CS, avoidance of shock usually deteriorates.

Readers are often somewhat skeptical about this conclusion and attribute the outcome to sources other than the CS–US procedure. For example, Mackintosh (1974) writes: "Roberts and Hurwitz (1970) and Hurwitz and Roberts (1971) observed rather consistent suppression. This may be related to difficulties often experienced in establishing lever pressing as an avoidance response in the first place" (p. 83). The evidence is otherwise. Avoidance in situations other than the lever-pressing apparatus also deteriorates under quite commonly used avoidance training procedures and CS–US arrangements. Which case one chooses to identify as normal and which as an abberation (a result of special circumstances) is not arbitrary but is a consequence of a theoretical commitment as well as of the probe operations selected as appropriate.

We shall therefore examine some of the theoretical bases (and biases) that have led writers to accept a finding that the conditioned aversive stimulus results in an increase in aversively motivated baseline behavior as the normal case. We shall outline an alternative theoretical model that suggests the reverse: deterioration of avoidance as normal and the enhancement of baseline as a special case. In this chapter, we examine what we call the "avoidance problem" from a historical perspective and in terms of the model we are presenting. Then we focus in turn on the "conditioned suppression" procedure, the theory of conditioned suppression, and issues of measurement as applied to avoidance baselines. A review of the literature concerning the effects of CS–US on avoidance behavior is given. Finally, we offer our conclusions and recast the issues in a non-Pavlovian paradigm.

Historical Antecedents

Escape and Avoidance

In this section we review—all too briefly—some of the historical and theoretical reasons an escape learning situation has been selected as prototypical of adaptive (motivated) learning and as a formal model for avoidance learning.

To escape is to remove oneself from a situation. This implies intentionality and suggests that an individual's wants are related to the nature of the situation in which it finds itself. Typically, the situation underlying escape is hurtful, harmful, noxious, or injurious, as when the rat is forced to swim an underwater alley (Broadhurst, 1957). Because there is something "compelled" about the nature of the behavior evoked by such situations, the vocabulary and conceptual models developed during nineteenth century science, with its strongly deterministic overtones, seemed particularly appropriate. Psychologists who adopted a deterministic view (for example, a stimulus–response model) advocated that the escape experiment provided an ideal paradigm for the experimental and theoretical analysis of behavior. The advantages were many, not least that the experimenter could determine, unambiguously, what the stimulus to action was, thereby eliminating much guesswork about internal processes. The behavior responsible for a return to quietus could also be identified. There was an additional bonus: Compared to T-maze learning for food reward, the escape situation resulted in relatively little variability in the data. Finally, the criterion response could not be construed as being part of a decision-like process that would inevitably have led to the adoption of a cognitive model.

Thorndike (1911), whose experiments with cats in a puzzle box provided the original impetus to study principles of adaptive behavior, summarized his findings by proposing that responses were mechanically strengthened whenever they led to appetitive satisfiers. He was less certain about the case where responses lead to noxious events and he did not, in his early speculations, consider the case of avoidance. It was left to later theorists to suggest that avoidance learning was a special case of escape learning and that escape learning was "really" just another case of leading to appetitive satisfiers.

Among the first was Hull. His early (Hull, 1929) attempt to integrate the gradually developing literature on Pavlovian conditioning, animal learning and human memory relied heavily on Pavlovian principles (and the concept of redintegration). However, Hull found that Pavlovian principles were too inadequate in their commitment to the notion that behavior is adaptive. He asserted that behavior was related to organismic needs, a position strongly expressed in his principle of reinforcement: according to this principle responses are differentially strengthened when they are proximal to a reduction in need (later, drive), a revision of Thorndike's law of effect. Like Thorndike and Pavlov, Hull (1943) focused on the fate of the single criterion response in the belief that once the phenomenon of single response strengthening was understood it could be generalized to more complex behavioral situations. Reinforcement was viewed as a process that brings a single response under the control of a single stimulus. The assumption was made that reinforcement affects a response the origin of which lies in a random internal process. The environment plays on the organism until one of the randomly occurring responses results in reinforcement. This account of reinforcement is considered below because this "single response—reinforcement" relationship has had a dramatic and continuing effect on the theorizing of successive generations of psychologists.

However, the Pavlovian role in escape learning was not ignored; for example, the historic study by L. H. Warner (1932). Warner's central concern was to put to rest the idea that the conditioning procedure inevitably resulted in a transfer of an unconditioned response to a novel stimulus. The experiment required the rat to jump a small fence that divided the electrifiable grid floor of a chamber. A buzzer was sounded before each shock was administered and the animal could escape shock by jumping the fence; shock could be avoided by jumping during the buzzer interval:

> [The animal made a] . . . clean, neat jumping of the fence following the sound stimulus without hesitation and yet without haste. . . . This differed radically from a crossing

response to the shock. The latter was usually jerky, sometimes almost hesitant, involving one or more very rapid removals of the feet from the rods before the rat scrambled ungracefully over the fence. . . . The effect of the two responses was the same but the neuro-muscular mechanism employed were certainly not identical. . . . The training certainly modified the animal's behavior, but the neurological basis of the modification was surely not that indicated by the conditioned response diagram. [Warner, 1932, p. 87]

In a later experiment Warner repeated some of the procedures used previously but on this occasion the animal could not avoid the shock that always followed shortly after the warning signal had sounded. Again his focus of interest was whether the response to the warning signal was structurally identical to the response to shock. It was not. When the conditioned stimulus appeared the animal braced itself, altered its breathing rhythm, vibrated its vibrissae, etc., all of which responses were characterized by Warner as "getting ready for shock" (anticipatory). If future theorists wished to speak of avoidance as conditioned escape, the response so conditioned under the stimulus pairing, or Pavlovian, procedure must be central in location.

Mowrer (1950) extended this view by claiming that the central response was "motivational," a state that had autonomic system involvements. That is, a warning signal for shock is aversive and its termination reduces an acquired motivational state. In short, avoidance was viewed as the animal escaping from the lesser of two evils, that is, a distal (warning signal) versus a proximal (shock) stimulus. The gap between Pavlovian and instrumental learning was bridged by this two-factor theory. The experimental analysis of avoidance learning closely modeled that of the escape paradigm (for example, single response–reinforcement) even to the measures selected (for example, latency of the response). Such attempts to model an analysis of avoidance on an escape learning paradigm are open to question from both an empirical and a theoretical standpoint. The finding that subjects can learn sometimes complicated avoidance behaviors in the absence of warning signals (cf. Sidman, 1966); the role of a warning signal's termination, that is, fear reduction or feedback (cf. Bolles, 1971); and the notion of species-specific defense reactions and the avoidance requirement (Bolles, 1971) all question the efficacy of such an analytical strategy. Moreover, the original drive-reduction thesis (with its linkage to the classical conditioning model) lurks in the background as an inviolate principle. It is to this "single response–reinforcement" view that we now direct our attention, in contrast to an alternative formulation that we believe may be more appropriate to the avoidance situation.

Reinforcement

If reinforcement were defined initially as an operation only, namely, the operation that brings about a particular event via a behavioral event, the outcome is not necessarily to strengthen (or increase the probability) of a response but of a behavior repertoire consisting of many components, for example, an ordered set of responses. We shall call the behaviors that occur in a new experimental situation (such as the lever-pressing apparatus used in operant research) entry behaviors, and we shall now make the assumption that when such entry behaviors result in certain changes in the environment (such as a pellet of food?) the probability of the responses in the repertoire may be changed. This should happen only under some circumstances: Even a food-deprived rat does not repeat, without much ado, behavior that results in a food pellet. The rat has to learn that in a given situation food is provided and that its behavior is the instrument of attainment.

In other words, the behavior of the organism seems to be influenced by reinforcement in three ways. First, the organism learns about the availability of specific reinforcers (for example, food, water, shock), which we call incentive learning. Second, the organism learns that certain behaviors influence the availability of an incentive, which we call strategy learning. Finally, the strengthening of a specific response in a repertoire can be viewed as response shaping.

Instead of stressing "kinds" of learning that may develop under a reinforcement operation, we may be observing various functions of reinforcement selectively operating on the evolution of a behavioral pattern. These functions of reinforcement, detailed more fully below, can be summarized as follows:

1. Reinforcement may confirm that a positive or negative incentive is available.
2. Reinforcement may support an existing response strategy.
3. Reinforcement may reduce but not eliminate the probability of other response strategies.
4. Reinforcement may play an important role in a process that forms or that shapes a unit response (or response element).

1. Confirming an incentive condition. That reinforcement functions to confirm the availability of incentives supposes that the subject associates a situation with an incentive condition. Rats, for example, take time to learn that the lever-pressing apparatus is also a food apparatus; they are likely to take less time to learn that this apparatus is associated with shock. Not only does a subject learn that a certain type of incentive is available in a situation but, under some circumstances, may learn that the situation is associated with a particular incentive condition. By this we mean that a discrimination can be learned relating to the temporal distributional characteristics of the incentive. This notion has been current for many years but it has proven difficult to find an experimental situation to illustrate the idea until recently when Herrnstein and Hineline (1966) reported an experiment in which rats were exposed to a situation that delivered a high rate of shock. The animal chamber was equipped with a lever that, when pressed, reduced this rate. The rate of response that developed was found to be related to the degree to which such behavior was permitted to reduce the shock frequency, that is, change the incentive condition.

2. Supporting a response strategy. The second function of reinforcement listed deals with its supportive role for an existing response strategy. As stated earlier, the term response strategy refers to the idea that an animal, like the rat, may acquire over its lifetime a variety of behaviors that subserve a number of goals, consummatory acts, environmental situations, and crises. A "response strategy" is distinguishable from the common definition of an operant, which identifies the animal's behavior in terms of a simple or even a complex effect on the environment. In this respect the term "operant" is part of a language that attempts to relate the organism's actions to the environment, part of a functional description instead of a structural analysis of behavior.

We have suggested earlier that when a subject enters an environment, whether new or familiar, it enters not with a response repertoire but a behavior repertoire. The subject selects elements from the environment with which to interact, and the immediate consequences of such interactions determine what the subject does next, that is, what behavioral repertoire is brought into play. When an interaction creates the condition for incentive learning, the stage is set for the differential strengthening of response strategies. This notion plays a prominent role in our analysis and was first elaborated about 20 years ago.

Hurwitz (1955) suggested that one should study the rat's learning in a lever-pressing situation in terms of the acquisition of an optimal pattern of response. The apparatus used was equipped with two manipulanda, a hinged Plexiglas door and a lever. The door guarded a food tray and had to be nuzzled open. The lever was positioned a few inches to the left of the door. The apparatus has become known as the Campden box. Clearly the most efficient way of obtaining food was to press the lever once, shuttle to the tray, open it, and retrieve and eat the pellet of food. After eating, the subject would be expected to return to the lever and repeat the sequence. Subjects learned to obtain food in relatively few trials but they required an inordinate length of time and practice to optimize their strategy. Typically, they settled into a sequence that involved a further return to the tray after the pellet had been eaten. The empty tray had become a discriminative stimulus for a lever response, whereas the appropriate cue was an empty paw! In later experiments the development of a response sequence under a fixed ratio and a counting schedule was studied, and in all instances the subjects developed a sequence of response that minimized effort and that insured reinforcement. However, ineffective and inefficient sequences continued to occur even after very many training sessions. Later, changes in behavior under extinction were studied. The data indicated that in addition to a waning of responses there was a change in pattern: Patterns emerged that had not previously been seen.

In summary, situational factors play as a substantial role in determining the type and complexity of the response strategy as do the conditions of reinforcement.

3. Effect on other response strategies. The third function of reinforcement concerns the fate of response strategies other than those already described. We are suggesting that these other strategies may be reduced but not eliminated. Our statement is rather speculative because changes in "other" behaviors are not usually studied directly.

Consider the case of conditioned suppression. Typically, a signal (the CS) followed by response-independent shock (US) is superimposed on motivated behavior (cf. Estes & Skinner, 1941). The motivated behavior is found to be reduced, or eliminated, during that CS. Some investigators have attributed the suspension of behavior to a process called "suppression" and have assumed that this must be caused by a change in motivation (cf. McAllister & McAllister, 1971). However, it is possible that the change of behavior may be caused by a shift in response strategy as well as by a motivational shift. If the CS is followed by food and is presented while the animal is already engaged in food-related behavior, the latter declines; a similar result is found when the signal is followed by direct stimulation to the medial forebrain bundle (Azrin & Hake, 1969). It seems to us this represents a change in strategy and is related to the emergence of behavior during CS that can compete with baseline response rates. Unfortunately, Azrin and Hake (1969) did not report whether behaviors other than lever pressing were present during the CS.

4. Response shaping. The final function of reinforcement concerns its role in shaping a response. This aspect of reinforcement has been extensively discussed in the literature by writers interested in response topography (e.g., Antonitis, 1951), and behavioral stereotypy (Herrnstein, 1961). As indicated earlier, we feel that it has often been assumed that this function of reinforcement represents its only effect and is the cornerstone of much operant research.

Our discussion here is limited to one point. If all that is achieved by reinforcement is the fixing of a response to a stimulus, the assumptions must be made that (1) the response has dimensional (topographic) properties and (2) that the reinforcement process works on this dimension. What is reinforced is the relation between a differentiated stimulus and a point on some response dimension. The dimension is usually not stated but implicit. Why this is so has already been discussed: In operant research the response is defined in terms of its (timeless) effect on the environment. There are exceptions, notably the recent work to bring autonomic responses under stimulus control by operant procedures. Autonomic responses are specified in terms of the functional system they serve and in terms of a dimension by which the extent of their activity can be gaged. Our claim is that response differentiation has served as the hidden model of operant research throughout.[1]

[1] This statement may seem exaggerated. How can the rate of response measure be subsumed under a response-shaping principle? The early operant literature (e.g., Schoenfeld & Keller, 1950) suggests this to be so. The occurrence of an emitted response could be changed by working on the interresponse interval. IRT has dimensional properties and these come under control through reinforcement. Hefferline's (1958) experiments showed the other side of the coin, namely that the dimensional properties of any response were also suitable for bringing under reinforcement control, even responses of the autonomic system (see also Brener & Hothersall, 1966).

Summary. We have made two substantive claims: first that the experimental paradigm for motivated behavior was the escape learning situation. This paradigm has led to theoretical commitments that may be questioned on a number of grounds, including its suitability as an analog for avoidance learning. The second claim is that an operational and functional analysis of reinforcement suggests at least four effects, of which the learning of the characteristics of the incentive condition and the development of response strategies are likely to be more important than the function emphasized in many past and current writings, namely response shaping and strengthening.

Reanalyzing the Avoidance Problem

When our analysis is applied to the avoidance learning situation the following feature emerges: the subject brings to such situations entry behaviors. Some of these are very prosaic, such as the exploratory investigatory behaviors of rats in a new environment; others are relevant to the type of aversive event introduced, shock, strong light (Keller, 1941), or air blasts (Maier, 1949). Response strategies are almost immediately formed as a result of the interaction of entry behaviors with a negative incentive (see Hurwitz, Bolas, & Haritos, 1961). In this view, escape from the aversive stimulus is not essential for avoidance behavior to emerge; on the contrary, an animal that learns to escape may not learn to avoid. In order to establish an avoidance response, the subject has to learn about the operative incentive conditions, that is, something about the frequency and/or the condition under which a negative event occurs. The signaled avoidance situation illustrates the latter, the "condition under which a negative event occurs." Note that this procedure is relatively simple. From the frequency distribution learning point of view, the subject has only to learn: one signal, one shock! The free-operant avoidance schedule represents a different order of things: The subject may have to tune into the distributional characteristics of the negative incentive in order to relate the outcome of its behaviors to the avoidance of shock. The Herrnstein and Hineline experiment (1966) represents a more extreme example of the same problem. The occurrence of a particular response offers no hint that "avoidance" has been achieved and, in this respect, the situation between avoidance and escape learning is different *sui generis.* The effect of the avoidance response (the nonoccurrence of shock) is detectable only by changes in the distribution of the incentives within the situation. Such a detection of difference represents a formidable feat by the organism, not easily and not always achieved, and usually only acquired after extensive exposure to the experimental situation. We shall later point out that the response strategies may get in the way of learning about incentive conditions, but for the moment we must dwell on the positive side of the argument, namely that the response strategies facilitate avoidance.

Some entry behaviors clearly facilitate avoidance and therefore are reinforced by the change in negative-incentive distribution. Much depends on the experimenter, because it is he who arranges for the "operant." If an eye blink is the criterion response, one shock may be all that is needed to generate the criterion operant in sufficient strength. If the criterion response is *not* part of the entry behaviors, however, learning about the temporal distribution of the incentive may become increasingly important and successful avoidance depends on the evolution of an appropriate response strategy.

Our view, the reader will note, does not rely on an emotional state (such as fear) as an explanatory construct. The next section centers on this question in more detail, but we can briefly note that the positing of such an emotional state may not be necessary to an analysis of avoidance.

Fear learning relates specifically to the acquisition by a stimulus, or by a set of stimuli, of control over distinctive properties of arousal of central processes that in their turn command a wide range of behaviors. The popularly held theoretical view is that the training condition for fear learning is the one described by Pavlov and consists of the pairing of stimuli, within temporal constraints.[2] The issue is whether the typical signaled avoidance learning situation (in which a CS precedes an avoidable shock) is a case of Pavlovian conditioning, learning a response strategy, or both. That is, is the subject responding because of a conditioned emotional state, or because a learned response strategy reduces the negative-incentive condition. The answer must be empirical, not definitional, and must be based on unambiguous criteria (dependent variables) for establishing that classical conditioning has or has not occurred. Simply employing the classical conditioning procedure is not satisfactory and using non-Pavlovian measures (such as the rate of an operant) should be ruled out.

Our analysis has implications for the conditioned suppression phenomenon. If the subject has learned a response strategy to avoid shock and is subsequently exposed to a situation where shock is not avoidable, the subject may give up its avoidance strategy for the duration (or part of the duration) of the CS. Such a change in strategy may not be very adaptive and may, in fact, worsen the situation (from the subject's point of view): Instead of receiving only the shock associated with the termination of CS, the subject may also receive shocks that can have been avoided. Such a change in strategy may have extensive implications for behavior during non-CS periods as well.

The next section, on the theory and measurement of conditioned suppression, considers these issues in more detail.

Conditioned Suppression: Theory and Measurement

Procedure

The usual experimental arrangement for demonstrating conditioned suppression involves two stages. Animals are first trained to perform a simple instrumental

---

[2] Liddel (1944) went so far as to claim that Pavlovian conditioning always involved the conditioning of emotional response. A more recent statement by Liddel (1965) is worth noting: "Pavlovian conditioning is primarily concerned with the emotional context of behavior. It is an emotionally charged episode of behavior bracketed between two primitive stereotyped forced reactions [p. 128] ."

task. The subjects are subsequently exposed to a classical conditioning procedure. This involves that a neutral stimulus be presented (e.g., tone), followed shortly by a response-independent shock. If classical conditioning trials are given while the animal is engaging in an instrumental appetitive behavior, a dramatic delince in the behavior is usually found during the CS. Most researchers subscribe to the view that this disruption of ongoing behavior is caused by a shift in the motivational state of the individual (cf. McAllister & McAllister, 1971).

The literature on conditioned suppression goes back 35 years (e.g., Estes & Skinner, 1941). Davis listed approximately 120 titles in his 1968 review, but the number of studies directly concerned with either the determinants of the phenomenon or that simply have used the procedure as an experimental technique for investigating pharmacological, physiological, and behavioral variables may soon reach 1,000.

Theory

To Richard Solomon and his associates (Rescorla, Black, Seligman, LoLordo, and Maier, among others) must go the credit for formulating a theory detail that brings together classical conditioning and instrumental learning. In doing so they extended Schlosberg's (1937) and Mowrer's (1950) earlier analyses of the question. In their view, the learning of instrumental response as the subject's way of solving problems the sources of which are motivational in nature. Classical conditioning, in contrast, seemingly represented an appropriate paradigm for the acquisition of motivational states, tendencies, or forces. This view is probably best articulated in a formulation by Rescorla and Solomon's (1967): When a CS is paired with a US (shock), an emotional response becomes conditioned to the CS. Subsequently the presence of the CS arouses a motivational state (a CER, anxiety, fear, and the like) when presented on its own; but more importantly if presented against a background of already present "emotionality," the CS increases the motivational state. This formulation can be viewed as a variant of a drive-summation hypothesis. With an appetitive instrumental response, the emotional state evoked by the CS attenuates the appetitive state and in some instances may overshadow it.

Implicit in this theoretical model is an assumption that is seldom stated but that has wide ramifications: An increase in aversive motivation intensifies behaviors that have been acquired as solutions. For example, if the aversively motivated behavior involves wheel turning, the wheel is spun faster; if lever pressing is the requirement, the rate of response increases. That is, the level of motivation during the CS is positively correlated with, and can be inferred from, changes in the response measure.

Rescorla and Solomon then attempted to organize the relationships between response measures and the effect of the CS-induced and instrumental, motivation interactions (1967; Table 8.1). By categorizing the instrumental motivation parameter (appetitive or aversive) and Pavlovian USs (appetitive or aversive), the

TABLE 8.1
Instrumental Procedures

Pavlovian procedures		Appetitive		Aversive	
		No S^D	$S^D - S^A$	No S^D	$S^D - S^A$
Appetitive	CS+	1 ↑	5 ↑	9	13
	CS−	2 ↓	6 ↓	10	14
Aversive	CS+	3 ↓	7	11 ↑	15 ↑
	CS−	4 ↑	8	12 ↓	16 ?

matrix was formed.[3] The focus of the present discussion concerns the inter-action between an unsignaled avoidance behavior (free-operant avoidance) and CS–shock US (that is, Cell 11 of Table 8.1). The reported effect of such an interaction was to increase the behavior, as indicated by a directional arrow and as predicted by a drive-summation hypothesis.

We do not wish to dwell extensively on the data summarized in that table. We recognize that it was mainly meant to indicate the interaction possibilities between different procedures and reinforcers (or USs). At the same time, however, there is a real danger of an oversimplification of complex results; results cannot be summarized by an upward or downward pointing arrow. That is, parameter changes in either the Pavlovian or the instrumental procedure result in new phenomena, the properties of which are possibly determined by new and/or different processes. For example if a CS–US (shock) is superimposed on an aversive instrumental baseline, the direction of the result observed during CS can depend on whether the CS–US interval is short or long. In the first case it may indeed be true, as two-factor theory predicts, that an emotional state becomes conditioned to the CS, which summates to increase the rate of avoid-ance. In the second case the emotional state may be severely attenuated, with the degree of attenuation depending on the class of behavior permitted during the CS interval. A later section examines several of these parametric questions as they apply to the change in behavior recorded during the CS. To anticipate, not only are these parametric questions important to the development of condi-tioned suppression, but the data call into question a basic premise of the two-factor theory: the drive-summation hypothesis.

Measurement: Conditioned Suppression

One of the problems in answering questions about the outcome of a Pavlovian-instrumental interaction is that we have not yet settled on a system of measure-ment that allows comparisons between experiments. Rescorla and Solomon

[3] The matrix also considered the presence or absence of a CS for the instrumental behavior and whether the CS was paired or unpaired with US, that is, a CS+ and CS−. These refinements do not concern the present discussion.

(1967) used directional arrows to indicate whether the effect of the "conditioning training combination on the amount of instrumental response" is to increase or decrease it. Presumably they meant these arrows to stand for an increase or decrease in the ratio of response during CS periods as against an estimate of the "normal" response rate under the instrumental training procedure, that is, a conditioned suppression ratio. This measure does not do under some circumstances, especially not for the case where US is shock and the baseline represents a response rate established under an aversive schedule.

Two computations of a suppression ratio are common. In one the number of responses (or rate of response) during CS (A) is used as numerator and the rate of response during a selected non-CS period of the session (B) serves as the denominator, i.e., A/B. Many investigators prefer to use the second, $A/A + B$. A represents the CS period and the B involves a non-CS period of comparable length, sometimes before and sometimes after the termination of CS.

The problems inherent in suppression ratios have been outlined elsewhere (Roberts & Hurwitz, 1970; Seligman, 1968) but can be mentioned briefly. First is the dilemma of dealing with zero entries (a problem concerning the former method). Second, the ratios have no inherent meaning other than a gross estimate of directionality, i.e., being above or below baseline. Third, we do no know if the resulting ratio could reflect a change in non-CS as well as the CS response frequency. Finally, the CS—US procedure can alter behavior in general, i.e., compared to measures obtained prior to CS—US training, which would not be reflected in the ratios (cf. Davis, Memmott, & Hurwitz, 1976). In short, a ratio transformation, especially if considered independently of the obtained behavioral measures themselves, can lead to incorrect interpretations of the data. This possibility is even more likely when CS—US and an aversively motivated behavior interacts.

Measurement: Free Operant Avoidance

Procedure. The negatively motivated behavior most often used in conjunction with Pavlovian conditioning is the free-operant avoidance baseline. We shall briefly note the procedure and note pecularities of this schedule that pose measurement problems, especially with respect to ratio transformations. Sidman (1953) initially described the procedure in which a brief shock was delivered at regular intervals, the shock—shock (S–S) interval,[4] unless a criterion response occurred. Each response postponed shock for a fixed period of time, the response—shock interval (R–S). Thus interresponse latencies less than the R–S interval successfully postponed (that is, avoided) shock. Sidman claimed that the rate of response resulting from this schedule is a function of the R–S interval:

---

[4] The shock—shock interval is one of the most unfortunate independent variables used. It was introduced solely to get the subjects moving on the lever instead of remaining frozen, as under an escape procedure. No further reference to this variable made here.

short intervals produce high rates; long intervals produce low rates. Actually, the subject usually performs many more responses than necessary to avoid shock.

Once an animal has developed a rate of response the stage is set for the exploration of a variable. The free-operant avoidance behavior has been used as the baseline for assessing the effects of a Pavlovian conditioning stimulus with a variety of different criterion responses: lever pressing (Hurwitz & Roberts, 1971), shuttle responding (Rescorla & LoLordo, 1965), wheel turning (Weisman & Litner, 1969a), and panel pressing (LoLordo, 1967). Although arranging a free operant avoidance schedule and generating shock-postponement behavior is relatively straightforward, measuring the behavior is another matter.

Measurement. At present, rate of response continues to be the favored measure of performance under a free-operant avoidance procedure. At least two reasons seem to undergird this choice. First, there is the tradition of operant research, stemming from work with appetitive baselines, in which response rate is the primary dependent variable. Given this long history, new experimental results can be readily integrated with old. Second, rate of response generally is believed to be inversely related to the length of the R–S interval. That is, the rate of response is presumed to reflect the degree of successful avoidance.

Another consideration, however, not present with appetitive baselines, is present with shock-postponement procedures: the behavioral effect of the reinforcer, shock. When an unavoided shock is delivered, a subject tends to produce a "burst" of short-latency lever responses. These responses are often included in, and thus artificially inflate, the overall response measure. We must therefore consider also the rate of unavoided shock.

Although response and shock rate values are undoubtedly interrelated, important differences exist between the two. As noted, the response measure could reflect a failure to avoid (that is, responses elicited by unavoided shock); in contrast, the response measure could reflect that responses occurred within the R–S interval. In other words, the distribution of responses, rather than the absolute number of responses, is related to shock postponement. The response rate value itself presents no information on either possibility; a concurrent consideration of the shock rate value can given an indication of the distribution of responses with respect to shock postponement. The lower the shock rate, the more optimally distributed the responses must be.

Whereas we may intuitively expect that relatively high response rates are associated with lower shock rates, this relationship may not materialize. In the lever-pressing situation, the response rate may reach a peak value in considerably fewer sessions than the shock rate value reaches its low (cf. Roberts, Porter, & Porter, 1974). Indeed, a peak rate may occur at an early stage in training when most of the shocks under the R–S contingency are delivered (Hurwitz & Bounds, 1968).

The lack of response and shock rate symmetry is vividly illustrated in Fig. 8.1. Each record in panel A shows 173 responses, but the upper record shows fewer

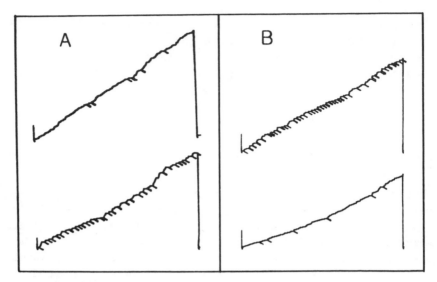

FIG. 8.1 Fifteen-minute portions of cumulative records obtained from avoidance training (Session 15) for four different subjects selected to illustrate the lack of correspondence between response and shock rates. Pen deflections indicate unavoided shock.

unavoided shocks than the lower record, six compared to 33. In Panel B, more responses were recorded for the upper record (183) than the lower (124), but unavoided shocks were also more frequent, 43 compared to six. Note that a large proportion of responses for the "poor" avoiders in each panel consisted of responses to unavoided shocks, that is, shock-elicited response bursts. These data show, quite clearly, that the rate of response as well as the consequence of that rate, the shock rate, must be considered jointly in evaluating the effects of an independent variable (such as CS–US) on avoidance behavior.

Let us return to the problem of suppression ratios calculated to show changes in avoidance behavior. Recall that A represents the response measure obtained during CS periods and B represents the measure in non-CS periods. In the lever-pressing apparatus, if a large number of shocks are received during CS compared to non-CS periods, the A value is likely to be inflated relative to the B value. Consequently, the suppression ratio would show elevation and lead to a conclusion that avoidance behavior was "enhanced" during the CS. It remains to be seen whether there is a "response burst" analog with shuttle- or wheel-turn response situations.

The Effects of CS–US on an Avoidance Baseline: Conditioned Suppression or Enhancement?

In this section we shall review the extensive literature on the effects of a Pavlovian training procedure when superimposed on an avoidance baseline. In addition to updating Davis's (1968) earlier review, the aim of the present survey is twofold: to answer the question whether or not the data support the claim made by two-factor theory that avoidance behavior is enhanced under these conditions; and to what extent the procedures used in these studies follow the criteria of Pavlovian conditioning. If it becomes clear that neither the result nor the procedures conform to guidelines for Pavlovian conditioning, then it may be reasonable when interpreting our results to look beyond interaction effects between Pavlovian and instrumental conditioning.

Pavlovian Training: CS–US Pairings

The Pavlovian training (CS–US) procedure has been outlined earlier: a CS is paired systematically with a shock–US. The CS–US pairing may be superimposed on avoidance behavior (cf. Hurwitz & Roberts, 1971) or may occur when the baseline behavior is prevented, i.e., off baseline. In the latter instance, the actual pairings of CS and US may be given in the avoidance training environment (cf. Riess & Farrar, 1973) or in a separate Pavlovian training environment (cf. Weisman & Litner, 1969a).

The effects of CS–US training may be tested by one of two methods. In one, common with on-baseline training, the probes are taken during each CS–US pairing. In the second, common with off-baseline training, the CS is presented with the US omitted. Such probes may be done with the avoidance schedule in operation (Weisman & Litner, 1969a) or under avoidance extinction (Rescorla & LoLordo, 1965).

Conditioned Suppression of Avoidance: Illustrative Studies

Several of the issues touched on in the previous section can be illustrated by an experiment reported some time ago (Hurwitz & Roberts, 1971). Three groups of rats were lever trained to postpone a .1-sec shock (R–S = 20 sec) under one of three shock intensities: 0.8, 1.4, or 2.0 mA. When the subjects were efficient avoiders, receiving less than one shock per minute, the CS–US procedure was introduced. A 60-sec clicking CS followed by a shock US of the same intensity as baseline shock, but of longer duration (1 sec), was given at irregular intervals. We recorded the number of responses and shocks in 1-min periods preceding the CS (our baseline measure) and during the CS.

The interesting results of the CS–US avoidance schedule interaction came from our low- and high-intensity shock conditions. With the less intense shock, response rate during the CS periods were above baseline during the first few sessions but then drifted below baseline and remained at a reduced level (by 20–40%) over the remaining CS–US sessions. However, shock rate during the CS increased substantially over baseline levels. The cumulative records in Fig. 8.2 illustrate the disruption in avoidance under the less intense shock. The bottom record clearly shows the clusters of unavoided shock during the CS–US interval, which is indicative of "suppressed" avoidance.

The subjects trained under the more intense shock (2 mA) showed slightly different changes in behavior during this CS: Both response and shock rates were elevated during CS. Only in the final sessions did the response rates during CS and baseline become comparable. Even with the increased rate of response, however, shock rate was dramatically increased over most of the CS–US sessions. This is, of course, typical of the case where the unavoided shock is responsible for substantial increases in response rate (cf. Fig. 8.1). The degree of shock rate increase between the two groups was seemingly unaffected by baseline shock intensity.

Several changes in avoidance (not found in Fig. 8.2) can be seen in Fig. 8.3, This rat was trained to postpone a .3-sec, .8-mA shock (R–S = 15 sec); Pavlovian

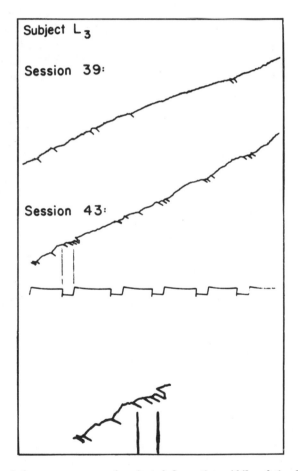

FIG. 8.2 Cumulative response records selected from the middle of the final avoidance session (No. 39) and the fourth CS–US session (No. 43). Reflections of the recorder pen indicate the occurrence of shock; deflections in the horizontal line correspond to the CS period. An enlarged portion of Session 43 record is given in the inset (based on Hurwitz & Roberts, 1971).

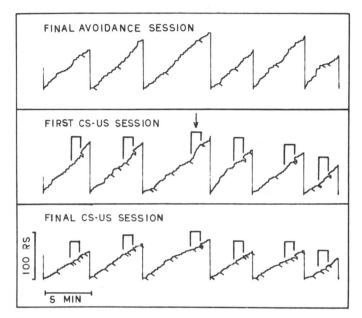

FIG. 8.3 Cumulative records from the same subject obtained from the middle of the final avoidance session (upper panel), the first CS–US session (middle panel), and the final CS–US session (lower panel). The brackets above the records indicate the CS period. The recorder pen reset 1 min following the US.

training involved a 60-sec clicking CS followed by a 1-sec, .8-mA shock US; 15 CS–US sessions were given. In the final avoidance training session (upper panel) the response rate was 16.5 per minute, and unavoided shocks were being delivered at the rate of .3 per minute. The record in the middle panel was taken from the first CS–US session. Avoidance responding was "enhanced" (by one-third) during the CS (note the arrow), whereas shock rate was reduced by one-third, both compared to baseline. In the final CS–US session (lower panel) two changes in avoidance are noteworthy. First, relatively more shocks were being delivered during the CS. Specifically of the 32 min of the session sampled in the record, 12 unavoided shocks were recorded during the 6 min of CS (a rate of 2 per minute). In the remaining 26 min, 19 unavoided shocks occurred, or a rate of .7 per minute. The second change concerns baseline behavior, itself. The effects of CS–US training have generalized to non-CS portions of the session; compared to avoidance training response rate was diminished (by 40%), whereas the rate of shock had doubled.

A further demonstration of the suppressive control acquired by the preshock CS comes when that CS was presented without US, that is, a Pavlovian extinction procedure. The general results found under the CS-alone procedure were (1) a reduction of shock rate (both in baseline and CS periods) and (2) an increased response rate during the CS, often above baseline. Both outcomes are illustrated in Fig. 8.4 which samples records from the subject also used to illustrate Fig. 8.2.

Our brief review has provided ample evidence to support the general conclusion that a CS–US superimposed on an avoidance baseline generally results in a deterioration of avoidance; however, CS–US does not necessarily result in the "suppression" of the avoidance response rate. The extent of the deterioration depends most probably on parameters of Pavlovian training as well as factors influencing the response rates (and response strategies) established under the avoidance schedule. These two factors are considered in the next section.

Parameters of CS–US and Avoidance Training

Avoidance baseline. The most consistent effect of the preshock CS reported above was the increase in the number of unavoided shocks present during CS presentations. We suggested that, compared to baseline, the response measure obtained during CS probably included a disproportionate number of shock-elicited responses. This possibility was examined in an experiment in which the avoidance schedule was suspended during the preshock CS, thus eliminating the occurrence of responses elicited by unavoided shock (Roberts & Hurwitz, 1970). The avoidance training and CS–US parameters were identical to the Hurwitz and Roberts (1971) study discussed previously. The cumulative response records given in Fig. 8.5 were obtained from a rat avoiding low (.8 mA) shock and

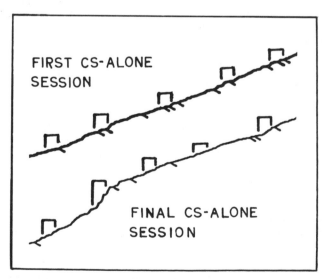

FIG. 8.4 Cumulative records sampled from the first (upper) and final (lower) CS-alone session from the same subject from which Fig. 8.2 records were obtained. The brackets indicate the CS period.

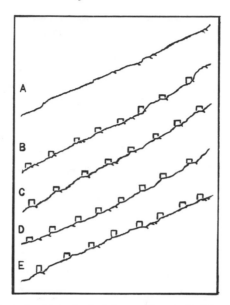

FIG. 8.5 Cumulative records obtained when the avoidance schedule was suspended during CS periods (brackets). Records were obtained from the middle of the final avoidance training session (A), the first and last CS–US sessions (A and C, respectively), and the first and last CS-alone sessions (D and E, respectively).

typifies performance found during the experiment. By the final CS–US session (Record C) response rate during the CS was characterized by a burst of responses to the onset of the CS followed by almost complete suppression of response rate. That the subject's behavior was under the control of the CS–US pairings, instead of signaled extinction, was demonstrated when the US was withheld. Record E was obtained from the final CS-alone session and shows that response rate had recovered during the preshock CS; that is, although less than baseline, response rate was considerably above the level found during CS–US. Once again we come up with the finding that the imposition of CS–US leads to a depression of "baseline" response rate, given that our reference point is the rate of response observed during the final training sessions.

The interaction between CS–US and the avoidance baseline is identified further in Fig. 8.6, which presents response rate patterns during consecutive 12-sec periods of baseline and the preshock CS. The data are given for the .8-mA shock subjects of the two Hurwitz and Roberts studies discussed above: when the avoidance schedule was present (upper panels) and suspended (lower panels) during the CS. The response patterns in the early portions of CS are strikingly similar under both conditions; an increase in response rate is followed by a sharp decrease. The degree of reduction was most pronounced when the avoidance schedule was not present. The data in the upper panels suggest that shock

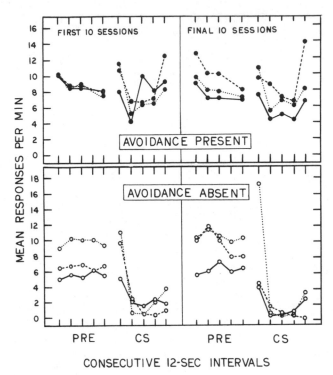

FIG. 8.6 Mean response rates during five consecutive 12-sec intervals preceding the CS (PRE) and during the CS period. The means were based on the first and final 10 sessions of CS–US. For the upper panels, the avoidance schedule was operative during the CS (based on Hurwitz & Roberts, 1969). In the lower panels the avoidance schedule was suspended during the CS (based on Roberts & Hurwitz, 1970).

postponement responding was disrupted but not "suppressed" to the point where shocks are continually delivered from the S–S timer.

Collateral behavior during the CS. The formal observation of avoidance behavior during the CS usually is confined to the single-criterion response, that is, lever pressing, shuttle responding. Roberts, Richey, and Cooper (1975) describe a study in which changes in a variety of noncriterion response classes are examined during the preshock CS. This revealed that rats held the lever less, locomoted more, or remained immobile (either on all fours or in a semierect stance) during the CS than when the CS was not present. Moreover, a response class not observed previously (which was called a "darting" response) developed over CS–US sessions: from a semierect position (4–5 cm in front of the lever) the rat emitted two to three short-latency responses and returned to the semierect position. In other words, the preshock CS produced changes in the style of lever pressing. In contrast, with an appetitive baseline the preshock CS controls an almost complete suppression of all overt behaviors (cf. Stein, Hoffman, & Stitt, 1971).

Avoidance—Extinction Baselines

Given the difficulties in analysis when the preshock CS is superimposed on the avoidance baseline (that is, response bursts) the reader may wonder why the avoidance schedule is not removed altogether in favor of an avoidance—extinction condition. This proposal leads to problems of its own. First, lever avoidance extinction is rapid and considerably variable (Roberts, Greenway, & Hurwitz, 1972), both of which pose problems in evaluating the effects of preshock CS; an analysis of changes in behavior over sessions is precluded for the same reasons. Weisman and Litner (1969a) have noted the same difficulties with wheel-turn extinction behavior. Intense shock levels can function to retard lever-press extinction (Boren, Sidman, & Herrnstein, 1959) but does not seem to reduce behavior variability. Moreover, intense shocks may interact with CS—US training in a manner different from less intense shocks (see below). Data of shuttle—avoidance extinction is unavailable.

A second problem stems from the interaction of a shock US with avoidance—extinction, itself. Sidman, Herrnstein, and Conrad (1957, Phase 2) and Hurwitz, Roberts, and Greenway (1972) demonstrated that shock US would reinstate an extinguished lever—avoidance response. Furthermore, if a CS preceded the US, Sidman et al. (1957) found the reinstated response rate to be greater during the CS than in baseline. In both experiments, the US and baseline shock characteristics were identical; it remains to be seen whether these results are replicable with US and baseline shock having differing characteristics.

Our choice for retaining the avoidance baseline during the CS is based on the view that data are not confounded by a changing behavioral baseline or by interactions between US permutations and an avoidance—extinction phenomenon. In addition, the effect of the CS can be gaged by a joint consideration of response and unavoided shock measures.

Duration of the CS

Figure 8.6 has shown that response rates (and probably shock rates) can take on characteristic patterns during a CS of fixed duration. With off-baseline CS—US training, the development of such patterns probably can be precluded. If the CS if of variable duration (cf. Martin & Riess, (1969) the effect of superimposing pairings of a variable-duration CS with US on an avoidance baseline remains to be studied. In contrast to Fig. 8.6, Rescorla (1967a) found that shuttle responding (R—S = 30 sec) was below baseline in the initial portion of a 30-sec CS and increased monotonically over the CS period. The cumulative record presented by Sidman et al. (1957, Fig. 3) is suggestive of a monotonic increase in lever responding during a 5-min preshock CS.

The experiments by Pomerleau (1970) and Shimoff (1972) stand alone as studies in which different CS durations were systemally examined in the same experiment. In both studies, monkeys were trained to lever press under an adjusting avoidance schedule. This schedule differs from free-operant avoidance in that a response briefly delays shock for a fixed period; each subsequent response, up to a predetermined maximum, adds to that delay. Once the maximum delay is reached, additional responses serve to maintain the delay period. For example, given a shock delay of 5 sec, 10 responses maximize the shock delay at 50-sec; additional responses maintain the 50-sec delay. Pomerleau (1970) used a visual preshock CS and reported a peak in the response rate pattern 12–16 sec following the onset of CS. With a tone CS, Shimoff (1972) found the peak in response rate shortly after onset of the CS followed by a lessening of response rate. The response pattern became less differentiated (following the initial peak) as CS duration was increased. However, both Pomerleau (1970) and Shimoff (1972) observed an interaction beween US duration and the shock-delay period (see below). Thus, a patterning in response rate does develop during a protracted CS, with the exact shape of the pattern under the control of several training parameters, possibly including the modality of the CS, itself.

Behavior Changes between CS Durations

A variety of CS durations has been used: 5 sec (Rescorla & LoLordo, 1965), 10 sec (Kamano, 1970), 30 sec (Rescorla, 1967a), 60 sec (Hurwitz & Roberts, 1971), 2 min (Scobie, 1972), 3 min (Bryant, 1972), and 5 min (Sidman *et al.*, 1957). Substantial differences in training and probe operations make direct comparisons on the effect of differing CS durations difficult. Pomerleau (1970) and Shimoff (1972) seem to be the only investigators to compare different CS duration effects on avoidance-maintained behavior.

Pomerleau (1970) found that changes in avoidance during a CS followed immediately by US was related to the maximum shock delay possible during the CS. Response rate was lower than during baseline, when CS was shorter (12 sec) than the postponement interval. Response rate increased over baseline when the US duration exceeded the shock-delay period. The latter instance resulted in the pattern of response rate noted above. Pomerleau (1970) also reported that the shock rate increased when the shock-delay period was less than the CS duration, a circumstance and result analogous to the Hurwitz and Roberts (1971) experiment discussed earlier.

Finally, both Pomerleau (1970) and Shimoff (1972) noted that the response rate during a short CS (for example, 10 sec) was lower than during a corresponding period of a longer CS (for example, the first 10 sec of a 40-sec CS).

Another source of difficulty in comparing the effects of CS durations on avoidance relates to the type and amount of CS–US training given: whether the CS is studied over sessions (typical of on-baseline training) or for relatively fewer sessions (typical of off-baseline training). The prominent differences between the two are that, in the latter, relatively few CS probes are involved and the probes are obtained on an avoidance—extinction baseline.

Given these cautions, the following observations concerning CS duration can be made. Increased response rates have been found during a preshock CS that is relatively brief (5 sec), irrespective of whether the avoidance baseline is present (Weisman & Litner, 1969a, b) or absent (Rescorla & LoLordo, 1965). Both experiments used off-baseline training and, in contrast to the Pomerleau (1970) and Shimoff (1972) results, found an increase in response rate when CS duration was shorter than the R—S interval. Increases in response rate have been found during a 10-sec CS with an R—S interval of 30 sec (Kamano, 1970), and when the CS matched the R—S interval, irrespective of the nature of the baseline behavior (cf. Kamano, 1968; Rescorla, 1967a). The studies noted above paired the brief CS with US in an off-baseline condition and gave relatively few CS probes. The 30-sec CS used by Rescorla (1967a) stands as the shortest CS used in on-baseline pairings [although Shimoff (1972) used a 10-sec CS, the first 50 CS—US pairings were given off-baseline]. Data on the development of the control of a brief preshock CS over ongoing avoidance are vital to our understanding but are not presently available.

The avoidance changes reported when CS duration is longer than the shock-postponement period have been inconsistent, particularly with on-baseline CS—US training. Data that demonstrate avoidance deterioration have been noted previously. In contrast, Sidman et al. (1957, Phase 1) reported increased lever responding (R—S = 20 sec) during a 5-min preshock CS. This increase lessened with additional CS—US training. Blackman (1970) also reported elevated lever responding (R—S = 20 sec) during a 2-min preshock CS, but response rates in CS and baseline were comparable if the subject were "warned" that the R—S interval was about to elapse. Unfortunately, shock rate data, which would be invaluable in comparing these findings with earlier experiments and would help in evaluating the effects of the preshock CS, were not given. Finally, Scobie (1972) found that a 2-min CS could control either increased or suppressed shuttle responding (R—S = 30 sec), depending on US intensity relative to baseline shock (see below).

Parameters of US

Although intense sounds (LoLordo, 1967; Riess, 1971) and food (Davis & Kreuter, 1972) have served as the US, this discussion focuses on shock—US parameters, namely (1) when US and baseline shock have identical characteristics, (2) when US and baseline shock differ in intensity, and (3) when US and baseline shock are of different durations.

The US identical to baseline shock. There have been many studies that have dealt with the CS effects on avoidance as a function of the US intensity. Surprisingly, shock duration has not been similarly investigated. Operationally, a

3-mA shock seems to be "intense" for the rat (cf. Boren *et al.*, 1959) and 6–8 mA defined as "intense" for the dog (cf. Rescorla, 1968); a comparable definition has not been located for monkeys.

As noted previously, when CS–US was superimposed on baseline, the response rate in CS was increased temporarily. Using .8-mA shock additional training diminished the response rate below baseline (similar results have been obtained with shock of 1 mA). The lessening in CS responding was more gradual with a more intense shock, that is, 2 mA, and often remained above baseline. With "moderate" shock intensity (1.4 mA) equivocal outcomes have been reported: Response rate reduced rapidly for some subjects and slowly for others. However, irrespective of the shock intensity used shock rates in CS were elevated above baseline; that is, avoidance in CS deteriorated. The study by Blackman (1970), which appeared to conflict with our results, used a 2-mA shock, which might account for the elevated response rates he reported. In short, the available data indicate that shock intensity can affect how rapidly impaired avoidance responding develops, but the data do not support a conclusion that the final outcome is differentially affected by different shock intensities. Turning to off-baseline training, reports that the CS controls increased response rate (noted in the previous section) can be found when baseline shock and US are identical (cf. Weisman & Litner, 1969 a, b).

Intensity differences between US and baseline shock. There seems to be no question that relative differences in shock intensity differentially affect avoidance during the CS. Is this change one of degree or is it qualitative in nature? To illustrate, Martin and Riess (1969) trained rats to shuttle to postpone (R–S = 30 sec) a .975-mA baseline shock. A variable-duration CS was paired off-baseline with one of four US intensities: .25, .56, 1.9, or 4.9 mA. One-minute CS probes (with US omitted) were superimposed on avoidance extinction and the effect of CS assessed by a supression ratio measure. Ratios under each US reflected increased responding during the CS, with the magnitude of the ratios directly and monotonically related to US intensity. Riess and Farrar (1973) replicated the procedures of the previous experiment but with a 1.5-mA baseline shock; US intensities were .25, 1.25, 2.85, and 4.9 mA. The avoidance baseline was present during CS probes (given without US) and ratios from each US reflected increased CS responding. The degree of increase was directly and monotonically related to US intensity. However, shock data were not given. These results suggest that the degree to which the rate of response change during CS is related to the absolute intensity of the US. However, recent experiments by Scobie (1972) suggest an alternative view.

The two experiments reported by Scobie (1972) showed that avoidance suppression was not a function of the absolute intensity of the US; rather, the US–baseline shock relationship seemed to control qualitative changes in avoidance during the CS: avoidance could be suppressed when the US was stronger, or increased when the US was weaker, than baseline shock. Comparable experiments systematically studying relative shock intensity differences with lever-pressing baselines have not been performed (although Bryant, 1972, found suppressed lever avoidance when US was more intense than baseline shock, 7.5 mA compared to 1.5 mA).

We should note that Scobie (1972) did not find systematic changes in avoidance during CS when US and baseline shocks were identical. In an experiment recently completed we found impaired shuttle responding (R–S = 20 sec), using 1-mA shocks, when US and baseline shocks were identical. As with the Scobie (1972) procedure, CS–US training was superimposed on avoidance. However, when measures of avoidance in CS were compared with their respective baselines, both response rate and shock rate had increased during CS, by 20 and 90%, respectively.

In short, when we attempt to reconcile the conflicting reports of "enhancement" versus "suppressive" control of the CS, two procedural considerations must be taken into account. First, "enhanced" avoidance during CS is often reported using a US less intense than baseline shock; for example, Rescorla and LoLordo (1965) used a 6-mA baseline shock and a 3-mA US. Second, differences between the Riess and Martin and the Scobie studies suggest that the presence of the US during CS probes can affect the observed outcomes.

Duration differences between US and baseline shock. Differences in shock durations can also be found; most often the US is of longer duration than baseline shock (e.g., Kamano, 1968). Sometimes the US may be more intense and longer than baseline shock (cf. Rescorla, 1967a), a combination most often observed with off-baseline training. Only a few experiments have systematically investigated CS control over avoidance as a function of relative US duration. The US duration–intensity interaction (brief, "intense" US versus long, "weak" US) in the CS control over avoidance has not been studied as yet.

Riess and Farrar (1973) trained rats to shuttle respond to postpone (R–S = 20 sec) a .2-sec, 2-mA shock. During off-baseline training, a variable duration CS was paired with a 1-mA US having one of four durations: .05, .3, 1, and 3 sec. CS probes (30-sec, with US omitted) were made on avoidance-maintained behavior. All ratio values reflected increased responding during the CS with the magnitude of the ratios monotonically related to US duration; significant differences between ratios were reported for the .3- and 1-sec US durations. Shock rate data were not presented.

Roberts and Porter (1974) examined relative US durations when CS–US pairings were given on-baseline. Rats lever pressed to postpone (R–S = 15 sec) a .5-sec, 1-mA shock; the US, which followed a 60-sec CS, was of the same intensity but with five different durations: two shorter than (.25 and .38 sec), two longer than (.75 and 1 sec), and one identical (.5 sec) to baseline shock. The cumulative records shown in Fig. 8.7 were obtained from different rats under

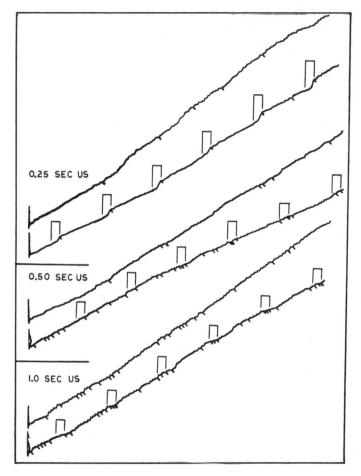

FIG. 8.7 Cumulative response records under three durations of US: .25 (upper pair), .50 (middle pair), and 1.0 sec (lower pair). The records were obtained from different subjects and were sampled from the middle of the session. The top record of each pair is from the final avoidance training session; the bottom record is from the final CS–US session.

the .25-, .5-, and 1-sec US durations. Quite clearly, avoidance was impaired under the .5- and 1-sec US (middle and lower pairs of records) as shock rates in CS were $2\frac{1}{2}$ times greater than baseline. Similar results were obtained under the .75-sec US. In contrast, avoidance was markedly improved when US was .25 sec, that is, shorter than baseline shock. In the session sampled, response rate during CS was twice the baseline value and positively accelerated (see also Linton & Roberts, 1974).

The CS–US Relationship

Rescorla (1967b) suggestion that random and independent presentations of the CS and the US serve as the appropriate control operation for CS–US training is based on the view that the contingency between CS and US, rather than CS–US pairings per se, is the important variable in the CS acquiring control over responding. Experiments using this operation consistently find that changes in avoidance do not come under the control of the CS (cf. Rescorla, 1967b). The efficacy of the "randomly unpaired" arrangement of CS and US as the "proper" control procedure is beyond the scope of this review, but the finding that the subject's behavior is affected by a relationship between the CS and US is important. Within Rescorla's (1967b) framework we have in earlier sections examined changes in avoidance when US delivery is contingent on a preceding CS. Two other possibilities concern changes in avoidance when the occurrence of US is (1) sometimes contingent on CS (i.e., partial reinforcement) and (2) never contingent on CS. Our survey of the literature failed to uncover a systematic investigation of the former using an aversive baseline.

The CS expressly unpaired with US. Many experiments where CS–US is closely paired (usually identified as a CS+) also present a different CS that is not followed by a US (identified as a CS–). The general result is that the CS– produces a change in avoidance exactly opposite that of the CS+. For example, Rescorla and LoLordo (1965) reported increase shuttle responding during a 5-sec CS+ and reduced responding during the CS–. Grossen and Bolles (1968) found shorter interresponse times (IRT) to a 5-sec CS+ and longer IRTs to a 5-sec CS–, relative to baseline IRTs.

Rescorla (1968, Experiment 2) used a free-operant avoidance schedule, one in which each response was followed by a 5-sec CS (and thus separated from shock: CS–); a second response was presented with CS 5 sec before shock (CS+). When the respective CSs were superimposed on avoidance behavior, response rate increased during the CS+ and reduced during the CS–. In both conditions, response rate levels were maximally reduced immediately following the CS. The reduced response rate to a CS– was also found when the CS– training in Experiment 2 was given following avoidance acquisition, when avoidance performance was stable (Rescorla, 1968, Experiment 3).

There are data which suggest that the CS– control over avoidance is not a mirror image of CS+ control. Following wheel-turn avoidance training Weisman and Litner (1969b, Experiment 1) presented CS+ and CS– training off baseline. During later on-baseline probes, the response rate immediately increased during the CS+ (with US withheld). A reduction in response rate to the CS– developed only gradually. Interestingly, the point of maximum response rate change occurred in the interval immediately following CS presentation and not to CS (see also Rescorla, 1968). When the control of the CS+ and CS– were allowed to extinguish (Experiment 2), the control of the CS+ extinguished rapidly, with about 100 presentations. In contrast, the control acquired by the CS− extinguished relatively slowly, and required over 200 presentations.

The effect of a CS− on avoidance can depend on how that CS− is scheduled to interact with the avoidance baseline. When presented independent of behavior the CS− may reduce the response rate; when given on a response-contingent basis, the response rate can increase or decrease depending on the nature of that contingency (Weisman & Litner, 1969b). Although a CS−US contingency may be reflected by avoidance changes during a superimposed CS− (or CS+), therefore, the effect can be modulated when that CS is given on a response-contingency basis. Similarly, a response-produced CS+ can either increase or decrease an avoidance response rate depending on whether suppression or enhancement has been previously found during that CS+ (Linton & Roberts, 1974).

Although the issues above may seem to have digressed from the topic, they serve to illustrate possible differences between the operational and functional meanings of CS+ and CS−. In this section, we have followed the traditional (operational) terminology: the CS+ referring to the CS−US contingency and the CS− to a CS−no US contingency. Clearly, both meanings for CS+ are upheld during off-baseline training. Often, however, probes for the effect of CS−US training involves the US being withheld; operationally, the CS+ then becomes a CS−. In other words, as we change the conditions of Pavlovian conditioning, changes in the functional attributes are likely to be found. The question concerns the extent to which the CS+ may acquire a CS− function. The results of several experiments are relevant. First, the extinction data reported by Weisman and Litner (1969b, Experiment 2) indicated that although a CS+ function was maintained over the first 20 probes it subsequently weakened. The rate of attenuation was seemingly related whether CS− training also had been given. Second, data presented in a previous section (cf. Fig. 8.5) showed that a CS which at one time was followed by US (and controlled suppression) showed a reversal in function when the US was withheld, that is, controlled enhancement. This function was not immediate but developed slowly over sessions.

Although avoidance behavior may be under the control of the CS−US contingency, therefore, the behavior is altered as the contingency changes. Whether the rate of change is rapid enough to help reconcile the discrepant outcomes from CS−US probes compared to CS-alone probes remains to be investigated.

The interval between CS and US.   Two procedures have been used for CS− training. In one, the CS+ is followed either by the US, or by a second stimulus, the CS− (cf. Rescorla & LoLordo, 1965). In the second, the CS always follows a US-free interval. Unfortunately, the length of the US-free period is not usually stated. The experiment by Shimoff (1972), using a trace-conditioning procedure, stands as a notable exception. Four intervals between CS offset and US were used: 0, 5, 20, and 80 sec. In general avoidance response rates were suppressed during a CS with a short trace interval, up to 20 sec. However, response rate was elevated above baseline during the 5- and 20-sec intervals, themselves. Rescorla (1968, Experiment 1) also reported an elevation in response rate in the 25 sec between a 5-sec CS and US. The 80-sec CS–US interval did not produce changes in response rate, during either the CS or the interval. If we view a CS that was separated from US by 80 sec to be a CS–, the reduction in response rate often reported to a CS– was not found.

CS–US training and multiple baselines. We must briefly mention some of the experiments in which more than one reinforcement schedule is employed. The review is restricted to cases in which at least one schedule involved avoidance training. The experiments may be classified into two categories: (1) when training under two or more reinforcement schedules have been given over consecutive blocks of sessions and (2) when two or more reinforcement schedules are present in the same block of sessions, that is, in operant technology language, a multiple schedule.

CS–US and consecutively trained baselines. Herrnstein and Sidman (1958, Experiment 1) first superimposed a 5-min CS followed by US on food-maintained behavior and found suppression during the preshock CS. Then, free-operant avoidance training (R–S = 20 sec) was given. When CS–US was again superimposed on the appetitive baseline, CS controlled an increased rather than a suppressed response rate. When Herrnstein and Sidman (1958, Experiment 2) trained and extinguished an avoidance response rate prior to appetitive baseline training, the appetitive response rate was suppressed during the preshock CS. After the avoidance baseline was retrained, the preshock CS controlled an increased appetitive response rate.

Morris (1974) presented a block of wheel-turn avoidance sesions (R–S = 20 sec). Then, signaled-avoidance sessions were given. For one group, a shuttle response during a 10-sec warning stimulus (CS+) produced a 10-sec safety stimulus (CS–); A group of yoked subjects received the CSs and shock on a response-independent basis. Subsequent CS+ probes (without US) produced an increased wheel-turn response rate for both groups. The CS– produced a reduced response rate only for subjects given relatively more signaled-avoidance training. Similar outcomes were obtained when signaled-avoidance sessions preceded free-operant avoidance training.

Finally, Scobie (1972, Experiment 4) found that the suppressive control of a CS over an appetitive operant produced an enhancement in avoidance responding. But the reverse was not found: a CS that controlled enhanced avoidance failed to show suppression with an appetitive baseline. We should note that the Scobie (1972) experiment did not involve consecutively trained baselines, but the appetitive and avoidance training sessions were alternated over days.

CS—US and simultaneous baselines. Sidman (1960) reported on monkeys trained under a concurrent appetitive and avoidance (R—S = 20 sec) schedule, with each schedule using a different response requirement. When a preshock CS was superimposed, both response rates increased during the CS. However, when the two schedule requirements were made more distinct (by requiring more than one response for appetitive reinforcement), the CS controlled a suppressed appetitive response rate, whereas the avoidance response rate remained elevated. Lewis (1973) recently confirmed that when the two schedule requirements are clearly differentiated (by a multiple schedule in which the appetitive and avoidance components alternate) the CS controlled a suppressed appetitive response rate. Unfortunately, the effect of CS was not probed on the avoidance baseline.

Belleville, Rohles, Grunzke, and Clark (1963) demonstrated "concurrent" transfer between simultaneous avoidance baselines. A number of reinforcement schedules were used, including a shock-postponement (R—S = 10 sec) component. When CS—US was given, response rate was increased during the CS, but the increase lessened over sessions. When the CS—US arrangement was modified so that US could be avoided by a different response requirement (that is, a concurrent schedule), the elevated free-operant avoidance response rate diminished. Once again, arranging the US to be response independent reinstated the elevated avoidance response rate during the CS.

Separately signaled reinforcement schedules, rather than concurrent procedures, have been used on a number of occasions. For example, Waller and Waller (1963) reported a experiment using an avoidance (R—S = 20 sec), an extinction, and an appetitive schedule in series A 60-sec CS followed by the US (identical to baseline shock) was superimposed on each baseline. During the CS, the previously extinguished response rate reappeared (see also Belleville *et al.*, 1963), whereas the appetitive baseline was suppressed. Responding during the avoidance component was generally elevated, especially during the CS. When the US was removed, the CS control over the increased avoidance response rate lessened gradually, compared to the more rapid loss in control over the other two baselines. Finally, giving CS—US on an avoidance—extinction baseline reinstated the response rate during CS periods only (see also Sidman *et al.*, 1957, Phase 2).

Kelleher, Riddle, and Cook (1963) reported a series of experiments using two identical appetitive components. In Experiment 1, the appetitive response rate was found to be increased during the preshock CS; during extinction the response rate lessened only when the US was withdrawn. Avoidance—extinction was examined in Experiment 2, so that the appetitive component of the multiple schedule was the only component not signaled by the preshock CS. As long as the US was not delivered, response rates under extinction were diminished. However, reinstating the CS—US contingency reinstated the response rate during the preshock CS.

Conclusions

It was a difficult choice whether to first present the data on the change in an avoidance baseline under CS–US and tackle theoretical issues later, or whether to reverse this order. We hope our decision to give first consideration to historical and theoretical issues has prepared the reader for the conclusion that must now be drawn: The experimental evidence does not support the widely held claim that signal–shock (CS–US) imposed on an avoidance baseline enhances avoidance.[5] This conclusion is not limited to rats in the lever-pressing apparatus, as Mackintosh (1974) among others has suggested, but applies to a variety of operant situations and species.

Part of the problem, as noted earlier, lies with our methods of assessment, including the designation of "baseline" behavior. We have concluded, reluctantly, that a rate of response alone cannot be considered a reliable measure for assessing the interaction between classical and instrumental procedures. Moreover, because the majority of studies are exclusively described by reference to the rate of response, we are on the horns of a delimma: whether to ignore all the data because they do not completely meet our measurement standards or whether to select only such data as fit into the author's theoretical conceptions.

Indeed, the question is not whether the avoidance response rate changes (enhances or suppresses) during a preshock CS, for this is likely to be a pseudo-question, if not a red herring. Instead, the question is what changes in shock-postponement behavior occur during the preshock CS; and one should keep in mind that the response rate is but one aspect of that behavior. Our conclusion from the literature review is that avoidance (shock postponement) deteriorates during CS–US under certain conditions of signal–shock training and avoidance training. We are not yet in a position to offer possible boundary conditions, as more research is needed. However, avoidance deterioration seems to be the normal, not the aberrant, case. We have suggested that the findings about enhancement of response rate, from which the opposite conclusion can be inferred, often represents a transitional phase in the development of a phenomenon the ultimate stable point of which is deterioration of avoidance.

In short, we view the effect of a CS–US procedure imposed on an operant baseline to be a behavior change, and in this respect we are in agreement with drive-summation views. Such behavioral change can take a variety of forms. For present discussion it is important to point out that a given criterion response can be a member of several different behaviors. Thus "lever pressing" is a functional

---

[5] We have given evidence that CS only imposed on an avoidance baseline elevates the rate of response and improves avoidance. It may be a transitory phenomenon or may be caused by a functional reversal of the stimulus, from being a Pavlovian excitatory stimulus to an inhibitory one. Because of these two considerations one should not assign to such experiments paradigmic status (the role of a reference experiment) and delegate nonconforming instances to special cases.

specification of a response in terms of describing the effect of the subject's action on its environment. This response can occur as part of a pattern of action eventuating in food or as part of a pattern of action that results in the lessening, or even prevention, of shock. The two patterns can be appropriate and functional within the same situation and even concurrently. We have called such a pattern of action (but not its component responses) response strategy. As experimenters we often choose to simplify our problems, and our labors, by focusing on one element of such a strategy, a particular response. However, the context in which the behavior is seen to occur may then have to be used to determine the membership of the response in a particular strategic arrangement.

If a warning signal for shock is presented to the subject while it is working for food, the previously developed response strategy changes. This rule would apply also to a subject working to avoid shock. The question to be answered (experimentally) is under what conditions a change in strategy occurs. Stated differently, what manipulations in known parameters produce such an effect. The literature supports the idea that if the US is different from the reinforcer (incentive) which maintains instrumental activity, the probability of a change in response strategy is high. It certainly appears to work for the case where the US is food and the incentive condition involves shock postponement (Davis & Kreuter, 1972). There is also evidence that when the US is food, a change in response strategy occurs (Azrin & Hake, 1969). Finally, we have documented the case for asserting that when the US is shock and the incentive condition is the avoidance of shock, a change in response strategy can be induced. This last case is of special importance to the drive-summation hyothesis. That is, the data suggest that a change in motivational state (increase or decrease) does not necessarily lead to a corresponding change in the behaviors that have previously been selectively reinforced or strengthened in that situation. This aspect is especially emphasized by the experiments imposing CS—US on multiple baselines.

The procedures of CS—US can just as easily be recast along a "discriminated avoidance" learning model (with the modification that avoidance is not possible), in which case we can examine the response strategies that develop during CS—US training. When such training is joined (either at the outset or following off-baseline training), the net effect may be an interference between separately acquired response strategies and the emergence and development of new strategies. It would account for the transitory enhancement found in the early CS—US sessions, that is, an "avoidance" strategy being applied to the CS—US situation. This view receives support from the observation that rats that have practically ceased responding on the lever during CS when the avoidance schedule during CS was suspended resumed responding (but primarily to each unavoided shock) when the avoidance procedure was restored.

Although we criticized the unilateral use made of rate of response data, no alternative method of measuring the effects of the interaction of procedures is suggested here. We have used shock rate data in much of our own work and have found this to yield more consistent and meaningful results. However, the analysis of the learning situation we have proposed makes the selection of this measure a temporary compromise. Ideally a system of measurement is required that takes account of the notion that what the subject has learned under the two training procedures are response strategies. The experimental problem is to develop situations and measures that tap into such learning more directly.

There is no reliance in our analysis on a mediating emotional state that may have developed during CS–US training and that may interact with extant baseline states. Our view is that behavior changes under CS–US can be predicted by knowledge of the conditions of training and identification of response strategies. We do not see the need for an assumption that emotional states mediate these behavior changes via classical conditioning. Moreover, we are not certain whether the behavior changes should be considered a product of a "Pavlovian"–instrumental conditioning interaction. That is, the pairing of stimuli does not necessarily meet the requirements of the classical conditioning procedure. The constraints on the types of stimuli and their temporal relations appear to be considerable if the gross phenomena attributable to the classical conditioning procedure are to be demonstrated. These procedural constraints have not been met in many studies that may otherwise fit the "Pavlovian procedure," although results from such studies have been accepted as evidence in support of predictions based on the assumption of an emotional state, that is, two-factor theory.

Our alternative, discussed in this chapter, can be considered a first-order approximation to a non-Pavlovian model in which the interpretation of CS–US– baseline behavior interactions is equally tenable. We believe that our model may establish more contact points with more broadly based general theories of behavior.

References

Antonitis, J. J. Response variability in the white rat during conditioning, extinction and reconditioning. *Journal of Experimental Psychology*, 1951, **42**, 273–281.

Azrin, N. H., & Hake, D. F. Positive conditioned suppression: Conditioned suppression using positive reinforcers as the unconditioned stimuli. *Journal of the Experimental Analysis of Behavior*, 1969, **12**, 167–173.

Belleville, R. E., Rohles, F. H., Grunzke, M. E., & Clark, F. C. Development of a complex multiple schedule in the chimpanzee. *Journal of the Experimental Analysis of Behavior*, 1963, **6**, 549–556.

Blackman, D. E. Conditioned suppression of avoidance behavior in rats. *Quarterly Journal of Experimental Psychology*, 1970, **22**, 547–553.

Bolles, R. C. Species-specific defense reactions. In F. R. Brush (Ed.), *Aversive conditioning and learning*. New York: Academic Press, 1971. Pp. 183–233.

Boren, J. J., Sidman, M., & Herrnstein, R. J. Avoidance, escape, and extinction as functions of shock intensity. *Journal of Comparative and Physiological Psychology*, 1959, **52**, 420–425.

Brener, J. M., & Hothersall, D. Heart rate control under conditions of augmented sensory feedback. *Psychophysiology*, 1966, 4, 1–6.

Broadhurst, P. L. Determinance of emotionality in the rat. *British Journal of Psychology*, 1957, 48, 1–12.

Bryant, R. C. Conditioned suppression of free-operant avoidance behavior. *Journal of the Experimental Analysis of Behavior*, 1972, 17, 257–260.

Davis, H. Conditioned Suppression: A survey of the literature. *Psychonomic Monograph Supplement*, 1968, 2, 283–291.

Davis, H., & Kreuter, C. Conditioned suppression of an avoidance response by a stimulus paired with food. *Journal of the Experimental Analysis of Behavior*, 1972, 17, 277–285.

Davis, H., Memmott, J., & Hurwitz, H. M. B. Effects of signals preceding and following shock on baseline responding during a conditioned suppression procedure. *Journal of the Experimental Analysis of Behavior*, 1976, 25, 263–277.

Estes, W. K., & Skinner, B. F. Some quantitative properties of anxiety. *Journal of Experimental Psychology*, 1941, 29, 390–400.

Grossen, N. E., & Bolles, R. C. Effects of a classical conditioned "fear signal" and "safety signal" on nondiscriminated avoidance behavior. *Psychonomic Science*, 1968, 11; 321–322.

Hefferline, R. F. The role of proprioception in the role of behavior. *Transactions of the New York Academy of Science*, 1958, 20, 739–764.

Herrnstein, R. J. Stereotypy and intermittent reinforcement. *Science*, 1961, 133, 2067.

Herrnstein, R. J., & Hineline, P. M. Negative reinforcement as shock frequency reduction. *Journal of the Experimental Analysis of Behavior*, 1966, 9, 421–430.

Herrnstein, R. J., & Sidman, M. Avoidance conditioning as a factor in the effects of unavoidable shocks in food-reinforced behavior. *Journal of Comparative and Physiological Psychology*, 1958, 51, 380–385.

Hull, C. L. A functional interpretation of the conditioned reflex. *Psychological Review*, 1929, 36, 498–511.

Hull, C. L. *Principles of behavior.* New York: Appleton-Century, 1943.

Hurwitz, H. M. B. Response elimination without performance. *Quarterly Journal of Experimental Psychology*, 1955, 8, 1–7.

Hurwitz, H. M. B., Bolas, D. R., & Haritos, M. Vicious-circle behavior under two shock intensities. *British Journal of Psychology*, 1961, 62(4), 377–383.

Hurwitz, H. M. B., & Bounds, W. Response specification and the acquisition of free operant avoidance response. *Psychological Reports*, 1968, 23, 483–494.

Hurwitz, H. M. B., & Roberts, A. E. Suppressing an avoidance response by a pre-aversive stimulus. *Psychonomic Science*, 1969, 17, 305–306.

Hurwitz, H. M. B., & Roberts, A. E. Conditioned suppression of an avoidance response. *Journal of the Experimental Analysis of Behavior*, 1971, 16, 275–281.

Hurwitz, H. M. B., Roberts, A. E., & Greenway, L. Extinction and maintenance of avoidance behavior using response-independent shocks. *Psychonomic Science*, 1972, 28, 176–178.

Kamano, D. K. Effects of an extinguished fear stimulus on avoidance behavior. *Psychonomic Science*, 1968, 13, 271–272.

Kamano, D. K. Types of Pavlovian conditioning procedures used in establishing CS+ and their effect upon avoidance behavior. *Psychonomic Science*, 1970, 18, 63–64.

Kelleher, R. T., Riddle, W. C., & Cook, L. Persistent behavior maintained by unavoidable-shocks. *Journal of the Experimental Analysis of Behavior*, 1963, 6, 507–517.

Keller, F. S. Light aversion in the white rat. *Psychological Record*, 1941, 4, 235–250.

Lewis, J. Conditioned suppression of a VI baseline using a two-bar multiple VI shock-avoidance schedule. *Animal Learning and Behavior*, 1973, 1, 247–250.

Liddell, H. S. Conditioned reflex method and experimental neurosis. In J. McV. Hunt (Ed.), *Personality and the behavior disorders.* New York: Ronald Press, 1944.

Liddell, H. S. The challenge of Pavlovian conditioning and experimental neurosis. In J. Wolpe, A. Salter, and L. J. Reyna (Eds.), *Animals in the conditioning therapies.* New York: Holt, Rinehart & Winston, 1965. Pp. 127–148.

Linton, L., & Roberts, A. E. Changes in unsignalled avoidance behavior when a preshock CS is response-produced. *Psychological Reports,* 1974, 35, 1251–1258.

LoLordo, V. M. Similarity of conditioned fear response based upon different aversive events. *Journal of Comparative and Physiological Psychology,* 1967, 64, 154–158.

Mackintosh, N. J. *The psychology of learning.* New York: Academic Press, 1974.

Maier, N. R. F. *Frustration, the study of behavior without a goal.* New York: McGraw-Hill, 1949.

Martin, L. K., & Riess, D. Effects of UCS intensity during preliminary discrete delay conditioning on conditioned acceleration during avoidance extinction. *Journal of Comparative and Physiological Psychology,* 1969, 69, 196–200.

McAllister, W. R., & McAllister, D. G. Behavioral measurement of conditioned fear. In F. R. Brush (Ed.), *Aversive conditioning and learning.* New York: Academic Press, 1971. Pp. 105–179.

Morris, R. C. M. Pavlovian conditioned inhibition of fear during shuttlebox avoidance behavior. *Learning and Motivation,* 1974, 5, 424–447.

Mowrer, O. H. *Learning theory and personality dynamics.* New York: Ronald Press, 1950.

Pomerleau, O. F. The effects of stimuli followed by response-independent shock on shock avoidance behavior. *Journal of the Experimental Analysis of Behavior,* 1970, 14, 11–21.

Rescorla, R. A. Inhibition of delay in Pavlovian fear conditioning. *Journal of Comparative and Physiological Psychology,* 1967, 64, 114–120. (a)

Rescorla, R. A. Pavlovian conditioning and its proper control procedures. *Psychological Review,* 1967, 74, 71–80. (b)

Rescorla, R. A. Pavlovian conditioned fear in Sidman avoidance learning. *Journal of Comparative and Physiological Psychology,* 1968, 65, 55–60.

Rescorla, R. A., & LoLordo, V. M. Inhibition of Avoidance Behavior. *Journal of Comparative and Physiological Psychology,* 1965, 59, 406–412.

Rescorla, R., & Solomon, R. L. Two process learning theory: relation between Pavlovian conditioning and instrumental learning. *Psychological Review,* 1967, 74, 151–182.

Riess, D. The buzzer as a primary aversive stimulus: III. Unconditioned and conditioned suppression of bar press avoidance. *Psychonomic Science,* 1971, 24, 212–214.

Riess, D., & Farrar, C. H. UCS duration, conditional acceleration, multiple CR measurement and Pavlovian R-R laws. *Journal of Comparative and Physiological Psychology,* 1973, 82, 144–151.

Roberts, A. E., Greenway, L., & Hurwitz, H. M. B. Extinction of free-operant avoidance with and without feed back. *Psychonomic Science,* 1972, 28, 176–178.

Roberts, A. E., & Hurwitz, H. M. B. The effects of a preshock signal on a free operant Avoidance Response. *Journal of the Experimental Analysis of Behavior,* 1970, 14, 331–340.

Roberts, A. E., & Porter, A. G. The conditioned suppression of avoidance: The duration of US. Paper presented at the meetings of the Southeastern Psychological Association, Hollywood, Florida, May 1974.

Roberts, A. E., Porter, J. W., & Porter, A. G. Stability of behavior in rats over 120 free-operant avoidance sessions. *Psychological Reports,* 1974, 34, 927–930.

Roberts, A. E., Richey, T., & Cooper, K. G. Collateral behaviors of rats during avoidance training and the conditioned suppression procedure. Paper presented at the meetings of the Southeastern Psychological Association, Atlanta, Georgia, March 1975.

Schlosberg, H. C. The Relationship between success and the laws of conditioning. *Psychological Review,* 1937, 44, 379–394.

Schoenfeld, W. N., & Keller, F. S. *Principles of psychology.* New York: Appleton-Century, 1950.

Scobie, S. R. Interaction of an aversive Pavlovian conditional stimulus with aversively and appetitively motivated operants in rats. *Journal of Comparative and Physiological Psychology*, 1972, 79, 171–188.

Seligman, M. E. P. Chronic fear produced by unpredictable electric shock. *Journal of Comparative and Physiological Psychology*, 1968, 66, 402–411.

Shimoff, E. Avoidance responding as a function of stimulus duration and relation to free shock. *Journal of the Experimental Analysis of Behavior*, 1972, 17, 451–461.

Sidman, M. Two temporal parameters of the maintenance of avoidance behavior in the white rat. *Journal of Comparative and Physiological Psychology*, 1953, 46, 253–261.

Sidman, M. Normal sources of pathological behavior. *Science*, 1960, 132, 61–68.

Sidman, M. Avoidance behavior. In W. K. Honig (Ed.), *Operant behavior: Areas of research and application*. New York: Appleton-Century-Crofts, 1966. Pp. 448–498.

Sidman, M., Herrnstein, R. J., & Conrad, D. G. Maintenance of avoidance behavior by unavoidable shocks. *Journal of Comparative and Physiological Psychology*, 1957, 50, 553–557.

Stein, N., Hoffman, H. S., & Stitt, C. Collateral behavior of the pigeon during conditioned suppression of key pecking. *Journal of the Experimental Analysis of Behavior*, 1971, 15, 83–93.

Thorndike, E. L. *Animal intelligence*. New York: 1911.

Waller, M. B., & Waller, P. F. The effects of unavoidable shocks on a multiple schedule having an avoidance component. *Journal of the Experimental Analysis of Behavior*, 1963, 6, 29–37.

Warner, L. H. The association span of the white rat. *Journal of Genetic Psychology*, 1932, 41, 57–90.

Weisman, R. G., & Litner, J. S. Positive conditioned reinforcement of Sidman avoidance in rats. *Journal of Comparative and Physiological Psychology*, 1969, 68, 597–603. (a)

Weisman, R. G., & Litner, J. S. The course of Pavlovian excitation and inhibition of fear in rats. *Journal of Comparative and Physiological Psychology*, 1969, 68, 667–672. (b)

DISCUSSION

A debate emerged over which dependent variable was most sensitive to the conditioned suppression of avoidance procedure. Hurwitz began by arguing that rate of response, although traditionally employed, probably "did the animal a disservice." Instead, Hurwitz proposed that shock rate was a more sensitive measure of the degree to which the animal was coping with the avoidance schedule and the motivational effects of the Pavlovian procedure on this behavior. He noted that although rate of response variously had been reported to increase, decrease, and remain unchanged during the conditioned suppression procedure, shock rate almost invariably had been shown to increase during presentations of the warning signal.

Seligman: You talk about rate of response, resistance to extinction, spontaneous recovery, and number of shocks. There are correlations between all of these measures. I don't see the logic of selecting one over all others as getting at the problem. It seems to me that there are a lot of different problems.

Hurwitz: Well, it would be nice if all of these measures correlated very highly . . .

Weisman: It isn't even a question of whether they correlate highly or not. It's a question of whether we're going to do a thorough job of describing behavior.

Hurwitz: If you want to do a decent job of describing behavior in the avoidance situation, don't use the rate of lever pressing. Why not instead take the time that the animal stays on the lever?

Weisman: I'm willing to use that too. But I think the argument that shock rate is *the* variable ignores most of the behavior that happens in the chamber.

Hurwitz: But you've been ignoring that behavior for years. The only behavior you've been focusing on is whether or not the lever microswitch clicks, which is not even behavior in a sense.

Seligman: Neither is shock rate. It's really a derived measure.

Hurwitz: So is response rate in this situation.

Davis: I think the argument against response rate is that you're measuring as much of the properties of your instrument as you are of the animal's behavior.

Weisman: That's a better argument for building better instruments. However, it isn't a good argument for not using response rate any more.

Davis: If the instruments are known to be insensitive at present, then why continue measuring the properties of the instrument and reporting them as if they were behavior?

Seligman: Shock rate can also be construed as a property of the instrument.

Davis: Shock rate obviously reflects input from the animal's behavior.

Weisman: So does response rate.

Staddon: You should be measuring the interresponse times, from which you can get both response and shock rate data.

Hurwitz: Interresponse time data wouldn't do it either because of the evidence we saw yesterday from Davis (chapter 9). It's pretty clear that the animal in the avoidance situation is remaining almost continuously in contact with the lever. All we would be picking up would be the oscillations in force.

Jenkins: I don't see how you can have a serious discussion about which behavior to measure unless you've laid down clearly which question it is you're trying to answer. Then you can argue about whether one dependent variable answers the question better than another.

Hurwitz: I'm not as concerned with the ultimate question of which is the best measure, as I with the fact that a number of theoretical conclusions with which I disagree have been drawn directly from data whose validity I question. Perhaps an interresponse time distribution analysis, as John Staddon has suggested, would have shown us that the animal's behavior during the CS was substantially different from its behavior during non-CS portions of the session. In short, the animal ceases to be a good avoider during the CS.

Weisman: Do you believe that, in general, animals cease to be good avoiders when you superimpose warning signals on their avoidance sessions, or is it restricted to the lever-press avoidance situation?

Hurwitz: We have evidence that animals deteriorate in their avoidance performance in both lever press and shuttlebox situations.

Weisman: We have similar data using a wheel-turning apparatus which suggest deterioration of avoidance. However, we also have data from the same apparatus which indicate change in response rate without any appreciable effect on shock rate. Had I accepted your earlier argument about the importance of shock rate I would have had to conclude that the CS had no effect on the animal's behavior in these situations. This obviously wasn't the case. I think it would be as foolish to ignore shock rate altogether as it would be to focus only on response rate.

Black: I think the question of importance here is one which Harry [Hurwitz] has raised. Mainly, do animals avoid less well, regardless of which measure you use?

In response to a question from Seligman as to which variables were functionally related to whether conditioned suppression or conditioned acceleration was the outcome, Weisman suggested the following formulation.

Weisman: There is no simple outcome which results from superimposing a tone—shock pairing on an avoidance baseline. Instead, there is an interaction between the unconditioned response to shock (the US) and the manner in which this feeds into the topography of the avoidance response.

Weisman identified both shock density (the number of shocks per unit time) and shock intensity as powerful determinants of the UR, and ultimately of response rate. He suggested that Scobie's data (1972) showed that high-intensity shock often resulted in conditioned suppression of avoidance, whereas low-intensity shock often produced a conditioned acceleration effect.

Davis: At what point does the analysis that Weisman has just suggested differ from the analysis that Seligman proposed earlier? Weisman claims that more intense shock leads to a particular form of UR, which in turn has particular, probably suppressive, effects on response rate. Earlier, Seligman suggested that more intense shock would lead to greater fear, which in turn would produce increased suppression of response rate.

Weisman: I think our explanations of this phenomenon are closely related.

Davis: However, your levels of analysis are entirely different. Marty's is a strictly motivational analysis, which stresses the role of fear, and your's is an entirely empirical analysis, which stresses the topography of the unconditioned response to shock. It's incidental that you've made the same prediction about the direction of response rate change.

Seligman: Hank may be right. I can think of an experiment that might lead us to entirely different predictions. Brooks Carber once thought up an experiment when we were in graduate school. We never did it for a number of reasons. If a

CS were paired with a tetanizing shock and this CS were then superimposed on an avoidance baseline, what would be it's effect on the rate of response? The fear analysis would suggest accelerated responding because of the intense fear associated with the highly intense shock. On the other hand, because the UR to tetanizing shock is completely incompatible with the avoidance response your prediction would probably be a decline of responding.

Weisman: Yes it would.

There was further discussion about the relationship between the UR to shock and the lever-press response.

Garcia: The shock intensity parameter has a lot to do with where the current goes. There are deep convulsion centers that obviously produce a response which is quite different from getting a mild zap on the skin.

Weisman: That's exactly what I'm saying. The URs to those different shocks are different, and probably the CRs are different. You end up conditioning something that either does or does not feed into the topography of the avoidance response. When I was a graduate student, two fellows named Trabasso and Thompson (1962) observed the rat's response to a wide range of shock intensities. Their results were very clear. Different intensity shocks produced topographically different URs. If we knew more about the rat we'd also find out why, for example, the rat jumps in response to certain shock intensities but not others.

Garcia: Put your finger in a light socket. You'll find out why.

Staddon: There is one problem with this analysis if you just keep it at the level of single URs. There is no reason in lever-press avoidance why any shock should produce a UR that facilitates lever pressing.

Weisman: The lever press is not pristine, you know. We're pretty sure it isn't an arbitrary operant.

Staddon: I'm not convinced.

Mackintosh: There are solid data on this point. Shocking an animal can produce lever pressing.

Staddon: From foot shock in a normal apparatus?

Davis: What about the postshock response burst data?

Staddon: However, the subjects which you reported to us about were sitting on the lever.

Weisman: It wouldn't be necessary for them to be on the lever.

Davis: I agree. There are clear data on this point. I believe that Joe Pear at Manitoba (1972) has demonstrated quite nicely that you can induce attack behavior directed at the lever simply by shocking rats in an operant chamber.

Staddon:: I'm curious about how the rats have learned to identify the lever as a source of shock. Do they do that without any prior training? If they do then I'm wrong.

Weisman: I'd like to restress the point that the autoshaping data as well as Hank's data on SSDRs and lever pressing argue quite strongly that the lever-press response is not an arbitrary operant at all. If the URs that are part of the lever-press response are like those URs that are generated by certain shocks, then the two systems are compatible. From this we can make some pretty convincing predictions about changes in response rate. We clearly need to know quite a bit more about what underlies the lever press.

Staddon: I'm sympathetic to that argument in general, but I'd rather see it stated in the following way. If you have an extremely strong shock as a US, then the range of behaviors that the animal is free to engage in is considerably restricted in comparison to the behaviors that can occur when weak shock is used. Rather than make your analysis in terms of a particular similarity between classes of URs, it seems more reasonable to say that if you have a very strong shock, then the responses the subject can show are stereotyped and will result in an extremely restricted set of avoidance responses. The broader range of behavior that weak shock allows might include a relatively high rate of lever-press avoidance responding.

Hurwitz suggested the possibility that we might account for and analyze conditioned suppression of avoidance in terms of the fact that animals in the CS–US situation are learning alternative response strategies, which can and do change the nature of the US. In his words, "The mere fact that we are presenting a Pavlovian situation is no guarantee whatsoever that the responses of the animal will not interfere with and ameliorate the US. If they do, then we have to realize that we are dealing with instrumental behaviors which may actively interfere with the instrumental behaviors which underlie our baseline."

Seligman: I think there is a serious theoretical deficit if you have to make the move to an interference model. I believe that's the last theoretical move that I would want to make. It forces you to invoke notions of response competition and interference in the absence of any hard body of knowledge. I know of no *a priori* psychology that tells me what response competes with what, what interferes with what. I know only of a *post hoc* invocation of these general notions in the absence of any substantial data. Why would you want to make such a move?

Hurwitz: I do so for two reasons. First, because I'm equally dissatisfied with the motivational analysis. Second, I know I can't do these things a priori. However, it's an analytical technique I'm developing. It's true I don't have a formal response competition theory at this point, but I can make pretty inspired guesses as to what classes of behavior are going to interfere with other classes of behavior under certain conditions.

Davis: I'm quite surprised at Marty's strongly negative reaction to Harry's use of a competitive or interference model. Aren't interference and competition of motives at the very heart of Seligman's "safety signal hypothesis?"

Seligman: They may be. However, I would argue that although we have virtually no information about competition between different motor behaviors, we have some semblance of a psychology involving the competition of motives. I think we do have a psychology in which fear and inhibition of fear have some competitive relationship we understand and can make predictions about.

Davis: Perhaps intuitively.

Seligman: But on an a priori level as well.

Staddon: We also have that sort of a priori information about the competition of motor behavior. It's entirely reasonable to say, for example, that competition exists between a rat's jumping over here and bar pressing over there. In fact that sort of incompatibility seems a good deal more intuitive than our making intuitive statements about the competitive status of fear and no fear. The only level at which those motives are clearly incompatible is logically.

Seligman: I think perhaps the logical level is the most important of all. And very rarely does the response incompatibility notion come down to incompatibility between two physical locations as in your example.

Staddon: However, at least here you have a situation that you can look at in order to determine whether two particular response topographies can or cannot occur at the same time. One can hardly do that with motives.

With regard to Hurwitz' critical analysis of two-factor theory, the following comments were made:

Seligman: Rescorla and Solomon's (1967) two-factor theory was not meant to deal with situations such as yours in which responses may produce stimulus changes which, in turn, might affect behavior. The appropriate situation in which to test their theory would be a situation in which there were no possibility of motoric competition. If the only interaction were between an elicited motivational state and a behavioral baseline then presumably all of their predictions might be affirmed.

Further discussion explored whether such a situation might ever occur.

Black: Perhaps this particular two-factor theory is saying nothing about the sort of data which Hurwitz has been reporting. It may only be relevant to what occurs during the first session or perhaps during the first presentations of the CS before elicited behaviors might begin to feed into the system. Under such relatively pure conditions the motivational predictions could be tested.

Weisman: I disagree. I never saw that limitation even in the fine print of the Rescorla and Solomon article. It certainly changes the nature of their theory so that it is no longer a general theory of what animals do, but a special theory of what they do in the test tube. To me that makes it of considerably less interest.

Black: Is that any different from what goes on generally in the Skinner box.

Weisman: It's worse than what goes on in the Skinner box. It's what goes on in a Skinner box when the animals have the good taste to refrain from showing any elicited behaviors.

Staddon: Once they admit that elicited behaviors might interact with and affect baseline behavior in a manner opposite to their motivational predictions, then one might as well forget about the entire motivational analysis.

Everyone generally agreed that data could be generated to contradict all of the predictions of Rescorla and Solomon's two-factor theory.

Black: It's important to know whether the data that contradict the predictions in this theory take 20 to 30 sessions in order to produce. Do they take 2 hours worth of running before they appear? Will you get data that support these predictions if you consider only the first day or two? The first minute or two?

Jenkins: Well, let's consider those cases in which the theory appears to be confirmed. For example, what do you think actually happened when we observed acceleration of avoidance?

Hurwitz: We were not given trial by trial data and it becomes very hard to answer that question.

Davis: I can think of at least one scenario to fit those data. Kreuter and I did a study (1972) in which we found that a lot of rate acceleration during the CS was produced by postshock response bursts. Consider a situation in which the animal is working on an avoidance baseline. A CS is presented, perhaps for the first time. Its initial effect is a suppression of responding, perhaps induced by a startle response or an orienting reflex. This pause in responding allows an avoidance schedule shock to occur which promptly results in a flurry of responses at the lever. Once this pattern of pause and burst is established, it's entirely reasonable that response rate increases would occur.

Weisman: I don't believe that. It's a nice hypothesis but it doesn't fit all the rat data that I've seen. Of course it happens sometimes, but you also get acceleration without showing any increases in shock rate.

Hurwitz: I don't see how we're going to solve this argument. Roberts and I claim on the basis of a literature review that there are very, very few instances in which response rate acceleration is not accompanied by shock rate increases. In the first place, very few people have ever reported whether or not they get shock rate acceleration. Second, in the situation where response rate acceleration is not accompanied by shock rate acceleration there are usually special procedural conditions during the test stage which make it very hard to interpret the basis for the response rate acceleration. Let's assume that this literature is in a pretty well-advanced state of chaos. I doubt that a single theory, such as the Rescorla and Solomon theory, is going to get us out of this mess.

Seligman: Two-process theory, in my understanding of it, is primarily a theory of avoidance behavior. It's concerned with origins and transitions, not steady states. There are occasional references in the Rescorla and Solomon paper to the use of CS probes on steady-state avoidance behavior. However, how this relates to the original focus of two-factor theory is very loose indeed. We're talking about the effects of CS probes on asymptotic avoidance behavior, which has very little relevance to the essential premises of two-factor theory. I think this discussion, by in large, has been about a very loose deduction from two-factor theory. And two-factor theory, in the form proposed by Rescorla and Solomon, has already been shown to be wrong on other grounds.

Davis: Does this mean that we are going to have to come up with two separate theories of avoidance or conditioned suppression? One to account for acquisition and the other to account for steady states?

Staddon: At the very least, we've learned that two-process theory accounts successfully neither for acquisition nor for maintenance of avoidance.

References

Davis, H., & Kreuter, C. Conditioned suppression of an avoidance response by a stimulus pared with food. *Journal of the Experimental Analysis of Behavior,* 1972, 17, 277–285.

Pear, J. J., Moody, J. E., & Persinger, M. A. Lever attacking by rats during free-operant avoidance. *Journal of the Experimental Analysis of Behavior,* 1972, 18, 517–523.

Rescorla, R. A., & Solomon, R. L. Two process learning theory: Relationships between Pavlovian conditioning and instrumental learning. *Psychological Review,* 1967, 74, 151–182.

Scobie, S. R. Interaction of an aversive Pavlovian conditional stimulus with aversively and appetitively motivated operants in rats. *Journal of Comparative and Physiological Psychology,* 1972, 79, 171–188.

Trabasso, T. R., & Thompson, R. W. Shock intensity and unconditioned responding in a shuttlebox. *Journal of Experimental Psychology,* 1962, 63, 215–216.

9
Response Characteristics and Control During Lever-Press Escape

Hank Davis

University of Guelph

INTRODUCTION

Using a variety of less than orthodox procedures, Davis and his colleagues have explored the lever-press escape procedure for the past several years. The following chapter summarizes the major findings of this research program and relates a view of lever-press escape with the broader issues of the conference. Unlike explanations of other aversively controlled behaviors, the analysis proposed by Davis does not stress the role of conditioned responses and negative reinforcement but relies heavily on elements of species-specific and reflexive behavior.

There is less research on lever-press escape than on any other conventional aversive control procedure (punishment, discriminated and free-operant avoidance, conditioned suppression). Presumably this reflects a corresponding lack of interest, which we find quite puzzling, given our involvement in escape conditioning research during the past several years.

Informally, one hears from colleagues that lever-press escape is too simple; that no important questions remain. We feel that the notion of simplicity is worth a second look. Certainly the escape procedure is relatively simple. Unlike punishment, conditioned suppression, and avoidance, there is no need to preestablish stable behavioral baselines, conditioned stimuli, or warning signals. Escape conditioning involves only presenting an aversive stimulus and training the subject to terminate it. Most subjects do, in fact, learn to terminate the aversive stimulus quite rapidly. However, the manner in which they do it belies the simplicity of the procedure.

In terms of several recent behavior theories (e.g., Bolles, 1970; Denny & Adelman, 1955), the escape subject may actually be rewarded for doing what it would have done naturally. This relative ease of conditioning, however, has not increased the popularity of escape research. Instead, it appears to have taken its toll by stigmatizing lever-press escape as being too trivial to investigate. As Seligman (1970) and Seligman and Hager (1972) have observed, investigators concerned with traditional or arbitrary learning are generally uninterested in phenomena that are located too close to either extreme of the "preparedness" continuum.

Lever-press escape, like virtually all other aversive control procedures, presumably involves elements of both operant and Pavlovian conditioning, as well as learned and unlearned factors. Moreover, as with other aversive control procedures, no investigator has yet established the manner in which these elements interact to produce characteristic escape performance. Rather than rushing to uncover these fundamental mechanisms, however, an unfortunate hiatus occurred between Keller's original investigation of lever-press escape (1941) and a subsequent series of studies by James Dinsmoor and his colleagues, which began appearing 15 years later (e.g., Dinsmoor & Hughes, 1956; see also review by Dinsmoor, 1968).

The judgement that lever-press escape is overly simple is based largely on evidence derived from studies employing conventional response frequency and latency measurement. We now have reason to believe that such traditional measurement techniques may be less than sensitive to important features of escape behavior. Our essential concern in the research reported in this chapter has been to provide a fuller analysis of the properties and sources of control of responding during lever-press escape. (As described later, our investigations of escape have led us, on several occasions, to examine lever-press avoidance as well.) The data we have collected, which supplement traditional "discrete" response measurement, have also led us to speculate about some of the more theoretical aspects of lever-press escape and avoidance; for example, their relation to species-specific defense reactions (SSDRs; Bolles, 1970).

The results of a number of our earlier experiments have been previously published. These, along with the outcomes of ongoing and recently completed (unpublished) work are summarized and presented in sequence in order to share the development of a number of our interests and questions about the dynamics of lever-press escape.

Background

We began about four years ago examining leverpress escape behavior in a conventional manner. With few exceptions, lever-press escape experiments have used male albino subjects. Although we began by sharing this bias, we have since (Davis, Porter, Burton, & Levine, 1976) systematically compared the leverpress escape behavior of male and female Wistar albino and Long Evans hooded rats. We found significantly shorter escape latencies, less between-subject variability, and significantly more on-lever behavior in Long-Evans females, the least frequently used subjects in our comparison. Male albinos showed the longest escape latencies of all subjects tested. We initially used a commercially available test chamber, lever, grid floor, and shock scrambler. We found, as had virtually all our published predecessors, that subjects learned rapidly to escape (terminate) shock with a lever-press response and maintained inordinately low escape latencies, generally averaging a fifth of a second and dropping at times below .1 sec. Even more impressive was the degree to which our subjects held on to the lever. Most spent in excess of 90% of each experimental session in contact with the lever despite the fact that our reinforcement contingency required only a momentary depression of the lever. Subjects held the lever before shock onset, during shock, and, following each shock-induced flurry of activity, after shock offset.

We discovered that most previous investigators beginning with Keller (1941) had also observed lever holding. Some investigators (e.g., Dinsmoor and his colleagues) apparently had their interest in escape conditioning deflected and had begun to systematically approach lever holding as a phenomenon in itself (e.g., Dinsmoor, Matsuoka, & Winograd, 1958; Campbell, 1962). Most approached lever holding with a curious degree of reverence and annoyance and attempted either to explain it or to eliminate it. Explanatory techniques involved neurological models, such as "after discharge" (Keller, 1941), or stressed the "preparatory" or "perseverative" aspects of lever holding (e.g., Campbell, 1962; Keehn, 1967a). Suppressive techniques in the battle with lever holding ranged in sophistication from implementing a punishment contingency (e.g., Migler, 1963) to prodding the subject off the lever with a pencil (Feldman & Bremner, 1963). None of these methods was overly successful.

In addition to the persistence of lever holding, a number of additional facets of our own early results began to suggest to us that lever-press escape was not a simple operant procedure. One experiment (Davis & Hirschorn, 1973) provided evidence, in quite an unexpected fashion, that it might be wise to reconsider which behaviors underlay lever-press escape and how we were to best go about measuring them. In this study we paired various combinations of escape-trained and naive rats. We were interested not only in how the escape procedure would affect the pattern of social interaction but also in how social behavior might shed light on some of the less understood aspects of individual escape behavior. Our primary finding concerned the "reflexive fighting" phenomenon previously demonstrated by Ulrich and Azrin (1962). We discovered that the level of shock necessary to induce aggression was dependent on whether or not subjects in the pair had previous escape experience. When both subjects had been trained to escape shock, and a fair degree of competition for the lever had presumably been established, relatively mild shock (e.g., .4 mA) was capable of reliably inducing aggression of the order reported by Ulrich and Azrin. During one such bout of aggression, the more submissive animal remained "frozen" on its back with its right front paw extended. After it had taken several consecutive shocks in this position we became concerned for the animal's safety and terminated the session in order to examine the subject. When a nose twitch revealed that some degree of life remained, we carefully placed our still frozen subject, right side up, back on the grids. His extended front paw fit perfectly over the lever and resulted in a lever press and "hold" that lasted for several trials after the session resumed.

A number of other aspects of paired performance in this experiment suggested that escape conditioning involved, at the very least, something more than conventional aversive control. We noted, for instance, that pretrained subjects with low individual escape latencies were extremely difficult to distinguish from naive subjects and appeared to be without skill in escaping shock in the presence of another animal. Observers reported the absence of any "purposeful movement" directed at the lever, even in situations where subjects were stationed on or immediately adjacent to the lever at the moment of shock onset. In several cases, behaviors that when directed at the lever had been previously reinforced were now being redirected at the second animal in the chamber. Observers reported instances in which subjects made manual responses on each other that had topographies similar to lever-press and lever-hold responses.

In a number of previous experiments we had similarly explored the loss of efficiency of operant behavior in a variety of "social situations" that included avoidance, extinction, and various schedules of positive reinforcement (e.g., Davis, 1969; Davis & Donenfeld, 1967; Davis & Wheeler, 1966; Wheeler & Davis, 1967). In each of these experiments, although we had demonstrated some degree of disruption from previously measured individual performance, in no case had the efficiency of a presumably learned behavior been so drastically affected by the presence of a second subject.

The SSDR Analysis of Escape: Its Adequacy

Because a number of our observations within the social situation had involved reference to highly stereotyped and possibly innate patterns of behavior (e.g., freezing), we became interested in a view of lever-press escape behavior that looked beyond traditional mechanisms of reinforcement. Bolles and McGillis had published a paper in 1968 in which they had, as they put it, proposed a "heresy" regarding the basis for extremely low-latency escape responses. Their account of lever-press escape traded heavily on and anticipated notions that were later elaborated in Bolles' (1970) seminal paper on species-specific defense reactions (SSDRs). Bolles and McGillis proposed the following scenario to account for the acquisition of lever-press escape. The rat, when first placed in the chamber, spends considerable time exploring. At shock onset the subject scrambles about and attempts to escape (in the purest sense of the word). According to SSDR theory it is essential to suppress fleeing, a competing SSDR. At some point the subject comes into contact, albeit accidentally, with the lever and some semblance of a "response" is made. This of course stops stock as well as the rat's movement. At the moment of shock offset, therefore, the rat is positioned on the lever where he remains frozen (another SSDR) throughout the following intertrial interval until onset of the next shock begins this sequence again. What are subsequently recorded by the experimenter as lever-press escape responses are, according to Bolles and McGillis (1968), based on momentary breaks in the lever-holding sequence that are caused by ". . . either a reflexive lurch (to shock onset) or perhaps a direct current-induced muscular contraction that results in the bar being released and depressed [p. 261]."

This picture of lever-press escape based on innate and reflexive components is a far cry from the historical notion of a discrete aversively maintained operant response. Interestingly, it is not the only such suggestion in the literature. Myers (1959), discussing the "emotional reactivity" of his subjects, observed that lever-press avoidance performance was facilitated by the onset of a buzzer that served as a CS. He reported that ". . . Ss early learn to hold the bar much of the time between trials. . . . Performance is facilitated because, after receiving a few shocks, Ss also exhibit a tendency to startle to the onset of the buzzer, these startle responses being sufficient to operate the bar and qualify as avoidance responses [p. 384]." Hurwitz and Dillow (1968) similarly noted that the use of a buzzer as a warning signal favored avoidance acquisition by producing a momentary break in lever holding, which resulted in a response being recorded.

In addition, the learned helplessness phenomenon, extensively described by Seligman (1975) and Maier, Seligman, and Solomon (1969), also bears on the nonlearned nature of lever-press escape. Typically, subjects that are exposed to inescapable shock (that is, are taught to be "helpless") have subsequent difficulty learning to escape, even when this behavior becomes possible. Maier (personal communication, 1975) has noted two interesting limitations on this interference effect: (1) if the escape response is of a highly reflexive nature, such as the lever-press response described in the present experiments, then early helplessness training does not interefere with later escape acquisition, and (2) providing the opportunity for an escape response during early shock experience typically blocks helplessness and allows the subject to learn. However, if the escape response is reflexive in nature, it does not immunize the subject against later helplessness.

Before we pursue any further our own sequence of escape experiments and their relevance to SSDR theory, it is advisable to take a closer look at what an analysis of lever-press escape learning in terms of SSDRs actually means. The term "SSDR," as well as the mechanism it implies, is in considerable vogue and accordingly suffers the misfortunes of overuse. At the outset we argue that an analysis of the acquisition of lever-press escape solely in terms of SSDRs is probably as untenable as one in which the role of this class of behavior is ignored. It should also be pointed out that an SSDR analysis of escape learning is not necessarily incompatible with the notion of operant conditioning, although aspects of escape previously attributed to reinforcement have been supplanted by SSDRs and reflexes.

What Bolles and McGillis (1968) have proposed can be summarized in the 2 X 2 table in Fig. 9.1. Two aspects of what is actually learned may be distinguished: (1) the topography of the response and (2) the location in which this behavior occurs. Response topography may be dichotomized into freezing, as opposed to all other behaviors, and location may be dichotomized into the lever, as opposed to all other possible areas of the test cage. As previously noted, "freezing on the lever," cell A in the matrix, is the ideal combination for the rapid acquisition of lever-press escape according to the SSDR analysis. This combination of behavior and location leads automatically to the form of lever-press escape responding proposed by Bolles and McGillis.

The "other behaviors," referred to in matrix cell B, are presumably also SSDRs, given the aversive properties of the stimulus situation that initially confronts the subject during escape training. It is unlikely, however, that either fleeing or fighting, the remaining SSDRs, can result in stable or consistent leverpress escape responding.[1] Cell C, that is, freezing in some location other than the lever, is unlikely to occur given the necessity of the subject's contact with the lever in order to terminate shock and the subject's tendency to freeze at the moment of shock offset (Bolles, 1970). It is worth noting the manner in which reinforcement is invoked in cells A and C in determining the location of the subject's behavior. According to the analysis proposed by Bolles and McGillis, it is not positive reinforcement associated with shock termination but the continuous presence of unescaped shock that differentially punishes responses in all locations other than the lever.

Cell D, the occurrence of behavior other than freezing in locations other than the lever, represents the least likely outcome given the simultaneous presence of species-specific predispositions and the reinforcement contingency inherent in lever-press escape conditioning. Finally, it should be stressed that the contribution of operant reinforcement to escape learning stops short of accounting for the low-latency escape responses that are recorded early in training. Despite how reinforcing these responses are to the investigator, they may be artifactual because, according to SSDR analysis, they are essentially reflexive in nature.

---

[1] The notion of aggression directed at the lever has considerable precedent in the aversive control literature (e.g., Azrin, Hutchinson, & Hake, 1967; Boren, 1961; Pear, Moody, & Persinger, 1972). In fact, our own data have indicated occasional instances of "postshock response bursts" during escape. These responses (described in a later section), however, are readily distinguishable from "normal" escape responding and at no time occurred reliably enough to warrant serious consideration within the SSDR analysis of escape.

RESPONSE

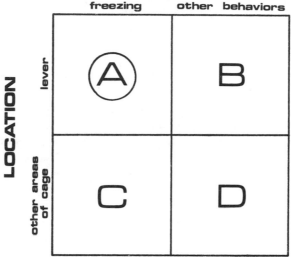

FIG. 9.1 Conditions underlying the acquisition of lever-press escape behavior according to an analysis that stresses the role of freezing, a species-specific defense reaction. See text for explanation.

The SSDR Analysis of Escape: Its Inadequacy

In at least one important way the SSDR analysis of lever-press escape is unsatisfactory. It is one thing to argue that a frightened animal in a novel and aversive situation is likely to freeze; it is quite another, however, to argue that the situation remains both novel and aversive. By definition, at some point the situation will cease to be novel. In addition, the rapidly decreasing escape latencies along with the predictibility of shock onset (assuming regular intertrial intervals are used) will reasonably begin to reduce the level of aversion.[2] It is here that SSDRs, by definition, become less likely. However, evidence does not suggest that "freezing on the lever" undergoes a corresponding reduction in

[2] The notion that the level of aversion is reduced with increased exposure to lever-press escape is not sheer speculation. We have recently collected data (Davis, Porter, Livingstone, Herrmann, & Levine, in press) on the rat's pituitary–adrenal response to escape conditioning. Activation of the pituitary–adrenal system, reflected in raised levels of plasma corticosterone, is traditionally used to infer the degree of "stress" experienced by an organism (e.g., Levine, 1971; Mason, 1968). Examined over 15 consecutive escape conditioning sessions, all rats showed significant elevations of plasma corticoids from basal (resting) level to levels recorded on sessions 1, 5, and 10, which did not differ. A significant decrease was recorded for all subjects between Session 10 steroid levels and those recorded on Session 15.

likelihood. What, then, continues to maintain this class of behavior if SSDRs are fading from the situation? Consider that "freezing on the lever" has been accompanied all along by a relatively potent reinforcement contingency. Although this class of behavior may originally have occurred for reasons quite removed from the rapid and efficient shock escape it afforded, it is now reasonable to propose a shift in the basis of control from SSDR to operant reinforcement. In fact, the case may be stated more strongly. Given a situation in which a rat has been exposed to lever-press escape for 10, 30 or 50 daily sessions in the same apparatus during which shocks have been reliably terminated at latencies averaging less than .2 sec, it is unreasonable to invoke the raw terror inherent in SSDRs to continue to explain the subject's performance. Arguably, the model proposed by Bolles and McGillis seems less and less appropriate as escape conditioning becomes part of the subject's daily routine (cf. Petersen & Lyon, 1975). In fact, Bolles (1971) himself has discussed the effects of continued exposure to the escape conditioning situation in terms of reaching ". . . a critical stage . . . in which fear begins to dissapate and as it does the restriction upon the subject's response repertiore relaxes . . . [p. 188]." The problem of course is to identify the point at which this "critical stage" or transition from SSDR to operant control occurs. The situation is further complicated by the fact that there is no reason to assume that a corresponding and readily measureable change in response topography must occur during this transition.[3]

We are therefore proposing a situation in which a specific sequence of behavior may remain essentially unchanged in topography despite a fundamental change in its source of control. This situation is by no means unique in the behavioral literature. It is gratuitous to note that by definition all operants were, prior to the first delivery of reinforcement, under the control of "other factors." Perhaps a more vivid example of what we are proposing is the case of experimentally induced polydipsia, the excessive drinking behavior observed under various temporally defined schedules of reinforcement. For example, Segal and Holloway (1963) and others have repeatedly demonstrated that when rats are differentially reinforced for low rates of response (a DRL schedule) they typically spend large amounts of time drinking in order to space their responses efficiently for reinforcement. Although initial drinking following the ingestion of 5 or 6 gm of dry food may stem largely from thirst, adventitious reinforcement, which has been available all along, may gradually exert control of this behavior until a point is reached when thirst per se is no longer a tenable explanation for the degree of drinking that occurs. As in our situation with lever-press escape, the moment when biological factors give way to consequential

---

[3] We have collected data which suggests that at least one aspect of leverpress escape, namely response force, may shift at the point when SSDRs give way to operant control. The data, which are presented later in the chapter, are far from conclusive, however.

control has not been identified with the gross measurement techniques currently employed. In both the lever-press escape and polydipsia situations, the fact that the behavior to be reinforced is virtually identical to one of the most inherently probable responses likely accounts for both the speed of acquisition and ubiquity of these response characteristics (Bolles, 1970; Denny & Adelman, 1955).

Pavlovian Analysis of Escape?

Throughout this chapter we continually allude to a distinction between operant and reflexive elements in the lever-press escape sequence. We spend considerable time, for example, discussing the importance of the reflexive lurch. The notion of "reflexive" has extensive meaning, however, probably far in excess of what we intend, and it is necessary to limit our definition before we go any further.

Our use of the term "reflex" derives more from Sherrington than from Pavlov. In short, we are concerned with its mechanical (that is, nonassociative) properties, and not with its potential for entering into associative bonds. There is, however, considerable precedent for introducing a Pavlovian analysis once a reflexive bond has been identified in the behavior of the subject. For example, Turner and Solomon (1962), in their analysis of traumatic avoidance learning, describe a dimension of "reflexiveness" on which the lever-press escape response would lie comfortably. They then use this dimension to elaborate the operant–Pavlovian distinction.

There is an obvious conflict here insofar as Turner and Solomon have, on the one hand, moved directly from identifying reflexive responses to offering a Pavlovian analysis and we, on the other hand, carefully avoid any mention of Pavlovian processes throughout our discussion of lever-press escape. The most obvious basis for this difference lies in the fact that Solomon and Turner have employed an avoidance procedure in which a warning signal is presented. Because this stimulus was frequently followed by shock, the raw ingredients for Pavlovian conditioning were well in evidence. In contrast, there is no formal CS presented in any of the lever-press escape procedures we describe. To the extent that we have designated any behavior as "reflexive," it is likely to remain, in strict analytical terms, an unconditioned reflex (UR).

It is still possible to pursue the Pavlovian analysis of escape in the absence of a formal CS. Because all of the escape conditioning studies we describe here involve regularly scheduled deliveries of shock (fixed-intertrial intervals), it is reasonable to liken our procedure to temporal conditioning. Pavlov described experiments in which an unconditioned stimulus, either food or acid, was presented at regular intervals. Despite the absence of an exteroceptive CS, the regular delivery of either of these stimuli led to the occurrence of an appropriate response, its conditioned nature being demonstrated on those trials when the US was withheld. As further evidence that a CR has been established to the passage of time alone, Pavlov (1927) noted that the reflex occurred at regularly spaced intervals and that the intertrial interval contained "... not the least sign of any ... reaction [p. 41]."

A second consideration, that some element of lever-press escape may have become a CR in the absence of a formal CS, depends on the possibility that the test cage itself may have taken on associative properties. Pavlov described precisely such a situation, which he claimed would lead to the development of a "synthetic environmental reflex".

> ... when conditioned reflexes are being established in dogs for the first time, it is found that the whole experimental environment, beginning with the introducing of the animal into the experimental room acquires at first conditioned properties. This initial reflex could be called, therefore, a conditioned reflex to the environment. But later on, when the special reflex to a single definite and constant stimulus has appeared, all the other elements of the environment gradually lose their significance ... [Pavlov, 1927, p. 115].

It is not unreasonable to assume that, in the absence of a "single, definite and constant stimulus," some aspect of the test cage or testing situation has functioned as a CS. The question remains, however, as to which aspect of the escape behavior sequence is a likely candidate for status as a CR. If we focus on reflexive acts, our behavior of choice is obviously the reflexive lurch. Can we reasonably argue, however, that what was once a shock-induced lurch from the lever may continue to occur in the absence of shock? Although the conditioning of such behavior, of sufficient magnitude to generate reliable lever-press responses, seems unlikely, such an outcome may not be without precedent in the literature.

Hurwitz (1974) first established stable responding on a Sidman avoidance schedule. Tone–shock (CS–US) pairings were then superimposed on this baseline. Postshock response bursts, previously elicited by shock onset, continued to occur at CS termination even after shock had been discontinued during a Pavlovian extinction procedure. It is arguable, however, that postshock responding in Hurwitz's study is not equivalent to the reflexive lurch in our escape experiments. Unfortunately, none of our data bore directly on whether the reflexive lurch, which occurred consistently throughout our escape experiments, was a CR or a UR. Because our view of lever-press escape did not give serious consideration to conditioning the reflexive lurch, either to regular passage of time or to the test cage itself, we made no systematic test to see whether we had established a conditioned reflex. Our escape extinction data (Davis & Burton, 1975; Hirschorn, 1972) are of some relevance to this possibility, however, although no reliable indication of any behavior resembling the reflexive lurch appeared following regular intervals or during periods in which the test cage–CS was "presented" and shock–US withheld.

There is another element of lever-press escape behavior that may lend itself to a Pavlovian analysis. If, as Bolles (1970) has suggested, the freezing response is a naturally occurring consequence of threatening or aversive stimuli, then perhaps freezing may be viewed as a UR. Bolles has not dealt directly with the question of whether SSDRs and URs may be functionally equated.[4] His theory proposes only that an SSDR may be readily conditioned as an avoidance response. It is unclear, however, whether such a conditioned avoidance response is established via operant reinforcement or because SSDRs are readily transferred from US to CS. It is the latter case that bears directly on the possibility of a Pavlovian analysis of lever-press escape.

Consider the following example: The subject is placed in a hostile environment (US), which elicits a hierarchy of defensive reactions (SSDRs). This hierarchy may be termed a UR to the generally aversive environment. Repeated exposure to the situation allows the subject to identify specific features of the environment (CSs), which gain differential control over freezing, a selected element of the SSDR complex that may be viewed as a CR. Therefore, the transition from general to specific, in terms of both the environment and the subject's behavior, may represent the transition from unconditioned to conditioned elements.

The above analysis is still not satisfactory. For one thing, it retains the "terror" inherent in SSDRs but shifts its source from the general US to specific features of a CS. Our original objection to retaining "fear" indefinitely to account for freezing still pertains. Similarly, the focusing on freezing from the SSDR hierarchy does not suggest that the role of "fear," per se, has been reduced. We would therefore prefer to see the effects of increased exposure to the situation reflected in a gradual reduction of "fear" or "terror," not in a change in the stimuli that caused them.

If we are correct in assuming that the subject gradually adapts to the aversion of the escape conditioning situation (that is, the US–UR relationship is eroded), then the continued presence of freezing is likely to reflect some source of control other than SSDRs or a related Pavlovian process. Several explanations related to operant reinforcement have been offered. Campbell (1962) has argued that freezing on the lever is ultimately controlled by the "topographical advantage" it offers in escaping shock. Keehn (1967a) has stressed the role of reinforcement in causing the animal to "perseverate" at the lever; that is, maintain the response topography that has occurred immediately prior to reinforcement.

---

[4] The concept SSDR is both generic and functionally defined. Most Pavlovian URs (e.g., salivation, leg flexion) have neither of these attributes, therefore suggesting the dissimilarity of these two categories. There is an arguable relationship, however, between the investigatory reflex (which is both generic and functionally defined) and the class of events known as SSDRs. Pavlov (1927), however, did not treat the investigatory reflex as a typical UR and regarded it as "unsuitable as a basis for the study of the analyzing activity of the nervous system" (p. 112).

Research on SSDRs and Escape

The following experiments derive from our fundamental concern with the relationship between SSDRs and lever-press escape behavior. Our strategy in the first study (Davis, Hirschorn, & Hurwitz, 1973) was to separate, if possible, the lever-press response from its underlying SSDR component: freezing. If the probability of freezing was high in an escape situation, we wanted to be able to measure it independently of the lever-press response. In order to do this we constructed a lever that had to be lifted rather than pressed. Our reasoning was simple: As long as lever holding might occur for reasons other than freezing, the conventional lever-press requirement did not allow for direct or adequate assessment of either the amount of freezing or the SSDR analysis of escape learning.

The results of this experiment were quite revealing. Lever-lift subjects escaped shock by positioning themselves under the lever and thrusting their backs upward into contact with the lever at shock onset. All subjects in the lever-lift group learned to escape and their latencies did not differ from a control group of "normal" lever-press subjects. A significant difference did appear, however, in the degree of lever holding recorded under the two procedures; whereas the lever-press procedure resulted in a mean of 85.5% of session time, not surprisingly lever holding was virtually eliminated under the lever-lift procedure (mean = 6.5% of session time). There was no decrease, however, in the amount of freezing observed for lever-lift subjects, who spent the majority of session time immobile under the lever. That lever holding might decrease dramatically while freezing per se remained a dominant feature of escape performance was taken in support of the analysis of escape behavior that stressed the importance of SSDRs.

The results of our next experiment (Davis & Kenney, 1975) were something of a mixed blessing. On the one hand, they amplified our understanding of the SSDR–lever-press escape relationship; on the other hand, however, we found that this model for escape learning was not always appropriate. Prior to this experiment all of our research had been conducted in Lehigh Valley test chambers. As our interest in escape and the number of studies proliferated, we were faced with the need for more equipment. We turned to a British supplier, Campden Instrument Company, and bought six elaborate two-lever test chambers. These were pressed immediately into service and within a week my assistant, working on his first escape conditioning project, came to me insisting that (a) no subject would lever hold and (b) that escape training was not proceeding as smoothly as expected. Despite my initial scepticism I found that he was right on both counts. Lever-press escape behavior, what there was of it, looked entirely different in our Campden chambers.

We were faced with the sobering question of whether everything we had learned about escape to date applied only to test chambers manufactured by Lehigh Valley Electronics. We decided that this issue took precedence over all others and began a systematic study of the difference between escape behavior in Lehigh Valley and Campden test chambers. It was obvious that we would need more than latency and response frequency data and so we decided to supplement these conventional measures with videotape records of each session. Subjects were then run, in either A–B–A or B–A–B sequence, in the Campden and Lehigh Valley chambers.

Our results indicated that although all subjects learned to escape shock regardless of in which chamber they were tested, there was a pronounced difference in the form this behavior took. In short, cage topography affected response topography. Our videotape records from the Lehigh Valley chambers revealed the expected sequence of behavior we had observed previously. Subjects were seen holding the lever continuously between shock deliveries; at the moment of shock onset they were bounced briefly off the lever and back, thereby terminating shock and beginning the next intertrial lever-holding sequence. Things did not go quite so smoothly, however, in the Campden chamber. Although all subjects appeared to lever hold early in Sessions 1 and 2, no subject spent the majority of these, or any subsequent sessions, in continuous contact with the lever. Our previous observations in the Lehigh Valley chambers had revealed a variety of postures underlying the lever-holding response (see Fig. 9.2). None of these topographies, however, appeared as awkward or inefficient as the postures we observed as subjects tried to lever hold in the Campden chamber. These responses are illustrated in Fig. 9.3. Once subjects abandoned their attempts to lever hold within the Campden chamber, a second escape "strategy" emerged. At this point subjects typically responded as if a discriminated operant procedure were in effect: At the onset of shock (the discriminative stimulus) the subject, which had been "waiting" midcage, leaped forward toward the lever and made a discrete operant response that was reinforced by shock termination. This sequence is illustrated in Fig. 9.4. It is essential to note that this pattern of escape behavior, which is far more consonant with the original conception of escape, appeared only after the "lever-holding–reflexive lurch" strategy had been tried and abandoned. It also appears that the initial effects of a test chamber on response topography may set some limit on the later flexibility of response strategies. For those subjects that spent Phase I of the experiment in the Lehigh Valley chamber, lever holding was reduced to approximately 30% of session time when they were exposed to the Campden chamber during Phase II of the experiment. Subjects exposed to the Campden chamber in Phase I, for whom lever-holding was reduced to approximately 8% of session time, never recovered to more than 15% during later exposure to the Lehigh Valley chamber.

Despite folklore to the contrary, the results of this experiment strongly suggested that the notion "a Skinner box is a Skinner box" is a convenient bit of myopia. Experimental environments can be as crucial in determining behavior as the equally ignored consideration of the subject's natural history (see related

FIG. 9.2 Illustrative views of lever-holding postures by a variety of escape-trained subjects in a Lehigh Valley chamber.

discussion by Schwartz, 1974). The critical difference between the Campden and Lehigh Valley test chambers appears to have been the location of the lever. The lever in the Lehigh Valley chamber is positioned in the center of the front wall and allowed the subject to brace itself comfortably and securely against the corner or side wall during the intertrial interval and reflexive lurch. The position of the lever in the Campden chamber, however, which is far closer to the side wall, does not allow subjects to brace themselves similarly during the reflexive lurch or while lever holding. Therefore, subjects in the Campden chamber were often thrown backward by shock onset and had to scramble across electrified grids, often from the rear of the chamber, in order to reach the lever. It took

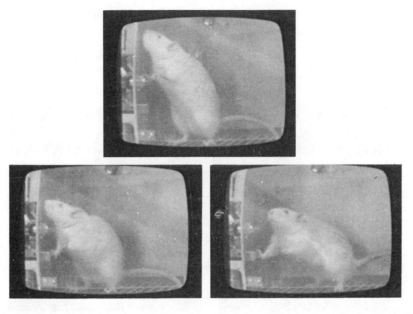

FIG. 9.3 Early attempts at lever holding by subjects in a Campden test chamber. Note the awkwardness of the postures, which include contact with the lightbulb above the lever. (From Davis & Kenney, 1975.)

relatively few such trials for subjects to abandon this "strategy" and to position themselves off the lever until shock onset, at which point they moved forward, often leaping, and terminated shock with a lever press.

Instead of confining the generality of our previous findings, the results of this experiment may in fact strengthen the SSDR-based model we have been evolving for escape learning. By having accidentally provided an unsupportive experimental environment we were able to watch the suppression of one escape strategy and the emergence of a second. The fact that all subjects first attempted to lever hold strongly suggested the "naturalness" of this strategy, a keynote feature of SSDRs. The eventual suppression of this behavior by the Campden chamber suggests an interesting possibility regarding other forms of escape behavior. Whenever an alternate "strategy" or response sequence is observed during lever-press escape, it is conceivable that some aspect of the experimental environment or procedure has differentially suppressed escape behavior based on the more highly probable lever-holding–reflexive lurch pattern.

Stemming largely from the research reported to this point we had evolved a working model of lever-press escape—its acquisition, and to some extent, its maintenance—based largely on SSDRs. Because our analysis of lever-press escape was far from conventionally operant in scope, we were coming to believe that

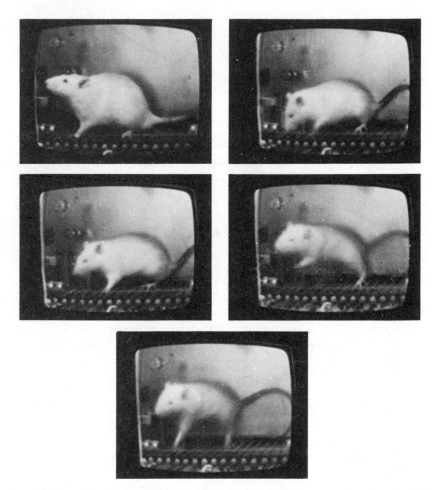

FIG. 9.4 Illustrative "strategy" for lever-press escape by subjects in a Campden chamber. Subject spends the majority of the intertrial interval off-lever. At shock onset, the subject leaps toward and makes contact with the lever, thereby terminating the shock. (From Davis & Kenney, 1975.)

recording and measurement techniques that were similarly unconventional were of greatest relevance and sensitivity.

Development of a Continuous Measurement Technique

The concern for sensitive measurement had yet to make its presence felt in one of the most fundamental aspects of lever-press escape: lever holding. Momentarily sidestepping the issue of why lever holding occurs, it does appear to be a fact of life in the lever-press escape situation. Although we had previously been able to suppress lever holding by imposing unsupportive conditions (for example, a lever-lift manipulation; the Campden chamber), its ubiquitous presence in an impressively wide array of "normal" test chambers suggested that lever-holding may be as essential a characteristic of escape conditioning as the escape response itself.

All of this left us facing the simple question: given the consistent presence of lever holding, how is it best measured? Initially investigators had only been concerned with the first 50 msec of what might otherwise be a 30-sec lever hold. This form of recording required a pulse former and yielded response rate data. As interest in lever holding per se deepened, however, continuous counters had been pressed into service. Our own technique (e.g., Davis, Hirschorn, & Hurwitz, 1973) involved an elapsed-time counter that advanced in tenths of a second as long as the subject depressed the lever. This technique told us how much time the subject had spent on the lever, but not when in the session this lever holding had occurred. To this end, event recorders were employed. The length of each pen deflection told us not only the duration, but also the exact location in time of each lever contact. These data were helpful insofar as they went beyond simple latency and response rate measurement, but they left us wanting more information. We watched our subjects and considered our event recordings and counters. It was clear that something was missing.

We recalled that a similar problem had been described by Donald Mintz when he studied fixed-ratio responding in rats. Mintz (1962), like others before him, had pondered the unsatisfying result that no change in the subject's rate of response occurred as it approached reinforcement on a fixed-ratio schedule. Because there was ample reason to believe that the animal could anticipate when reinforcement was due, it was unlikely that the resultant "excitement" would not show up in its behavior. If response rate data were insensitive to this effect, where would sensitive measurement lie? Mintz decided to measure the force of each response and found, not surprisingly, that subjects were hitting the lever harder and harder as each reinforcement was neared. In a series of subsequent experiments, Notterman and Mintz (1965) employed the response force measurement technique across a variety of procedures and provided some valuable insights into characteristic performance. Their range of techniques, however, did not include escape conditioning.

We decided that the information to be gained from continuous measurement of lever contact during escape behavior far outweighed the frustrations of designing a force transducer circuit. Along with our technician Daniel Whitley, my assistant Jo-Ann Burton and I worked to establish a recording technique that would give us continuous measurement of the force of all on-lever behavior.[5]

___

[5] J. D. Keehn has pointed out to me that Mowrer's interest in intertrial behavior during avoidance conditioning led him to employ the wheel-running response which, like response force, allowed for a continuous behavior record. J. D. Keehn (1967b) has explored the analogy between wheel-running and lever-holding behavior during avoidance.

Our ultimate design (described in detail in Davis & Burton, 1974) involved mounting a lever on a strain gage force transducer so that all downward pressure exerted by the subject produced a small voltage change. We then ran these voltages through a Schmitt trigger, which allowed us to select any force criterion (e.g., 15 gm) by simply finding its voltage equivalent and defining all voltages equal to or above this level as a "response." Lever contact of less than criterion value simply did not operate the escape program and its recorders, timers, and counters. Regardless of whether responses were above or below criterion, we took the voltage equivalent of all lever contact and fed this information directly into a physiograph so that the pen tracings provided us with a continuous record of the time, duration, and force of all on-lever behavior. In our earlier experiments, measurement such as mean response force was taken directly off physiograph records. In more recent research, the continuous voltage from the force transducer has been fed directly into a computer that is able to sample response force on line several times a second. This methodology has been the backbone of virtually all of our subsequent research. At the least it has provided us with traditional measurement of lever-press escape and has complemented these data with an additional dimension of performance. At times it has also produced unexpected insight into escape performance and has led us to pursue lines of inquiry that would have been impossible had traditional discrete response measurement been employed.

Response Force and Lever-Press Escape

Our initial efforts using this technique were concerned with simply establishing the pattern of on-lever behavior that occurred during lever-press escape. We had a number of preliminary questions in mind. What was the mean force of lever contact? Was the force of lever contact stable over trials? Over sessions? How would the "reflexive lurch" appear in terms of continuous measurement? (Would it appear at all on our force records?) Most of these questions were answered in relatively short order. We were struck, and still continue to be, by how few between-subject differences there are and by how readily "characteristic" lever contact records can be obtained. The composite record shown in Fig. 9.6 is typical in that literally thousands like it have been obtained in our laboratory. This is doubly impressive considering the potential sensitivity involved in continuously recording the force, duration, and time of on-lever behavior.

Figure. 9.5 shows a sequence of six consecutive trials during an escape conditioning session. Figure 9.6 presents an enlarged composite illustration of the major characteristics of the initial 5-sec portion of a 30-sec intertrial interval. Examining Fig. 9.6, one can envision the following sequence of activity. Prior to shock onset the subject was in contact with the lever at approximately 48-gm force. Immediately following shock onset (Point A), a reflexive lurch, which

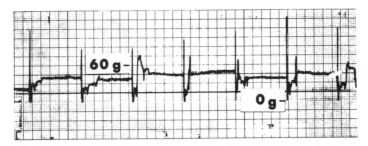

FIG. 9.5 Response force recording made of lever contact during six consecutive lever-press escape trials. The heavy horizontal ruling represents the 15-gm response force criterion. The vertical grid lines indicate 5-sec increments; horizontal grid lines indicate 15-gm increments in force.

appears on virtually all escape records, occurs (Point B). This appears on the lever contact record as a brief spike of peak force, typically in excess of 100 gm and occasionally reaching values above 150 gm. As a consequence, the subject is briefly out of contact with the lever, during which time the force record returns to 0 gm (Point C). The subject typically returns to contact with the lever rather quickly, which appears as a rapid increase in force followed by a short period of

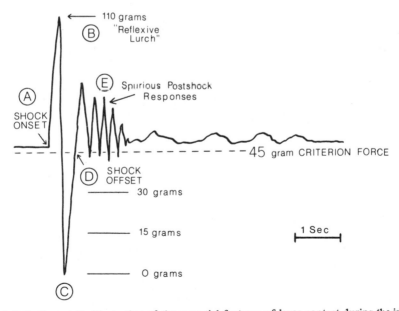

FIG. 9.6 Composite illustration of the essential features of lever contact during the initial portion of a lever-press escape trial. See text for explanation. (From Davis & Burton, 1974. Copyright 1974 by the Society for the Experimental Analysis of Behavior, Inc.)

erratic contact. As the rapidly increasing force first passes from 0 through the criterion value, a "response" is recorded and shock is terminated (Point D). This entire portion of the sequence typically occurs in less than one-half second. The brief period of erratic force that follows shock offset may result in a spurious "discrete" response count (Point E) if the force values associated with lever contact are centered near the criterion (as illustrated in Fig. 9.6). Relatively minor shifts in posture may result in responses being recorded each time the force of lever contact drops below and again passes through criterion. As suggested in Fig. 9.5 and illustrated more clearly in Fig. 9.6, the force of lever contact for the remainder of the intertrial interval is typically quite constant, varying as little as 5 gm for the remaining 25-sec period. Figure 9.7 illustrates an occasion in which the force of lever contact over this period varied less than 2 gm. Throughout all of our research, no pattern, either of increasing or decreasing force, characterized the majority of on-lever behavior reported either on particular trials or throughout a session.

In examining a variety of continuous recordings of lever contact during escape, we have become aware of at least two situations which suggest that traditional discrete response measurement may be less than accurate. The first is illustrated in Fig. 9.6 (Point E), where unstable lever contact may result in discrete

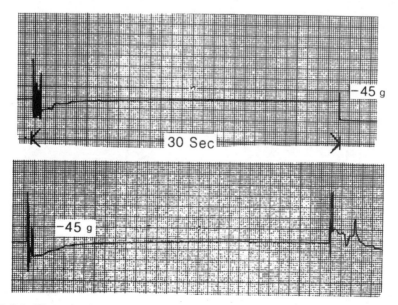

FIG. 9.7 Illustrative lever contact records obtained during an escape conditioning trial. Note the stability in the force of lever holding in both records. Despite continuous lever contact, approximately half of the on-lever behavior in the upper record and all the on-lever behavior in the lower record would be lost (i.e., would fail to operate programming and recording equipment) if the response force criterion equaled or exceeded 30 gm.

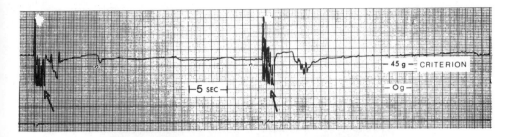

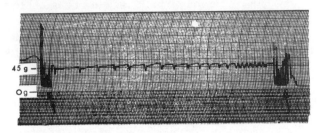

FIG. 9.8 Characteristic pattern of response force produced by postshock response bursts (at arrows). In addition to response counts produced by such behavior, the lower record also illustrates a response force pattern produced by respiration, which becomes more rapid as the 30-sec intertrial interval elapses. Twenty-two "responses" at a 45-gm criterion were recorded following the postshock response burst on the lower record, despite the subject's sustained contact with the lever. (From Davis & Burton, 1974. Copyright by the Society for the Experimental Analysis of Behavior, Inc.)

response counts despite the fact that the subject has not left the lever. Such effects were far from rare. Figure 9.8 illustrates further examples of artifactually produced discrete response counts in a situation that continuous measurement has revealed to be sustained lever contact. The rhythmic changes in response force, such as those illustrated on the lower record in Fig. 9.8, resulted from metabolic activity (respiration) of a subject that was otherwise motionless on the lever while "anticipating" shock. Figure 9.8 also illustrates that spurious response counts may result from postshock response bursts, a widely observed phenomenon under aversive control procedures (e.g., Azrin et al., 1967). Using continuous measurement of response force, the distinctive pattern of such lever contact is readily identifiable and may be distinguished from other forms of on-lever behavior. In the experiment by Davis and Burton (1974) the force of these brief spikes of activity rarely exceeded the force of the reflexive lurch and ranged between 50 and 75 gm. Only one of three subjects showed this behavior reliably. Between Sessions 24 and 44, postshock response bursts occurred on approximately 70% of trials per session, but prior to and following this period such behavior rarely occurred on more than 15% of any session's trials.

A second form of inaccuracy that has been revealed by continuous recording of on-lever behavior concerns lever contact which may have occurred at force values lower than the arbitrarily selected criterion. As illustrated in Fig. 9.7, lever contact of considerable stability may fail to operate counters simply because its force falls below the criterion set by the investigator. Because "lever holding" has been of considerable historical interest in escape conditioning studies, its accurate measurement seems to be essential. At least one example can be offered, however, in which inaccurate measurement of lever contact may have resulted in a questionable conclusion. In an attempt to modify the amount of lever holding, Winograd (1965) examined the effects of varying the response force criterion during escape. He found that raising this threshold to 60 gm, an unusually high value, reduced lever holding to approximately 2% of session time. It now appears conceivable, however, that the main effect of raising the force criterion to 60 gm may have been to render the apparatus insensitive to the presence of on-lever behavior that occurred below this force instead of reducing its frequency.

In our initial continuous measurement work with lever-press escape (Davis & Burton, 1974), Jo-Ann Burton and I pursued this issue by varying the response force criterion. We wondered specifically whether the subject could discriminate changes in force criterion and whether these differences would affect the properties of on-lever behavior, either during the intertrial interval or the shock termination sequence. There had appeared, at first, to be some reason to explore the relationship between response force criterion and the general properties of lever-press escape. One might envision, for example, a rather simplistic view of lever-press escape in which subjects might show intertrial lever holding at a force near criterion in order to "prepare," in a manner suggested by a number of investigators (e.g., Campbell, 1962), to execute a low-latency escape response. Despite our best intentions and most elaborate experimental techniques, neither the force of lever-holding behavior nor the escape sequence itself illustrated in Fig. 9.6 revealed the slightest control by the response force criterion manipulation, at least within the range we examined (15–45 gm).

Although we were initially surprised by this lack of effect, it has come to make more sense to us. Our reasoning is the following: If the actual response that terminates shock in spurious, that is, part of a reflexive sequence that requires only that the subject be on-lever at the moment of shock onset, then once the subject is in contact with the lever at virtually any force, the reflexive lurch and resultant shock termination are guaranteed to occur. Turner and Solomon (1962) have suggested precisely such a negative relationship between the reflexiveness of an aversively controlled response and "awareness" of the stimulus contingencies that govern this behavior.

Some time after we had completed work on this project, it was suggested that subjects might be responsive to changes in response force criterion if this value were above the average force level reached during the reflexive lurch. Again making reference to Fig. 9.6, it does appear reasonable that if such a criterion is in effect, neither the peak force value reached during the reflexive lurch nor the level reached during the return to the lever can result in shock termination. Under these conditions, then, some class of on-lever behavior would have to be altered if shock were to be terminated. The average response force recorded during the reflexive lurch might therefore suggest the minimum value at which manipulating the response force criterion would consistently affect lever-press escape behavior. Similarly, manipulations of force values below this level would be, as we found them, ineffective.

Because most subjects lever held at forces typically averaging more than 45 gm regardless of which criterion was in effect, we began to wonder why subjects had not learned to restrict on-lever behavior to values below the force criterion. It follows that had the subject been holding the lever at some force below criterion, shock would have been terminated by the initial lurch from the lever instead of by the lever contact that followed it (Point A vs. Point D). We ultimately concluded that this potential improvement in efficiency was never learned because either (1) the properties of lever holding, its force and topography, were rooted more deeply in SSDRs than in consequential control or (2) the relatively small decrease in escape latency that would have resulted from this change in strategy was so minor as to be either indiscriminable (.05 sec versus .20 sec) or, loosely speaking, simply not worth the trouble.

Our original data (Davis & Burton, 1974), along with the results of a later experiment (Davis, Porter, Burton and Levine, 1976), contained a compelling suggestion that bears directly on the notion discussed earlier that lever-press escape may undergo a "change in control" over sessions. The mean force of lever contact recorded over the first three escape sessions appeared (and continues to appeal in later experiments) to be considerably higher in force (averages ranging from 75 to 93 gm) than in later sessions (averages typically declining to near 40 gm). Before glibly relating this change in force to the change from SSDR to operant control, it should be noted that considerable variability underlies each of these means. For example, during an early session in which response force may average 85 gm, it is not uncommon to find that intertrial lever holding may also occur at between 30 and 40 gm on as many as 30% of the trials in this same session. There are simply a larger number of trials in initial than in later escape sessions on which the force of on-lever behavior is quite high. This trend has been apparent in virtually every subject we have run and is most apparent if one examines the records of the first escape session. Our conclusion, tentative and qualified by the variability of our data, is that "pure" SSDRs, that is, the "raw terror" of freezing, is more likely to result in a "heavy-handed" lever press than is the lever-holding behavior of a subject that has become reasonably "relaxed" in the escape situation and is now under control of the escape reinforcement contingency.

Because we have postulated that the presence of shock is necessary in order to catalyze lever-holding behavior into "discrete" responses, it follows that elimination of shock from the experimental situation should leave the subject holding the lever with relatively few responses for his effort. We have evidence to this effect stemming from two different approaches to elimination of shock.

The first concerns the use of a formal extinction procedure, which we have examined on two separate occasions. In one study (Hirschorn, 1972), we looked, almost as an afterthought, at whether lever holding would persist once periodic presentations of shock were discontinued. Following 15 half-hour escape sessions, subjects were "primed" by receiving 15 regular escape trials, after which shocks were withheld altogether. All subjects remained on the lever for longer than the previous intertrial interval (30 sec) and showed total lever-holding times averaging 1,201 sec during a 5-hr extinction session. The duration of the initial lever-hold following shock offset averaged 429 sec. In a later replication (Davis & Burton, 1975), Jo-Ann Burton and I obtained essentially similar results despite several procedural differences. Although we were able to eliminate lever holding or reduce it to 8% of session time by the end of a second 30-min extinction session, we did record lever holds ranging between 120 and 780 sec at the start of the first extinction session.

Our second, somewhat less sophisticated, method for examining lever contact in the absence of shock results from a fact of life in our laboratory. Some of our levers do not retract automatically and, following the end of the session, the subject must remain in the chamber until the experimenter removes him. On most occasions, this sequence lasts less than a minute. Occasionally, however, the experimenter's reaction time is considerably slower and we are afforded an unplanned opportunity to observe our subject's behavior immediately following removal of shock. The record presented in Fig. 9.9 illustrates unpublished data collected in our laboratory by John Porter. The notable feature of this record is that on-lever behavior following shock termination appears virtually identical to its counterpart, recorded during shock presentations, except for the regular occurrence of shock-induced lurches from the lever.

In a study dealing with extinction, Malott, Sidley, and Schoenfeld (1963) have concluded that "... the present study indicates that 'escape' and 'avoidance' contingencies play minor roles in *maintaining* the behavior, within the limits of exposure used here. The importance of these two contingencies in the *establishment* of behavior is yet to be determined" [p. 371]. This analysis fits comfortably within the schema we are proposing. Shock per se results in "responses" (reflexive lurches from the lever) regardless of why shock has been programmed to occur. Therefore, "free shock" presented during an extinction procedure would presumably yield a "response" as readily as a shock that occurred during an escape schedule, provided the subject was on the lever at the time of its delivery. It is this latter point that makes the escape contingency important during the acquisition stage. The escape contingency not only assures the regular delivery of shock but, as previously discussed, virtually confines the presence of freezing to the lever by punishing this behavior in alternative locations.

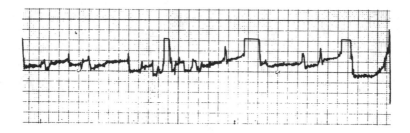

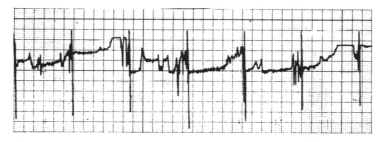

FIG. 9.9 Force recording of the lever contact obtained during the final six lever-press escape trials with an intertrial interval of 30 sec (lower record) and in comparable time period immediately following final shock (upper record). The horizontal grids represent 15-gm increments and vertical grids indicate 5-sec periods.

The Reinforcement of Lever Holding

As a consequence of our initial research, we had compiled a reasonably complete picture of the lever contact that occurred during escape conditioning (Davis & Burton, 1974). The lever holding behavior we had observed had occurred in the absence of an explicit reinforcement contingency. In fact, virtually all lever holding reported in the literature seemed to have emerged fortuitously as an indirect consequence of some aspect of the conditioning situation. We next wondered what the properties of lever holding would be, in contrast to the picture we had already obtained, if this behavior were explicitly required and reinforced.

In order to generate an appropriate procedure we borrowed an idea that had found relatively little favor since its introduction by Hefferline more than 25 years ago. In his original experiment, Hefferline (1950) had required rats to remain in continuous contact with the lever, that is, to lever hold, in order to avoid the onset of light. In our experiment (Davis & Burton, 1976), we similarly required rats to lever hold in order to forestall the delivery of shock, which would occur immediately on release of the lever. Unlike all of our research reported to this point, we were now working with an avoidance procedure. Shock could be totally avoided if the correct response were maintained. Our essential question was whether the properties of lever holding that occurred under the direct reinforcement of an avoidance procedure would be similar to those of lever holding that occurred "fortuitously" under the lever press escape situation.

All subjects learned to remain in contact with the lever continuously in order to avoid shock. Although no sessions were shock free, the amount of unavoided shock decreased across sessions until, in many instances, total shock duration recorded during an avoidance session was as brief as the latency typically recorded on a single escape conditioning trial (for example, less than .5 sec). The general properties of lever holding under the avoidance procedure are illustrated in Fig. 9.10. All subjects spent the majority of each session exerting considerably more force on the lever than was required to avoid shock. Subjects typically waited until shock onset at the start of the session before they initiated lever contact. During the remainder of the session shock onset resulted from subjects gradually decreasing the amount of force exerted on the lever until a value below criterion was reached or, more frequently, from the subject's "suddenly" releasing the lever while holding at a value in excess of the response force criterion.

As had also been the case during escape conditioning, the force of lever contact immediately following shock offset under the avoidance procedure tended to be erratic, showing frequent fluctuations in excess of 15 gm. During this period, brief decreases in the force of lever contact occasionally resulted in the delivery of shock. Such periods of erratic lever holding, which usually lasted no more than 10 sec, were typically followed by periods of relatively stable lever holding during which few fluctuations occurred throughout the remainder of the session. As illustrated in Fig. 9.10, it was not uncommon for avoidance subjects to show momentary "dips," varying between 5 and 15 gm, in the force of lever holding. These dips occurred during periods of otherwise stable lever contact and typically occurred at values above the criterion response force and therefore did not result in shock delivery. They were observed to occur anywhere between 0 and 15 times per session, with no consistent change in frequency either within or between experimental sessions.

The question of why lever-holding avoidance subjects consistently exerted greater force than was required is worth considering. Because lever holding was usually constant in force within a session, it might have been possible for subjects to maintain lever contact at considerably lower force values without substantially increasing the amount of shock. What we propose is that the additional margin of force exerted on the lever, although seemingly violating the principle of "least effort" (e.g., Tolman, 1932; Zipf, 1949), is actually tied to successful performance under the lever holding avoidance procedure. Perhaps by maintaining the force of lever contact well in excess of criterion, the frequent

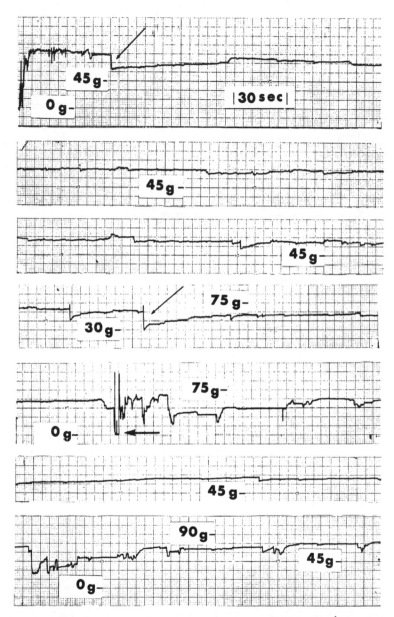

FIG. 9.10 Response force recordings obtained during seven consecutive $3\frac{1}{2}$-min segments at the start of a procedure in which shock avoidance was contingent on continuous depression of the lever. Characteristic "sudden" breaks in lever holding are indicated by thin arrows in Records 1 and 4. The heavy arrow in Record 5 illustrates a brief period of shock delivery that has occurred when the force of lever contact fell below the 15-gm criterion.

"dips" in response force that may well help to relieve muscular strain, "boredom," or other unpleasantries generated by the procedure are less likely to result in the occurrence of shock.

There is a considerable literature suggesting that avoidance responses are relatively difficult to learn and may be unstable even once initial learning has occurred (e.g., Meyer, Cho, & Wesemann, 1960; Anderson & Nakamura, 1964). In contrast to avoidance conditioning, in which discrete responses are reinforced, our work with lever-holding avoidance shows this response class to be readily learned and consistently performed. As is the case with lever-press escape, our success with lever-holding avoidance may well be related to the fact that sustained lever contact is profoundly related to freezing, an SSDR. A further reason for the rapid learning associated with lever holding avoidance may be the immediate and continuous feedback to which the subject is exposed. In contrast to the paucity of stimulus change that typically accompanies discrete avoidance response learning, the extensive feedback involved in lever-holding avoidance may be optimal for behavioral control (e.g., Bolles & Grossen, 1969). It is possible to view the lever-holding avoidance situation as analogous to that encountered by the little boy who averts the flood by keeping his finger in the dike. Providing fatigue effects do not take their toll, neither situation requires many trials to establish and maintain stable and effective avoidance performance.

Relationship Between Lever-Press Escape and Avoidance

We have recently completed an experiment to examine the relationship between lever-press escape and avoidance behavior. There is an extensive literature dealing with the manner in which these two behaviors (or learning processes) interact. Conclusions on this point run the gamut from escape experience being a necessary condition for successful avoidance learning (e.g., Petersen & Lyon, 1975; Solomon & Brush, 1956) to escape directly interfering with successful acquisition of avoidance (e.g., Hurwitz & Bounds, 1968; Turner & Solomon, 1962). In order to navigate this rather extensive literature, we will concern ourselves only with behavior generated by the procedures we will be using: lever-press escape and lever-press free-operant (Sidman) avoidance. Given these procedural limitations, the arguments seem to be fairly one sided. Escape behavior typically results in extensive lever holding; lever holding interferes with discrete responding and must be broken up before free-operant avoidance can progress (Feldman & Bremner, 1963; Hurwitz, 1967).

It follows from this argument that were we to expose subjects first to a lever-press escape procedure and later try to train them on a Sidman avoidance procedure, we should witness a substantial interference effect. We might also reverse the procedure in order to explore the effect of prior avoidance conditioning on the acquisition of lever-press escape. If the interference doctrine is correct, then avoidance experience, during which lever holding is presumably broken into discrete responses, should have deleterious effects on the development of escape behavior. These are precisely the issues that John Porter has recently investigated in our laboratory (Porter, 1976). Using an *A–B, B–A* design, Porter trained rats either on an escape or avoidance procedure and then reversed the conditions for each subject. Continuous recordings of on-lever behavior, as well as cumulative response records and response and shock frequencies, were obtained during each of 15 sessions under both procedures.

The results of this experiment do not support a strong reading of the interference theory of escape and avoidance. Such a view appears, in large measure, to have been based on an incomplete picture of the on-lever properties of avoidance behavior. For instance, if it were the case that successful avoidance depended on "discrete" lever contacts, then escape conditioning experience might indeed categorically retard avoidance acquisition. This analysis does not work for two reasons. First, subjects can show adequate avoidance behavior using a response topography considerably removed from the discrete responding envisioned by Bolles (1970), Hurwitz (1967), and others (illustrated in Fig. 9.11). Figure 9.12 shows an alternate response topography, which involves sustained lever contact but nonetheless resulted in the stable avoidance responding in Fig. 9.13. Second, the early portion of virtually all avoidance sessions contained the characteristic

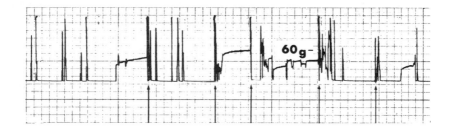

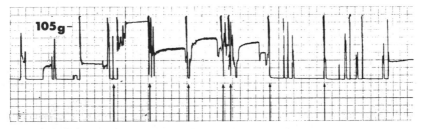

FIG. 9.11   Response force records obtained during two consecutive segments of a Sidman avoidance procedure. Discrete lever-press responses appear as brief spikes on the record. Approximately one-fourth of such responses (indicated by arrows) occurred contiguously with the shock delivery.

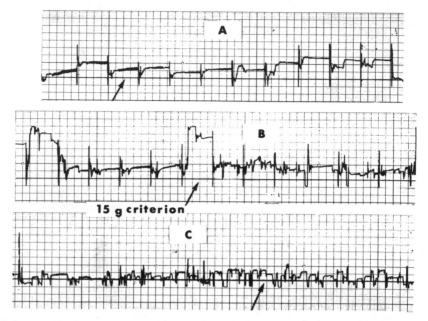

FIG. 9.12 Transition in the form of lever contact observed during three segments of a shock-avoidance session. Record A shows the characteristic warmup effect obtained at the start of a session. Note the relative stability in the force of lever contact between regular occurrences of shock-induced "reflexive lurch" from the lever. During the midportion of the session, shown in Record B, the shock rate is essentially unchanged and shock termination still occurs as a consequence of "reflexive lurch," although the force of lever contact between shock deliveries has become less stable. Because fluctuations in force, which predominate in the later session, occur near the criterion force value, a fairly high response rate is recorded in Record C and shock rate is reduced, despite the fact that "discrete" avoidance responses rarely occur. The heavy horizontal ruling at the arrows indicates the 15-gm response force criterion.

"warmup" effect, widely observed by other investigators (e.g., Powell, 1972). From our continuous records of on-lever behavior, we have learned that the properties of lever contact during warmup are essentially identical to those observed during escape (compare Figs. 9.5 and 9.12a). Therefore, whether lever holding is specifically fostered by preexposure to escape or not, it is still likely to be part of avoidance conditioning (cf. Petersen & Lyon, 1975; Hurwitz, 1967).

This latter point indicates that the interference view of escape to avoidance is far from unreasonable. In fact, further evidence supporting this view comes from lever contact records we recorded during the occasional deterioration of avoidance performance (cf. Anderson & Nakamura, 1964; Hurwitz & Bounds, 1968). During these periods, lever contact typically reverted to the characteristic

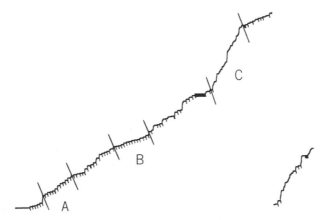

FIG. 9.13 Cumulative response record obtained during the same avoidance session shown in Fig. 9.12. Segments A, B, and C correspond to Records A, B, and C in Fig. 9.12. The blips below the response record indicate the delivery of shocks.

sustained holding observed during escape. It is essential to note, however, that although most poor avoidance was characterized by escape-like holding behavior, it was not necessary to eliminate the essential character of escape lever contact in order to produce reasonably good avoidance. For instance, there did not appear to be any difference between escape pretrained and naive subjects in response rate or shock rate recorded during any of the 15 avoidance sessions. Moreover, these two groups did not differ in the percentage of session time spent in warmup.

Porter's data also failed to reveal any consistent decrement in escape performance caused by prior avoidance training. This is perfectly reasonable because the avoidance procedure did not, as previously noted, "break up" lever-holding behavior to a degree that may have affected escape performance. There was ample opportunity for avoidance subjects to develop and retain essential features of lever holding both during warmup and in the topography shown in Fig. 9.12, which they could employ gainfully during subsequent escape conditioning.

Conclusion

The data and techniques described in this chapter reflect a *zeitgeist* in animal learning research. We are no longer quite so cavalier in accepting at face value the behavior that results from our traditional array of laboratory procedures. In fact, we are becoming less complacent about some of our time-honored procedures.

In our experiments we have supplemented, even supplanted at times, conventional measures with alternative and, it is hoped, broader views of behavior. In so doing, we hope to have learned more not only about the behavior that emerges under lever-press escape and avoidance procedures, our primary concern, but also about possible errors that have been made in the classification and analysis of these procedures.

For nearly 30 years, investigators have reported striking similarities in the topography of lever-press escape behavior, not only in the escape response but also during the presumably unstructured intertrial interval. Although the operant test cage admittedly does not allow for extensive movement or behavioral variety, this degree of stereotypy may have been seen, as it does in retrospect, as a signal to look beyond the realm of reinforcement. We can now conclude that the development of escape, like other highly "prepared" behaviors (Seligman, 1970), involves learning to such a minimal degree that to classify escape as an operant aversive control procedure is to stress what may be its least relevant source of control and minimize what is likely its fundamental character.

Acknowledgments

Thanks are due to R. C. Bolles, Harry M. B. Hurwitz, J. D. Keehn, J. L. Mottin and Andrew S. Winston for their crital comments in an earlier version of this chapter.

References

Anderson, N. H., & Nakamura, C. Y. Avoidance decrement in avoidance conditioning. *Journal of Comparative and Physiological Psychology*, 1964, 57, 196–204.

Azrin, N. H., Hutchinson, R. R., & Hake, D. F. Attack, avoidance and escape reactions to aversive shock. *Journal of the Experimental Analysis of Behavior*, 1967, 10, 131–148.

Bolles, R. C. Species specific defense reactions and avoidance learning. *Psychological Review*, 1970, 77, 32–47.

Bolles, R. C. Species-specific defense reactions. In F. R. Brush (Ed.), *Aversive conditioning and learning*. New York: Academic Press, 1971. Pp. 183–233.

Bolles, R. C., & Grossen, N. E. Effects of an informational stimulus on the acquisition of avoidance behavior in rats. *Journal of Comparative and Physiological Psychology*, 1969, 68, 90–99.

Bolles, R. C., & McGillis, D. B. The non-operant nature of the bar-press escape response. *Psychonomic Science*, 1968, 11, 261–262.

Boren, J. J. Isolation of post-shock responding in a free operant avoidance procedure. *Psychological Reports*, 1961, 9, 265–266.

Campbell, S. L. Lever holding and behavior sequences in shock-escape. *Journal of Comparative and Physiological Psychology*, 1962, 55, 1047–1053.

Davis, H. Social interaction and Sidman avoidance performance. *Psychological Record*, 1969, 19, 433–442.

Davis, H., & Burton, J. The measurement of response force during a leverpress shock escape procedure in rats. *Journal of the Experimental Analysis of Behavior*, 1974, 22, 433–440.

Davis, H., & Burton, J. An analysis of two extinction procedures for leverpress escape behavior. *Bulletin of the Psychonomic Society*, 1975, 5, 201–204.

Davis, H., & Burton, J. Reinforcement of leverholding by avoidance of shock. *Bulletin of the Psychonomic Society*, 1976, **8**, 61–64.

Davis, H., & Donenfeld, I. Extinction induced social interaction in rats. *Psychonomic Science*, 1967, **7**, 85–86.

Davis, H., & Hirschorn, P. Social behavior in rats during escape from shock. *Canadian Journal of Psychology*, 1973, **27**, 262–271.

Davis, H., Hirschorn, P., & Hurwitz, H. M. B. Lever holding behavior during a leverlift shock escape procedure. *Animal Learning and Behavior*, 1973, **1**, 215–218.

Davis, H., & Kenney, S. Some effects of different test cages on response "strategies" during leverpress escape. *Psychological Record*, 1975, **25**, 535–543.

Davis, H., Porter, J. W., Burton, J. & Levine, S. Sex and strain differences in leverpress shock escape behavior. *Physiological Psychology,* 1976, **4**, 351–356.

Davis, H., Porter, J. W., Livingstone, J., Herrmann, T., & Levine, S. Pituitary-adrenal activity and lever press shock escape behavior. *Physiological Psychology,* in press.

Davis, H., & Wheeler, L. Social interaction between rats on different schedules of reinforcement. *Psychonomic Science*, 1966, **4**, 389–390.

Denny, M. R., & Adelman, H. M. Elicitation theory: I An Analysis of two typical learning situations. *Psychological Review*, 1955, **62**, 290–296.

Dinsmoor, J. A. Escape from shock as a conditioning technique. In Marshall R. Jones (Ed.), *Miami symposium on the prediction of behavior 1967: Aversive stimulation.* Coral Gables: University of Miami Press, 1968. Pp. 33–75.

Dinsmoor, J. A., & Hughes, H. L. Training rats to press a bar to turn off shock. *Journal of Comparative and Physiological Psychology*, 1956, **49**, 235–238.

Dinsmoor, J. A., Matsuoka, Y., & Winograd, E. Barholding as a preparatory response in escape-from-shock training. *Journal of Comparative and Physiological Psychology*, 1958, **51**, 637–639.

Feldman, R. S., & Bremner, F. J. A method for rapid conditioning of stable avoidance bar pressing behavior. *Journal of the Experimental Analysis of Behavior*, 1963, **6**, 393–394.

Hefferline, R. F. An experimental study of avoidance: Experiment 3: "Holding": The effects of different reinforcement components of the bar-pressing response. *Genetic Psychology Monographs,* 1950, **42**, 263–283.

Hirschorn, P. Fixed and variable intertrial intervals and the maintenance of leverholding in shock escape conditioning. Unpublished master's thesis, University of Guelph, Ontario, Canada, 1972.

Hurwitz, H. M. B. Leverholding under free operant avoidance. *Journal of the Experimental Analysis of Behavior*, 1967, **10**, 551–554.

Hurwitz, H. M. B. A note on the conditioned stimulus control of postshock responding. *Bulletin of the Psychonomic Society*, 1974, **4**, 554–556.

Hurwitz, H. M. B., & Bounds, W. Response specification and acquisition of free operant avoidance. *Psychological Reports*, 1968, **23**, 483–494.

Hurwitz, H. M. B., & Dillow, P. V. The effects of the warning signal on response characteristics in avoidance learning. *Psychological Record*, 1968, **18**, 351–360.

Keehn, J. D. Is bar-holding with negative reinforcement preparatory or perseverative? *Journal of the Experimental Analysis of Behavior*, 1967, **10**, 461–465. (a)

Keehn, J. D. Running and bar pressing as avoidance responses. *Psychological Reports*, 1967, **20**, 591–602. (b)

Keller, F. S. Light aversion in the white rat. *Psychological Record,* 1941, **4**, 235–250.

Levine, S. Stress and behavior. *Scientific American*, 1971, **224**, 26–31.

Maier, S. F., Seligman, M. E. P., & Solomon, R. L. Pavlovian fear conditioning and learned helplessness: Effects on escape and avoidance behavior of (a) the CS–US contingency and

(b) the independence of the US and voluntary responding. In B. A. Campbell & R. M. Church (Eds.), *Punishment and aversive behavior.* New York: Appleton-Century Crofts, 1969. Pp. 299–342.

Malott, R. W., Sidley, N. A., & Schoenfeld, W. N. Effects of separate and joint escape and avoidance contingencies. *Psychological Reports,* 1963, **13**, 367–371.

Mason, J. W. A review of psychoendocrine research on the pituitary-adrenal cortical system. *Psychosomatic Medicine,* 1968, **30**, 576–607.

Meyer, D. R., Cho, C., & Wesemann, A. F. On problems of conditioning discriminated leverpress avoidance responses. *Psychological Review,* 1960, **67**, 224–228.

Migler, B. Experimental self-punishment and superstitious escape behavior. *Journal of the Experimental Analysis of Behavior,* 1963, **6**, 371–385.

Mintz, D. E. Force of response during ratio reinforcement. *Science,* 1962, **138**, 516–517.

Myers, A. K. Avoidance learning as a function of several training conditions and strain differences in rats. *Journal of Comparative and Physiological Psychology,* 1959, **52**, 381–386.

Notterman, J. M., & Mintz, D. E. *Dynamics of response.* New York: John Wiley and Sons, 1965.

Pavlov, I. P. *Conditioned reflexes.* (Translated by G. V. Anrep.) London: Oxford University Press, 1927.

Pear, J. J., Moody, J. E., & Persinger, M. A. Lever attacking by rats during free-operant avoidance. *Journal of the Experimental Analysis of Behavior,* 1972, **18**, 517–523.

Petersen, M. R., & Lyon, D. O. An application of the species-specific defence reaction hypothesis. *Psychological Record,* 1975, **25**, 21–37.

Porter, J. An analysis of lever contact during transition from leverpress escape to avoidance. Unpublished master's thesis, University of Guelph, Ontario, Canada, 1976.

Powell, R. W. Analysis of warm-up effect during avoidance in wild and domesticated rodents. *Journal of Comparative and Physiological Psychology,* 1972, **78**, 311–316.

Schwartz, B. On going back to nature: a review of Seligman and Hager's Biological Boundaries of Learning. *Journal of the Experimental Analysis of Behavior,* 1974, **21**, 183–198.

Segal, E. F., & Holloway, S. M. Timing behavior in rats with water drinking as a mediator. *Science,* 1963, **140**, 888–889.

Seligman, M. E. P. On the generality of the laws of learning. *Psychological Review,* 1970, **77**, 406–418.

Seligman, M. E. P. *Helplessness.* San Francisco: W.F. Freeman, 1975.

Seligman, M. E. P., & Hager, J. L. *The biological boundaries of learning.* New York: Appleton, 1972.

Solomon, R. L., & Brush, E. S. Experimentally derived conceptions of anxiety and aversion. In M. R. Jones (Ed.), *Nebraska symposium on motivation.* Lincoln, Nebraska: University of Nebraska Press, 1956. Pp. 212–305.

Tolman, E. C. *Purposive behavior in animals and man.* New York: Appleton-Century-Crofts, 1932.

Turner, L. H., & Solomon, R. L. Human traumatic avoidance learning: theory and experiments on the operant-respondent distinction and failures to learn. *Psychological Monographs,* 1962, **62**(40, Whole No. 559).

Ulrich, R. E., & Azrin, N. H. Reflexive fighting in response to aversive stimulation. *Journal of the Experimental Analysis of Behavior,* 1962, **5**, 511–520.

Wheeler, L., & Davis, H. Social disruption of performance on a DRL schedule. *Psychonomic Science,* 1967, **7**, 249–250.

Winograd, E. Escape behavior under different fixed ratios and shock intensities. *Journal of the Experimental Analysis of Behavior,* 1965, **8**, 117–124.

Zipf, G. K. *Human behavior and the principle of least effort.* New York: Hafner, 1949.

DISCUSSION

A fair degree of criticism arose concerning the notion of SSDRs and the extent to which this model accounted for the characteristic pattern of lever-press escape behavior. Discussants occasionally offered their own analyses of lever-press escape in terms that involved different premises and vocabularies. To clarify his own view, Davis made the following statement:

"I'm not sure there is anyone who would seriously suggest that the entire escape pattern is based upon SSDRs. There are two distinctions which must be made. The first concerns where the animal goes versus what he does when he gets there. It is primarily the latter for which I am invoking SSDRs. The second distinction concerns the establishment versus the maintenance of escape behavior. The SSDR–reflexive lurch model speaks most clearly to the establishment of lever-press escape. It's quite unreasonable, for example, to argue that a subject who has been run for 25 or 50 escape sessions is still lever holding for reasons of "pure terror," as he was in session number two. At some point in training he becomes competent, so to speak, and the role of SSDRs becomes less and less central. As I pointed out earlier, there are contingencies out there, both operant and Pavlovian, and it's hard to believe that these operations don't eventually begin to govern the subjects' behavior. The questions of interest to me are at what point does this "second level" of control occur, and does it yield forms of behavior that are measurably different?

Seligman: I'm troubled by the notion of SSDRs and by analyses which take off from this position. I can understand flight or running away as an SSDR and how the one-way shuttlebox taps into these behaviors. However, I can't think of a naturalistic situation where, in order to escape, the rat has to stand in one place and manipulate something. In other words, how does the lever-press escape situation relate to natural settings and SSDRs?

Davis: I'd like to respond in two ways. One, I don't believe it's logically necessary to find the perfect laboratory analog to wildlife situations in order to justify using SSDRs in one's analysis. Bolles described aversive situations in general when he spoke of the necessary conditions for SSDRs. We've chosen escape conditioning and freezing, not because the two necessarily go together in nature, but because escape conditioning is one way we know of inducing aversion in the lab and because freezing is one of a hierarchy of responses that is brought to the fore according to Bolles' analysis. If we create an aversive circumstance and find the animal repeatedly engaging in a behavior previously described as an SSDR, then this analysis is at least worthy of consideration.

The second part of my reply concerns your description of an animal "standing in one place and manipulating something." I don't believe this is what our subject does at all. It's true we record lever-press responses, but as I've said before I believe these to be highly artifactual. Only because our subject happens to freeze on the lever do we end up recording what may be viewed as a manipulative response.

Boakes: The only reason you're not willing to accept it as a manipulative response is that it looks different from how rats lever press for food. You're ruling it out because of preconceived notions of how rats ought to lever press.

Davis: Perhaps. However, I would argue that a lever press should and is conventionally assumed to result from a depression of the lever, not a current-induced lurch from it.

Boakes: There's another way to view your escape situation. The operant is defined simply as pressing a piece of metal down. Because there are few topographical constraints on the form of this behavior, the nature of the reinforcer will play a major role in determining its topography. When shock is involved, as in the escape situation, fear will inhibit casual wandering around, sniffing in corners, and a variety of other behaviors that might affect lever pressing when food is the reinforcer. It's more likely that "staying still" will become dominant, which is what you observe and call "freezing." This analysis may be nothing more than you're saying; I just don't see that calling these behaviors SSDRs buys you very much.

Seligman: I'd like to try to "unpack" the notion of SSDRs. I'm curious about which of three possible readings you're giving the term. I don't believe Bolles distinguishes among these three possibilities. The general message of SSDR theory, as I understand it, is that the presence of pain or a related Pavlovian process, e.g., "fear," facilitates the learning of an avoidance response. This can happen in at least three ways:

1. The response that is caused by the pain or fear is synonymous with the operant.

2. Pain or the related Pavlovian process facilitates sampling the operant contingency. It increases the probability that the animal will make the operant response and will therefore be reinforced and learn.

3. The third is to me the most interesting from the "preparedness" point of view. Pain or fear have a different rate parameter which governs their acquisition than do alternate responses which are not related to the SSDR hierarchy. For example, given one occasion of freezing and being reinforced, the animal associates that faster with reinforcement than he would some arbitrary response such as chain pulling.

If these three readings of SSDR are clear to you, in which way are you using the term?

Davis: From the point of view of my data, I find the first most interesting and would argue that the escape situation, initially, falls within that category. I realize once I align myself with that reading of SSDR theory I have possibly produced the most trivial outcome. One can argue "what are we doing as learning theorists? The animals came prewired and we design so-called conditioning situations which produce little more than what the subjects were bound to give us anyway." Nevertheless, I believe the operant data we collect early in escape training are largely artifactual, and consequently your first version of SSDR theory is a good approximation of what's going on. The only additional consideration in this case is that we've got to get the animal to make his prewired response in the right place. The rat is highly attuned to spatial cues at this point and some mechanism, be it place learning, punishment, and/or whatever, plays its role. Once he's in the right place, however, your definition applies: What he is wired to do is going to pay off.

Your second reading of what SSDRs mean probably applies to the maintenance of lever-press escape rather than to its establishment. I believe you're saying that because of pain or fear, certain behaviors will occur more frequently and inevitably will be hooked by the reinforcement contingencies. That's close enough to my description of the maintenance of escape, provided you stress that the subject cannot be thoroughly responsive to contingencies for lever pressing, if he is still caught up in the "raw terror" which characterizes the SSDR state. A subject in that condition is simply a closed shop; he's not interested in sampling contingencies, evolving strategies, or processing feedback. He is reduced to prewiring. It's a good thing that what he was equipped to give us is what we've defined as a successful response, or else the first rat in the first escape experiment would still be taking the first shock.

Jenkins: What kind of things cause rats to freeze in nature?

Davis: Sudden stimuli, loud noises, novelty . . .

Black: But only for a while.

Davis: That's right. There's a habituation effect and that's why I believe there must be a transition in the control of freezing within the escape situation. Novelty is tremendously important in the rat's coping behavior and the escape situation, by definition, can only be novel for a limited period of time. Something has to maintain that freezing or lever holding after terror or fear have been reduced.

Seligman: Freezing may be confined to a particular type of aversive stimulus which can't readily be localized. Shock might tie into this by coming up through the floor rather than being centered in any one area. An experiment was done in which shock was confined to a small area; I believe it was delivered by a cattle prod type of apparatus. Its effects, for instance the amount of freezing, were quite different than those usually produced by grid shock.

Jenkins: In Davis's experiments the lever may come to act as a safe place because it is associated with less shock than is the rest of the box. The rat literally hangs on to this place. Localizing this as a safe place shows that his behavior is sensitive to contingencies. They may not be response contingencies, but they are spatial stimulus contingencies. I think this account, which is of course speculative, is different from the one Hank has proposed. He has said that the rat happens to be in a particular location when the shock goes off, namely at the lever. This becomes a trial and error account of why he spends so much time there. What I'm suggesting emphasizes the possibility that the lever becomes a relatively shockfree place which is good to hang onto because of its safety value.

Black: I think any situation in which you study escape behavior without taking into account the importance of spatial learning is unfortunate. That's why the lever-press procedure has lead to so many difficulties in interpretation.

Garcia: That depends on the kind of shock you use. If the shock source allows for localization, then you should make provision for observing spatial behavior. However, the shock might be of a highly general kind, in which case spatial cues would be relatively unimportant. Then freezing and other factors, such as temporal cues, become important. Depending on which receptors the shock stimulates, you'll get entirely different classes of behavior.

Weisman: It's surprising after all these years of shocking rats, how little we really know about the way they react to shock.

Davis: Myer has a chapter in Brush's book (1971) on the unconditioned effects of shock. Offhand, it's the most systematic work I can think of on this topic.

The notion of preparation has been raised quite frequently in the literature on lever-press escape and has been the focus of several critical experiments (e.g., Keehn, 1967). The question of whether or not animals prepare in some way to lever press in order to escape shock was raised during the discussion of Davis' paper.

Davis [In reference to the lower record in Fig. 9.8] : Strangely enough, this is about the only evidence we have for anything resembling "anticipation" on the part of the subject. We've been quite surprised by this. When Bob Bolles was here recently, I showed him these data. He too was surprised at the fact that our measures were picking up no evidence of anticipatory conditioning, despite the fact that regular intertrial intervals (ITIs) were in effect. If some form of temporally based preparation is going on, it doesn't seem to be at the level our response measures are sensitive.

Staddon: Have you looked at the effects of running variable intertrial intervals?

Davis: We ran a study like that some time ago, using ITIs that varied between about 5 and 75 sec with a mean of 30 sec. The results were virtually identical to our fixed 30-sec groups. The temporal regularity or "predictability" factor just didn't seem to be important.

Staddon: Your intervals were still fairly short. Have you looked at what happens with longer ITI's?

Davis: That may be an important variable. Peter Keehn has shown some effects of long ITIs on leverholding, in avoidance behavior (Keehn and Walsh, 1970). We currently have two studies in progress; one deals with the effects of long ITIs and the other examines the effects of long session times, up to 3 hours. We haven't progressed to the point where I can report data to you, although there are some clear indications of fatigue—such as effects on lever holding in the long sessions.

Seligman: I'm not sure I agree with your conclusion that the behavior you observed reveals no form of preparation. Some years ago we ran dogs in a panel-pressing situation. That, too, is an extremely reflexive-looking response, with latencies around .1 sec. It seemed that the only thing the dog learned was to position itself close to the panel during the intertrial interval in order to make its reflexive panel-press response. I thought of its posture during the ITI as being a preparatory response. The best it could do was to get itself into position to make, via the reflexive mode, the so-called instrumental response. Is there anything wrong with regarding behavior during the entire intertrial interval as a preparatory response?

Davis: No. I agree with you about preparation taking the form of learning where to be. This is not unlike the analysis proposed by Campbell (1962) and Bolles and McGillis (1968), and which I reiterate in my chapter. The question, however, is why the animal ends up giving you this behavior for the entire ITI after he's learned that shocks regularly occur 30 sec apart. Perhaps John Staddon's point is relevant here. If the ITI were longer, say 3 min, then subjects might move freely around for the first half of the interval and only in the final minute would they move into position to execute the reflexive response. Looking at such a distribution of lever contact, I'd have to consider preparation as a viable explanation for what was going on. Within the constraints of the 30-sec ITI we've been using, however, we don't have the differential conditioning effects to support the preparation hypothesis.

Seligman: If the animal were to be somehow paid off for not lever holding, and the frequency of this behavior dropped, wouldn't that suggest to you that lever holding was a voluntary or operant preparatory response?

Davis: It would certainly strengthen that argument. Unfortunately, though, there have been a number of experiments that have reinforced "getting off the lever" and the results have not been positive. For example, Migler (1963) published a study in which he punished intertrial lever contact and found it virtually impossible to suppress it. In fact, on occasion the rate increased. In a sense we're paying off our subjects for not lever holding as well. The lever has to be pressed to terminate shock and it can't be pressed if the subject is already on it. We've got an implicit release—press requirement which should logically decrease lever holding, but it doesn't. We've also required subjects to explicitly release the lever to terminate shock and not affected the amount of leverholding.

Davis presented data bearing on the relationship between lever-press escape and avoidance and argued that discrete responding was not the only class of on-lever behavior that resulted in stable avoidance rates. A number of records were presented that illustrated an intermediate class of lever holding: one in which sustained lever contact of erratic force resulted in periodic response counts when the force fluctuations passed regularly through the criterion value. In addition to its relevance to the argument that lever holding must categorically interfere with successful avoidance behavior (cf. Feldman & Bremner, 1963), the following observation was made:

Hurwitz: These data don't sit very well with Anger's (1963) proposal about the control of nondiscriminated avoidance behavior. Anger argued that the behaviors which occur when the animal is off the lever are the source of the conditioned anxiety necessary to maintain avoidance. The subject terminates that anxiety by getting back on the lever and responding. Your data show that nothing of that kind is going on since he's on the lever most of the time in any case.

References

Anger, D. The role of temporal discriminations in the reinforcement of Sidman avoidance behavior. *Journal of the Experimental Analysis of Behavior,* 1963, 6, 447–506.

Bolles, R. C., & McGillis, D. B. The non-operant nature of the bar-press escape response. *Psychonomic Science,* 1968, 11, 261–262.

Campbell, S. L. Lever holding and behavior sequences in shock escape. *Journal of Comparative and Physiological Psychology,* 1962, 55, 1047–1053.

Feldman, R. S., & Bremner, F. J. A method for rapid conditioning of stable avoidance bar pressing behavior. *Journal of the Experimental Analysis of Behavior,* 1963, 6, 393–394.

Keehn, J. D. Is bar holding with negative reinforcement preparatory of perseverative? *Journal of the Experimental Analysis of Behavior,* 1967, 10, 461–465.

Keehn, J. D., & Walsh, M. Bar holding with negative reinforcement as a function of press- and release-shock intervals. *Learning & Motivation,* 1970, 1, 36–43.

Migler, B. Experimental self punishment and superstitious escape behavior. *Journal of the Experimental Analysis of Behavior,* 1963, 6, 371–385.

Myer, J. S. Effects of noncontingent aversive stimulation. In F. R. Brush (Ed.), *Aversive conditioning and learning.* New York: Academic Press, 1971. Pp. 469–536.

10

Conditioning Food—Illness Aversions in Wild Animals: *Caveant Canonici**

John Garcia
Kenneth W. Rusiniak
Linda P. Brett

University of California, Los Angeles

INTRODUCTION

The chapter by Garcia, Rusiniak, and Brett and conference presentation by John Garcia are of interest on two separate fronts. The first concerns the range of wild animals in which the bait shyness phenomenon can be demonstrated. This has obvious relevance of both an academic (that is, comparative) and applied nature. The applied interest in bait shyness is epitomized in the furor over coyote control, which has generated dialog in media ranging from Time *magazine to* Science *(1974).*

The second front on which the work of Garcia et al. *bears interest is perhaps of more immediate concern to the conference proceedings. The issue of how bait shyness is accomodated by traditional learning theory is dealt with in the final portion of their chapter and pursued in the discussion that follows. When the bait shyness or taste-aversion data first came to the general attention of psychologists, it reached them through what have been referred to as "non-blue ribbon" journals. The data were simply not credible to those who held fast to the tenets of traditional learning theory. The phenomenon of taste-aversion learning is now well established, however, and learning theory has struggled to accomodate it (e.g., Seligman, 1970). The struggle is far from over (e.g., Krane & Wagner, 1975). It is hoped that this chapter and discussion focus the issues and bring the*

*Let theoreticians beware.

synthesis between taste aversion and more traditional forms of learning further along.

Historical Notes on Bait Shyness

Bait Shyness, Poisons, and x Rays

It seems appropriate that the use of feral predators and the comparison of diverse species are recent major trends in flavor–toxicosis conditioning research. After all, some of the earliest notions of this form of conditioning exist in the folklore concerning the use of poisons. Wild animals that survived poisoning became so wary and wise to the ways of the human exterminators that a battle of wits ensued between man and beast. Time and time again, poison baits scattered in the field to eliminate varmints met with an initial success, then gradually lost their efficacy. Effectiveness of the poison baits plotted over time resembled the classical negatively accelerated learning curve based on group mean errors, because that was precisely what it was. A similar continuous function was recently generated by Gustavson, Kelly, Sweeney, and Garcia (1976), who scattered dog food baits laced with toxic lithium chloride and observed bait consumption by a population of free-ranging coyotes, *Canis latrans* (see Fig. 10.1). Lithium chloride produces acute malaise and vomiting but no fatalities, and one bout of illness is enough to condition an aversion in captive coyotes; therefore, the individual learning curves resemble a discontinuous function (see Fig. 10.2); (Gustavson, Garcia, Hankins, & Rusiniak, 1974).

We owe much of our knowledge of this phenomenon to research workers interested generally in wild rat behavior and specifically in the practical problem of eradicating wild rats in the domiciles and food stores of man. Richter (1953) stressed the importance of using poisons that the rats could not taste in his efficient campaign against rat infestations in Baltimore. His research (Richter, 1945) also demonstrated the remarkable "neophobia" of the wild rat (*Rattus norvegicus*); 3 years after he eradicated rats in Baltimore that city was still "rat free," indicating that invasion of the empty territory by rats from outlying areas was a cautious, time-consuming process.

Rzoska (1953, 1954) conducted the pioneering studies in bait shyness to devise strategies for clearing wild rats out of Khartoum. He laboriously fed rats by hand in an operant conditioning manner. First, he gave them a pellet of bread paste containing poison and then periodically fed them quarter pellets of unpoisoned bread paste to observe the development of the aversion for the bread base, or "bait" as it came to be called later. Rzoska varied poisons, devised baits and concluded that the surviving rats became "bait shy" rather than "poison shy." That is, changing the food bait and using the same poison was more effective than using the same bait and changing the poison. He seemed aware of the two major characteristics of flavor–aversion conditioning: Flavor is the critical CS and delayed illness is an effective US. Barnett's (1963) excellent

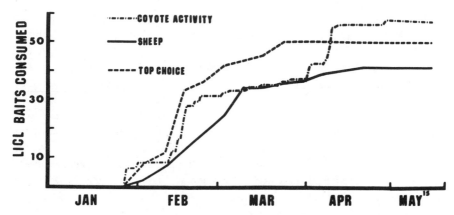

FIG. 10.1 A cumulative learning curve generated by free-ranging wild coyotes feeding on lithium-treated sheep carcasses and sheep flavored dog food (Top Choice) baits in the fields. Coyote activity was established by visual sighting and fresh tracks (After Gustavson *et al.*, 1976).

treatise on the rat provides a more detailed analysis of the rat's behavior in coping with toxins and other problems in natural as well as laboratory settings.

Research on the effects of ionizing radiation, another applied research area ushered in by the atomic age, provided the final impetus that gave flavor—toxicosis conditioning a legitimate place in behavioral research. Gamma rays and high-energy x rays proved to be a pervasive stimulus for behavioral research. Radiant energy penetrating the nasal cavity produces chemical byproducts, probably ozones and peroxides in the mucosa, that mimic an odor. A few milliroentgens can arouse the rat from sleep or signal a shock in a conditioned emotional response paradigm (Garcia & Koelling, 1971).

Although rats can perceive the deadly rays, they make little effort to escape. Instead of moving away from the source of radiant energy, they alter their dietary regime, as if they have been poisoned. If they are exposed to radiation in conjunction with drinking saccharin-flavored water, they develop an aversion that is functionally related to the radiation dose. Furthermore, rats exposed to massive doses ingest earth and fecal matter, just as poisoned rats do, apparently in an adaptive attempt to absorb poison in the gut. The impact of the radiant energy apparently releases histamine-like substances within the tissues which ultimately stimulate the evolutionary mechanism designed to cope with ingested poison (Garcia, Kimeldorf, & Koelling, 1955; Levy, Ervin, & Garcia, 1970).

Bait Shyness and the Nature—Nurture Issue

Bait shyness has profound evolutionary significance. Most natural poisons are bitter; perhaps 20% of all plant species contain bitter toxic glycosides and alkaloids. The prevalence of these toxic plants all over the world is matched by a widespread tendency in the animal kingdom to reject flavors that we describe as bitter. We have tabulated a sample of the reaction of a variety of species to bitter in Table 10.1. The list includes primitive protozoans, sponges, worms, and molluscs, as well as that "living fossil" the horse-shoe crab.

We do not imply that the rejection of substances bitter to man is mediated by the same sensory mechanisms in these diverse species, but simply that the ubiquitous toxic plants have supplied the selective pressure for toxiphobic behavior in most living species (Garcia & Hankins, 1975). In fact, much of the information necessary for survival is already encoded into the genome. By and large, men and other mammals survive by eating substances that taste good and rejecting those that taste bad. Ripe fruits and vegetables rich in carbohydrates taste sweet. The blood and flesh of prey taste salty. Green fruit and spoiled food are sour. Toxic plants are bitter.

Negative hedonic reactions to bitter are widespread in phylogeny and appear early in ontogeny. In man and other mammals, toxiphobic behavior is primarily mediated by gustatory receptors sensitive to the bitter flavors of toxic alkaloids and glycosides, which trigger a natural rejection response. This basic motivational function is subserved by midbrain mechanisms with intimate connections rostrally to the hypothalamic system and caudally to the brainstem reticular formation. Even neonate humans will reject bitter before they have received their first meal after parturition (Pfaffman, 1973). In contrast, they savor sweet substances, displaying adaptive hedonic reactions. The relative palatability of substances introduced into the mouth therefore protects the neonate before he acquires any experience or cognitive insights into the relationships between flavors and illness.

The bitter–toxiphobic system is often elaborated by learned responses. For example, primitive peoples have developed methods of processing poisonous plants, such as the cassava root. To remove fatal concentrations of glycosides and make the starch available for food, they wash and pound the pulp until it no longer tastes bitter (Montgomery, 1969). Similar elaborations have been observed in other plant–animal relationships. The milkweed *Asclepiga curassavica* contains a toxic glycoside that protects it against herbivores. The larva of the monarch butterfly has evolved the capacity to feed on the milkweed and utilizes the glycoside for its own protection against predation. Avian predators that become ill after eating monarch butterflies learn to reject the monarch on the basis of visual cues. The nontoxic viceroy butterfly, which resembles the monarch in its visual patterning, also achieves a measure of protection through mimicry (Brower, 1969).

The evolutionary contingencies that have shaped the hereditary structure of a successful species resemble those environmental contingencies that shape the coping responses of the successful individual; otherwise neither species nor individuals would survive. In essence, genetic and environmental influences are necessarily confounded in every step of the developmental sequence and the genetically acquired bitter—toxiphobic system in mammals is accompanied by a plastic capacity to adjust the hedonic tone of arbitrary flavors commensurate with their visceral aftereffects. This intimate relationship between inherited and acquired toxiphobias is illustrated in the marked similarity of the animal's conditioned responses to poisoned food and his unconditioned responses to bitter substances.

Evolution is opportunistic, and the confounding of nature and nurture provides a multiplicity of options. The "tabula rasa" is inherited just as surely as is the fixed action pattern. Constancies in the environment during development can serve the same function as constancies in the genome, for if, under almost all circumstances in its natural niche, the first moving thing the gosling sees is its mother, then a plastic posthatch imprinting tabula serves the gosling's survival as well as would an inherited imago. When Lorenz (1937) substituted himself for the mother goose, the nature—nurture confound in the gosling's development became apparent in a form amenable to research. If, under almost all circumstances in its natural niche, the white-crown sparrow nestling can hear the adult's territorial song, then all the characteristics of species song need not be programmed genetically. When Marler (1972) interfered with the natural niche, it became obvious that environmental opportunity for sensory experience, infantile memory, response rehearsal, and sensory feedback were all necessary for developing normal species-specific song. Abnormal niches can produce abnormal songs as surely as can abnormal genes.

The analysis posed above is by no means original with contemporary scientists. Its implications were debated in detail by Locke, Berkeley, Hume, Kant, and other philosphers of the seventeenth and eighteenth centuries. The "tabula rasa" was not a fatuous error made by the British empiricists. It was their insight into the nature—nurture confound. Given a variety of acute senses, an impressionable sensorium, and the capacity to explore objects in their temperospatial context, the relatively constant structured environment could explain man's percepts, his behavior, and his social station without recourse to his heritage.

Simple impressions of an object obtained by visual inspection were complicated by impressions from other sense modalities and converted into ideas by associations with past experience. Exploratory movements bringing peripheral modalities into contact with distally perceived objects created impressions of space and time. Repetitious coincidence of sensory events gave impressions of causality. This relentless march of "pure reason" led to Kant's defensive "critique" which, after all, argued that only time and space impressions were a priori intuitions, a far retreat from the Platonic position that all knowledge existed a priori.

Behavioral technology and sophisticated instrumentation have taken the nature—nurture confound directly from philosophy into science, where the goal of assigning a general attribute of behavior proportionately to one side or the other has been abandoned. Neural cells of cats and frogs are asked to respond to

TABLE 10.1
Unconditioned Rejection of Bitter[a]

Phylum (example)	Substance	Response	Reference
Protozoa (unicellular) *Stentor caeruleus*	Quinine-soaked food	Contraction and "withdrawal"	Schaeffer (1910)
Porifera (sponge) *Stylotella heliophila*	Strychnine $(2 \times 10^{-4}\ M)$	Ostia and ocula closure	Parker (1910)
Coelenterata (anemone) *Metridium*	Quinine in gelatin capsule	Eversion of gastric sac	Hodgson (personal communication, 1970)
Annelida (worm) *Lumbricus terrestris*	Quinine $(10^{-5}\ M)$	Withdraw from prostomial application	Laverack (1960)
Arthropoda *Limulus limulus* (horseshoe crab)	Quinine	Mandible sensitive	Barber (1956); Patten (1894)
Apis (honey bee)	$8 \times 10^{-4}\ M$ quinine in $1M$ sucrose	Rejection	von Frisch (1934)
Porthoteria dispar (butterfly larvae)	Quinine	"Spit out"	Dethier (1937)
Mollusca *Ostria virginica* (oyster)	Quinine sulfate $(4.6 \times 10^{-6}\ M)$	Retraction	Hopkins (1935)
Octopus vulgaris	Quinine sulfate $(1.5 \times 10^{-7}\ M)$	Behavioral task discrimination	Wells (1963)

Echinodermata *Synaptula hydriformis* (sea cucumber)	Quinine (10^{-4} M)	Withdrawal	Olmstead (1917)
Chordata Tunicata *Ascidia atra* (sessile)	Quinine sulfate (5×10^{-5} M)	Siphon retraction	Hecht (1918)
Osteichthyes many, e.g., minnow (*Phoxinus phoxinus*)	Quinine (5×10^{-9} M)	Avoidance reactions, ejection through gills	Sheldon (1909); Herrick (1904); Bardach and Case (1965); Bardach and Atema (1971)
Amphibia *Triturus* (salamander)	Many bitter substances	Avoidance	Bardach (1967)
Avia (*Columba Livia*)	Quinine (2×10^{-3} M)	Rejection	Duncan (1960)
Mammalia (*Rattus norvegicus*)	Quinine (8×10^{-6} M)	Rejection	Many, e.g., Cicala and McMichael (1964)

[a] Based on Garcia and Hankins (1975).

categorical inferences as well as perceived properties of an object (Lettvin, Maturana, McCulloch, & Pitts, 1959; Hubel & Wiesel, 1962). Kittens are reared in a world of controlled visual inputs to see whether their neural cells respond differently (Hirsch & Spinelli, 1970). Others are placed in a Berkelean world of space, time, and movement and deprived of specific empirical feedback to disrupt their capacity to cope with objects in "natural" space and time (Held & Bossom, 1961). Apes are reared with restricted sensory channels to the same end and the infant monkey's mother object has been functionally fractionated into nutritive, tactual, and kinetic dimensions (Riesen, 1961; Harlow & Suomi, 1970; Mason & Kenney, 1974). Learning in the adult animal is not only constrained by the phylogeny of his species but by his own ontogeny. Perhaps early and repeated exposure to flavor–visceral correlations facilitates bait shyness learning, as Mackintosh (1974) suggests.

Comparative Bait Shyness

Coyotes, Wolves, and Stimulus Substitution

European zoologists, as well as English philosophers, have supplied us with fundamental concepts in the study of behavior. They described the rich species-specific behavior of wild animals in their natural niche, developing the ethogram, a record of expressive gestures and intention movements of animals in response to changing stimulus conditions. Pavlov also described the intention responses of his dogs to illustrate his notion of stimulus substitution. He said his dogs were attempting to eat the CS that signaled a food US. With increasing demands of quantification, emanating principally from Yale, Iowa, and other American universities, qualitative descriptions gave way to rates, latencies, and amplitudes of responses. Recently some operant conditioning researchers in Canada have spent more time looking at the pigeon's response than at the cumulative recorder. Like Pavlov, they found that pigeons reinforced with food were attempting to eat the key and those reinforced with water were trying to drink it (Jenkins & Moore, 1973; Jenkins & Sainsbury, 1969). We have also been observing the dramatic expressive movements of feral carnivores to test the general validity of the stimulus substitution hypothesis in classical and operant conditioning. Specifically, we are observing the reactions of the predator to prey following prey flavor–illness conditioning.

Captive wild mammals proved to be highly susceptible to flavor–illness aversions, as illustrated in Fig. 10.2. The main objective of these studies on feral canines, reported in 1974 and 1976 by Gustavson and his associates, was to test the generalization of a food aversion to living prey. Various types of lithium baits were employed, and if a single lithium treatment was not effective, then a second treatment was applied. No animal received more than two treatments.

Let us first consider the effects of a single treatment following consumption of a meal where the form and the motion of the living prey animal was completely

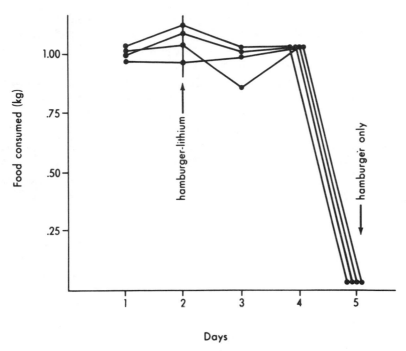

FIG. 10.2 Individual learning curves generated by captive coyotes eating lithium-treated hamburger on one trial and untreated hamburger 3 days later. Dog food was provided on alternative days. (From Gustavson *et al.,* 1974. Copyright 1974 by the American Association for the Advancement of Science.)

obliterated. In the Gustavson, Garcia, Hankins, and Rusiniak (1974) study, three coyotes were given chopped mutton wrapped in raw sheep hide containing lithium chloride capsules. In the Gustavson, Kelly, Sweeney, and Garcia (1976) study two wolves received the same mutton, wool, and lithium treatment and two coyotes received a fresh rabbit skin packet containing dog food and lithium chloride capsules. In all seven cases the gross anatomical features of the prey were eliminated but the flavor and superficial textural cues were obviously unchanged.

One mutton—lithium trial, which incidentally produced vomiting, was sufficient to inhibit attack on live sheep in one coyote and two wolves. After its single treatment the coyote ran up to the lamb, sniffed it, turned away, and retched, indicating conditioned emesis to the odor of sheep. Prior to lithium treatment, the two wolves, who were always tested together, seized sheep in their jaws, pulled them down, and killed them with prolonged biting. After treatment, they charged the sheep and made oral contact several times with their characteristic flank attacks but immediately released their prey. During the next half hour, the sheep became dominant as the wolves gave way whenever the sheep threatened with short charges. Gradually the wolves withdrew and responded to the sheep like submissive pups. Apparently the conditioned taste aversion blocked feeding and the now inedible sheep elicited social behavior from its former predators (see Fig. 10.3). Similar "inappropriate" responses to living prey were observed in coyotes, who tend to be much less "social" than wolves. When the lamb approached, the coyote retreated and growled threateningly with ears laid back in a fighting stance.

Four of the seven feral canines killed the live prey after one flesh–fur–lithium packet, but feeding on the prey was inhibited in two cases and blocked in the other two. One more lithium treatment suppressed killing in all four coyotes. After the second treatment, the odor of the prey appeared to be the sufficient cue to block attack. Perhaps odor acts as a second-order CS if we consider taste to be the original CS and illness to be the US.

Another five coyotes received a rabbit carcass perfused with lithium chloride. In this case, the form of the prey was intact but prone and motionless during acquisition; however, it was upright and active during the test. Two coyotes refused to kill after sniffing the live rabbit. Three coyotes killed the rabbit immediately but eating was markedly retarded. An additional treatment suppressed killing in these three coyotes as well. These results were remarkably similar to the previous series in which the flesh and fur of the prey was presented in a packet during acquisition; apparently the visual cues arising from the gross morphology of the dead prey are not potent conditioned stimuli.

FIG. 10.3 Wolves yielding and giving way to sheep after the flavor of sheep was made aversive by pairing it with lithium. (Copied from films by Gustavson *et al.*, 1976.)

Finally, two coyotes were given two rabbit—lithium treatments before being tested with live prey. Rabbit attacks were suppressed in one coyote. The other coyote, an extremely shy wild animal, was tested in its home cage, where it killed the intruding rabbit without eating it. After she had killed six rabbits without eating a single one, this timid creature was finally coaxed into an outdoor choice arena containing a tethered rabbit and a tethered chicken. She sniffed the rabbit thoroughly but left it unharmed; she then took the chicken to her home cage and ate it. This behavior clearly indicates that killing for predatory consumption must be differentiated from killing for territorial defense or other reasons. The expressive posture of the coyote during attack is diagnostic; when it attacks prey, it charges with ears pointed forward and tail up. When it threatens intruders, its ears are laid back, its tail is down, and it growls ominously.

Extinction, which was studied only in coyotes, proved to be variable depending on test conditions. In the Gustavson *et al.* (1976) study, six coyotes were tested in a choice area shaped like a T maze made of chain-link fence containing a tethered rabbit in one arm and a tethered chicken in the other. Under these conditions, no extinction was noted in 6—9 trials conducted over several weeks. The killing attack seemed completely suppressed, although on numerous occasions the coyotes thoroughly investigated the rabbit, smelling it all over. Invariably they would turn away, seize the chicken, and carry it home to eat.

In the Gustavson *et al*. (1974) study, five coyotes were tested in a simple enclosure without a choice of prey. Of the two coyotes averted to lambs, one coyote attacked the lamb after 2 weeks but broke off the attack without killing; another did not attack for 8 weeks, after which testing was discontinued. Both these coyotes exhibited displacement behavior, snapping and biting grass and plants in the presence of the lamb. The three coyotes averted to rabbits killed at 1 week, 2 weeks, and 4 weeks. All three showed identical recovery patterns of rabbit consumption. They first carefully ate the ears of the rabbit and then waited about half an hour. They returned to eat the head of the rabbit and again waited about another half-hour before returning to eat the remainder of the rabbit. This sampling behavior is in marked contrast to the pattern observed prior to aversive conditioning, when the coyotes started eating the neck and consumed the entire rabbit in one continuous bout.

The distinctive flavor of meat is found in its fatty acids, which provide both its characteristic taste and its characteristic odor. The coyotes probably ate the ears first because they had the least fat content. Because this small meal was not followed by malaise, their aversion was attenuated. They next ate the head, avoiding the large deposits of subcutaneous fat in the body. This second meal was not followed by malaise; instead, it was followed by nutritious effects that further reduced the aversion. The coyote therefore returned to consume the now palatable rabbit.

The responses that emerge after conditioning can be divided into three classes. First, there are conditioned illness responses, retching for example, which resemble the unconditioned vomiting caused by lithium chloride, following the classic Pavlovian doctrine of stimulus substitution. Second, there are conditioned disgust responses reflecting the changed hedonic tone of the prey flavor. For example, the coyotes either urinated on, buried, or rolled on fresh meat to which they had been averted. These disgust responses resemble the uncondi- tioned responses of dogs to putrid offal or fecal matter. The 1976 study provides another example. After a single vension–lithium meal, which did not induce vomiting, a cougar (*Felis concor*) was strongly attracted to the sight and smell of the venison but apparently the taste of venison blocked consumption. He spent the better part of an hour examining the meat. He turned over his dish and mouthed each chunk of meat. Finally he left it, shaking each paw in rotation as cats do when they contact something unpleasant. Third, there are conflict responses that are directed to other stimulus properties of the prey. This class of response was dramatically evident in the social behavior of the wolves toward the sheep, its former prey. Ultimately, the male wolf might be expected to attack and kill the sheep in a contest for dominance of the "pack," which now includes the sheep. Similarly, one coyote averted to rabbits killed rabbits thrust into its cage, but refused to eat them, as if it were defending its territory. This third class of responses has also been observed in appetitive conditioning by Timberlake and Grant (1975). Rats direct social responses, not eating responses towards a stimulus rat which is used as a CS prior to a food US. The authors conclude that the results support Konrad Lorenz' (1969) hypothesis that an entire species specific behavioral pattern is conditioned rather than a single reflex. These novel responses are also reminiscent of the confabulations with which human brain damaged patients "fill-in" lacunae to cope with paradoxes resulting from mem- ory loss. The hungry carnivores are also forced to cope with the paradox of a prey they cannot eat; in doing so they also appear "abnormal" or "disturbed."

Attack, Consummation, and the Red-Tailed Hawk

The visual world of the bird appears to be similar in many respects to that of man. Birds possess a greater resolving power by virtue of very densely packed retinal cones, although their visual acuity relative to man has sometimes been exaggerated. Raptorial birds, for example, have an especially large number of cones, and probably exceed humans in acuity by a factor of 2 or 3. In addition to seeing stationary objects in greater detail, birds also appear to have a much lower threshold for movement detection than does man. Avian and human color vision are approximately equivalent (Pumphrey, 1961).

On the other hand, the perceptual world of the bird appears to be quite different from that of laboratory rats and wild carnivores, in which bait shyness has been studied most extensively. These mammals rely heavily on olfaction in a number of situations, including food getting, mating, and evading predators. Birds, however, have generally less well-developed chemical senses. Although there are a few bird species, such as the kiwi and turkey vulture, that have demonstrated a good ability to locate food on the basis of odor cues, most avian species do not appear to use olfaction in this way (Wenzel, 1971; Stager, 1964). Birds also have few taste receptors relative to mammals. They probably discriminate the four basic tastes to which humans are sensitive, although individual and species differences are apparent (Kare, 1965).

Because birds possess keen eyesight and a paucity of taste buds, they may rely more heavily on visual cues than on taste cues when selecting nourishing foods and avoiding toxins. For example, Wilcoxin, Dragoin, and Kral (1971) studied learned aversions in the bobwhite quail and found these birds could associate illness with either blue or sour water. However, quail presented with a compound blue and sour stimulus during acquisition subsequently avoided the color but not the taste. The quail visually forages for seeds, which are covered by a tough, relatively bland seed coat and are swallowed whole. Unlike the rat, which chews and tastes seeds in the mouth, the quail grinds up seeds in its gizzard after ingestion. Therefore, the quail may have developed visual mechanisms to discriminate toxic foods.

Avian predators that capture live prey with their beaks are more comparable to mammalian predators. Brower's (1969) previously mentioned study of the blue jay (*Cyanocitta cristata*), which preys on the monarch butterfly (*Danaus plexippus*), is an example of a naturalistic bait shyness experiment. The toxic butterfly is colorfully and distinctly marked, providing a rich visual display. The blue jay becomes sick and vomits after it eats the butterflies and in a few trials learns to avoid monarchs on sight. When pressed by hunger, the jay seizes butterflies in its beak, consuming the safe ones and releasing the toxic ones, presumably because of their bitter flavor. This indicates the primacy of taste cues in aversion learning for this avian species.

The feeding behavior of carnivorous raptors differs from both the quail and the blue jay. Although they also hunt their prey using their excellent vision, they seize prey with taloned feet and thus kill without tasting. What is more, they expend considerable energy at great risk in swooping down from high altitude to strike their victim. In this peculiar niche, a visual mechanism for rejecting prey unfit to eat would seem extremely advantageous. So Brett, Hankins, and Garcia (1976) selected large broadwing hawks (*Buteo jamaicensis, Buteo lagopus*) as their subjects in a bait-shy study.

Black and white mice served as visually distinct prey, and a mild quinine solution was used to impart a distinctive flavor to the mice on some occasions. To begin a trial, mice, usually dead, were tossed onto the floor of the large "walk in" cage in full view of the bird sitting on its waist-high perch. Ordinarily the hawk would immediately pounce on the mouse and seize it in its talons. This latency was recorded as attack time. Usually the hawk would begin to feed promptly. The total time from the beginning of the trial to the end of the meal was recorded as consume time.

Attack time, which provides a measure of the effectiveness of visual cues, is illustrated for three birds in Fig. 10.4. After a period of habituation to eating white mice, the first bird (TC2) was given a black bitter mouse, which he

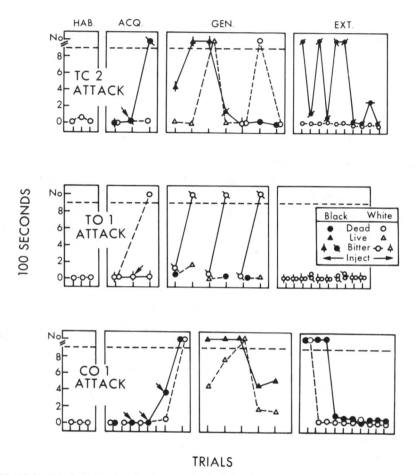

TRIALS

FIG. 10.4 Attack latencies in three red-tailed hawks during habituation, acquisition, generalization, and extinction of a mouse aversion. TC means that during acquisition the poison prey differed from the safe prey in taste and color. CO and TO refer to color only and taste only, respectively.

promptly attacked and consumed. Several days later he was given another black bitter mouse and was then injected with lithium chloride. He became ill and vomited about an hour later. A week later, he refused a black bitter mouse, frantically fluttering away from the offering and crying out in alarm and distress.

After this single acquisition trial he was given a generalization test with a variety of live and dead mice. He vacillated in his attack and showed a slight preference for white mice. During extinction he attacked white mice immediately but vacillated when confronted with black bitter mice. He would seize one black bitter mouse, taste it, and refuse to consume it. On the next trial he would refuse to come down off his perch for the black bitter mouse (see Fig. 10.4).

The second bird (TO1) in Fig. 10.4 was not given a color cue; her poison mice differed in taste only. Her behavior in acquisition and generalization was remarkably similar to that of hawk TC2, who had both taste and color cues. During extinction, she immediately seized any white mouse and promptly tasted it. She ate the unflavored mouse with dispatch, but her aversion for bitter white mice took 17 trials to extinguish.

The third hawk (CO1) in Fig. 10.4 had only the mouse's black coat as a cue for poison. She was at a definite disadvantage compared to the birds with taste cues. Three injections were required in the acquisition phase. However, she acquired a general aversion for mice of both colors, showing only a slight preference for white mice in the generalization and extinction trials.

Consume scores for the same three hawks, shown in Fig. 10.5, confirm the impression that the taste cue was prepotent. The first two birds, TC2 and TO1, displayed a profound aversion for bitter mice, after a single acquisition trial, that was manifested in the generalization series and endured in extinction. Hawk TO1 took 17 trials to extinguish but TC2 did not extinguish in 42 trials. Hawk CO1, which had the color cue only and acquired a taste aversion for mice in general, extinguished in 16 trials. (Fig. 10.4 does not include all the extinction trials.) Data from three more hawks not illustrated here confirmed these impressions.

In general, the hawk behaves like the blue jay and the coyotes, forming a strong primary aversion for the taste of the poison prey. The color cue seems to become secondarily aversive by association with the aversive taste in the mouth. The data from hawk TC2 may contradict this two-phase hypothesis; he did not attack the first black mouse offered to him after his single acquisition, presumably because he did not like the look of it. Recall that the birds vomited during acquisition. The coat color was plainly visible in the vomitus, so there was an opportunity to experience color, taste, and illness together. The relative potency of the visual cues *vis à vis* taste cues is difficult to assess in any of these bird studies because their relative intensity is unknown. Perhaps bitter taste is a more intense cue than black color for the hawk and, by the same token, blue may be more intense than sour for the quail.

Rats, Ferrets, and Domestication Pressure

Coyotes and wolves are superb subjects for predation studies, but they are large resourceful animals, heavily armed with stabbing teeth set in powerful jaws. They would be ideal if they weighed about 500 to 1,000 gm because obviously they would be cheaper to maintain and much less hazardous to handle. Two laboratory animals that meet these criteria are the common laboratory rat (*Rattus norvegicus*) and the laboratory ferret (*Mustela putorius*). Feral rats are omnivores and notorious for eating grain and food stores of man, but they are

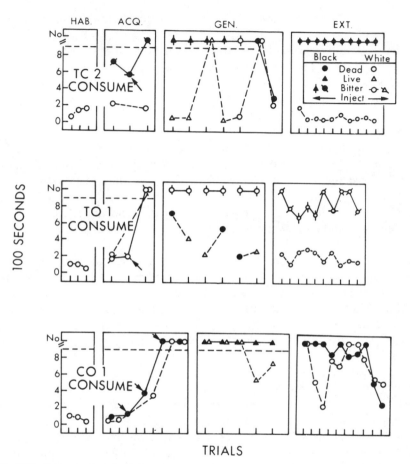

FIG. 10.5 Consumption times for three hawks in the mouse aversion study. See Fig. 10.4 for experimental conditions. (After Brett *et al.*, 1976.)

also active predators, feeding on small birds, mammals, and invertebrates. The laboratory ferret belongs to a large carnivorous family (*Mustelidae*), including the North American black-footed ferret (*Mustela nigripes*), which preys on rabbits, rodents, and birds in its natural niche. Both animals are descendants of generations of laboratory breeding and are tractable in laboratory experimentation.

There has been a good deal of research on the rat's predatory behavior toward the laboratory mouse (*Mus musculus*). Although some laboratory rats kill mice, others do not (Karli, 1956). Both types of rats consume mice when hungry (Paul & Posner, 1973). Predatory aggression as an explanation is somewhat controversial. The killing response per se seems to have some autonomy from factors known to affect feeding. First, it seems relatively independent of the level of deprivation, because mouse killers kill while satiated (Paul, 1972). Second, satiated mouse killers press a bar for the opportunity to kill a mouse (Van Hemel & Meyer, 1970), Third, rats poisoned for killing and eating mice develop an aversion for the flavor of mouse flesh that blocks consumption but they continue to attack the mouse, which is no longer a food item (Berg & Baenninger, 1974; Krames, Milgram, & Christie, 1973).

One consistent result is that habituation to the flavor of mouse flesh or simple experience with a food deprivation schedule potentiates killing. The deprivation experience itself seems to be the most important factor because it matters little whether mouse flesh, pellets, or powdered food is given during the deprivation period. Yet, paradoxically, the single consistent difference between killer and nonkiller rats seems to be that killers regard mice as food more often than nonkillers. Mouse killers tend to start eating sooner and eat more of the mouse than nonkillers and more often begin with the brain. Responses to other types of foods appear to be similar (Paul, 1972; Paul, Miley, & Baenninger, 1971).

Mouse killing rats resemble predatory house cats in some ways. The rat–mouse relationship is susceptible to the same types of socialization effects that Kuo (1930) has demonstrated for the cat–rat relationship. Rats raised with mice are less likely to kill than mouse-naive rats (Denenberg, Paschke, & Zarrow, 1968). Apparently, this is caused by some type of habituation to the odor of mice, because exposing rats to mice or to mouse cages also reduces killing. In addition, mouse killers typically spare rat pups on the basis of odor differences between the pups and mice (Avis & Trendway, 1971; Meyer, 1964; Paul, Miley, & Mazzagatti, 1973).

With these findings in mind, Rusiniak, Gustavson, Hankins, and Garcia (1976) set out to study the behavior of the rat in an experimental situation modeled after the predatory situation in field conditions. As did the researchers before them, they found that an aversion for the flesh of a dead mouse, established in a few trials, did not suppress the attack on living prey. When the predatory attack was followed by lithium illness, mouse killing was suppressed in a few trials. Still, a number of questions remained unanswered. Would the aversion for the taste of the prey generalize to the odor trail (spoor) of the prey? In addition, they wanted to determine whether an aversion for artificial flavors would protect prey soaked in that flavor.

The apparent independence of the consummatory and the attack responses of the rat stands in marked contrast to the integrated predatory behavior of the feral canine, who immediately stopped killing prey to which it had been aversively conditioned. The behavior of the laboratory rat resembles the wanton killing of sheep by domestic dogs, who rarely feed on their victims. Alternatively, mouse killing in the rat may be an act of territorial defense, because in most studies the aversive mouse is thrust into the rat's home cage. Similar defense of the home cage by a coyote against a rabbit was noted above. Neither predator ate the intruder.

Rusiniak *et al.* (1976) also tested rats in a T maze where alternate prey were available. One mouse was candied, that is, wet with a saccharin peppermint solution, and the other mouse was plain. The maze had spoor trails, reaching from choice point to goal box, which consisted of the respective odor of the mouse in each goal box. After the rat trailed its prey from choice point to goal box and made its kill, it was moved along with its prey to its home cage (territorial lair) to feed on its prey. Feeding on one prey, usually the candy mouse, was followed by experimentally induced lithium illness. Under these conditions, trailing, killing, and eating appear to be an integrated sequence. The left panel of Fig. 10.6 illustrates the acquisition of the avoidance reactions to the poison prey in this two-choice situation. Initially, the rats chose the poison spoor 50% of the time and then killed and ate their prey. During acquisition, feeding dropped out rapidly, closely paralleled by a similar decline in killing. However, the odor avoidances continued to rise during extinction, when killing and feeding were asymptotic. Apparently rats are slow in learning to relate the distal cues at the choice point to the aversive tastes in the goal box.

The contrast between the omnivorous laboratory rat and the carnivorous feral coyote are remarkable even when we make allowances for the training and testing differences. The coyotes and wolves were tested in simultaneous or successive situations where they were free to take either or both prey, whereas

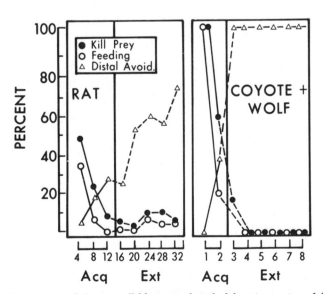

FIG. 10.6 Comparison of the prey–lithium aversions in laboratory rats and feral canines. "Distal avoid" refers to the percentage of avoidances made on the basis of olfactory, visual, or auditory cues without oral contact. The rats were limited to the choice of one prey, whereas the feral canines could take both prey; the baselines are therefore 50% and 100% respectively, for killing and feeding. (After Rusiniak *et al.*, 1976.)

the rat was limited to a single choice of either prey. The lithium treatment of the coyotes and wolves followed a meal of the flesh of dead prey, whereas rats were made ill after killing and eating a mouse made distinctive with an artificial sweet minty flavor. These differences were calculated to make the rats' task easier, yet the rats required more training and treatment than the feral canines. On the right panel of Fig. 10.6 we have plotted by estimate and extrapolation the coyote and wolf data in the same graphic format as the rat data. When compared in this manner, the species differences appear to be merely quantitative at first glance. However, the feral canines learn to avoid the poison prey on the basis of the distal cues in three trials. The rats are not making effective use of distal cues after 30 trials. This leaves us with the strong impression that there is a qualitative species difference in the dependency relationship between the appetitive and consummatory phases.

Because the laboratory rat is an omnivore and the feral coyote is a carnivore, perhaps it is more appropriate to consider the behavior of the carnivorous laboratory ferret. The independence of mouse killing and mouse eating was even more striking in the ferret than in the rat. The left panel of Fig. 10.7 compares the suppression of mouse killing in rats after an average of three punishing illnesses and the increased efficiency of mouse killing in the ferret after five similar punishments. After killing is punished by illness the rat gives up killing mice even in its home cage. The ferret does not give up mouse killing even though the mouse becomes extremely aversive. After repeated illness the ferret retches as he bites the mouse and literally stomps the mouse with its forefeet and then retreats in disgust. The right panel summarizes an experiment demonstrating that repeated shock punishment slows down the ferret's attack in the shock box, but not in an arena in which it has not been shocked. This increased latency extinguishes immediately, even in the shock box. The independence between the appetitive and consummatory phases therefore appears to be even more profound in this laboratory carnivore than in the laboratory omnivore (Rusiniak *et al.*, 1976).

The difference beween the laboratory species and the captive feral animals may reflect the selective pressure of domestication. Such characteristics as tameness and docility lead to successful reproduction in the breeding farm. Food is plentiful but exercise is at a premium in the cage. In contrast, neophobia and intractable behavior lead to survival in the natural niche. Energy and food cannot be wasted in the pursuit and slaughter of animals that cannot be eaten. These differential selection pressures could lead to independence of attack and consummation in domestic species and to dependence of the two patterns in wild species.

Man, Monkey, Salamander, Fish, Snake, and Slug

Food aversions have been investigated in a wide variety of species (see Table 10.2). The ubiquity of these palatability shifts commensurate with visceral aftereffects suggests that selection pressures molded this coping ability from

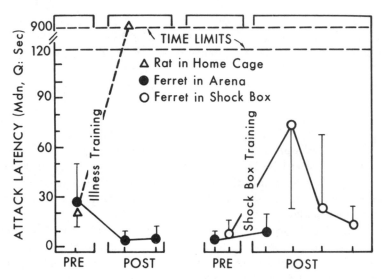

FIG. 10.7 Results of attempts to suppress mouse killing in the laboratory ferret. On the left, attack latencies for ferrets increase despite punishment of killing with lithium illness. In contrast, the same response is suppressed in the rat. On the right, shock punishment inhibits the ferret's attack only in the box where shock occurred and extinguishes rapidly. (After Rusiniak *et al.*, 1976.)

ancestral species in antiquity. There is some neurological evidence suggesting that these behavioral phenomena are not merely analogous reactions to a common selection pressure but may indeed represent a divergence from a common source. Herrick (1948) describes the neuropil in the brain of the tiger salamander, which receives afferents from the gustatory receptors and from the viscera; the outflow is to the smooth musculature of the viscera. In the mammalian brain, the nucleus solitarius is remarkably similar in structure and function, thus linking a wide variety of species from man to salamander.

Recently, Garb and Stunkard (1974) conducted a rigorous interview survery of aversions in man. Their sample included 696 subjects, ranging in age from 6 to 60. Several interesting but not unexpected findings emerged. Of the 256 people reporting aversions, 87% stated that gastrointestinal upset had followed the consumption of the averted food by 0–6 hours. Very few, 4–6%, developed an aversion for visual or auditory events that also preceded the bout of illness. Although most subjects attributed their illness to the food, Seligman (1972) has pointed out that knowledge that the food did not cause the illness does not attenuate the aversion in the most rational of creatures.

Aversions were remarkably robust and specific, with novelty of the food contributing substantially to their formation and persistence. Neither sex nor body weight were correlated with aversion incidence or characteristics, but Garb and Stunkard suggested that age might be an important determinant. Most subjects reported that their aversions were acquired between the ages of 6 and 12. Aversion incidence at older ages was remarkably lower. In addition, the aversions of youngsters tended to be stronger than those of adults and old people. A critical period for aversion in animals has not been demonstrated; however, several factors may potentiate aversions in children. The young inexperienced subject is much more likely to encounter novel flavors and, because taste sensitivity declines with age, the young encounter more intense tastes. Both novelty and intensity facilitate acquisition of aversions (Garcia, Hankins, & Rusiniak, 1974; Revusky & Bedarf, 1967).

Treatment for alcoholism with chemical aversion therapy provides another source of information on human aversions (Lemere & Voegtlin, 1950; Mottlin, 1973). On the whole, treatments in which alcohol consumption is followed by illness induced by emetic agents seem more effective than other behavioral procedures. The patient under illness treatment is much more likely to form an aversion for alcohol than for the experimental setting, the clinician, or the bottle. However, the treatment is not nearly as effective with humans addicted to alcohol as it is with coyotes addicted to lamb. Humans ingest substances that taste bad, presumably in anticipation of rewarding aftereffects. The coyote, who is not so intellectually gifted, does not swallow anything that tastes bad.

Aversions in monkeys have been studied over the last 15 years. For example, Harlow (1962) reported that monkeys developed aversions for distinctive fluids and fruit juices consumed during exposure to X-rays, which cause delayed radiation illness. More recently several investigators have demonstrated that monkeys can develop avoidance reactions to color cues paired with delayed illness. For example, Johnson, Beaton, and Hall (1975) have reported such aversions in vervet monkeys. Thirty minutes after they drank water from tubes colored either blue or yellow, monkeys received an injection of lithium chloride. The four experimental animals subsequently avoided drinking from the color associated with poison for up to 5 days, with yellow tubes being avoided longer than blue tubes. Gorry and Ober (1970) have also reported that squirrel monkeys given similar treatments with tinted water acquired aversions. However, those aversions reportedly dissipated in a few trials. Although direct visual cue—illness learning in these highly visual animals is certainly interesting, the theoretical implications are sometimes confusing, as is discussed in the final part of this chapter.

Let us now consider the other end of the phylogenetic continuum. When the garter snake (*Thamnophis sirtalis*) is punished with lithium after consuming an extract of earthworm, it develops an aversion for earthworm (Burghardt, Wilcoxin, & Czaplicki, 1973). Because the snake is constantly sampling airborne chemicals with its flickering tongue, it may be able to taste its prey at a distance without relying on secondary cues, such as vision. Similarly, fish are constantly sampling the soup of the sea with their chemical senses, but vision is also

TABLE 10.2
Conditioned Aversions throughout the Animal Kingdom

	Food/flavor cue	Illness consequence	Delay, trials[a]	Comments
Vertebrates				
Primates				
Man (*Homo sapiens*)	Variable, novel flavors	Visceral upset	0–6hr,1	Specific aversions in individuals from a survey of 969 people in six different populations–novelty and age contribute strongly (Garb and Stunkard, 1974)
	Alcoholic drink	Emetine	0,4–6	Follow-up conditioning trials 6 months later; 44% still averted when tested 1yr. later (Lemere and Voegtlin, 1950)
	Alcoholic drink	Many	Var	Chemical aversion therapy in alcoholics (Mottlin, 1973)
Rhesus (*Maccaca*)	Cherry Kool-Aid	X ray, 30–150 r/45 min	0,3	One trial effect (Harlow, 1962)
	Apple Juice	X ray, 30–150 r	0,5	One trial effect (Harlow, 1962)
Green monkey (*Ceropitheus sabaeus*)	Blue/yellow tubes, water	LiCl (i.p.), 32 mg/kg, 64 mg/kg	1hr.,1	32 mg/kg threshold effect–64 mg/kg 5 day aversion (Johnson *et al.*, 1975)
Squirrel monkey	Red water	LiCl	0.5hr.	Gorry and Ober (1970)
Monkeys	Peanut, carrot raisin, apple, bread	X–ray, 100–400 r	0,12	Successive choices between two foods during irradiation; general anorexia followed by persistent avoidance of peanuts especially (Leary, 1955)

Canines				
Coyote (*Canis latrans*)	0.12 *M* LiCl/0.12 *M* NaCl	LiCl (or)	0–30 min,3	No aversion to salt; all vomited 20–50 min after drinking lithium (Gustavson, 1974)
	Chicken-flavored dog food	LiCl (i.p.) (0.12 *M*), 50–250 ml	10–15 min, 1–5	One coyote learned in one trial following 50-ml dose; two required five trials with progressively increasing dose (Gustavson, 1974)
	Raw hamburger	LiCl (or caps), 2.7–6.0 gm	0,1	Vomiting occurred $2\frac{1}{2}$–6 hours after meat consumption (Gustavson *et al.*, 1974)
	Minced lamb in hide	LiCl (or caps), 6.0 gm	0,1	Vomiting 80 min after meal; also suppressed attack of live lamb (Gustavson *et al.*, 1974)
	Minced lamb in hide	LiCl (or) + LiCl (i.p.), 6.0 gm + 2.5 gm	10–15 min,1	Vomiting 30–42 min after meal; also suppressed attack of live lamb (Gustavson *et al.*, 1974)
	Rabbit carcass	LiCl (or) + LiCl (i.p.) 5.0 gm + 2.5 gm	10–15 min,2	Suppressed attack and consumption of live rabbit (Gustavson *et al.*, 1974)
	Rabbit carcass	LiCl (or), 6.0 gm	0,1	Suppressed rabbit attack (Gustavson *et al.*, 1976)
	Dog food in rabbit hide	LiCl, 3.0 gm	0,2	Suppressed rabbit attack (Gustavson *et al.*, 1976)
Timber wolf (*Canis Lupus*)	Sheep flesh in hide	LiCl (or caps), 6.0 gm	0,1	Suppressed attack of fully grown sheep (Gustavson *et al.*, 1976)

(continued)

TABLE 10.2 *(continued)*

	Food/flavor cue	Illness consequence	Delay, trials[a]	Comments
Felines				
Cougar (*Felis concolor*)	Deer meat	LiCl (or), 6.0 gm	0,1	Observed conditioned emesis on posttest with plain deer meat (Gustavson et al., 1976)
Cat (*Felis domesticus*)	Chocolate milk	x ray, 106 r/1hr	0,3	Safe food, plain milk; weak effect after one trial, big effect after three (Kimeldorf, Garcia, and Rubadeau, 1960)
	Cottage cheese	LiCl (i.p.)	5 min,4	Gradually increasing dose; vomiting 30–60 min after each injection (Brett, unpublished observations 1975)
	Beef kidney	LiCl (i.p.)	5 min,3	One trial effect (Brett, unpublished observations 1975)
Mustelids				
Ferret (*Mustela putorius furo*)	Salt water	0.12 *M* LiCl (or)	0,5	Reduced very high preference to water consumption level, vomiting and diarrhea observed (Rusiniak et al., 1976)
	Dog food	LiCl (i.p.), 70–100 mg/kg	5–10 min,1	Big effect (Rusiniak et al., 1976)
	Mackerel	LiCl (i.p.), 70–100 mg/kg	5–10 min,1	Prior experience with illness did not attenuate effect (Rusiniak et al., 1976)
	Mouse	LiCl (or caps), 1.6 gm	5–10 min,5	Illness after killing without consumption induced aversion, no effect on killing (Rusiniak et al., 1976)

Rodents				
Gerbils (*Tatera indica, Meriones hurrianae*)	Millet with groundnut oil	Zinc phosphide (Zn_3P_2) (or)	0,4 days	LD_{50} determined (approx. 64 mg/kg) but animals allowed to free feed on poison (Prakash & Jain, 1971)
Guinea pig (*Cavia porcellus*)	.05% HCl, 1% saccharin, red water, blue water, red tubes, blue tubes	LiCl (i.p.), 127 mg/kg	1h,1	Aversions to both color of fluid and taste of fluid (Braveman, 1974)
	Var saccharin + 5 drops red dye, .15% saccharin + var red dye	LiCl (i.p.), 127 mg/kg	0,1	Taste stronger cue than color; color aversions only when taste cue is very familiar (Braveman, 1975)
Golden hamster	Vaginal secretion 1% saccharin	LiCl (i.p.)	0,1	Johnston and Zahorick, (1975)
Mouse (*Mus musculus*, CF1)		x ray, 119 r/3h	0,3	One-trial effect (Kimeldorf et al., 1960)
	Crickets	LiCl (i.p.), 127 mg/kg	0–30 min, 1–5	Suppression of cricket eating and killing (Lowe & O'Boyle, 1975)
Black rat (*Rattus rattus*)[b]	Millet seed	Zn_3P_2 (or), 2 mg/10 gm food 4 mg/10 gm food	0,6–8 days	Free consumption over several days was reduced; anosmia does not reduce avoidance (Barnett, Cowan, Radford, & Prakash, 1975)
Brown rat (*Rattus norvegicus*)[b]	Grains	Common pesticides	0,many	Free-consumption studies (Thompson, 1954)

(continued)

TABLE 10.2 *(continued)*

	Food, flavor cue	Illness consequence	Delay, trials[a]	Comments
Half-wild rats and laboratory strains[b]	Saccharin, sucrose, NaCl, HCl, quinine, coffee, vinegar, apple juice, and others; many levels	x ray, LiCl, apomorphine, cyclophosphamide, i.v. saline, many psychoactive drugs, thiamine deficiency and others; many levels	0–12 h,1–5	One-trial effects are common. See the reviews below for extensive treatments of the problem and original papers giving exact parameters (Rzoska, 1953; Garcia et al., 1974; Revusky & Garcia, 1970; Rozin & Kalat, 1972; Riley & Baril, 1976)
	Mouse flesh, mouse dipped in sweet–minty fluid	LiCl (i.p.), 127 mg/kg	0–0.5h,1–11	Mouse eating always reduced, killing sometimes, if tested in choice situation (Krames et al., 1973; Berg & Baenninger, 1974; Rusiniak et al., 1976)
Avians				
Red-tailed hawk (*Buteo jamaicensis*)	Black mouse, black + bitter mouse, bitter mouse	LiCl (i.p.), 213–320 mg/kg	5–10 min, 1–3	Taste learned better than color; rapid chaining of color to taste (Brett et al., 1976)
Blue jays (*Cyanocitta cristata bromia*)	Monarch butterflies	Cardiac glycoside, .028–.167g	0,1–10	A one- to three-trial effect, depending on prey food containing the glycoside (Brower, 1969; Platt, Coppinger, & Brower, 1971)
Bobwhite quail (*Colinus virginianus*)	Blue sour water, blue water, sour water	Cyclophosphamide (i.p.), 132 mg/kg	30 min,1	Both taste and color learned in 1 trial (Wilcoxon et al., 1971)
Chicken (*Gallus gallus*)	Red mash/blue mash	10% NaCl (or), 2 ml	0,6	Reduced preference (Capretta, 1961)

			Delay, trials	
Pigeon (*Columba*)	Red water, saccharin water, red + saccharin water	LiCl (i.p.), 127 mg/kg	5–10 min, 1–5	Both color and taste learned (Homer & Rusiniak, unpublished observations, 1975)
Black-capped chickadee (*Parus atricapillus*)	Mealworm	Quinine sulfate (or)	0,1–8	Vomiting 5–10 min after poison worm consumption; multiple daily trials; avoidance of seed covers and mimics also (Alcock, 1970a)
White-throated sparrow (*Zonotrichia albicollis*)	Mealworm	Tartar emetic (or)	0,6–22	Vomiting 5–10 min after eating poison worm; multiple trials on same day; refused to even turn over seed covering mealworm (Alcock, 1970b)
Osteichthians				
Atlantic cod (*Gadus morhua* L.)	Liver, squid	LiCl (i.p.), 636 mg/kg	0.5h,1	Some sensitization effects (Mackay, 1974)
Reptilians				
Garter snakes (*Thamnophis sirtalis*)	Earthworm extract	LiCl (i.p.) 570 mg/kg	0.5hr,1	Apparently mediated via Jacobson's organ (Burghardt *et al.*, 1973)
Invertebrates				
Molluscs				
Land slug (*Limax maximus*)	Mushroom, cucumber	CO_2, 5 min	0,multiple; 1hr, multiple; 3hr, multiple	One-trial effect; Marginal effect; Sensitization, possible effect (Gelperin, 1975)
Coelenterates				
Anemone (*Aiptasia anulata*)	Shrimp	Quinine (or)	0,1	True "discriminative learning" not yet unequivocally demonstrated (Haralson and Haralson, personal communication 1974)

[a] or caps = lithium chloride in gelatin capsules; or = oral, ingested or by stomach tube; i.p. = intraperitoneal injection; var = variable. Delay, trials column first gives the CS–US delay and then the number of acquisition trials.

[b] Studies of bait shyness in wild, hybrid, and domestic rats, are so numerous that only a few representative samples are presented here.

important. Mackay (1974) found that when Atlantic codfish (*Gadus morhua*) consumed a piece of squid or liver and were injected with lithium chloride, two things occurred. At first there was a generalized rejection of all food; this was followed by a gradual acceptance of safe food and rejection of the food that preceded the lithium treatment. Because the appearance and the chemical properties of the food were confounded, it is not certain whether the fish were avoiding the appearance or the flavor of the food.

Recently, Gelperin (1975) demonstrated rapid food aversions to a variety of vegetables in the terrestrial slug (*Limax maximus*). He gassed the slugs with carbon dioxide, which induces withdrawal, rolling up, and copious secretion. Yet even with delays up to an hour, marginal aversions developed. One might argue that the gas treatment served more as a peripheral insult than as a postingestional effect of the food. However, CO_2 is indeed toxic to the slug and anesthetizes and kills the mollusk if the dose is too large. Experiments to determine the specificity of the US, that is, using shock or a pin prick, should solve this question.

How far from man, along the phylogenetic array, can bait shyness be found? Hodgson (personal communication, 1970) related some incidental observations indicating that coelenterates may acquire bait shyness. He fed sea anemones capsules containing food that they accepted after a brief habituation. Later he substituted quinine for the food in the capsule. The anemones first accepted the capsule and then "vomited" it by inverting their sacs. Subsequently they refused further capsules. In a similar incident, Haralson and Haralson (personal communication, 1974) relate how they inadvertantly fed their anemones shrimp colored with a bitter food dye. After this the anemones refused food. These anecdotes are intriguing but it still remains to be demonstrated conclusively that anemones can acquire bait shyness in a few trials. The natural rejection of bitter seems well-established in these coelenterates, with their rudimentary nerve nets and sensory palpocils (Jennings, 1905). Furthermore, Parker (1896) alternately fed sea anemones (*Metridium*) bits of crab meat or filter paper soaked in crab meat and reported that they formed an appropriate discrimination, rejecting the paper and accepting the crab meat. Bait shyness may yet be found in this primeval form of animal life.

The Status of Bait Shyness
in Learning Theory

Students of conditioning and learning phenomena are sometimes discouraged by the ease with which ingenious experimenters can demonstrate learning that runs counter to the general propositions they laboriously have established by sweat of arm and brow. Nevertheless, confidence in general propositions can only be established by diligently seeking to overthrow them. This empirical process should lead to clarification and limitation, so, at this point, let us turn to the

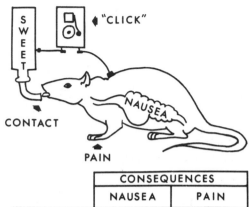

FIG. 10.8 The cue to consequence paradigm, a fourfold experimental design where two cues, taste or auditory stimuli, are paired with two consequences, illness or pain. Learning is more probable in the cells indicated and the conditioned responses are qualitatively distinct. (From Garcia, Clarke, & Hankins, 1973.)

		CONSEQUENCES	
		NAUSEA	PAIN
CUES	SWEET	AQUIRES AVERSION	DOES NOT
	"CLICK"	DOES NOT	LEARNS DEFENSE

original cue–consequence paradigm (Garcia and Koelling, 1966). Some confusion has arisen, perhaps because of overgeneralization. Figure 10.8 illustrates the fourfold design of the original experiment in which two specific cues (CS) were pitted orthogonally against two punishing consequences (US). More generality than this was implied. The auditory click is a member of a class of cues by which the animal locates his position in time and space and includes visual, olfactory, and tactual stimuli. Ultimately we will find a specific role in conditioning for each of these external sensory channels. For example, there is some evidence that odors may play a favored role in sexual conditioning (Carr, Krames, & Costanzo, 1970; Marr & Gardner, 1965), and it is our impression that auditory signals are favored over visual signals for cutaneous pain. However, for the moment, we concede that they appear equivalent in the cue to consequence paradigm. Taste cues appear to be in a class by themselves, probably because taste is the only peripheral sensory system that projects directly to the nucleus solitarius.

Nausea can be induced by a broad class of agents, such as emetic drugs, toxins, x rays, and motion sickness. Other agents that appear similar, such as general anesthetics, opiates, and anoxia, may not be very effective, even in the near lethal range, for perhaps two reasons. These agents may incapacitate the central associative mechanisms, or they may not produce an effective gut-referred malaise involving the nucleus solitarius. Similarly, pain refers not only to electrocutaneous shock specifically but includes any noxious stimulus on the peripheral surface of the animal that causes it to move away promptly (Garcia & Ervin, 1968; Garcia *et al.*, 1974).

When the complete four-cell design has been carried out in rats, learning becomes asymptotic in the sweet–nausea and the click–pain cells before any learning is evident in the sweet–pain and the click–illness cells (Garcia & Koelling, 1966; Garcia, McGowan, Ervin, & Koelling, 1968; Domjan & Wilson, 1972; Green, Bouzas, & Rachlin, 1972). This indicates that associative learning is specialized to some degree, or as Seligman (1972) says, animals are prepared to make some associations and not others. They are prepared to associate external sounds with painful attacks on the skin, but not with illness. They are prepared to form aversions for the taste of a meal, but not for an auditory signal warning them that the food is poisoned. This "preparedness" is assumed to be neurological, although experience during development can play a critical role. If learning were found to occur with equal facility in all four cells, we would have to conclude that there exists a general capacity to associate equipotentially any perceptible signal to any reinforcer as a function of the classical principles of contiguity, frequency, and intensity.

It is a rank overgeneralization to assume that no learning will appear in the other two cells of the fourfold schema under any conditions. On the contrary, such learning has been demonstrated even in the laboratory rat. For example, external cues (visual and tactual) have been effectively paired with delayed illness from radiation exposure. Rats tended to avoid the radiation compartment in a two-compartment shuttlebox in a series of experiments in which taste cues and ingestion were not involved. The dose required to produce avoidance of visual and tactual cues was 10 times that required to produce a taste aversion, and the compartment avoidance quickly extinguished (Garcia, Kimeldorf, & Hunt, 1957, 1960). Similar effects were obtained with apomorphine (Green & Garcia, 1970). For another example, morphine addiction studies have demonstrated that rats that have suffered morphine withdrawal in a distinctive compartment subsequently exhibit symptoms of withdrawal when they are returned to the chamber in the absence of addiction. The external compartmental cues were classically conditioned to the withdrawal syndrome (Wikler & Pescor, 1967).

Finally, learning has been obtained in the taste–shock cell also. Anosmic rats learned to avoid shock in a discrimination situation where taste was the only cue. However, anosmic rats perform much better in auditory–shock than in taste–shock conditioning (Hankins, Garcia, & Rusiniak, 1973; Hankins, Rusiniak, & Garcia, 1976). If we broaden the experimental arrangements, therefore, we can only say learning appears to be more probable in those cells where "stimulus relevance" holds, to use Capretta's (1961) terms. However, when the rat is free to choose either cue, the probability of an association in the alternative irrelevant stimulus cells appears to be near zero, whereas learning is near certainty in the relevant cells. In addition, extinction is more rapid when irrelevant stimuli are associated.

The qualitative differences in the learning observed in the four cells should not be overlooked. In the relevant sweet–nausea cell, a hedonic shift occurs. Operationally speaking, the experimenter may arrange an association between sweet and nausea, but psychologically speaking, the rat does not acquire an association. Sweet does not signal pending illness. Instead, sweet becomes distasteful even in situations where illness did not occur. After conditioning, the taste CS elicits disgust reactions, not coping reactions to anticipated illness. This hedonic shift occurs even if the illness is applied while the rat is under anesthesia or while the animal's cortical electrical activity is depressed by KCl (Roll & Smith, 1972; Davis & Bures, 1972). In contrast, a true association is acquired in the relevant click—shock cell. The external CS warns the rat that shock is imminent. The rat prepares to cope with the painful US and these coping responses are limited to that specific spatiotemporal context. Furthermore, the shock US is extremely unlikely to be effective if delivered under anesthesia or cortical spreading depression.

When learning is achieved in the irrelevant sweet—pain cell, the rat does not acquire an aversion for the taste CS; instead, it uses taste as a signal to defend against the pain in the experimental context. After sweet—shock pairing it may suppress drinking sweet water in the experimental chamber, yet drink it avidly in the home cage (Garcia, Kovner, & Green, 1970). If the rat smells the fluid, it quickly learns an odor—shock avoidance that may be mistaken for a taste aversion. For example, Krane and Wagner (1975) recently published a paper entitled "Taste Aversion Learning with a Delayed Shock US." They erred in labeling their effect a taste aversion, because they used an odorous .7% saccharin solution as a CS followed by intense (4.0 mA for 1.5 sec) shock. Rats can smell this solution, and when strong shock is used they can avoid the smelly spout without licking (Hankins et al., 1976). This obviates the authors' explanation that the taste of saccharin has more enduring memory traces, because the odor of saccharin provides lingering physical traces.

We have classified odor as an external cue in the same category as an auditory click, but aversions may be formed when gaseous odorants, directed at the muzzle of the rat, are followed by delayed illness (Taukulis, 1974). Here again, taste and odor may be confounded, because gaseous odors can go into solution on the moist surface of the tongue and stimulate the taste receptors. Other investigators have reported that odor cues are not effective when paired with delayed visceral effects (Hankins et al., 1973; Barnett, Cowan, Radford, & Prakash, 1975; Lovett, Goodchild, & Booth, 1968; Simson & Booth, 1973). It is clear that when fluids with both taste and odor properties are paired with illness, anosmic rats are not handicapped compared to controls with the sense of smell. This indicates that anosmic rats have not been deprived of cues relevant to illness. On the other hand, when the same fluid is paired with shock, anosmic rats are extremely handicapped, indicating they have been deprived of a cue relevant to shock (Hankins et al., 1973; Hankins et al., 1976). Thus we have assigned odors to the external cue category.

In the final click—illness cell, classical stimulus substitution conditioning appears as, for example, when the formerly drug-addicted rats are again returned to the compartment where they suffered morphone withdrawal (Wikler & Pescor,

1967). Coyotes will retch at the sight and smell of the aversive lamb and then turn away (Gustavson *et al.*, 1974). Similar avoidance responses to the external features of the radiation chamber are exhibited by previously irradiated rats. These motor responses, which do not resemble illness responses, are motivated by the hedonic shift generated through stimulus substitution.

Of all the stimuli associated with food, taste is the prepotent stimulus for food aversions in the rat, who has notoriously poor vision. This unique position of taste is often challenged in animals that depend more on vision. For example, when a monkey is made sick after drinking colored water it may reject colored water on sight on the next trial. This result demonstrates that if irrelevant cues are made novel and intense, and if an expert problem solving subject is used, then improbable associations are made more probable (Gorry & Ober, 1970; Johnson *et al.*, 1975). This result does not demonstrate that visual cues are prepotent over taste cues for the sick monkey; that can only be demonstrated with a fourfold design. Only one cell was examined for the monkeys. When we look at two cells, the prepotence of taste over vision becomes evident. For example, Braveman (1974, 1975) demonstrated that guinea pigs could associate colored water directly with delayed illness, with the effect lasting about 3 days. However, subsequent experiments, using parametric variations in color and taste intensity, showed that color was used as a cue only when taste cues were absent or very familiar. Aversions to the taste were stronger and lasted longer than those to the color cue. If four cells are examined, it becomes apparent that monkeys and guinea pigs have the same bias as rats and men. Subtle taste cues serving food aversions do not adequately serve place avoidance. Conversely, subtle visual cues serving shock avoidance do not adequately serve food aversions.

Prepotency of vision over taste was recorded for the bobwhite quail (*Colinus virginianus*) in the previously mentioned two-cell study. This experiment gains power because rats were also tested with the same cues: blue and sour presented in water and paired with illness (Wilcoxon *et al.*, 1971). The data showed that the birds could use the visual cue and the rats could not. These results with the seed-eating quail conflict with the results obtained with carnivorous hawks and bluejays. Both these species can avoid toxic prey on the basis of visual cues, but taste cues are prepotent as far as consumption is concerned. It would be interesting to see these birds tested in the fourfold design with stronger taste cues or weaker color cues.

Ethologists make a distinction between appetitive and consummatory behavior which is roughly comparable to that between instrumental and classical conditioning. Consider the food selection sequence of any large complex animal. In the appetitive phase, the forager searches out its food guided by signals (CS) received via its visual, olfactory, and auditory telereceptors. The ultimate reinforcement (US) of this plastic coping phase is the taste of food in the mouth. Good tasting food rewards the instrumental learning, whereas bad tasting food punishes it. The consummatory phase that follows resembles a fixed action pattern. This stereotypic phase is guided by gustatory receptors and is reinforced by the visceral feedback provided by the monitors of the internal milieu.

The psychological difference between the learning in these two phases has been previously emphasized. To reiterate, in the appetitive instrumental phase, the animal gains specific information concerning the spatiotemporal relationship of signals (CS) to reinforcers (US) and he subsequently adjusts his behavior accordingly. Attention to both the CS and the US is critical in the appetitive phase. In the consummatory phase, the hedonic value of the taste CS is altered by the visceral feedback US. Feedback from illness decreases palatability and feedback from nutrition increases palatability. Attention must be directed to the taste CS but not to the visceral US, for this feedback is effective even if the animal is asleep, a common state after consummation in nature. In the laboratory hedonic adjustment of the taste CS also occurs when the illness US is delivered under anesthesia. This mechanism, that is, hedonic adjustment of peripheral sensation in the service of internal homeostatic demands, is not limited to gustation. The cutaneous temperature sense apparently works the same way. A warm stimulus feels pleasant if the internal core temperature is low. The same warm stimulus feels unpleasant if the internal core temperature is high. This hedonic shifting causes the animal to select an appropriate environment and it thereby corrects internal imbalances by seeking peripheral comfort (Garcia et al., 1974).

In the predatory sequence gustation plays a mediating role, because it is a reinforcer (US) for appetitive tactics and the CS for visceral feedback. Alternatively, we could consider visceral feedback as the true US and consider taste as CS_1, that is, a first-order CS. The distal (for example, visual) cue would then be CS_2, a second-order cue. In either case, this analysis leads us to several problems. First, some of the evidence discussed above indicates that some animals appear to avoid the poisoned food on the basis of visual or olfactory cues without tasting the CS again after one food—illness pairing. We have conceded that this may be possible, but other possibilities also exist. Vomiting can pair these distal cues (CS_2) with a newly acquired taste aversion (CS_1) and an illness (US). Sensory preconditioning is yet another possibility. The distal CS_2 is repeatedly paired with the gustatory CS_1 when a food is habitually consumed. When the familiar food is paired with an illness US, the distal CS_2 is associated with the taste CS_1 through sensory preconditioning and thus is avoided without oral contact. In the laboratory, sensory preconditioning is a weak effect (see Weisman, Chapter 1, this volume). Nonetheless, it is a genuine effect and may play a greater role in natural settings for the reasons we discuss below.

The difference between laboratory species and captive wild species raises another problem if we consider the appetitive phase of predation to be higher order conditioning. In the laboratory, once higher order conditioning has been established, it appears to be independent of changes in the underlying first-order conditioning. The CS_1 can undergo extinction so that it no longer elicits its CR, yet the CS_2 can continue to produce its respective CR (see Rescorla, Chapter 6, this volume). Laboratory-bred predators respond in the same way. Distal cues (CS_2) elicit attack, which stimulates taste (CS_1) and consumption. If taste (CS_1) is paired with illness and becomes aversive, the eating response is blocked, but the distal cues (CS_2) continue to elicit the attack response. The attack response must be directly punished if it is to be suppressed at all. In feral animals, the story is quite different. When the taste of the prey (CS_1) is paired with an illness (US), the distal cues (CS_2) are so quickly associated with the now aversive taste (CS_1) that attack responses require no direct punishment to suppress them. We have suggested that the difference between feral and laboratory species may be caused by differential selection pressure exerted by the natural niche and the breeding farm. As a result of the laboratory breeding, the gene pools controlling behavioral patterns undergo change, so that behavioral principles derived from laboratory species may have little predictive value when applied to wild species. In contrast, passive observation of wild species in their natural niches does not reveal the mechanisms by which they achieve their adjustments. That can only be done when we bring laboratory manipulations to the natural niche or wild animals into the laboratory.

Acknowledgments

This research was supported by USPHS-NIH Research Grant, 1-RO1-NS-11618 and USPHS Program Project Grant, HD-05958.

References

Alcock, J. Punishment levels and the response of black-capped chickadees (*Parus atricapillus*) to three kinds of artificial seeds. *Animal Behaviour*, 1970, **18**, 592–599. (a)

Alcock, J. Punishment levels and the response of white-throated sparrows (*Zonotrichia albicollis*) to three kinds of artificial models and mimics. *Animal Behaviour*, 1970, **18**, 733–739. (b)

Avis, H. H., & Treadway. J. T. Mediation of rat–mouse interspecific aggression by cage odor. *Psychonomic Science*, 1971, **22**, 293–294.

Barber, S. Chemoreception and proprioception in *Limulus. Journal of Experimental Zoology*, 1956, **131**, 57–73.

Bardach, J. The chemical senses and food intake in the lower vertebrates. In M. Kare & O. Maller (Eds.), *The chemical senses and nutrition*. Baltimore: John Hopkins Press, 1967. Pp. 19–43.

Bardach, J., & Atema, J. The sense of taste in fishes. In L. Beidler (Ed.), *Handbook of sensory physiology*. Vol. 4. New York: Springer-Verlag, 1971. Pp. 293–336.

Bardach, J., & Case, J. Sensory capabilities of the modified fins of squirrel hake (*Urophycis chuss*) and searobins (*Prionotus carolinus* and *Prionotus evolans*). *Copeia*, 1965, **2**, 194–206.

Barnett, S. A. *The rat: A study in behavior*. Chicago: Aldine Press, 1963.

Barnett, S. A., Cowan, P. E., Radford, G. G., & Prakash, I. Peripheral anosmia and the discrimination of poisoned food by *Rattus rattus* L. *Behavioral Biology*, 1975, **13**, 183–190.

Berg, D., & Baenninger, R. Predation: Separation of aggressive and hunger motivation by conditioned aversion. *Journal of Comparative and Physiological Psychology*, 1974, **86**, 601–606.

Braveman, N. S. Poison-based avoidance learning with flavored or colored water in guinea pigs. *Learning and Motivation*, 1974, **5**, 182–194.

Braveman, N. S. Relative salience of gustatory and visual cues in the formation of poison-based food aversions by guinea pigs (*Cavia porcellus*). *Behavioral Biology*, 1975, **14**, 189–199.

Brett, L. P. Unpublished observations, 1975.

Brett, L. P., Hankins, W. G., & Garcia. J. Prey–lithium aversions: III. Buteo hawks. *Behavioral Biology*, 1976, in press.

Brower, L. P. Ecological chemistry. *Scientific American*, 1969, **220**, 22–29.

Burghardt, G. M., Wilcoxon, H. C., & Czaplicki, J. A. Conditioning in garter snakes: aversion to palatable prey induced by delayed illness. *Animal Learning and Behavior*, 1973, **1**, 317–320.

Capretta, P. J. An experimental modification of food preference in chickens. *Journal of Comparative and Physiological Psychology*, 1961, **54**, 238–242.

Carr, W. J., Krames, L., & Costanzo, D. J. Previous sexual experience and olfactory preference for novel *vs* original sex partners in rats. *Journal of Comparative and Physiological Psychology*, 1970, **71**, 216–222.

Cicala, G., & McMichael, J. Quinine aversion thresholds in rats as a function of age and psychophysical procedure. *Canadian Journal of Psychology*, 1964, **18**, 28–35.

Davis, J. L., & Bures, J. Disruption of saccharin aversion learning in rats by cortical spreading depression in the CS-US interval. *Journal of Comparative and Physiological Psychology*, 1972, **80**, 398–402.

Denenberg, V. H., Paschke, R. E., & Zarrow, M. X. Killing of mice by rats prevented by early interaction between the two species. *Psychonomic Science*, 1968, **11**, 39–40.

Dethier, V. Gustation and olfaction in lepidopterous larvae. *Biological Bulletin*, 1937, **72**, 7–23.

Domjan, M., & Wilson, N. E. Specificity of cue to consequence in aversion learning in the rat. *Psychonomic Science*, 1972, **26**, 143–145.

Duncan, C. The sense of taste in birds. *Annals of Applied Biology*, 1960, **48**, 409–414.

Garb, J., & Stunkard, A. Taste aversions in man. *American Journal of Psychiatry*, 1974, **131**, 1204–1207.

Garcia, J., Clarke, J. C., & Hankins, W. G. Natural responses to scheduled rewards. In P. P. G. Bateson and P. H. Klopfer (Eds.), *Perspectives in ethology*. New York: Plenum Press, 1973, 1–41.

Garcia, J., & Ervin, F. R. Appetites, aversions and addictions: A model for visceral memory. In J. Wortis (Ed.), *Recent advances in biological psychiatry*. Vol. 10. New York: Plenum Press, 1968. Pp. 284–293.

Garcia, J., & Hankins, W. G. The evolution of bitter and the acquisition of toxiphobia. In D. Denton (Ed.), *Fifth international symposium on olfaction and taste*. New York: Academic Press, 1975. Pp. 39–45.

Garcia, J., Hankins, W. G., & Rusiniak, K. W. Behavioral regulation of the milieu interne in man and rat. *Science*, 1974, **185**, 824–831.

Garcia, J., Kimeldorf, D. J., & Hunt, E. L. Spatial avoidance in the rat as a result of exposure to ionizing radiation. *British Journal of Radiology*, 1957, **30**, 318–321.

Garcia, J., Kimeldorf, D. J., & Hunt, E. L. The use of ionizing radiation as a motivating stimulus. *Psychological Review*, 1960, **68**, 384–394.

Garcia, J., Kimeldorf, D. J., & Koelling, R. A. A conditioned aversion towards saccharin resulting from exposure to gamma radiation. *Science*, 1955, **122**, 157–159.

Garcia, J., & Koelling, R. A. Relation of cue to consequence in avoidance learning. *Psychonomic Science*, 1966, **4**, 123–124.

Garcia, J., & Koelling, R. A. The use of ionizing rays as a mammalian olfactory stimulus. In L. Beidler (Ed.), *Handbook of sensory physiology*. Vol. 4. New York: Springer-Verlag, 1971. Pp. 449–464.

Garcia, J., Kovner, R., & Green, K. F. Cue properties versus palatability of flavors in avoidance learning. *Psychonomic Science*, 1970, **20**, 313–314.

Garcia, J., McGowan, B. K., Ervin, F. R., & Koelling, R. A. Cues: Their relative effectiveness as a function of the reinforcer. *Science*, 1968, **160**, 794–795.

Gelperin, A. Rapid food aversion learning by a terrestrial mollusk. *Science*, 1975, **189**, 567–570.

Gorry, T. H., & Ober, S. E. Stimulus characteristics of learning over long delays in monkeys. Paper presented at the 11th Annual Meeting of the Psychonomic Society, San Antonio, Texas, 1970.

Green, K. F., & Garcia, J. Role of reinforcer in selecting and responding to cues. *Proceedings of the 78th Annual Convention of the APA*, 1970, 251–252.

Green, L., Bouzas, A., & Rachlin, H. Test of an electric-shock analog to illness-induced aversion. *Behavioral Biology*, 1972, **7**, 513–518.

Gustavson, C. R. Taste aversion conditioning as a predator control method in the coyote and ferret. Unpublished doctoral dissertation, University of Utah, 1974.

Gustavson, C. R., Garcia, J., Hankins, W. G., & Rusiniak, K. W. Coyote predation control by aversive conditioning. *Science*, 1974, **184**, 581–583.

Gustavson, C. R., Kelly, D. J., Sweeney, M., & Garcia, J. Prey–lithium aversions: I. Coyotes and wolves. *Behavioral Biology*, 1976 (in press).

Hankins, W. G., Garcia, J., & Rusiniak, K. W. Dissociation of odor and taste in baitshyness. *Behavioral Biology*, 1973, **8**, 407–419.

Hankins, W. G., Rusiniak, K. W., & Garcia, J. Dissociation of odor and taste in shock-avoidance learning. *Behavioral Biology*, 1976, in press.

Harlow, H. F. Effects of radiation on the central nervous system and on behavior–General survey. In T. J. Haley & R. S. Snider (Eds.), *Responses of the nervous system to ionizing radiation; second international symposium*. Boston: Little Brown, 1962. Pp. 627–644.

Harlow, H. F., & Suomi, S. J. Nature of love–Simplified. *American Psychologist*, 1970, **25**, 161–167.

Hecht, S. The physiology of *Ascidia atra* (*Leseur*). *Journal of Experimental Zoology*, 1918, **25**, 261–299.

Held, R., & Bossom, J. Neonatal deprivation and adult rearrangement: Complementary techniques for analyzing plastic sensory-motor coordinations. *Journal of Comparative and Physiological Psychology*, 1961, **54**, 33–37.

Herrick, C. J. The organ and the sense of taste in fishes. *Bulletin of the United States Fish Commission*, 1904, **22**, 237–272.

Herrick, C. J. *The brain of the tiger salamander–Ambystoma tigrinum*. Chicago: University of Chicago Press, 1948.

Hirsch, V., & Spinelli, P. Visual experience modifies distribution of horizontally and vertically oriented receptive fields in cats. *Science*, 1970, **168**, 869–871.

Hopkins, A. Sensory stimulation of the oyster, *Ostrea virginica*, by chemicals. *Bulletin of the United States Bureau of Fisheries*, 1935, **47**, 249–261.

Hubel, D. H., & Wiesel, J. N. Receptive fields, binocular interaction and functional architecture in the cat's visual cortex. *Journal of Physiology*, 1962, **160**, 106–154.

Jenkins, H. M., & Moore, B. R. The form of the auto-shaped response with food or water reinforcers. *Journal of the Experimental Analysis of Behavior*, 1973, **20**, 163–181.

Jenkins, H. M., & Sainsbury, R. S. The development of stimulus control through differential reinforcement. In N. J. Mackintosh & W. K. Honig (Eds.), *Fundamental issues in associative learning*. Halifax: Dalhousie University Press, 1969. Pp. 123–161.

Jennings, H. Modifiability in behavior: 1) Behavior of sea anemones. *Journal of Experimental Zoology*, 1905, **2**, 447–472.

Johnson, C., Beaton, R., & Hall, K. Poison-based avoidance learning in nonhuman primates: Salience of visual cues. *Physiology and Behavior*, 1975, **14**, 403–407.

Johnston, R. E., & Zahorick, D. M. Taste aversions to sexual attractants. *Science*, 1975, **189**, 893–394.

Kare, M. R. The special senses. In P. Sturkie (Ed.), *Avian physiology*. (2nd ed.) Ithaca, New York: Cornell University Press, 1965. Pp. 406–446.

Karli, P. The Norway rat's killing response to the white mouse; an experimental analysis. *Behavior*, 1956, **10**, 81–103.

Kimeldorf, D. J., Garcia, J., & Rubadeau, D. O. Radiation-induced conditioned avoidance behavior in rats, mice and cats. *Radiation Research*, 1960, **12**, 710–718.

Krames, L., Milgram, N. W., & Christie, D. P. Predatory aggression: Differential suppression of killing and feeding. *Behavioral Biology*, 1973, **9**, 641–647.

Krane, R. V., & Wagner, A. R. Taste aversion learning with a delayed shock US: Implications for the generality of the laws of learning. *Journal of Comparative and Physiological Psychology*, 1975, **88**, 882–889.

Kuo, Z. Y. The genesis of the cat's response toward the rat. *Journal of Comparative Psychology*, 1930, **11**, 1–35.

Leary, R. W. Food-preference of monkeys subjected to low-level irradiation. *Journal of Comparative and Physiological Psychology*, 1955, **48**, 343–346.

Laverack, M. Tactile and chemical perception in earthworms-I. Responses to touch, sodium chloride, quinine and sugars. *Comparative Biochemistry and Physiology*, 1960, **1**, 155–163.

Lemere, F., & Voegtlin, W. L. An evaluation of the aversion treatment of alcoholism. *Quarterly Journal of Studies on Alcohol*, 1950, **11**, 199–204.

Lettvin, J. Y., Maturana, H. R., McCulloch, W. S., & Pitts, W. H. What the frog's eye tells the frog's brain. *Proceedings of the IRE*, 1959, **47**, 1940–1951.

Levy, C., Ervin, F. R., & Garcia, J. Effect of serum from irradiated rats on gastrointestinal function. *Nature*, 1970, **225**, 463–464.

Lorenz, K. Z. The companion in the bird's world. *Auk*, 1937, **54**, 245–273.

Lorenz, K. Z. Innate bases of learning. In K. H. Pribram (Ed.), *On the biology of learning*. New York: Harcourt, Brace & World, 1969. P. 47.

Lovett, D., Goodchild, P., & Booth, D. Depression of intake of nutrient by association of its odor with effects of insulin. *Psychonomic Science*, 1968, **11**, 27–28.

Lowe, W. C., & O'Boyle, M. Conditioned suppression and recovery of cricket killing and eating in laboratory mice. *Animal Learning and Behavior*, 1975, in press.

Mackay, B. Conditioned food aversion produced by toxicosis in atlantic cod. *Behavioral Biology*, 1974, **12**, 347–355.

Mackintosh, N. J. *The psychology of animal learning*. New York: Academic Press, 1974.

Marler, P. A comparative approach to vocal learning: song development in white-crowned sparrows. In M. E. P. Seligman & J. L. Hager (Eds.), *Biological boudaries of learning*. Englewood Cliffs: Prentice-Hall, 1972. Pp. 336–376.

Marr, J., & Gardner, L. Early olfactory experience and later social behavior in the rat: Preference, sexual responsiveness, and care of young. *Journal of Genetic Psychology*, 1965, **107**, 167–174.

Mason, W. A., & Kenney, M. D. Redirection of filial attachments in rhesus monkeys: Dogs as surrogates. *Science*, 1974, **183**, 1209–1211.

Meyer, J. S. Stimulus control of mouse-killing rats. *Journal of Comparative and Physiological Psychology*, 1964, **58**, 112–117.

Montgomery, R. Cyanogens. In I. Liener (Ed.), *Toxic constituents of plant foodstuffs*. New York: Academic Press, 1969. Pp. 143–158.

Mottin, J. L. Drug-induced attenuation of alcohol consumption. A review and evaluation of claimed, potential or current therapies. *Quarterly Journal of Studies on Alcohol*, 1973, **34**, 444–472.

Olmsted, J. The comparative physiology of *Synaptula hydriformis* (Leseur). *Journal of Experimental Zoology*, 1917, **24**, 333–379.

Parker, G. H. The reactions of *Metridium* to food and other substances. *Bulletin of the Museum of Comparative Zoology*, Harvard, 1896, **29**, 107–119.

Parker, G. H. The reactions of sponges with a consideration of the origin of the nervous system. *Journal of Experimental Zoology*, 1910, **8**, 1–42.

Patten, W. On the morphology and physiology of the brain and sense organs of limulus. *Quarterly Journal of Microscopical Science*, 1894, **35**, 1–96.

Paul, L. Predatory attack by rats: Its relationship to feeding and type of prey. *Journal of Comparative and Physiological Psychology*, 1972, **78**, 69–76.

Paul, L., Miley, W. M., & Baenninger, R. Mouse killing by rats: Roles of hunger and thirst in its initiation and maintenance. *Journal of Comparative and Physiological Psychology*, 1971, **76**, 242–249.

Paul, L., Miley, W. M., & Mazzagatti, N. Social facilitation and inhibition of hunger-induced killing by rats. *Journal of Comparative and Physiological Psychology*, 1973, **84**, 162–168.

Paul, L., & Posner, I. Predation and feeding: Comparison of feeding behavior of killer and non-killer rats. *Journal of Comparative and Physiological Psychology*, 1973, **84**, 258–264.

Pfaffman, C. R. Abstract of comments; Panel on gustatory aversive conditioning, 6th Annual Conference on Brain Research, Vail, Colorado, 1973.

Platt, A. P., Coppinger, R. P., & Brower, L. P. Demonstration of the selective advantage of mimetic *Limentis* butterflies presented to caged avian predators. *Evolution*, 1971, **25**, 692–701.

Prakash, I., & Jain, A. P. Baitshyness of two gerbils, *Tatera indica* Hardwicke and *Meriones hurrianae* Jerdon. *Annals of Applied Biology*, 1971, **69**, 169–172.

Pumphrey, R. J. Part I. Sensory organs: Vision. In A. J. Marshall (Ed.), *Biology and comparative physiology of birds*. Vol. 2. New York: Academic Press, 1961. Pp. 55–86.

Rescorla, R. A. Pavlovian second-order conditioning: Some implications for instrumental behavior. Paper presented at the Conference on Operant-Pavlovian Interactions, Guelph, Ontario, 1975.

Revusky, S., & Bedarf, E. Association of illness with prior ingestion of novel foods. *Science*, 1967, **155**, 219–220.

Revusky, S., & Garcia, J. Learned associations over long delays. In G. Bower (Ed.), *The psychology of learning and motivation: Advances in research and theory*. Vol. 4. New York: Academic Press, 1970. Pp. 1–84.

Richter, C. P. The development and use of alpha-naphthyl thiourea (antu) as a rat poison. *Journal of the American Medical Association*, 1945, **129**, 927–931.

Richter, C. P. Experimentally produced behavior reactions to food poisoning in wild and domesticated rats. *Annals of the New York Academy of Sciences*, 1953, **56**, 225–239.

Riesen, A. H. Stimulation as a requirement for growth and function in behavioral development. In D. W. Fiske & S. R. Madd (Eds.), *Functions of varied experience*. Homewood, Ill.: Dorsey Press, 1961. Pp. 57–80.

Riley, A. L., & Baril, L. L. Conditioned aversions: A bibliography. *Animal Learning and Behavior Supplement*, 1976, **4**, 15–135.

Roll, D. L., & Smith, J. C. Conditioned taste aversion in anesthetized rats. In M. E. P. Seligman & J. L. Hager (Eds.), *Biological boundaries of learning*. Englewood Cliffs, N.J.: Prentice-Hall, 1972. Pp. 98–102.

Rozin, P., & Kalat, J. W. Learning as a situation-specific adaptation. In M. E. P. Seligman & J. L. Hager (Eds.), *Biological boundaries of learning*. Englewood Cliffs, N.J.: Prentice-Hall, 1972. Pp. 66–96.

Rusiniak, K. W., Gustavson, C. R., Hankins, W. G., & Garcia, J. Prey–lithium aversions: II. Laboratory rats and ferrets. *Behavioral Biology,* 1976, in press.

Rzoska, J. Bait shyness, a study in rat behaviour. *British Journal of Animal Behaviour,* 1953, **1,** 128–135.

Rzoska, J. The behaviour of white rats towards poison baits. In D. Chitty (Ed.), *Control of rats and mice.* Vol. 2. Oxford: Clarendon Press, 1954. Pp. 374–394.

Schaeffer, A. Selection of food in *Stentor caeruleus* (Ehr). *Journal of Experimental Zoology,* 1910, **8,** 75–132.

Seligman, M. E. P. On the generality of the laws of learning. *Psychological Review,* 1970, **77,** 406–418.

Seligman, M. E. P. Introductory remarks. In M. E. P. Seligman & J. L. Hager (Eds.), *Biological boundaries of learning.* Englewood Cliffs, N.J.: Prentice Hall, 1972. Pp. 1–6.

Sheldon, R. The reactions of dogfish to chemical stimuli. *Journal of Comparative and Physiological Psychology,* 1909, **19,** 273–311.

Simson, P., & Booth, D. Effect of CS–US interval on the conditioning of odor preferences by amino acid loads. *Physiology and Behavior,* 1973, **11,** 801–808.

Stager, K. E. The role of olfaction in food location by the turkey vulture (*Cathartes aura*). *L. A. County Museum Contributions in Science,* 1964, **63,** No. 81. Pp. 1–63.

Taukulis, H. Odor aversions produced over long CS–US delays. *Behavioral Biology,* 1974, **10,** 505–510.

Thompson, H. V. The consumption of plain and poisoned cereal baits by brown rats. In D. Chitty (Ed.), *Control of rats and mice.* Oxford: Clarendon Press, 1954. Pp. 352–373.

Timberlake, W., & Grant, D. L. Auto-shaping in rats to the presentation of another rat predicting food. *Science,* 1975, **190,** 690–692.

Van Hemel, P. E., & Meyer, J. S. Satiation of mouse killing by rats in an operant situation. *Psychonomic Science,* 1970, **21,** 129–130.

Von Frisch, K. Über den geschmackssinn der biene. *Zeitschrift für Vergleichende Physiologie,* 1934, **21,** 1–156.

Weisman, R. G. On the role of the reinforcer in associative learning. Conference on Operant-Pavlovian Interactions, Guelph, Ontario, 1975.

Wells, M. Taste by touch: Some experiments with octopus. *Journal of Experimental Biology,* 1963, **40,** 187–193.

Wenzel, B. M. Olfactory sensation in the kiwi and other birds. *Annals of the New York Academy of Sciences,* 1971, **188,** 183–193.

Wikler, A., & Pescor, F. T. Classic conditioning of a morphine abstinence phenomenon. Reinforcement of opioid-drinking behavior and "relapse" in morphine addicted rats. *Psychopharmacologia* (Berlin), 1967, **10,** 255.

Wilcoxon, H. C., Dragoin, W., & Kral, P. A. Illness induced aversions in rat and quail: Relative salience of visual and gustatory cues. *Science,* 1971, **171,** 826–828.

DISCUSSION

Part of John Garcia's conference presentation involved a film that depicted conditioned taste aversions in a range of nonlaboratory animals. A truly striking sequence involved the reversal of the predator–prey relationship between wolves and sheep following the wolf's ingestion of a small amount of lithium chloride in a "sheep patty." Garcia stressed that the subcutaneous fat contained the characteristic taste of sheep, although the presence of wool was probably important in averting the wolf to the sight of the sheep, as well, via higher order conditioning from gustatory to visual cues.

Garcia noted that his was a motivational approach—an attempt to understand and modify the hedonic value of objects rather than directly to alter behaviors. He made the following observation:

"We could have faked the scenes in our films by putting shocks around and getting the coyote to run away. We'd spend a lot of time teaching the coyote "no matter where you encounter the sheep, you're going to get zapped." And the coyote would say "I'd better not eat the sheep. It tastes good but they zap me no matter where I find it." In the real world people spend a lot of time doing just that to the coyote, and the coyote spends a lot of time trying to beat the system and eat the sheep. However, what happens when you change the coyote's motivation, not his behavior? The minute you make him dislike the sheep, you can leave him standing in the corral with the sheep. It doesn't matter. He doesn't want it anymore. It doesn't taste good to him. He's not going to eat it. He says, "You eat it. That's what the farmer wants."

Throughout much of the following dialog, Garcia expresses, at times implicitly, an alternate view of the mechanisms of Pavlovian conditioning. This becomes clearest in his answers, which deal with the notion of stimulus substitution, a traditional doctrine that received considerable assault at this conference (see, for example, Chapter 4 and related discussion by Boakes). Garcia's point seemed to be that flavor—illness conditioning produced a hedonic shift or change in the palatability of the food eaten before illness. As the animal attempts to cope with the now unpalatable food object, retching, which resembles the unconditioned illness response, may occur. Such behavior may be classed as stimulus substitution. However, other forms of behavior appear that cannot be so classified. These include (1) the natural responses of the animal to a disgusting object, and (2) social responses to the live aversive prey, which after conditioning elicits avoidance instead of approach.

Davis: In your film, the sheep makes threatening movements toward the wolf and the wolf retreats. I wonder if there are size limitations on the reversal of predator—prey behaviors. Could you produce a situation in which a rabbit chases a coyote or a mouse chases a hawk?

Garcia: No. This is related to the discussion of stimulus substitution which we've had over and over at this conference. In your example of a rabbit, illness and aversion are inappropriate behaviors and you won't see the coyote transfer those behaviors to the rabbit, no matter what stimulus substitution theory predicts. When the coyote is confronted with the CS, be it a rabbit or a sheep, it will show you all the behaviors it normally makes to that particular compound CS. All you've done by the conditioned aversion procedure is change the hedonic value of the CS, but it's still basically the same CS they're responding to. They may approach it, attack it, or shy away from it as a consequence of the hedonic shift, but there's no need to look for behaviors appropriate to the US in the presence of the CS.

Hurwitz: How do you think the wolf in your film would treat the sheep over time, once it was clear the predator–prey relationship was no longer in order?

Garcia: I think the wolves would treat the sheep as a pack member, giving him a place in the hierarchy.

Hurwitz: The wolf actually affiliates with the sheep!

Garcia: Yes, I think so. The wolves have to do something with the sheep. It's possible that ultimately the dominant member of the wolf pack will challenge the sheep and probably kill him, but for reasons quite removed from feeding or predation. [See Chapter 10, pages 281–284, for elaboration on this point by Garcia *et al.*–Eds.]

Garcia made an interesting speculation about the relationship between ana-otmy and the characteristic temporal relationship found in associative learning involving odor and taste.

"We have an anatomy in which the nose is located 500 msec from the mouth. This structural relationship appears repeatedly throughout the animal kingdom. The result is that you get conditioning very rapidly–the mouth teaches the nose–that a particular substance is bad. It's an example of higher order conditioning. If you put the nostrils on the top of the head you'd get some really weird behavior. If you followed the model of early auditory perception experiments where they used a pseudophone, and physically separated the nose and mouth, you'd find out that this anatomical relationship is extremely important. It's not because of internal connections, it's simply external structure. Having the nose just above the mouth saves a tremendous amount of hard wiring inside. Somewhere in the head there really is a continuity program that says 'If two things are 500 msec apart, no matter how crazy it seems, they are causally connected.' That's the conclusion that Hume came to in deciding what causality is about. Experimental psychologists have reached the same conclusion. They've gotten to the point of successfully pairing events which are only arbitrarily related simply because they're separated by that special interval for temporal contiguity: 500 msec.

Seligman: I wonder if I can pin you down on what I see to be one of the major explicit questions this conference is about? What is your thinking about whether there is a general process of associative learning vs. specific types of learning for specific situations?

Garcia: The primary thing you learn from taste aversions is that you're shifting motivation. Time–space relationships are in a sense discarded. What's really happening is that you're changing the hedonic tone of a stimulus irrespective of where or when that stimulus may occur. It's independent of spatial context and time. The organism doesn't learn an if–then relationship. "If I take this stuff I'm going to get sick at time *t* in place *p*." All he learns is that he doesn't like this stuff anymore.

Weisman: How is that different from normal Pavlovian conditioning? Couldn't you say that's what happens in general?

Garcia: Yes. I think so.

Black: No. You're also saying that under some same conditions animals can learn about temporal relationships.

Garcia: They can do that too.

Weisman: But what I'm asking is whether Pavlovian conditioning in general is explained by changing the hedonic value of the CS? Or does that only apply to taste aversion learning?

Garcia: No. For example it also happens in the "instinctive drift" data. [See Breland and Breland, 1961—Eds.] The important aspect of those results is not that there was instinctive drift, but that the racoons were acting to plastic tokens as if they were crayfish. The hedonic value of the tokens was changed.

At this point Boakes and Davis argued that this seemed to be a departure from Garcia's previous analysis. Instead of a shift in the hedonic value of the token, the racoon's behavior appeared to be a classical example of stimulus substitution; i.e., by virtue of pairing the token with food, food-related behaviors were now transferred directly to the token. Garcia argued that the token and crayfish were sufficiently similar so that instinctive drift could be discussed in terms of a hedonic shift. If the CS (token) were markedly different from the US (crayfish) and instinctive drift were observed, then the hedonic shift would produce behavioral changes that could not be described as stimulus substitution.

Mackintosh: Your first statement was that bait-shyness learning differed from "ordinary" conditioning in that it represented a shift in hedonic tone independent of space—time relations. Later you seem to be saying that other forms of learning can be handled in exactly the same form. In fact you seemed to indicate to Ron [Weisman] that hedonic shift might be a reasonable general view of Pavlovian conditioning. You seem to be talking on both sides in response to Marty's [Seligman] question.

Garcia: That's a very important thing to be able to do [laughter]. It's known as getting your back to the wall and looking for the exit signs. [more laughter]. [In a more serious vein, Garcia deals with this issue in chapter 10, pp. 300—306.—Eds.]

Seligman: I'd like not only to press my question further, but also ask you whether you think the following four things are different in kind between taste-aversion learning and other forms of Pavlovian conditioning: (1) the long delays between CS and US, (2) resistance to extinction, (3) the role of redundancy in information, and (4) the plasticity of the physiological mechanisms that underly these forms of learning.

On balance, Garcia indicated that he saw no essential differences between taste aversion and other forms of Pavlovian conditioning along any of these four dimensions. Seligman registered his surprise at this answer.

Seligman: Within the operations of Pavlovian conditioning, it's possible that two very different outcomes or processes are engendered. One process is a hedonic shift. The other is an if–then relationship being learned bloodlessly. By analogy, consider two classes of people who won't go into crowded cities. One class of people don't walk into cities because they learn the probability is, say, 1 in 9 that they'll be the victim of some street crime. When that probability changes, it is possible to convince them to walk into the city. The other class may be called agoraphobics. When they think about or see crowd scenes it scares the hell out of them. They shiver, feel nauseous, cringe. I'm suggesting that this is a real distinction and it might be captured in different types of Pavlovian conditioning. The fact that we've got one class of procedure—CS paired with US—shouldn't lead us too readily to conclude that we've only got one possible outcome. I'd like to see us enumerate criteria that might differentiate between cognitive and noncognitive processes underlying Pavlovian conditioning.

Staddon: That seems like almost a mysterious thing to hypothesize for an animal. That it learns an if–then relationship. What does that mean?

Seligman: Operationally it means such things as if you change the contingency between CS and US, you get changes in behavior; or that redundancy blocks conditioning.

Staddon: But that can happen for many reasons. It doesn't necessarily suggest that the animal has made a logical analysis of the situation.

Garcia: No. Like Davis said earlier, these are metaphors to help explain why the animal behaves as it does. The if–then learning seems to apply more readily to the buzzer–shock situation than to the taste aversion learning, but I'm sure you could arrange the taste aversion situation so it applied. It still may not tell you how the behavior was really being controlled though.

Black: The point was made yesterday—it's one thing to be affected by a correlation and another to know about it or be able to verbalize it.

Staddon: I think I was put off because Marty's example about cities was an entirely verbal example. You tell people about crime statistics and they behave in such and such a way; that does not seem in any simple way to apply to the animal situation. I do recognize of course that animals can respond to more or less complicated situations. (For related discussion on "autocontingencies" see a paper by Davis, Memmott, & Hurwitz, 1975).

Seligman: I believe that some kinds of learning, maybe more than others, maybe to the exclusion of others, are correlation sensitive. I think that such sensitivity may be an indication of the importance of if–then relationships.

Discussion turned to the specificity of aversions and Garcia suggested an application of these principles to the behavior of the American drinker.

Seligman: The alcohol aversion people have said that one of the reasons you only get a 50% cure rate with making alcoholics sick is latent inhibition. That is, prior to therapy they've already had a lot of, say, Old Grandad without being sick. This suggests that if you switched them to another brand for a month prior to pairing illness with Old Grandad, you might increase your cure rate.

Garcia: I think so. There's a tremendous amount of evidence for the specificity of aversions. In the film we showed that a coyote's aversion to lamb does nothing to stop its attack on a rabbit. I think what happens to the American drinker is similar. He starts on sweet stuff and usually overdrinks and gets sick. He acts as if the mixer were making him sick and progresses away from it and finally winds up with scotch on the rocks. Nobody in his right mind who was starting out to drink would drink scotch on the rocks. But that's what happens when you get averted to everything that tastes good and end up drinking the stuff that tastes like medicine.

Seligman: The same problem may occur in treating cigarette smoking with aversions. You'd have to get the smoker off his regular brand for a while to get around the latent inhibition effects that will interfere with treatment.

Staddon: That appears to be very great specificity indeed. I would have thought the average person would have difficulty discriminating between brands.

Garcia: If you talk to most people, you find they have very specific tastes about drinking.

Staddon: They may think they do.

Garcia: They do at least with regard to different drinks. A woman may drink martinis, then become nauseated while she's pregnant. When she gets back to drinking she just won't drink martinis any more. She swears that martinis made her sick even though it had nothing to do with it. [Editor's note—see also Seligman, 1972]. American drinkers always swear that sweet drinks make them sick. You don't find that among European drinkers, though. There, little kids order sweet drinks and rarely overdrink. Because no aversion or the progression from sweet to bitter occurs, the European drinker remains an "omnivore" as far as booze is concerned.

References

Breland, K., & Breland, M. The misbehavior of organisms. *American Psychologist,* 1961, **16**, 681–684.

Davis, H., Memmott, J., & Hurwitz, H. M. B. Autocontingencies: A model for subtle behavioral control. *Journal of Experimental Psychology: General,* 1975, **104**, 169–188.

Seligman, M. E. P., & Hager, J. L. Biological boundaries of learning (the Sauce Bearnaise syndrome). *Psychology Today,* 1972, **6(Aug)**, 59–61, 84–87.

Author Index

Numbers in *italics* refer to the pages on which the complete references are listed.

A

Ackil, J. E., 72, 75, 87, *97*
Adelman, H. M., 234, 241, *265*
Ader, R. A., 175, *178*
Adkins, J., 172, *179*
Adler, N., 9, *19*
Alcock, J., 299, *306*
Allen, J. D., 70, *96*
Allison, J. A., 122, *126*
Allport, G. W., 151, *163*
Anderson, N. H., 260, 262, *264*
Anger, D., 272, *272*
Anokhin, P. K., 105, *126*
Antonitis, J. J., 195, *221*
Arabian, J., 173, 175, *176*
Atema, J., 279, *306*
Atkinson, J. W., 109, *126*
Averill, J. R., 169, 174, *176*
Avis, H. H., 289, *306*
Ayers, S. L., 104, 123, *127*
Azrin, N. H., 168, *177*, 195, 220, *221*, 235, 238, 253, *264, 266*

B

Badia, P., 168, 170, 172, 173, 174, *177*
Baenninger, R., 289, 298, *307, 310*
Barber, S., 278, *306*
Bardach, J., 279, *306*

Baril, L. L., 298, *310*
Barnes, L. W., 174, *177*
Barnett, S. A., 274, 297, 303, *306*
Baron, A., 168, *178*
Barrera, F. J., 18, *19*
Beaton, R., 293, 294, 304, *309*
Bedarf, E., 293, *310*
Belleville, R. E., 218, *221*
Bentler, P. M., 174, *178*
Berg, D., 289, *307*
Berlyne, D. E., 166, *177*
Berryman, R., 180, *187*
Besley, S., 104, *126*
Bindra, D., 50, *61*, 134, *163*
Birch, D., 109, *126*
Black, A. H., 28, 29, 38, *39, 40*
Blackman, D. E., 211, 212, *221*
Blanchard, E. G., 29, *39*
Blough, D. S., 108, 109, *126*
Boakes, R. A., 69, 82, 88, 95, *96*, 166, *177*
Bolas, D. R., 196, *222*
Bolles, R. C., 15, 17, 18, *19*, 38, *39*, 49, *61*, 166, 170, *177*, 192, 215, *221, 222*, 234, 236, 237, 238, 240, 241, 242, 260, 261, *264*, 271, *272*
Boneau, C. A., 116, 117, 118, *126*
Booth, D., 303, *309, 311*
Boren, J. J., 209, 212, *221*, 238, *264*
Bossom, J., 280, *308*
Bounds, W., 201, *222*, 260, 262, *265*

Bouzas, A., 302, *308*
Bowers, K. S., 175, *177*
Brady, J. P., 175, *177*
Brady, J. V., 29, *40,* 172, 173, *177*
Braveman, N. S., 297, 304, *307*
Breland, K., 18, *19,* 95, *96*
Breland, M., 18, *19,* 95, *96*
Bremner, F. J., 235, 260, *265,* 272, *272*
Brener, J. M., 29, *40,* 195, *222*
Brett, L. P., 285, 288, 296, 298, *307*
Brimer, C. J., 168, *177*
Broadhurst, P. L., 190, *222*
Brogden, W. J., 3, *20*
Brower, L. P., 276, 285, 298, *307, 310*
Brown, P. L., 9, *19,* 48, *62,* 68, 86, *96*
Brown, W., 153, *164*
Brush, E. S., 260, *266*
Brush, F. R., 70, *96*
Bryant, R. C., 210, 213, *222*
Buchanan, D. C., 170, *177*
Bures, J., 303, *307*
Burghardt, G. M., 293, 299, *307*
Burstein, K. R., 116, 117, 118, *126*
Burton, J., 234, 242, 250, 251, 253, 254, 255, 256, 257, *264, 265*
Byrum, R. P., 168, *178*

C

Campbell, B. A., 136, *164*
Campbell, S. L., 235, 243, 254, *264,* 271, *272*
Capretta, P. J., 298, 303, *307*
Carr, W. J., 301, *307*
Case, J., 279, *306*
Catania, A. C., 51, *62,* 106, 117, *126*
Caul, W. F., 170, *177*
Cho, C., 260, *266*
Christie, D. P., 289, 298, *309*
Cicala, G., 279, *307*
Clark, F. C., 218, *221*
Clarke, J. C., 301, *307*
Clayton, F. L., 3, *19*
Cleeland, C., 172, *179*
Coate, W. B., 157, *163*
Coker, C., 173, 174, *177*
Coleman, S. R., 28, *40*
Conrad, D. G., 209, 210, 211, 218, *224*
Cook, J., 174, *177*
Cook, L., 218, *222*
Cooper, K. G., *223*

Coppinger, R. P., 298, *310*
Costanzo, D. J., 301, *307*
Cott, A., 28, *39*
Cousins, L. S., 2, *19*
Cowan, P. E., 297, 303, *306*
Crespi, L. P., 152, *163*
Crisler, G., 9, *19*
Cross, D. V., 104, *126*
Culbertson, S., 168, 170, 172, 173, 174, *177*
Czaplicki, J. A., 293, 299, *307*

D

Daly, H. D., 152, *163*
D'Amato, M. R., 174, *177*
Davis, H., 104, *126,* 168, 169, *177, 178,* 187, *187,* 200, 202, 211, 220, *222,* 230, *231,* 234, 235, 236, 242, 244, 247, 248, 249, 250, 251, 253, 254, 255, 256, 257, *264, 265, 266*
Davis, J. L., 303, *307*
Davis, J. M., 123, 124, *126*
Davison, C., 70, *96*
Debold, R. C., 9, *20*
DeFisher, D., 175, *177*
Defran, R., 168, *177*
Denenberg, V. H., 289, *307*
Denny, M. R., 4, *20,* 159, *163,* 166, *178,* 234, 241, *265*
Desiderato, O., 173, 175, *176*
Dethier, V., 278, *307*
de Toledo, L., 38, *39*
de Villiers, P. A., 122, 124, *126*
DiCara, L. V., 28, 29, *40*
Dillow, P. V., 237, *265*
Dinsmoor, J. A., 234, 235, *265*
Domjan, M., 302, *307*
Donenfeld, I., 236, *265*
Doob, A. N., 168, *178*
Dragoin, W., 285, 298, 304, *311*
Driscoll, J. M., 174, *178*
Duncan, C., 279, *307*
Dunham, P. J., 123, *126*

E

Engle, B. T., 29, *39*
Ervin, F. R., 275, 301, 302, *307, 308, 309*
Estes, W. K., 12, *20,* 195, 198, *222*

Esty, J. F., 175, *177*
Ewer, R. F., 7, 8, 14, 16, *20*

F

Fantino, E., 151, *163*
Farrar, C. H., 203, 212, *223*
Farris, H. E., 9, 12, *20*
Farthing, G. W., 104, *126*
Feldman, R. S., 235, 260, *265,* 272, *272*
Fields, C. I., 31, *39*
Finch, G., 9, *20*
Findley, J. D., 29, *40*
Fleshler, M., 168, *178*
Friedman, S. F., 175, *178*
Frommer, G. P., 72, 75, 87, *97*
Furedy, J. J., 168, 173, *178*

G

Gamzu, E., 48, *62,* 69, 72, 82, 85, 87, *96,* *97,* 114, 115, *126, 127*
Garb, J., 292, 294, *307*
Garcia, J., 38, *39,* 151, *163,* 274, 275, 276, 279, 281, 282, 283, 285, 288, 289, 290, 291, 292, 293, 295, 296, 297, 298, 301, 302, 303, 304, 305, *308, 309, 310, 311, 316*
Gardner, L., 301, *309*
Gatchel, R. J., 29, *39*
Geer, J. A., 169, *178*
Geer, J. H., 169, *179*
Gelperin, A., 299, 300, *308*
Gibbon, J., 180, *187*
Gilbertson, D., 94, *96*
Gilliam, W. J., 29, *40*
Glass, D. C., 169, *178*
Glass, D. H., 152, *163*
Gleitman, H., 157, *164*
Glickman, S. E., 11, *20*
Gliner, J. A., 29, *40,* 170, 171, *179*
Gonzales, R. C., 157, *163*
Goodchild, P., 303, *309*
Gormezano, I., 8, *20,* 28, *40*
Gorry, T. H., 293, 294, 304, *308*
Gottlieb, S. H., 29, *39*
Grant, D. L., 95, *97,* 284, *311*
Green, K. F., 38, *39,* 302, 303, *308*
Green, K. S., 151, *163*
Green, L., 302, *308*

Greenway, L., 209, *222, 223*
Grossen, N. E., 215, *222,* 260, *264*
Grunzke, M. E., 218, *221*
Gumenik, W. E., 174, *177*
Gustavson, C. R., 274, 275, 281, 282, 283, 289, 290, 291, 292, 295, 296, 298, 304, *308, 311, 316*
Gutman, A., 70, *96*
Guttman, N., 103, 120, *126*

H

Hager, J. L., 234, *266*
Hahn, W., 29, *40*
Hake, D. F., 195, 220, *221,* 238, 253, *264*
Hall, K., 293, 294, 304, *309*
Halliday, M. S., 69, 88, *96,* 166, *177*
Hanford, P. Z., 153, *164*
Hankins, W. G., 274, 276, 279, 281, 283, 285, 288, 289, 290, 291, 292, 293, 295, 296, 298, 301, 302, 303, 304, 305, *307, 308, 311, 316*
Hanson, H. M., 120, *126*
Haralson, J., 299, 300, *308*
Haralson, S., 299, 300, *308*
Hare, R. D., 174, *178*
Haritos, M., 196, *222*
Harlow, H. F., 280, 293, 294, *308*
Harris, A. H., 29, *40*
Harrison, R. H., 116, *127*
Harsh, J., 173, 174, *177*
Haynes, M. R., 29, *39*
Hays, R. C., 170, *177*
Hearst, E., 7, *20,* 69, 71, 72, 75, 85, 87, 94, *96, 97,* 104, 115, *126*
Hecht, S., 279, *308*
Hefferline, R. F., 195, *222,* 257, *265*
Heiligenberg, W., 111, *126*
Held, R., 280, *308*
Hemmes, N. S., 70, *96*
Henke, P. G., 70, *96*
Herrick, C. J., 279, 292, *308*
Herrmann, T., *265*
Herrnstein, R. J., 193, 195, 196, 209, 210, 211, 212, 217, 218, *221, 222, 224*
Hershiser, D., 176, *178*
Heth, C. D., 12, *21,* 152, *164*
Hincline, P. M., 193, 196, *222*
Hinde, R. A., 3, 4, *19, 20*
Hirsch, V., 280, *308*
Hirschorn, P., 235, 242, 244, 249, 256, *265*

Hoffeld, D. R., 3, *20*
Hoffman, H. S., 168, *178,* 209, *224*
Hogan, J. A., 9, 11, *19, 20*
Holland, P. C., 136, 138, 139, 141, 143, 145, 146, 161, *163*
Holloway, S. M., 240, *266*
Holman, E. W., 151, *163*
Holmes, P. A., 168, *178*
Honig, W. K., 116, 117, 118, 125, *126*
Hopkins, A., 278, *308*
Horvath, S. N., 29, *40*
Hothersall, D., 29, *40,* 195, *222*
Houlihan, J., 175, *179*
Hubbard, J., 104, *126*
Hubel, D. H., 280, *308*
Hughes, H. L., 234, *265*
Hull, C. L., 134, 143, *163,* 191, *222*
Hunt, E., 302, *307*
Hurwitz, H. M. B., 169, *178,* 187, *187,* 190, 194, 196, 200, 201, 203, 204, 206, 208, 209, 210, *222, 223,* 237, 242, 244, 249, 260, 261, 262, *265*
Hutchinson, R. R., 238, 253, *264*

I

Imada, H., 169, *178*
Ison, J. R., 152, *163*

J

Jackson, D. E., 168, *178*
Jain, A. P., 297, *310*
Jasper, H., 3, 4, *21*
Jenkins, H. M., 7, 9, *19, 20,* 48, 49, 52, *62,* 68, 69, 71, 75, 85, 86, 88, 94, *96,* 105, 116, *126, 127,* 280, *308*
Jennings, H., 300, *309*
Jensen, D. D., 9, *20*
Johnson, C., 293, 294, 304, *309*
Johnston, R. E., 297, *309*
Jones, A., 174, *178*

K

Kalat, J. W., 298, *310*
Kalish, H. I., 103, *126*
Kamano, D. K., 210, 211, 213, *222*
Kamin, L. J., 168, *177*
Kare, M. R., 285, *309*
Karli, P., 288, *309*

Kause, R. H., 175, *178*
Keehn, J. D., 235, 243, 249, *265,* 270, *272*
Keele, S. W., 14, 17, *20*
Kelleher, R. T., 218, *222*
Keller, F. S., 195, 196, *222, 224,* 234, 235, *265*
Keller, K., 69, *97*
Kelly, D. J., 274, 275, 281, 282, 283, 295, 296, *308*
Kendall, S. B., 2, 3, *20*
Kenney, M. D., 280, *309*
Kenny, S., 244, 247, 248, *265*
Kimble, G. A., 8, *20*
Kimeldorf, D. J., 275, 296, 297, 302, *307, 309*
Knapp, R. K., 175, *178*
Koelling, R., 275, 301, 302, *307, 308*
Konorski, J., 81, *97,* 105, 106, *127,* 134, *163*
Kovner, R., 151, *163,* 303, *308*
Kral, P. A., 285, 298, 304, *311*
Krames, L., 289, 298, 301, *307, 309*
Krane, R. V., 273, 303, *309, 316*
Kreuter, C., 211, 220, *222,* 230, *231*
Kuhlman, C. K., 29, *40*
Kuo, Z. Y., 289, *309*

L

Lacroix, J. M., 30, 31, *40*
Lang, P. J., 29, *40*
Lanzetta, J. T., 174, *178*
Laverack, M., 278, *309*
Leary, R. W., 294, *309*
Lemere, F., 293, 294, *309*
Leong, C. Y., 111, *127*
Leslie, J. C., 72, *97*
Lett, B. T., 4, *20*
Lettvin, J. Y., 280, *309*
Levine, S., 234, 239, 255, *265*
Levis, D. J., 173, *179*
Levy, C., 275, *309*
Lewis, J., 218, *222*
Lewis, P., 168, 174, *177*
Liddell, H. S., 197, *223*
Lindberg, A. A., 146, *163*
Linton, L., 214, 216, *223*
Litner, J. S., 166, *180,* 201, 203, 209, 211, 212, 215, 216, *224*
Little, L., 70, *97*
Livingston, A., 170, *179*

Livingstone, J., *265*
Lockard, J. S., 173, *178*
Lockwood, M. J., 82, *96*
LoLordo, V. M., 166, *179*, 201, 203, 210, 211, 213, 215, 216, *223*
Lord, J., 70, *97*
Lorenz, K., 4, 6, 7, *20*, 277, 284, *309*
Lovett, D., 303, *309*
Lowe, W. C., 297, *309*
Lubow, R. E., 3, *20*
Lykken, D. T., 168, *178*
Lyon, D. O., 240, 260, 262, *266*
Lyons, J., 123, 124, *127*

M

MacDonald, L., 168, *178*
Mackay, B., 299, 300, *309*
Mackintosh, N. J., 2, 3, 14, *21*, 38, *40*, 49, *62*, 68, 70, 86, 87, *97*, 120, *127*, 157, *163*, 190, 219, *223*, 280, *309*
Maier, N. R. F., 196, *223*
Maier, S. F., 13, *21*, 166, 176, *178, 179*, 237, *265*
Mallott, R. W., 256, *266*
Maltzman, I., 175, *179*
Mandler, G., 29, *40*
Marler, P., 277, *309*
Marr, J., 301, *309*
Martin, L. K., 209, 212, *223*
Mason, J. W., 239, *266*
Mason, W. A., 280, *309*
Matsuoka, Y., 235, *265*
Maturana, H. R., 280, *309*
Mazzagatti, N., 289, *310*
McAllister, D. G., 195, 198, *223*
McAllister, W. R., 195, 198, *223*
McBane, B., 174, *177*
McCulloch, W. S., 280, *309*
McDougall, W., 105, *127*
McFarland, D. J., 8, *21*, 109, *127*
McGillis, D. B., 236, 237, 238, *264*, 271, 272
McGowan, B. K., 38, *39*, 302, *308*
McIntire, R. W., 168, *177*
McMichael, J., 279, *307*
Memmott, J., 169, *178*, 187, *187*, 200, *222*
Meyer, B., 168, 169, 170, 171, 176, *179*, 184, *187*
Meyer, D. R., 260, *266*
Meyer, J. S., 289, *309, 311*

Mezinskis, J., 170, 171, *179*
Migler, B., 235, *266*, 271, *272*
Miley, W. M., 289, *310*
Milgram, N. W., 289, 298, *309*
Miller, N. E., 9, *20*, 28, 29, *40*, 134, 157, *163*
Mintz, D. E., 249, *266*
Montgomery, R., 276, *309*
Moody, J. E., 227, *231*, 238, *266*
Moore, A. U., 3, *20*
Moore, B. R., 7, 10, 12, 15, *21*, 49, 50, *62*, 69, 88, *96*, 280, *308*
Moot, S. A., 170, *177*
Morgan, M. J., 151, *163*
Morris, R. C. M., 217, *223*
Mottlin, J. L., 293, 294, *310*
Mowrer, O. H., 15, *21*, 134, *163*, 192, 198, *223*
Myer, J. S., 270, *272*
Myers, A. K., 237, *266*

N

Nakamura, C. Y., 260, 262, *264*
Neisser, U., 2, *21*
Noirot, E., 4, *21*
Notterman, J. M., 249, *266*

O

Ober, S. E., 293, 294, 304, *308*
O'Boyle, M., 297, *309*
Obrist, P. A., 29, *40*
Olmsted, J., 279, *310*

P

Paré, W. P., 170, *179*
Parker, G. H., 278, 300, *310*
Paschke, R. E., 289, *307*
Patten, R. L., 72, *97*
Patten, W., 278, *310*
Paul, L., 288, 289, *310*
Pavloski, R., 29, *39*
Pavlov, I. P., 2, 6, 10, *21*, 105, *127*, 135, *164*, 242, 243, *266*
Pear, J. J., 70, *97*, 227, *231*, 238, *266*
Pennypacker, H. S., 116, 117, 118, *126*
Perkins, C. C., 88, *97*, 166, 173, 175, *178*, *179*
Persinger, M. A., 227, *231*, 238, *266*

Pervin, L. A., 174, *179*
Pescor, F. T., 302, 303, *311*
Petersen, M. R., 240, 260, 262, *266*
Peterson, G. B., 72, 75, 87, *97*
Petry, G., 174, *178*
Pew, R. W., 17, *21*
Pfaffman, C. R., 276, *310*
Pitts, W. H., 280, *309*
Platt, A. P., 298, *310*
Platt, J. R., 31, *40*
Poli, M., 69, 82, 88, 95, *96*
Pomerleau, O. F., 210, 211, *223*
Porter, A. G., 201, 213, *223*
Porter, J. W., 201, *223*, 234, 255, 261, *265*, *266*
Posner, I., 288, *310*
Posner, M. J., 14, *21*
Powell, R. W., 262, *266*
Prakash, I., 297, 303, *306, 310*
Pumphrey, R. J., 284, *310*
Pratt, C. H., 156, *164*
Preven, D. W., 29, *40*
Prewitt, E. P., 2, 3, *21*
Price, K. P., 169, 170, 171, 175, *179*
Prokasy, W. F., 176, *179*

R

Rachlin, H., 113, 114, *127, 302, 308*
Radford, G. G., 297, 303, *306*
Ramsay, A., 175, *179*
Ramsden, M., 13, *22,* 63, *66*
Rapport, D. J., 122, *127*
Ratliff, F., 111, *127*
Ratner, S. C., 4, *20*
Redford, M. E., 88, *97*
Renner, K. E., 175, *179*
Rescorla, R. A., 2, 3, 8, 12, *21,* 23, *26,* 42, *45, 62,* 68, *97,* 134, 135, 136, 138, 139, 141, 143, 145, 146, 152, 153, 158, 161, *164,* 166, *179,* 189, 198, 199, 201, 203, 209, 210, 211, 212, 213, 215, 216, 217, *223,* 229, 231, *310*
Revusky, S., 293, 298, *310*
Reynolds, G. S., 106, *126*
Richey, T., *223*
Richter, C. P., 274, *310*
Riddle, W. C., 218, *222*
Ridgers, A., 72, *97*
Riesen, A. H., 280, *310*
Riess, D., 203, 209, 211, 212, 213, *223*
Riley, A. L., 298, *310*

Rilling, M., 104, 115, *127*
Rinaldi, P., 29, *40*
Rizley, R. C., 2, *21,* 23, *26,* 135, 153, *164*
Roberts, A. E., 190, 200, 201, 203, 204, 206, 208, 209, 210, 213, 214, 216, *222,* 223
Roberts, L. E., 30, 31, 38, *40*
Rohles, F. H., 218, *221*
Roll, D. L., 303, *310*
Rosenn, M., 169, 174, *176*
Rozin, P., 298, *310*
Rubadeau, D. O., 296, 297, *309*
Rudy, J. W., 72, *97*
Rusiniak, K. W., 274, 281, 283, 289, 290, 291, 292, 293, 295, 296, 298, 301, 302, 303, 304, 305, *307, 308, 311, 316*
Rzoska, J., 274, 298, *311*

S

Sainsburg, R. S., 280, *308*
Savage, A., 72, *97*
Schaeffer, A., 278, *311*
Schlosberg, H. C., 156, *164,* 198, *224*
Schmidt, R. A., 17, *21*
Schoenfeld, W. N., 134, *164,* 168, *179,* 195, *224,* 256, *266*
Schwartz, B., 48, *62,* 69, 85, 87, *96, 97,* 114, 115, *127,* 246, *266*
Schwartz, G. E., 29, *40*
Scobie, S. R., 210, 211, 212, 213, 217, *224,* 226, *231*
Scott, R. W., 29, *39*
Segal, E. F., 240, *266*
Seidel, R. J., 2, *21*
Seitz, A., 110, *127*
Seligman, M. E. P., 13, *21,* 166, 168, 169, 170, 171, 176, *178, 179,* 184, *187,* 200, *224,* 234, 237, 264, *265, 266,* 273, 292, 302, *311, 316*
Seward, J. P., 157, *164*
Seymann, R., 173, *179*
Sharpless, S., 3, 4, *21*
Sheldon, R., 279, *311*
Sheffield, F. D., 82, *97,* 136, *164*
Shemberg, K., 170, 171, *179*
Shepard, R. N., 104, 113, *127*
Shepp, B. E., 157, *163*
Shettleworth, S. J., 18, *21*
Shimoff, E. H., 168, *179,* 210, 211, 216, *224*

Sidley, N. A., 256, *266*
Sidman, M., 192, 200, 209, 210, 211, 212, 217, 218, *221, 222, 223*
Siebert, L., 3, *20*
Siegel, S., 3, *21*
Silverman, P. J., 117, *126*
Simmelhag, V. L., 17, *22,* 105, 106, *127*
Simson, P., 303, *311*
Sines, J. O., 172, *179*
Singer, J. E., 169, *178*
Skinner, B. F., 6, 15, *21,* 104, *127,* 144, *164,* 195, 198, *222*
Slaughter, J., 29, *40*
Smith, J. C., 303, *310*
Snapper, A. A. G., 168, *179*
Soga, M., 169, *178*
Sokolov, E. N., 3, *21*
Solomon, R. L., 8, 9, 13, *21, 22,* 42, *45,* 68, *97,* 134, *164,* 166, 176, *178, 179,* 189, 198, 199, *223,* 229, *231,* 237, 241, 254, 260, *265, 266*
Spear, N. E., 152, *164*
Spence, K. W., 103, *127,* 134, 157, *164*
Spencer, R., 173, *179*
Specht, L., 175, *179*
Spigel, I. M., 175, *179*
Spinelli, P., 280, *308*
Spitzner, J. H., 152, *164*
Staddon, J. E. R., 17, *21, 22,* 63, *66,* 104, 105, 106, 107, 108, 109, 115, 123, *127*
Stager, K. E., 285, *311*
Stein, N., 209, *224*
Stern, R. M., 29, *40*
Stitt, C., 209, *224*
Strongman, K. T., 168, *180*
Stubbs, D. A., 117, *126*
Stunkard, A., 292, 294, *307*
Sturm, T., 9, *22*
Suboski, M. D., 2, *19*
Suomi, S. J., 280, *308*
Suter, S., 168, 174, *177*
Sutterer, J. R., 70, *96*
Sweeney, M., 274, 275, 281, 282, 283, 295, 296, *308*

T

Tait, R. W., 2, *19*
Taukulis, H., 303, *311*
Terrace, H. S., 8, *22,* 105, 115, *127*
Thompson, H. V., 297, *311*

Thompson, R. F., 2, 3, *20*
Thompson, R. L., 180, *187*
Thompson, R. W., 227, *231*
Thompson, T., 9, *22*
Thorndike, E. L., 16, *22,* 191, *224*
Thornton, D. R., 175, *177*
Thorpe, W. H., 13, *22*
Timberlake, W., 95, *97, 101,* 284, *311*
Tinbergen, N., 6, 8, *22*
Tolman, E. C., 6, *22,* 144, 157, *164,* 258, *266*
Trabasso, T. R., 227, *231*
Trapold, M. A., 176, *178*
Treadway, J. T., 289, *306*
Turner, L. H., 9, *21,* 241, 254, 260, *266*
Twentyman, C. T., 29, *40*

U

Ulrich, R. E., 235, *266*

V

Van Hemel, P. E., 289, *311*
Voegtlin, W. L., 293, 294, *309*
Vogel, J. R., *311*
von Holst, E., 8, 11, *22*
von St. Paul, U., 8, 11, *22*

W

Waddington, C. H., 5, *22*
Wagner, A. R., 68, *97,* 152, *164,* 273, 303, *309, 316*
Walsh, M., 270, *272*
Walters, B. C., 173, *178*
Warner, L. H., 191, 192, *224*
Wasserman, E. A., 10, *22,* 70, 86, *97*
Wearden, J. H., 4, *22*
Weisman, G., 63, *66*
Weisman, R. G., 9, 13, *22,* 166, *180,* 201, 203, 209, 211, 212, 215, 216, *224, 311*
Weiss, J. M., 168, 170, 171, 172, 173, 175, *179, 180*
Wells, M., 278, *311*
Wendt, G. R., 105, *128*
Wenzel, B. M., 285, *311*
Wesemann, A. F., 260, *266*
Westbrook, R. F., 69, 70, 88, *97*
Wheeler, L., 236, *265, 266*
Wiesel, J. N., 280, *308*

Wikler, A., 302, 303, *311*
Wilcoxon, H. C., 285, 293, 298, 299, 304,
   307, 311
Wilkie, D. M., 70, *97*
Williams, D. R., 28, *40,* 48, 49, *62,* 69, 72,
   82, *96, 97,* 115, *126*
Williams, H., 28, *40,* 48, *62,* 82, *97*
Wilson, N. E., 302, *307*
Winograd, E., 235, 254, *265, 266*
Wolbarsht, M. L., 111, *128*
Wolfe, R. R., 29, *40*
Wolff, C., 175, *179*
Woodruff, G., 9, *22*
Wright, M., 30, 31, *40*

Y

Yeandle, S. S., 111, *128*
Young, L. D., 29, *39*
Young, R., 38, *40*

Z

Zahorick, D. M., 297, *309*
Zamble, E., 2, *19,* 136, *164*
Zarrow, M. X., 289, *307*
Zener, K., 10, *22,* 75, *97*
Zimmer-Hart, C. L., 137, *164*
Zimmerman, J., 153, *164*
Zipf, G. K., 258, *266*

Subject Index

A

Activity, 136, 145
Activity
    class, 109
Adaptive Behavior, 190
Aggression, 235, 238, 312
Alcoholism, 316
Antagonism, Behavioral, *see* Competition,
    Behavioral
Anticipatory conditioning, 151, 159, 192,
    253, 270
Appetitive behavior, 6, 304
Attack behavior, 11, 227, 284–287
Autocontingencies, 169, 315
Autonomic responses, 27–45, 195
Autoshaping, 9, 25, 47–66, 69–101, 114,
    228
Avoidance behavior, 3, 18, 36, 134, 166,
    182, 189–231, 237, 241, 256–263, 268,
    271, 302

B

Backward conditioning, 137
Bait shyness, 273–316
Behavioral contrast, 69–71, 104, 113–118,
    124
Blocking, 4, 68, 137
Brain stimulation, *see* Electrical stimulation
    of the brain

C

Causality, 313
Central representation, 2, 18
Cigarette smoking, 316
Cognitive behavior, 10, 24, 314
Competition, behavioral, 103–131, 228
Conditioned acceleration, 187, 202, 219,
    226
Conditioned aversion, *see* taste aversion
Conditioned emotional response, *see*
    conditioned suppression
Conditioned enhancement, *see* Conditioned
    acceleration
Conditioned suppression, 4, 41, 68, 139,
    160, 168, 180–187, 189–231
Conservation, behavioral, 122
Consummatory behavior, 6, 87, 92–95, 98,
    304
Contrast, *see* Behavioral Contrast
Coping behavior, 170
Corticosterone, 239
Curare, 29, 31

D

Delayed conditioning, 137
Deprivation, 63, 78–81, 144, 149
Deterioration of avoidance, 211, 225,
    260–263
Discriminative stimulus, 28, 51, 60, 108,
    123, 194, 219, 245

Discriminated operant, *see* discriminative
  stimulus
Domestication, 287–291
Drive reduction, 185, 191
DRL Schedule, 240
Duration of CS, 180, 209

E

Electrical stimulation of the brain, 11, 195
Emotion, 41, 197
Entry behaviors, 192
Escape, 15, 190, 196, 233–272
Extinction, 4, 64, 87, 144, 153–158, 160,
  209, 218, 242, 255, 302, 314

F

Fear, 18, 41, 139, 165–187, 192, 197, 226,
  229, 239, 243, 268
Freezing, 236, 239, 242, 267–272
Functional autonomy, 151

G

Generalized reinforcer, 144
Goal event, 144, 147–153
Goal tracking, *see* Sign tracking

H

Habituation, 3, 6, 22, 269
Head positioning response, 54–60, 62
Heart-rate conditioning, 27–45
Hedonic shift, 311–316
Higher-order conditioning, *see* Second-order
  conditioning

I

Illness, conditioned, 140–144, 151,
  273–316
Implicit correlation, 47–66, 81–84, 99–101
Incentive learning, 192, 220
Incentive motivation, 133–164
Instinctive drift, 314
Interim activities, 103–131
Interresponse times, 225, 271
Intertrial interval, 181, 270
Investigatory reflex, 243

L

Latent extinction, 156
Latent inhibition, 3, 137, 316
Latent learning, 3, 14
Learned helplessness, 101, 237
Learning, general process view, 1–26, 313
Least effort, principle of, 258
Leverholding, 233–272
Leverlift response, 244
Locomotor activities, 6
Loop-pulling behavior, 88–92

M

Malaise, *see* Illness, conditioned
Memory, 11–14
Multiple schedule, 64

N

Nature-nurture issue, 275–280

O

Omission training, 18, 48, 61, 75, 90
Orienting response, 3, 7, 230
Origin hypothesis, 54, 65
Overshadowing, 4, 137

P

Peak shift, 104, 118–120, 125
Percentile reinforcement procedure, 31
Piggyback correlation, *see* Implicit
  correlation
Pituitary-adrenal system, 239
Polydipsia, 240
Postshock response bursts, 201, 227, 230,
  238, 242, 253
Predictability, 165–187, 270
Preparatory response, 165–187, 235, 253,
  270
Preparedness, 43, 65, 234, 264, 268
Punishment, 235, 256, 269, 271
Puzzle box, 191

R

Redundancy, 24, 314
Reflexive fighting, 235

Reflexive lurch, 233–272
Reinforcement density procedure, 30
Response additivity, 69
Response elasticity, 63
Response force, 225, 240, 248–266, 271
Response rate, 189, 200, 224–231
Response shaping, 195
Response strategy, 193, 206, 220, 228, 245, 269
Response system, 23, 38, 42, 44, 47–66
Response topography, 15, 118, 195, 226, 233–272

S

Safety, 165–187, 228
Satiation, 140–145, 147–151, 156
Satisfiers, 191
Sauce Bernaise Syndrome, 316
Second-order conditioning, 133–164, 312
Secondary correlation, see Implicit correlation
Secondary reinforcer, Extinction of, 154–156
Sensory Preconditioning, 2, 22–25
Shock avoidance, see Avoidance
Shock duration, 213, 269
Shock escape, see Escape
Shock frequency, 189–231
Shock intensity, 182, 203, 211–214, 227
Shock rate, see shock frequency
Shuttlebox, 201, 209, 226, 267
Sign tracking, 47–101
Skeletal response, 9, 29, 34, 37, 40–43
Social behavior, 98, 235, 312
Spatial learning, 269

Species-specific defense reactions (SSDR), 17, 192, 228, 233–272
Stimulus generalization, 2, 103–131
Stimulus substitution, 68, 94, 98–101, 280–284, 312–316
Stress, 41, 170–173, 175, 239
Successive contrast, 152
Superstitious behavior, 48, 81–84, 92, 98–101
Suppression Ratio, 199–202
Synthetic environmental reflex, 242

T

Taste aversions, 4, 23, 273–316
Terminal responses, 104–110, 125, 128–131
Temporal conditioning, 104, 241
Trace conditioning, 137, 216
Tray-entry behavior, 72
Two factor theory, 22, 42, 68, 134, 192, 198, 229–231

U

Ulceration, 170, 181
Uncertainty reduction, 165–187

W

Warm-up effect, 261
Weight loss, 175
Wheel turning, 201, 209, 217, 226

X

X-ray conditioning, 274

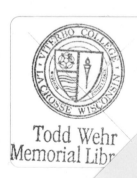